Hope
and
Honor

Hope
and
Honor

MAJOR GENERAL
SID SHACHNOW (U.S. ARMY, RET.)
AND
JANN ROBBINS

A Tom Doherty Associates Book
New York

HOPE AND HONOR

Copyright © 2004 by Sidney Shachnow and Jann Robbins

All rights reserved, including the right to reproduce this book, or portions thereof, in any form.

This book is printed on acid-free paper.

A Forge Book
Published by Tom Doherty Associates, LLC
175 Fifth Avenue
New York, NY 10010

www.tor.com

Forge® is a registered trademark of
Tom Doherty Associates, LLC.

ISBN 0-765-30792-8
EAN 978-0765-30792-7

First Edition: October 2004

Printed in the United States of America

0 9 8 7 6 5 4 3 2 1

To the women in my life—
my mother, Rose, my wife, Arlene,
and my four daughters, Shereen, Michelle, Denise, and LeeAnne

CONTENTS

ACKNOWLEDGMENTS

First and foremost, thanks to my wife, Arlene, and my daughter, LeeAnne, for inspiring and tenaciously insisting that I put my story down in writing.

My sincere appreciation to my cousin, Max Guefen, for tirelessly working to find a means to make this story a book, and for introducing me to Jann Robbins and Matt Cimber.

To my loyal partner, Jann Robbins, who never wavered and extracted events that were stored in the recesses of my mind that I did not want to reveal. This book would not be possible without you.

I cannot fully express my gratitude to Tom Doherty for his confidence and support; Linda Quinton, for her faith and precious guidance; to Elana Stokes, Eric Raab, and David Moench, who believed in this story and worked exceptionally hard to make it a success.

My gratitude to Bob Gleason, the talented executive editor, who labored incredibly hard and believed and understood what this book was all about. Your advice and mentorship was invaluable.

To Elizabeth Winick, the most professional agent, who worked tirelessly and steadfastly in promoting this story, I am deeply obligated to you.

I'd like to thank W.E.B. Griffin for coming up with the title *Hope and Honor* and Alison Lazarus for pointing it out to me.

Last but not least, to Ken Holland and Brian Heller, who have taken an unusual interest and have given this book their enthusiastic support.

And the wild regrets, and the bloody sweats,
None knew so well as I:
For he who lives more lives than one
More deaths than one must die.

—Oscar Wilde, *"The Ballad of Reading Gaol"*

PROLOGUE

I was sitting on the curb waiting for Samuel to start the race. I heard Lithuanian patriotic anthems playing in the background from an apartment above. I started to tap my foot. But when I saw Samuel step on top of the box we had placed in the middle of the cobblestone street, I jumped up and took my position at the starting line.

My legs were tired. But only one more race and I would break the record. I would be the king of the "tin-rim" races in the neighborhood. Each of us had our own customized tin-rim . . . some were deluxe models, taken from a bicycle wheel with the spokes removed . . . these were the sturdiest, but heavier to carry . . . mine was from a barrel . . . the ring that wrapped around the middle of the barrel. I had filed the edges of the rim to make it move faster.

Peter, my opponent, used a bicycle rim. He was an inch taller than me and some people thought he would be faster. He was eight years old and I was seven. He had been tin-rim champion for the past six months. But today, I knew I could beat him because I was faster. This was the first time I was his opponent.

Samuel looked down at me. "Schaja, are you ready?"

I nodded.

Samuel looked at Peter. "Ready?"

Peter nodded.

"Get set . . . and go!" Samuel shouted.

I was already a couple of paces in front of Peter. The tin-rim traveled as fast as I could run. It was moving so fast it was airborne . . . but then, I hit a chipped hole in the cobblestone and my rim almost fell to the ground. I used my stick on the rear roll of the rim to keep it upright. I had lost my lead. I raced to catch up.

I could hear my friend Mo rooting for me as Peter and I came close to the finish line. I glanced at Peter; his face was red and he was sweating even though it was getting cold. I was inches ahead of him.

"Schaja is the winner," Samuel announced as we pounded past the finish line. All of the kids were jumping up and down, screaming and yelling. It had been a close race. Peter sat down on the curb to catch his breath. I was still standing when Samuel came over and took my hand and lifted my arm in the air. "The new reigning king of tin-rim races!"

"Did you see the look on Peter's face?" Mo asked as we were walking to my house to play more games. Mo had on his yarmulke.

"Yeah," I said. "He thought he could beat me. He didn't know I'd been practicing. I knew I was faster than him."

Mo started laughing and holding my arm up like Samuel did. "Schaja is the king!"

We both looked at each other when we heard some older boys yelling at us. I couldn't understand what they were saying.

"Jew scum! Jew scum! Jew scum!"

This time I heard what they said. Mo and I started walking faster. We both kept our heads down. I heard the boys run across the street to walk behind us. Mo and I were frightened. We didn't know what to do. Then, one of the older boys hit Mo from behind and he almost fell down.

Another one grabbed his yarmulke and put it on his own head.

"Oh, no, I'll get Jew bugs in my hair!" he yelled and pulled the cap off and stomped on it.

Mo and I stood still as they circled around us. They started to shove both of us from one side to the other.

One of the boys stepped into the center of the circle and put his finger in the center of my chest. "What's your name?"

"Schaja," I said. I could hear my voice quivering.

"Schaja, you're a Jew scum," he said. He looked at me with such hatred. I didn't understand. He knew me from the neighborhood and I knew him. How could he hate me?

"Why are you saying that?" I asked.

They started kicking at my shins and then one of them punched Mo in the stomach. I bent down to help Mo and one of the boys punched me in the jaw. I swung my arms wildly trying to hit them back. I heard my nose crack when the next punch hit my face. I saw blood on my shirt.

Mo and I didn't have a chance. We both took off running in different directions.

This was the day my world changed from that of a carefree childhood to a battle that would follow me throughout life.

PART I

Into the Fire

1941–1945

ONE

I was standing at the bottom of the stairway jumping rope when my father came rushing into the house about eight o'clock in the morning. He had run several blocks and was gasping for breath. His wire-rimmed glasses were fogged and his black slicked-back hair fell across his forehead. Sweat was running down his face. He looked frantically at my mother. She quickly closed and locked the door behind him. Grandmother Rochel stopped playing the piano. We were all frightened.

"The Germans . . . the tanks, the troops . . . they're here in Kaunas," he gasped excitedly. "I was coming out of synagogue after prayers and walking across the street for a copy of *Der Amos* [*The Truth*, a Yiddish-Russian newspaper] and I heard loud noises and shouting in the street."

"Leon, catch your breath," Mother said, rocking my little brother, Mula, in her arms. "You're very pale."

He sat down on the cushioned chair in the living room. We all gathered around him. My grandmother held onto my hand.

"I looked down the street and I saw them, rows and rows . . . so many, I don't know. The tanks rolled over whatever was in their way," my father gasped, taking a deep breath as he collected himself. "Some people were crushed . . ."

Mother looked over at me and nodded toward my bedroom. "Schaja, go and clean your room." She tried not to show it but her eyes were filled with fear.

Grandmother took Mula from her to put him to bed in my parents' room.

I didn't want to leave. I wanted to know what was going on. I walked down the hallway and stopped before reaching my room. I sat down on one of the three-legged stools in the nook of the hallway. They couldn't see me from there. I sat and listened to the rest of my father's story. I could hear him pacing back and forth as he spoke. His voice sounded even more frantic as he continued.

I heard Abraham and Tili, my aunt and uncle, come down the stairs.

We had all moved into my grandmother's house about two months ago. There had been reports of Jews being murdered by Lithuanian Partisans who called themselves "freedom fighters." They didn't like the Russians who had invaded Lithuania last year. I didn't understand why Jews were being killed but my Uncle Willie, who knew almost everything as far as I was concerned, said it was for political reasons. Hitler wanted all Jews dead. He said the Partisans killed Jews because they wanted to get Hitler's attention. I didn't understand, but I remembered a few months ago when I was beaten up for being a Jew.

"Tili, Abraham, the Germans, they are here. When I went to synagogue there were only a few people, now I understand why. Rabbi said he heard on the radio they had entered the city at three o'clock this morning. He fears the Germans more than the Partisans. We may all die now. We should have listened to Willie. He wanted us to leave."

My mother gasped as Father spoke about death in such certain terms.

"The Germans are not animals. They are intellects. How can this be? What have we done?" Mother asked.

I couldn't sit alone anymore. I ran into the living room and sat on the sofa near my mother. No one told me to leave this time.

"They believe that we cause the ills of the world. It's insanity," Father said as he looked fearfully into the distance. "We should have listened to Willie when he told us we needed to leave." My father repeated this over and over again that day.

Uncle Willie came to our house several months ago and told my parents that he was trying to find a country where we could get a visa and escape Lithuania. He was afraid then that Hitler would take over Lithuania but my parents didn't believe him. Today they regretted that decision.

"He's been to every embassy. There was no place for us to go," my grandmother said. "How could we just uproot our life? We have lived here our entire lives. I don't believe that this is as serious as you or the rabbi believe."

"What can we do, Leon?" mother asked, in exasperation. "There must be an answer."

"We need to stay calm. The world is watching what Hitler is doing," Abraham said.

"With a blind eye," my father said, sarcastically.

"Why do they hate us because we're Jews? Aren't we just like everybody else?" I asked.

No one had an answer.

Uncle Willie came to see us later that afternoon.

"Hi, Uncle Willie," I said when he walked in.

"How's my young nephew?" he said. He tousled my hair as he smiled down at me.

My mother took his jacket. I looked at the hunting knife in the leather sheath that Uncle Willie always wore. The knife was held with a strap that hung below his belt, and tied securely to his thigh. It had a pearl handle with a serrated blade. When he walked, it sometimes looked like he had a splint on his leg.

He untied the knife from his leg and sat down. I watched as the knife swung like a pendulum below the chair. Willie took a sip of tea that my mother had placed in front of him.

"They murdered many Jews last night . . . in Villampole, outside of Kaunas," Willie said sadly. "The rabbis are having a meeting with the German authorities. Maybe they will come to some agreement . . . and save us . . ." His voice trailed off.

"How many have been murdered?" my mother asked.

"Too many . . ." Willie looked in my direction and stopped short of giving a number.

"The Soviets are not fighting back?" my mother asked and looked at me. I got up and left the room. But I still could hear them talking.

"They have been defeated," Willie said. "They have retreated, this is why hundreds of Jews were massacred last night. All through Lithuania, there were killings. Just stay in the house and don't go outside."

"All we can do is sit and wait . . ." my father said.

"And pray . . ." my mother added.

Several days later, a group of Lithuanians walked down our street. My father peeked out the window and saw that they were stopping at several houses close to us.

We all jumped in fear when we heard banging at our door. It was so loud it shook the glass in the inset of the front door. Uncle Abraham answered the knock. We could hear a short conversation and he came back carrying a notice of rules that Jews had to follow. I was told to go to my room.

At dinner that evening I was sipping hot chicken soup and dipping my bread into the creamy broth. It was the first real meal we had eaten in two days. Food supplies were scant. I let the crumbs drop into the soup and pushed the crumbs back and forth in my bowl with the spoon, imagining they were boats. My parents were talking to each other in Russian. I knew it was about something bad. They always spoke Russian, rather than Lithuanian, to each other when they didn't want me to hear or understand.

"Schaja, don't play with your food, please," my mother said irritably.

She was very nervous tonight. I stopped playing with my boats.

"Schaja, we need to tell you about some new rules we were given today that you must follow," Father said, holding a piece of paper in his hand.

"You must listen very carefully and obey these rules," my mother said.

"Who made the rules, Mama?" I asked.

Her eyes were filled with tears. "The Germans made the rules, Schaja," she said. "They are the government now and these are their rules. You must obey them."

I didn't understand why it was so important, but I listened.

My father began to read the rules. "We must always walk on the right side of the street in the gutter. Never walk on the sidewalk, Schaja."

"Why not?" I asked.

"That is what a rule is, Schaja, something that you cannot question," my father said, looking at me over his wire-rimmed glasses.

"Parks, squares, promenades, and benches are off limits for Jews," he continued. "We cannot use any public transportation . . . if you are outside never put your hands in your pockets."

Mother leaned across the table and handed me two yellow Stars of David. "You must always wear this on your left breast and back." She pointed out where I was to wear the star. "And we can no longer go to synagogue."

"Are these just for kids?" I asked.

"No, Schaja for all of us," my father answered.

I was confused by the rules. Why we were being treated worse than animals?

"These rules are only for Jews aren't they?"

"Yes, Schaja," my mother said.

"I'm sorry, Schaja. We have no choice."

What none of us knew at this point was that Partisans could now kill Jews for any reason; there was no accountability.

I shook my head.

"What about Mula?" I asked.

"Your little brother is too young to understand, but we'll make sure he follows all the rules."

There was a tension in our house that I had never before experienced. The lighthearted atmosphere had disappeared. About two weeks later in the middle of the night, I was jolted awake by a sound. I shot straight up in bed.

"Help . . . Help . . . Help," Uncle Abraham screamed. The sound of terror echoed through the whole house.

My heart pounded wildly in my chest after I heard the screams. Suddenly, my father burst into the bedroom and grabbed Mula and me.

"What's wrong?" I asked. My voice was shaking.

"Shhhh . . ." My father motioned for me to stay quiet.

He grabbed our hands and took us into a small windowless room on the side wing of the house. The doorway was hidden away behind a post. "Don't make a sound," he whispered frantically and shut the door.

I held Mula's hand and pressed my ear next to the door, straining to listen for any sound. Mula and I were barefoot in our pajamas, our entire bodies shaking. I heard a scuffle at the back of the house. Then I heard the crashing of glass breaking and loud voices demanding money and jewelry. Mula and I held on to one another.

Then I heard everyone screaming. The screams were so loud that Mula and I started screaming as loud as we could—disobeying our father's orders.

Somehow, over the screaming I heard a truck pull up in front of the house. I put my hand over Mula's mouth and listened. Within seconds there was more pounding at the door, this time at the front door. Then I heard sharp, distinct German commands. The back door commotion stopped.

"Go hide, get under the bed, or in the closet . . ." my mother hissed to the others as she ran to the front door. I heard the door open and my mother speaking German. "Help me, Captain," she said in a pleading, shaking voice.

I opened the door and told Mula to stay in the room and be quiet. I sneaked in the darkness to the front of the house. There were several German soldiers standing at the front door with the officer. He was surprised at my mother's fluent German. I could see he was complimented that she had called him Captain even though he said he was a lieutenant.

"We had a report of screams coming from this house . . ." the officer said.

"Yes, yes . . . I am so grateful that you stopped," she said, leading him into the house to the area where the men had been. "There were men trying to break into my back door."

The officer told his soldiers to search the backyard as he and my mother went to the back door. He looked at the broken glass on the floor then walked back to the front of the house.

"We found them hiding in the back, lieutenant," the soldiers said, dragging the two Partisans toward the officer.

They were unarmed now, their heads hanging down. The lieutenant shouted at them, but they didn't understand German. My mother offered to translate his questions into Lithuanian.

"Tell them that Lithuanian Partisans have no authority here," the lieutenant said.

My mother translated this to the men.

There was no response.

The officer didn't seem to like them and he grew impatient and ripped the Partisans' white bands off their arms. He shouted out more commands in a few clipped sentences. The soldiers quickly led the Partisans onto the back of the truck.

"We will resolve this problem, madam," he said politely to Mother. "You speak very good German. I commend you for that. You are a smart woman to learn our language," he said. "Have you spent time in Germany?"

"Yes, I have, sir," she smiled at him. "It's a very wonderful country."

He nodded in agreement. "How did you keep them from coming

through the door? It's not easy for one woman to keep two men from coming through the door."

My mother smiled at him. "They must not be very strong men."

He nodded, almost smiling, and turned toward the truck.

"Thank you again, Captain," Mother said, still insisting on using the higher rank. She quickly shut the door and locked it. I saw her breathe a sigh of relief. I walked up next to her and hugged her closely. I felt her shaking.

"What happened, Mama," I asked looking up at her. "Why was Uncle Abraham screaming?"

"The Partisans tried to break in but the Germans are going to take care of the problem. I think everything is going to be okay, Schaja . . ." she said optimistically. She called for everyone to come out.

Father, Aunt Tili, Uncle Abraham, and my grandmother came from their hiding spots in different parts of the house. In the distance I heard a small, whimpering cry.

"Mula!" I said and ran to get him from the room.

We all listened to my mother's newfound confidence in the kindness of the Germans. No one was able to sleep for the rest of the night. By early morning we were all convinced that things would get better.

Jacob was my father's youngest and only brother. He lived a few miles from Grandmother Rochel's house. He had a dark moustache and was short and stocky. He always dressed in a suit and white shirt that was buttoned at the top with a bow tie. Jacob had never worked. His only income was his share of the inheritance that his parents had left him. He was not rich, but he and his family were content.

Since we had moved to my grandmother's house, he came to visit at least once a month or he would send a posted letter. Uncle Jacob was very serious and didn't spend much time playing and socializing.

It had been almost a month since the Germans had invaded. We had seen him only a few days after the invasion. He was very frightened of the future under German rule. My father had invited him and his wife, daughter, and brother-in-law to come live with us, but he wanted to stay in his own home.

One of his neighbors knocked on our door early one morning. My father recognized him from Jacob's neighborhood. When my father opened the door the man was crying. He couldn't speak. He could only shake his head and look woefully at my father.

"What has happened, Lech?" my father asked. "Please, tell me."

"They are dead . . . all dead . . ." he whispered.

My father looked at him in shock. "What . . . what are you talking about? Who is dead?"

"I was sitting at my window and I saw Jacob standing in the hallway of his house. There was a loud knock at his front door. He jumped when he heard the sound. Our houses are so close and the windows were open because it was warm."

As Lech was talking tears were streaming down his face.

"It was late and no one ever came to his door this late. I wondered what kind of an emergency it might be. I saw him turn off the radio and take his glasses off. He went to the door. We had been listening throughout the day to the reports about Partisan activity since the Germans had authorized them to enforce the new laws. He was concerned about all the turmoil. I wondered why he was going to answer the door, but I heard my son calling me and went upstairs. I was gone for about twenty minutes . . ." He broke down and sobbed. "I'm so sorry. I could be of no help."

He finally composed himself and continued with the story. My mother had come into the room and was listening. She didn't ask me to leave.

"When I came back downstairs I was shocked by what I saw. I saw his brother-in-law on the floor. His throat had been slashed. Blood was everywhere."

I saw Lech's face turn chalky white. I thought he was going to be sick.

"I was sure that he was dead. I didn't see anyone else in the house and I ran outside toward the front door, but I stopped when I heard the barn door open. I went to the side of the barn and heard Jacob's voice. He was pleading for his life and for the life of his wife and daughter. The two monsters kept screaming about the stupidity of Jews. They demanded money. I couldn't see inside but the yelling continued . . . I heard Jacob scream and then only muffled sounds. Two men walked out of the barn, I saw the white band on their arms, and I hid. I was frightened," he said and broke down again.

"Lech," my father said through his tears. "What could you have done? . . . all of us are helpless . . ."

"I saw them laughing and walking away and they heard a baby's cry coming from the house. They went inside and were there for a few minutes and then they left. I waited for some time, afraid they might return . . ." He looked at my father and again tearfully spoke of his sorrow. "Then I saw what they had done . . . they had killed all of them. They stuffed Jacob's mouth with manure and killed . . . even the baby!"

I had never seen my father look so devastated. The cruelty inflicted on Uncle Jacob and his family was a massacre. It was my father's only brother. I felt his pain in my own heart as I watched the expression on his face.

The two men embraced each other and sobbed. Uncle Jacob's neighbor continued to cry as he spoke of his shame that he had done nothing to help. He had hidden. My father tried to comfort him, but he was inconsolable.

My parents immediately went to Uncle Jacob's house. They saw firsthand the horror inflicted on the family. They dragged Samuel, my uncle's brother-in-law, from the house to the barn to be buried with the others.

My mother brought the baby from his crib. His throat had been slashed the same as the others.

As they looked down at each member of the family in the barn, they began to pray. They placed each mangled body in a shallow grave that my father dug. The only epitaph was their agony.

They walked back into Jacob's home and began to look for things to salvage. My mother saw a letter that Jacob had recently addressed to all of us. She began to cry. They found jewelry and money hidden in the baby's bedroom. It appeared that the Partisans never intended to steal; they only wanted an excuse to kill Jews.

My parents gathered the food in the house. They couldn't speak about what they had seen. Without understanding why, they both sat down and ate the food they had gathered. As they ate, they cried.

My parents felt guilty about this moment for the rest of their lives.

This event was a deafening blow for all of us as things continued to get worse. Merchants that my parents had shopped with in the past had stopped selling food and clothing to Jews after the Germans invaded. Only Lithuanians were allowed to purchase any needed items. My father was forced to go out each day and beg for food at any price. It was degrading and demoralizing for him. Some shopkeepers violently turned him away at their door. Those he had done business with before just sorrowfully shook their heads and turned away.

If he was caught carrying food, Partisans beat and humiliated him and confiscated his food for themselves. He would plead with them that his family was starving, but they did not care. When he arrived home he was angry and frustrated. But Mother was grateful that he had not been murdered as so many others.

There were times when we had no food at all and he would travel miles to a black market dealer in a hidden area who sold food at exorbitant prices. The dealer changed locations periodically to keep the Partisans from discovering his business. Father would have to walk several hours to locate him. He aged before my eyes.

I secretly listened to many of my parents' conversations and the reports of Uncle Willie. At night when I went to bed I tried to remember their words to understand why we were hated. Each night I prayed to be a better person.

Two

Massacres of Jews became commonplace. Seven thousand Jews were taken from Kaunas, brutalized, and murdered by Partisans. The Lithuanian chief of police attempted to bury a Jewish doctor and his wife in sealed bricks while they were still alive. It was rumored that his wife went insane and was shot; the doctor escaped.

On June 28, 1941, Partisans paraded sixty Jews into the courtyard of an agricultural-machine co-op. They stuck air pumps and water hoses into their throats until their insides burst. If Partisans caught Jews they beat them to death with metal rods and billy clubs. They carried knives and axes now lying in wait to murder any Jew that passed them.

With each new wave of rumors and events I watched my parents dramatically change. Every day was a struggle. My mother no longer played games with me. She walked through the house saying very little, only shaking her head and crying. My father became timid, withdrawn, and bitter. I even missed his many lectures that he used to give. For me, I wanted life to be the way it was before.

I remembered my seventh birthday. All of my uncles and aunts came. My neighborhood friends were there and we played games. My grandmother made me a sugar icing cake. My parents had decorated our house in celebration. It was the last happy time I remembered. But even then there was a rumor about friends who had been killed. It was only discussed among the grown-ups. But I knew something terrible had happened to my friends.

My grandmother was the only person who broke the silence in the house. She tried to lift our spirits with her music, but the anxiety and fear was ever-present. If my parents spoke it was usually in recrimination about not leaving Lithuania earlier. They both were mistaken in believing the Germans would restrain the Partisans. I was living in a world that I did not understand.

Uncle Willie was the remaining strength of the family. Each day he continued to stand in line with hundreds of other Jews trying to obtain a visa. The lines were so long he never reached the door of many embassies. It was a hopeless gesture on his part. We all knew the Germans weren't going to allow us to leave.

I woke up early one morning and heard Aunt Tili crying. When I went into the kitchen I was told that Tili's parents were very ill. She was very concerned about her elderly parents and felt it would be best for she and Abraham to move in with them until they recovered. I didn't want them to leave. It would be very lonely without them.

On the day they moved we all walked together in single file to Tili's parents' home about ten blocks away. My father felt there was safety in numbers. Partisans with white bands on their arms were stationed along the way. They glared as we passed them. When we arrived at Tili's parents' home we left them at the curb and returned home.

The entire upper floor in my grandmother's house was empty now and filled with a deafening silence. My grandmother did not seem as concerned as my parents about what we were facing, but I don't think she really understood the severity of the situation. Whenever dire events were under discussion she would go to her piano and drown out the conversation. But even her spirits were broken after the next tragedy a short time later.

Willie's face was angry and defiant. We were all sitting in the living room listening to the radio when he appeared in front of us. Tears were in his eyes. My mother gasped and put her hands to her face; she knew from his expression it was more bad news.

"They have murdered them . . . all of them . . . Tili, Abraham, her parents . . ." He walked to my grandmother who was sitting in a stunned silence as he spoke.

"No! . . . How?" my mother asked.

"Why?" my grandmother whispered.

Willie looked at his mother. "They were burned, Ma, burned alive," he said through gritted teeth.

She could not speak after he told her. She rocked back and forth on the sofa and looked at each of us in the room frantically trying to understand.

My mother sobbed and ran to hold her.

"It happened early this morning. I talked to the people on the street where they lived. German officers led a group of Lithuanian Partisans to their house. But, no one had any idea what . . ." My Uncle Willie paced the floor. "They stopped in front of the house where you left them. The German commander ordered the men to surround the house. The neighbors thought they were going to be arrested.

"Elie, who lives next door, peeked out of his window. He said he couldn't believe his eyes when a small truck pulled up filled with wooden sticks tipped with a ball of material. One of the men jumped to the ground and lifted a large can of kerosene off the truck. He soaked the tip of the torch with the liquid, lit it, and handed three to each Partisan. They ran to the foundation of the house and placed each flaming torch at the base of the wooden house." Willie stopped. He sat down and put his hands to his face. After a few moments he continued the story.

"They could hear the screams," Willie sobbed. "And the heartless bastards just stood and did nothing. They stayed until the house had burned completely to the ground."

He went to my grandmother. She sobbed as he held her.

I heard her sobbing whispers over and over again. "Burned alive." I felt a pain in the pit of my stomach.

"They said that the house was contaminated with typhoid. The Partisans said it was done to protect the population. They felt justified in their actions."

I ran to my room and began to cry and beat the pillows. I loved Abraham and Tili and now they were gone. I wondered why God was punishing us. Why couldn't anyone stop this horror? Why couldn't we fight back? Where was God's miracle? I felt helpless. I heard my grandmother crying as each detail seemed to hit her and echo over and over again.

I heard my mother's pleas later that night. "Where is God, Leon . . . Where is God?" I lay awake listening to her repeated question. I prayed to God to do something.

Several weeks later, my brother and I had just gone to bed when we heard a knock at the door. My mother went to the window and cautiously peeked out. She saw a tall thin man in his thirties wearing a white band on his arm, a Lithuanian Partisan. She told my father to hide under my bed. The Partisans raided houses now looking for Communist sympathizers. It was a law now that all Jews were required to open the door, otherwise the Partisan had the right to apply force to enter a home and question the occupants using whatever means necessary.

My father forced himself under the bed, reluctantly.

"Good evening, officer, I'm sorry it took me some time to answer the door," my mother explained.

"Good evening, madam," he said and took a step into the house.

My mother could smell alcohol on his breath.

"I am a Lithuanian freedom fighter," he boasted. He looked around the room and peered down at my mother. "You are here alone?"

"Oh no, my mother and my children live here, sir," Mother answered politely.

The "freedom fighter" walked through the rooms of the house. He was nervous. "We have information that Bolsheviks are being hidden in this neighborhood," he said and began to lecture my mother about Lithuanian independence and the evils of Communism. He kept his eyes on the yellow Star of David that was sewn on my mother's dress.

She agreed with him politely, hoping if she were compliant he would leave.

He walked into our bedroom. I slammed my eyes shut after I saw what he looked like. He stood over my bed. Mother begged in whispered tones not to wake Mula or me as he walked over to our beds.

"Jew boys," he slurred.

My mother stiffened at his comment, but remained civil. When they went into the other room I heard him order my grandmother to get him something to eat.

"Do you not get lonely with no man in the house?" he said seating himself and leaning back comfortably on our sofa.

"Mother and I stay very busy with the children," she answered quietly.

"You have very beautiful hands," he said. He reached for her hands and held them in his grip.

She tried to pull them away.

When he felt her resistance, he put his hand firmly on her neck and moved her closer to him. My mother tried to fight him. Finally, he grabbed her face and kissed her. She struggled to free herself from his firm grasp.

He tore her clothing. He tore her Star of David off and threw it to the floor.

"No, please. No! My God! My God!" Mother pleaded.

I heard my mother's pleas and I wanted to help, but I was frightened and I had no idea how I could help.

When Grandmother Rochel walked into the room, my mother was partially naked on the sofa with the Partisan on top of her. Grandmother screamed and dropped the plate of food she had prepared. She fought to pull him off of her daughter. The Partisan, with his left hand, threw the tiny gray-haired woman against the wall.

I felt my father squirm, but he didn't come out from under the bed.

"I'll kill you old woman, I'll kill you!" the Partisan shouted.

I felt my father again under the bed shudder. He moved with each noise we heard from the other room. I wanted him to move out and help, but he stayed writhing in his own pain.

I was biting my lip so hard it began to bleed. I knew what was going on, but I was paralyzed with fear. Tears were stinging my eyes. Each time I heard my mother's terrified cries I felt angry and ashamed because I could do nothing to help her. Finally, there was silence. I clutched the sheets with tight, white-fisted knuckles. I wondered if he was going to kill all of us. I wanted to poke his eyes out with my fingers; every muscle in my body strained from adrenaline and fear. I felt like my rib cage was about to break wide open. I tossed and turned on top of the bed.

I thought my father would go out and help. He didn't. I thought he was a coward. Maybe I was a coward, too.

Sometime in the early hours of the morning the Partisan left. He was sober and polite.

I felt my father finally move out from under the bed after he heard the front door close. A few moments later I walked into the living room and I saw a scene that became permanently etched in my memory. My grandmother was cradling my mother in her arms, my father held both of them in his arms. My mother gazed into space in a blank, dead expression. Tears were rolling down their cheeks. I wanted to cry and I couldn't; all I could do was wonder why there was no help for us. Why didn't my father come to her rescue? Why couldn't we fight back?

These questions would stay with me throughout my life.

The next day Uncle Willie and his wife, Leni, moved into the upper floor of the house. I felt protected with him around. Willie was a man of action.

My mother now lived like a ghost, never changing expressions. She had not combed her hair or changed her clothes since the morning after the attack. She was in a world I could not reach . . . a world of silence. I tried to get her to smile . . . all I could do was hold her hand and wait for her pain to pass.

The tragic events of massacre, rape, and oppression against the Shachnowskis occurred during a very brief period of two months. Any one of these events alone would be a shock. These repeated, tragic blows would scar Leon and Rose throughout their lives. Schaja, on the other hand, began to find his courage through the tragedies.

THREE

The Partisans handed out notices in Jewish neighborhoods stating that all Jews residing in Kaunas would be relocated to Villampole, a newly established residence for Jews. It was actually a village about five miles across the river from Kaunas where many Jews had been massacred on the night of the German invasion. It would later be called Kovno Ghetto by some, but it was a concentration camp.[1]

Dating back to the sixteenth century, Italians created ghettos for Jews to protect them from the Christian population. Because of this, my parents looked at this move with relief. We would be provided a safe haven where our religious culture could survive and be practiced and we would no longer be at the mercy of the Partisans.

Our neighborhood had not been served with a notice. But we continued to hear rumors of this upcoming event. These rumors were always in conflict with the last one and this led to a roller-coaster existence concerning our future under the rule of the Germans. Now, many of the rabbis and influential leaders believed that political issues might be resolved and the

---

[1] *Ghetto vs. Concentration Camp:*

From a German point of view, Ghettos were holding pens for a subjugated population with no rights. Labor was to be exploited, goods and property confiscated. In late 1942 the Nazis began "liquidating" ghettos' remaining populations to extermination camps. It was a slow process that lasted the better part of two years.

The Kovno Ghetto was established in August 1941 and designated Concentration Camp #4, Kovno, in 1943. Records indicate that from a total Kovno population of 40,000 Jews, only 2,000 survived: 500 from the camp and 1,500 who were shipped out of the camp. Anti-Semitic Lithuanians went on a murderous rampage killing 10,000 Jews within one month and just prior to the establishment of the Kovno Camp.

On the other hand, the stated purpose of the concentration camps were threefold. They were penal colonies, a source of labor for special projects, and finally, the camps were used for "liquidation" or murder.

From a victim's perspective it is only semantics and any differences are transparent. Regardless of whether you are in a concentration camp or a ghetto, you were destined for destruction and death. Consequently, we will refer to the Kovno Ghetto as the Kovno Camp.

Jewish population would be safe. Uncle Willie believed that we might not be moved to a camp. They were all wrong.

I was lying on my bed one afternoon trying to stay cool as the breeze blew over me. It was hot and humid and all the windows in the house were wide open. The curtains were flapping back and forth against the wall. I heard the knock and then moments later the curtains were sucked outward. Someone had opened the door. I ran to the living room just in time to hear that we were being "vacated" as they called it.

Uncle Willie organized and instructed each of us that afternoon to take what we had discussed in our plan (we had spent several nights prior to this deciding on what each of us would take if we were forced to leave our home). I packed my favorite clothes, my extra pair of shoes, a wad of clay, and a square of chocolate that I had been saving, and put my bag over my shoulder. After I finished I went to my grandmother to help her pack. She had already finished most of her packing. She asked me to bring her sheet music from the piano bench. "Grandmother, I don't think we will have a piano where we're going."

I looked at the tears well up in her eyes. I ran and got the sheet music.

As I passed my parents' bedroom I saw them wrapping jewelry and money tightly in thin pieces of cloth and concealing them under their clothes.

Within a half hour we each came out of the house with our belongings. My father carried my brother's belongings as well as his own. We each wore our yellow Stars of David and stood in the yard waiting for further instructions.

I looked across the street and saw a Lithuanian family standing on the corner holding their possessions. I realized that they were waiting to move into our house. I stared at them angrily. None of them would look at me.

One of the Lithuanian officials in the yard knew Uncle Willie. He was kind to us but visibly embarrassed when Willie asked where we would be going. He told him very quietly that we were being moved into "adequate" housing. He explained that Jewish officials would be waiting for us at Villampole. For the first time since Mo and I had been attacked I saw a flicker of hope in my mother's eyes. She believed that if the Jewish officials were meeting us that this would be a safe and secure residence until the conflicts were resolved.

A horse-drawn flatbed wagon pulled up in front of our house and we were ordered to get in the back. It was very crowded with barely room to sit. I could hardly breathe during the ride since I was smaller and packed between two large men. Uncle Willie and Leni were walking beside the wagon, protecting my grandmother sitting on the edge. My mother and father were face-to-face trying to protect Mula, who was in my father's arm.

The wagon trip was bumpy, hot, and dusty. The driver stopped after we crossed the bridge a couple of miles later and told us to walk the remaining distance to the camp. Following the rules, we walked in single file with our yellow stars in place.

As we neared the camp, tired and thirsty, we were shocked when we saw thousands and thousands of people standing in long lines clutching their meager possessions. Some carried a piece of furniture, some held photographs, a few carried supplies of food.

As we came nearer the entrance after standing for hours, we saw people showing their papers to the guards and entering the gates of the camp. We realized that we had been lied to again. The guards were not Jewish officials, but Lithuanian guards. A scuffle broke out at the entrance gate with one of the guards. We all watched as the guard confiscated a gun that a man had tried to bring into the camp. He ordered the soldiers standing nearby to take the man away. They dragged him by his arms into a building about twenty yards away.

I looked up at Uncle Willie and then down to the shining pearl handle of his knife. I noticed a patina of sweat on his forehead as he saw a Lithuanian guard move up the line in our direction. He very smoothly took the knife's sheath from his belt and started to throw it into the bushes, but it was too late and he realized the officer would see the weapon.

I was standing in front of him and held the back of my pants open. He quickly slipped the knife into the pants and pulled my shirt down. I could feel my heart pounding as the guard walked past me.

When we reached the gate moments later, the guard took our papers. I looked at him. His brutality mirrored from his eyes. I didn't care; I stared back. He directed us to our quarters. I smiled as I passed through the gate. He never knew I had the knife. After we entered, Uncle Willie discreetly took the knife and I never saw it again while we were in Kovno Camp.

The small houses in the camp were built with flimsy wood slats and large gaps appeared in the wall where they had warped. Each house was constructed differently. Some had foundations, but most did not. The floor of our house had no foundation, only thin boards on top of damp ground. There were two ten-by-ten rooms for five of us. There was no plumbing, no water pipes, and a wood-burning stove sat in a dark corner of the kitchen with a canopy to vent the smoke. There were countless cockroaches near the stove.

We had to share an outhouse with many others and there was no facility for bathing. It was not the Utopia that we had hoped for.

Uncle Willie and Leni lived in a house nearby. Their house had running water and a bathroom and was shared with several other families.

No one spoke as we settled inside our house. There were no beds, only a light blanket for each of us. Before I lay down to go to sleep that night

I hugged and kissed my mother on the cheek and smiled up at her. "Mama, please don't worry, we'll all be safe here."

She smiled back at me and I saw tears in the corner of her eyes.

"I know, Schaja, I know. We must be strong."

I hugged my father and laid down on the floor and used my small blanket as a pillow. I prayed that night that my parents wouldn't give up. I was never going to give up.

The historical facts state that Hitler and the hierarchy of the Lithuanian Church had exacted their hatred upon Jews more completely in Lithuania than in any other nation in the world. It is believed the Lithuanian intent was to "gain points" with Hitler in their effort to become independent . . . To root out Jews from the world for the death of Christ . . . to cleanse Lithuania of Jews for their exploitation financially of the country . . . and the anti-Semitism that related Bolshevism to Jews. At the end of the war over 96 percent of the Jewish population had been killed in Lithuania.

At a very young age, Schaja was becoming a support to his family that would continue throughout his life. The Shachnowski family had no inkling of what horrors awaited them. The camp that had given them momentary hope turned out to be economic isolation, exploitation, and near destruction of an entire Jewish race.

There is no other period in history when such a large group of people experienced so much humiliation, terror, and psychological helplessness. Over thirty thousand prisoners were placed in Kovno; an area meant for seven thousand five hundred. There was no infrastructure, no water pipes, no sewage system, and no access to running water. Not only the brutality of the Gestapo, but the threat of disease was an ever-present terror to the population.

FOUR

I sat and listened attentively to my grandmother's story.

"And when the handsome young prince became king, he made a new law in his village of Sugarhill because he loved all the children in the village and he wanted them to be happy."

"What's the new law, Gram?" I asked.

"I wanted to save this delicious treat until last, Schaja. You must be patient," she smiled and patted my leg. "Every day each child would receive five cookies . . . that was the new law."

Mula heard the word *cookie* and clapped his hands and giggled.

"Each day, Veronica, the king's finest baker would deliver warm chocolate cookies with white icing, and gingerbread cookies with brown sugar icing, and vanilla cookies with cherry icing to all of the children in the village . . ." she continued in her lilting voice.

I couldn't listen any longer; my mouth was watering and my stomach was growling. All I could think about were the cookies. I could almost taste the warm, dripping icing.

Since our arrival several months ago, we were given meager portions of food. Each of us received ten pieces of stale bread, four ounces of horse meat, and two ounces of lard once a week. On few occasions we were provided with fruits and vegetables, usually half rotted. The Jewish Council that had been formed after we arrived was a governing body that communicated with the German authorities about any complaints from the inmates. They begged for an increase of food since some of the older inmates had already died of malnutrition, but their pleas fell on deaf ears.

It was four more days before I would receive any food. I had finished my ration yesterday and was starving. But I wasn't the only one. We were all hungry and it was strange because our favorite topic of discussion was food and eating. We reminisced about past dinners and desserts we had feasted on so long ago. The thing we found most lacking in our existence became an object of fascination. It was a constant demand from the body that pounded into our brain twenty-four hours a day. I wondered how I would last until the next delivery of rations.

The sun had just disappeared from the sky when Grandmother Rochel finished her story. My father was still out with his assigned work crew. All inmates able to work had been assigned to work detail. They were usually taken outside the camp to do construction or cleanup work. Some nights my father didn't return home until ten or eleven o'clock. Mother would pace the floor, wondering if he was still alive. The rumors of Jews being killed for no reason while out on their work crews threaded their way through the camp every day.

I walked over to my sleeping spot to lay down. I closed my eyes and began to dream about food. Sleep was a great escape, but occasionally sleep wouldn't come between the gnawing hunger and my desire to eat . . . eat anything available!

As I tried to force my eyes to stay closed I thought about the vegetable garden I had seen today when Moishe and I were walking near the fence that surrounded the camp. We liked to hide and watch the guards walk along the fence in case anyone tried to escape. Sometimes they would throw their cigarette butts in our direction. Moishe was nine years old and he liked to smoke. If the butt came close enough, he would crawl out from under the bushes and snatch it while the guards had their backs turned. We laid there for hours and made plans about how we could escape the camp.

Moishe had dark black, curly hair and he was a little pudgy. He said he could roll under the fence and look like a ball. I had grown about an inch since our arrival and I was very thin. I told him I was so skinny that I could turn sideways and they would never see me. We covered our mouths when we laughed to keep them from hearing us.

When we returned to our houses later in the day, Moishe showed me the vegetable garden. It was hidden by trees from the road and surrounded by a short barbed-wire fence. We crept past the trees to investigate. I saw potatoes, carrots, and some other vegetables. Moishe said it belonged to the Jewish Council. He said it was guarded at night. I took his word.

After I had gone to bed, pains started shooting through my stomach. I couldn't stand the feeling of hunger any longer. I looked around the room in the darkness and saw Mula and my grandmother sleeping. I was relieved when I heard my father snoring. I had not heard him when he returned from work crew. I was sure my mother was asleep.

I had to get to the vegetable garden. I knew I was taking a chance but it had been over a day and a half since I had eaten. It was my only chance for food unless I stole food from my family and I couldn't do that. I hadn't told my parents that I had already devoured my entire ration. They would have shared their food with me, but they needed it more than I did. They had to have energy to work.

I looked out the window and up at the moon. It was partly covered by clouds so there was not much light on the street. I checked one more time to see if everyone was asleep and wiggled out the window. I quietly edged against the houses as I walked toward the garden. When I got closer to the field, I crouched in the bushes. It was so quiet I could hear myself breathe.

I spotted where the guard was stationed. In a few minutes, I heard footsteps and saw him pacing on the east side of the garden. Then he crossed the center of the garden and continued to walk down the path away from me. I saw him sit down and light a cigarette. This was my chance. I rushed as fast as I could into the center of the garden. I looked around and spotted the potatoes. I dug a hole into the ground beside the potatoes. The dirt was soft as I dug a hole long enough and deep enough for me to lie in. When I was almost finished digging, I heard sounds that I couldn't identify. I pressed myself against the ground in the hole I had dug and tried to discreetly look around.

My heart leaped into my throat when I saw a second guard turning the corner on the west side of the garden. He was close enough that I could hear him humming a tune.

I nestled into the ground as best as I could, facing the sky with my back on the ground. I put handfuls of fresh dirt over my body and pressed dirt onto my face. I kept my eyes closed. I could hear his footsteps on the soil nearby and held my breath until I almost passed out. Then, I heard footsteps pass at the end of the row where I was hidden. I waited a few minutes, sat up, and looked around. It was all clear. I dug into the ground and grabbed a potato. I brushed the dirt from the skin and sunk my teeth into the potato. It was hard and crunchy but that raw potato tasted like heaven to me. I ate two more potatoes and left the vegetable garden with a small carrot in my pocket. I noticed the two guards in the street talking with each other as I skirted past them and back to my house. I munched on the carrot as I ran home with new energy and a full stomach.

I crawled into the window and back to my sleeping spot. I thought about the dangers that I had encountered but I'm sure I was smiling as I went to sleep. I had found a way to quench my hunger, temporarily.

I was outside near the Jewish Council (*altestenrat*—a wise, old advisory group) building eavesdropping on conversations between two elderly men about the state of affairs in the camp. They were interrupted when an official came out on the steps of the building to make a request. "Col. Fritz Jordan, SS commander of our camp, has requested that we provide him with twelve spades. Does anyone have spades or can any be made in the workshop?" he asked some men.

"The council is worried about spades for gardening . . . please, worry about food that we can put in our stomachs now!" One of the men said in disgust.

There were always crowds of people outside the council building. This was where most rumors took root, and most had no factual basis. The two old men went back to their conversation, dismissing the request for the spades. They wrapped their coats around them as a gust of cold wind blew.

But I couldn't dismiss what had been requested. I wondered why. Then it dawned on me. The vegetable garden must belong to the Germans, not the Jewish Council. They needed the spades for the garden I had stolen from. Suddenly, I felt my palms get wet when I realized that the guards were not Jewish police.

Several days later my parents were whispering to each other. I heard something in their conversation about spades. I had become very good at eavesdropping on conversations since I arrived; after all, information is power. I could look in the other direction and still comprehend what was being said many feet away from me.

"Don't worry about the spades," I said. "I was at the council building when they requested them."

My mother looked at me. "This is nothing that concerns you, Schaja," she said and smiled. But she had a worried look on her face.

"They are for the garden," I said.

"Schaja, what are you talking about?" Father asked me.

"I know why they want the spades," I said.

"You're too young, Schaja, to worry about these things. You are not old enough to understand everything you hear. Most of it is rumor," my mother said, becoming impatient when Mula started to cry.

"I know about the spades," I said, trying to get through to them.

"What do you know, Schaja?" father asked.

"I know they need the spades for the garden, just like I said before."

My parents looked at me strangely.

"I saw the garden when I was walking around with Moishe several weeks ago," I said as casually as I could. I knew I had said too much, but I wanted my parents to believe me like they would another grown-up. I was tired of being treated like I shouldn't know anything or hear anything.

"Schaja, do you and Moishe go near that fence?" my mother asked in a frightened voice.

"I just know where it is and the vegetable garden is not far from the fence. What do you expect me to do all day?"

"I don't want you to go far from the house while we're not here," my mother said with a hushed tone. "Please, it's very dangerous for all of us. Schaja, you must be careful."

I thought I was pretty smart about all that went on in the camp, but I would discover that I was very naïve.

FIVE

I was outside playing with Moishe, Jochim, Samuel, and Anna. Every afternoon we played a game balancing on a log. It was a battle between two people and the winner was the one that stayed on the log without falling off. The streets were always crowded and we had a lot of spectators. My opponent was stronger and much better at this game than I. He sent me flying off the log and I landed in a pile of rocks. When I looked up, Meck was standing over me.

Meck, was much older, probably about twenty-something. I liked him, he always smiled and talked to my friends and me whenever he saw us outside. My parents knew his mother and father who had once owned a jewelry store in Kaunas.

Meck was confident and sure of himself. He reminded me of Uncle Willie. He didn't act like anyone else in the camp. He never walked with his head bowed down in defeat; he walked with a swagger of superiority. He wasn't ignorant of the difficulties we faced but he wasn't going to allow anything to keep him from being happy. I liked his attitude.

"Schaja, are you all right?" Meck asked.

My head hurt, but I didn't want to admit that to him. I wanted to be brave like him. "I'm okay, I just fell off." I started to get up but I was a little dizzy.

"Schaja, take it easy," Meck said, and helped me up by my arm. He walked with me to the sidewalk nearby and we sat down together.

"Schaja, you can be very good at that game," Meck said.

"I don't think so," I answered. "I'm not that strong. I'm shorter than most of my friends."

"Yes, yes, Schaja, you are strong . . . not with big muscles!" Meck said and stood up in a stance like a body builder. "Schaja, your strength is all here . . ." He put his hand above his belt on his stomach. "All of your strength comes from here," he said, patting his upper stomach where the ribs are. "This is your center. This is where you learn balance."

I looked at him and stood up. "Here," I pointed at the same spot.

"Yes," he said. "Stand on this stick." He grabbed a branch lying on the ground.

I stood on the narrow branch.

"Now walk carefully on the broadest part of the stick, and keep your center steady with your stomach muscles . . . you won't fall off."

I did as he told me. "You're right," I said, smiling and balancing myself on the branch.

"You see," Meck smiled and ruffled my hair. "There's a secret to everything, Schaja. Now go back and challenge your opponent."

I walked back over toward the log, but before I could challenge my opponent to play, the entire street froze with the sound of frantic screams.

"The hospital! The hospital! They are all burning alive!!! They're burning them alive," Mr. Levine, one of the inmates screamed as he came around the corner and into the street. He held his head as though he couldn't comprehend what he had seen. "Look, look up in the sky."

We all looked up and there was smoke billowing over the gray sky.

Someone else grimly told us that the hospital was burned to the ground because of a "typhus epidemic." "Everyone in the hospital was burned alive, including the nurses." The man broke down as he spoke and struggled to continue.

I heard later that a pit was dug surrounding the outside of the hospital. They were dug with the spades that had been requested by the German authorities. The elderly and orphans from the smaller side of the camp across the bridge were arrested and gunned down and then thrown into the pit and set on fire.

I was shocked: the spades were used to dig the pit beside the hospital.

After this incident, rumors surfaced about more deaths. Five thousand Jews had died in Vilnus. For many in the camp, this event caused them to lose hope. Every day was just one day closer to death.

There continued to be epidemics of typhus due to the unsanitary conditions of overflowing and open cesspools of sewage in the camp. Outhouses were exposed as people tore them down to use the wood to make fires and survive the increasingly frigid temperatures in Kovno. The latter epidemics were unreported and concealed by Dr. Brauns, chief medical doctor of the camp. He was confronted by a group of Lithuanian doctors from Kaunas about a sudden case of the deadly disease of typhus. He convinced them that there were only problems with a flu epidemic. Dr. Brauns, with the help of the Jewish Council, concealed over seventy cases of typhus from both the Lithuanians and the Germans.

Six

The smell of burning flesh seemed to hang in the air after the hospital "action." The street outside my house was rarely crowded. Fear was more deadly an epidemic than typhus. It affected everyone.

Starvation seemed less important now, but hunger still gnawed at my insides. After the hospital incident I had confirmed that the Jewish police were the guards for the vegetable garden and I made visits in the middle of the night when I couldn't bear the pains in my stomach.

Uncle Willie, my father, and my mother spent the evenings whispering about the possibilities of escape. Uncle Willie had arranged for Leni's escape, successfully. We all painfully understood that the Germans would use any excuse to kill a Jew and in order to survive we must escape. We were caged animals waiting for the next massacre.

I developed an instinct for survival. If I saw any kind of trouble, I hid. I learned to disappear into an alley, a doorway, or behind a shrub. If I saw a German or Lithuanian guard walking toward me I ran before he noticed me.

I didn't trust the Jewish police and would hide if I saw one patrolling our street. There had been rumors that Jewish policemen had killed other Jews. I already knew the Jewish Council was benefiting from the vegetable garden while the inmates were starving.

I woke up one morning to the sound of hammering outside. My parents had not gone to work yet. The three of us went outside and joined the others who were looking at a notice posted throughout the camp by the Jewish police. I couldn't read the notice, but my father read the posted note printed in Yiddish.

The Council has been ordered by the authorities to publish the following official decree to the camp inmates. All inmates of the camp, without exception, including children and the sick, are to leave their homes on Tuesday, October 28, 1941, at 6 A.M., and to assemble in Demokratu Square, and to line up in accordance with police instruction. The camp inmates are required to report by families, each family being headed by the worker who is the head of the family.

It is forbidden to lock apartments, wardrobes, cupboards, desks, etc.
After 6 A.M. nobody may remain in his apartment.
Anyone found in the apartments after 6 A.M. on this day will be shot
on sight.

My parents looked at each other and I could hear the others standing nearby beginning to mumble in a whispered tone. Several of the women started crying. My father squatted down and spoke to me. I looked at his tight, controlled expression as he explained to me what the notice said. He spoke to me in a very calm and gentle tone, but I felt the seriousness of the posted order.

"Are they going to kill us?" I asked. I had heard rumors that the population had to be decreased at Kovno because of the overcrowded conditions.

"Schaja, don't think such thoughts," my mother said to me.

"Why are people crying?" I asked.

"We are all frightened, Schaja, but we have to remain strong," my father answered.

I looked at him and his hands were trembling. He was right, we were all scared.

My mother took me by the hand. "We cannot think that we will die, we must only think of living," she said.

"They killed the old people, the sick people, and the babies and orphans. And I heard that they killed a lot of people in other countries, too. Moishe's parents told him that we would probably all die. He said we are being tested by God."

"Schaja, remember what you told me the first night we arrived here?"

I shook my head. When I looked into her eyes, I was suddenly afraid of being left with no parents.

My mother read my thoughts. "The first night we were here Schaja, you told me that everything was going to be all right. And we must stay strong and believe that we are going to be fine. Your father has a good education. I am strong and can work and we are all healthy, thanks to God. They need people to work, and we are lucky."

She said this with such confidence, I felt better. I nodded my head and tried to forget what Moishe's parents had told him. Maybe he just made it up.

"What about Grandmother Rochel? Can she work?" I asked.

"We'll protect her, Schaja," my mother answered in a less confident voice.

It was dark, damp, and cold as we began our journey to Demokratu Square. I could feel the icy mist hitting the top of my cap. We had to walk slowly because the road was congested with the mass of people. My father was carrying my brother, Mula.

I held my mother's hand as we walked with my grandmother on her other side. My father led the way. Streams and streams of people were converging toward the square. I never realized how many people there were in the camp. Most of them came in groups with their families and others were assembled in groups from their neighborhood. It looked like a funeral procession. Despite the massive amount of people, you could almost hear a pin drop as we came to a halt and stood obediently in the square waiting for further instructions.

"Form into columns," a Jewish policeman shouted as he passed us, tapping a short stick on his gloved palm.

When we heard the order we formed ourselves into columns. I saw one of the elderly people several yards across from me squat down on the ground from fatigue. Immediately, several people crouched to help her stand up. They continued to support her. No one wanted to look weak. I looked around and saw Lithuanian and German guards on the perimeter of the square, their guns hung to their side.

Occasionally, one of the soldiers would prop himself against his gun, take out a cigarette, light up, and chat with the other guards. They laughed and joked as we stood, somber and silent, waiting for life or death.

My stomach was empty, and I thought I was going to be sick. I was shivering from the cold or maybe because I was more terrified than I had ever been in my life. It is the cruelest agony of all to stand for hours waiting for the unknown. As I looked in the eyes of the guards, I saw no mercy, no hint of sorrow, no hint of compassion. I wondered if they had children of their own.

I looked around for Uncle Willie, but I couldn't locate him. After several hours the dawning rays of sun began to filter through the morning clouds. My mother looked down and saw me shivering. She motioned to me and I realized that I needed to stand straight. I watched my grandmother and saw her getting weak, at times gasping for breath.

I turned around and tried to distract myself from this barbaric moment, but scenes of cruelty were everywhere I looked. I saw old people trying to stay strong even though they were on the verge of collapse; mothers were holding their babies close to them and hushing them in fear of being killed for even the slightest sound.

I looked at my father when I heard him mumbling. He was saying prayers. He was praying as fervently as I ever remember. His head was down and he was racing through the prayers he knew, or even halfway remembered. He was reaching out to God with all of his heart.

I don't know why, but I started talking under my breath. "I wish I had never been born a Jew, I wish I had never been born a Jew." I kept repeating this over and over again. I wished more than ever that we had been born something else so we could be spared from this nightmare.

My mother heard me and shook her head. I saw tears in her eyes as she squeezed my hand.

I didn't care, I was angry and I stared back at my mother. "I hate being a Jew!" I whispered.

An elderly, very frail lady was standing in front of me. She was clutching her cane when I saw her fall. Her husband, who was as frail as she, grabbed her by the waist and tried to hold her steady. Her head was falling from side to side as she lost consciousness. I could see her husband tottering under her slight weight. I wanted to reach out and help him but the guards were hovering nearby with their weapons. Finally, her legs buckled and she crumpled to the ground. Her body lay still and lifeless. Her husband cried out desperately and fell on top of her. When he realized her life was gone, he convulsed into sobs of heartbreak.

I felt the weight of his heartbreak in my own heart. My soul was broken as was his. I hid my eyes in my mother's back to escape this sight of agony. I realized in that moment that life wasn't fair and there was no one you could trust.

No one could comfort the poor man in his sorrow without fear of being punished. I pressed closer to my mother for comfort, but there was no comfort for what I had seen; my life had changed forever. Deep inside, a part of me turned cold and numb. I watched the Jewish police drag the elderly couple away by their arms and legs.

My father, who only a short time ago was praying to God asking for help, was now cursing God, questioning his existence. This moment scarred each of us.

As the morning crept by in an endless eternity, we finally heard a stir at the front of the line as a Gestapo officer positioned himself on a mound and began barking out orders that we were unable to hear. It became apparent as people approached him that he was instructing them to go to the left or to the right.

The only sounds I could hear were the cries of pain and the cracking of bones. The square was littered with bodies. My head started to spin. I took deep breaths trying to keep myself from passing out. My mother quickly took my hand again. I kept my eyes on her face. I had to find a way to escape what I was seeing.

My mind wandered to the past and more pleasant times. I could almost taste the warm sugar icing on the cookies that my grandmother made . . . I thought about the gifts I had been given for my birthday. It was hard but I kept thinking about anything but the present and I started feeling better.

I was jolted out of my fantasy as we neared the Gestapo officer on the mound. Master Sergeant Rauca was acting as judge, jury, and executioner of each human life that passed before him. He held a swagger stick in his hand. As the line moved, he ordered each prisoner's fate. I noticed that he never made eye contact with his victims. He would simply snap his stick to the right or to the left: life or death. As he directed those ahead of us, I wondered which way was life and which was death . . . right or left. It appeared to me that right might be the good side.

When Rauca dismissed the person ahead of us I saw that my father was sweating profusely and he was close to panic. I held onto my mother's hand for dear life. She was also struggling to help my grandmother stand straight.

My father's glasses began to fog from perspiration and cold air as he moved toward Rauca. He could hardly breathe from anxiety as he approached the master sergeant. He moved forward and stumbled clumsily as he balanced my little brother in his right arm. I quietly gasped when I saw the expression on Rauca's face when he moved too close to him. He almost fell into him.

"Halt!" Rauca shouted and pushed my father away. I closed my eyes tightly. I was sure when I opened them my father would be lying on the ground, dead. "Recht!" he yelled angrily, and glared at my father as he pointed his stick to the right.

My mother let go of my hand and spoke to the master sergeant. "Guten Tag, and how are you today, Captain?" she said smiling, speaking in correct German diction. Every officer was always captain to my mother.

He looked at her with a puzzled expression on his face. It took him several seconds before he changed his mind. He then pointed his stick to the left.

My entire body froze when I saw this. I tried to take in a breath, but I was paralyzed with fear. I was sure that we had been directed to the death side. Why had my mother interfered? "Recht" was the safe side! I was sure of it! We all moved slowly to the line on the left. I felt defeated and dazed. I was going to die. I envied my little brother and wished that I was younger and didn't understand that I was going to die. I felt sick again. I looked at my parents and they were staring straight ahead, but they didn't even look concerned. Had they not realized that we were going to die?

When I looked at the other prisoners being directed to our line, I saw the stronger people were being sent to the left. I looked up at my mother and she was nodding her head in the affirmative without speaking to me. We were on the good side.

Thoughts began racing through my mind. Why? What saved us? Was it my mother's cheerful remarks to the Gestapo officer? I wondered if it had been God that swayed him? Did my father's German diploma change his mind? Was it my father's prayers earlier that had invoked this act of God? Did God want to prove to me that he existed? I didn't know why, I only knew that we had survived another day.

The Nazis exterminated approximately ten thousand Jews in the Demokratu Square "great action." In a death procession the Germans led the unlucky, the unhealthy, the mothers with innocent babies, the pregnant, and the elderly past their families who stood in helplessness as their loved ones were escorted to a waiting death sentence. The prisoners silently trudged through the mud with their heads down and their gaze forward as they had been ordered. Soldiers marched pointing rifles in their backs, prepared to shoot if they tried to escape. They were never heard from or seen again. The remaining prisoners at Kovno knew those taken would arrive at Fort IX for liquidation.

SEVEN

We were all drained when we returned home, and shocked to discover our entire house had been ransacked. Dishes were thrown out of the cabinet and broken. The small amount of valuables that were not concealed were gone. A few coins that Grandmother Rochel had hidden in the cotlike bed had been confiscated.

My father ran to the room where he and Mother slept. He pushed the small bed several feet and knelt down to a floorboard. He tapped one end of the board and then carefully pressed down on the other end. I peered over his shoulder. When he lifted up the board, I could see it was hollowed out. Then I saw the cloth that I had seen when my parents were wrapping the jewels as we left our home in Kaunas. My father took out each cloth and placed them on the floor.

I heard the door to our house open. My father threw himself over the jewelry. I looked up and saw it was Uncle Willie. I jumped up and ran to him. My mother and he hugged. He went to my grandmother, who was staring silently into space. When he approached her, she whispered to him.

"I can't go on any longer, son. I don't have the strength," her voice was weak with fatigue.

"You can, Mama. You're just tired, but I promise we will find a way out of this hell," Willie said softly. "Stay strong."

She just shook her head and continued to stare vacantly.

I held Willie's hand and walked with him to my father.

"Is it all here?" Willie asked. "The Partisans ransacked every home. They took any valuables they could find. They even took some people's rations."

My father had carefully laid out the jewels on top of the bed. He had unwrapped the sparkling gems. I saw green ones and sparkling white ones and red ones. They were made into brooches, rings, and necklaces. They were set in gold or platinum and some were loose gems without a setting.

"Are these ours?" I asked.

"Yes, some of these were your grandparents' that I inherited and some are your mother's jewelry."

I had never seen the jewels before. I was usually in bed when my parents dressed up to go out in the evening and when they came home it was dark. If they came into my room I was usually too sleepy to notice.

"This is something that you must never talk about with anyone, Schaja," Uncle Willie said looking at me sternly. "No one can know that we have these possessions."

"This is our ticket to freedom, Schaja. It takes money to escape . . . this is what we'll use for money," my father said. He counted each piece and acknowledged to Willie that no pieces were missing. He wrapped up each piece again and put them back in their hiding place.

I hoped that my parents and Uncle Willie could find a way for us to escape soon.

On October 21, 1941, during a diatribe, Hitler compared Jewish Christianity with Jewish Bolshevism, comparing the fall of the Roman Empire with latter-day Bolshevization through the Jews. "If we eradicate [ausrotten] the plague," he said in conclusion, "we will be carrying out a good deed for mankind, the significance of which our men out there can have no conception."

Four days later, while meeting with Himmler and Reinhard Heydrich, two of his secretaries (Heydrich had just been promoted on September 27 to deputy Reich protector, making him chief of security police and security service), the conversation again broached the subject of the Jews and Hitler's hatred for the race. "This criminal race has the two million dead of the World War on its conscience," he continued, "now again hundreds of thousands. Don't anyone tell me we can't send them into the marshes. Who bothers then about our people?" (There had been an attempt during the prior summer to drown all Jewish women in a German town in a marsh.)

> *Report by SS Col. Karl Jager, December 1, 1941 (sent to Hitler):*
> *"Today I can confirm that our objective, to solve the Jewish problem for Lithuania, has been achieved by Einsatzkommando 3. In Lithuania, there are no more Jews, apart from Jewish workers and their families in the Camps."*
> Hitler 1936–1945 Nemesis, *by Ian Kershaw*

JANUARY 20, 1942

It was a cold, wet, and gray morning as twelve Mercedes Benz staff cars carrying the secretaries of the Third Reich entered the gated circular driveway of the Wannsee Villa in Berlin. Each car had been stopped at the gate by a Nazi guard and waved through as the identity of each man was confirmed: Deputy

Reich protector Reinhard Heydrich, Dr. Alfred Meyer, Dr. Eberhard Schongarth, Dr. Rudolf Lange, Dr. Wilhelm Stukcart, Dr. Gerhard Klopfer, Dr. Roland Freisler, Erich Neumann, Dr. Martin Luther, Gen. Otto Hofmann, Col. Adolf Eichmann, Gen. Heinrich Muller, and Heidrich's stenographer. The secretaries considered themselves the real "doers" and crisis managers of the Third Reich.

During this meeting Heydrich gave to each secretary at the table a protocol entitled Conference of State Secretaries. This title would translate into a decision called "the final solution" as the meeting fully developed. It was a final plan to exterminate the entire Jewish population discussed in detail as these men ate their gourmet luncheon prepared by the finest chef in Berlin. As they chatted with each other over brandy and cigars, the room was thick with smoke and laughter and some derision between secretaries. As casually as a businessman would order the assembly plans of a product, these men planned the implementation for extermination of an entire race.

The meeting lasted a little over two hours, not once discussing the morality of their actions, but rather, the process and method of the extermination. The purpose of the meeting was kept within the high ranks of the Third Reich. The language of the extermination orders was softened in order that the public at large would never fully understand the intent that would be enforced.

EIGHT

Since the Demokratu Square "great action" my grandmother was not the same. She didn't tell Mula and me stories any longer. She had lost her hope for the future and nothing anyone could say changed her mind. My mother confided in me that she was very worried and asked me to try and be cheerful during the day while she and my father were gone on work crew. I took this responsibility very seriously and did everything I could to make my grandmother smile. I asked her to play games with me, but she just silently shook her head and stared vacantly into space. I told her corny jokes that I had heard from my friends, but it was as though she didn't even hear me.

She would sometimes sing lullabies to Mula and they both fell asleep for afternoon naps. I listened to the lullabies and waited until I was sure they were asleep then I put on my coat and went outside.

Each afternoon, Moishe and Michael would wait on the corner for me. We walked down the street to Spitz's house to play Territory. This game could sometimes take days to play and there were times when it would sometimes last only minutes. The purpose of the game was to gain land, like a land baron. To start the game, a rectangle was drawn on a decided square of land. The opponents had to agree on the spot. Next, it was decided where the line dividing the land was drawn across the rectangle. The next point of negotiation was who would go first. Once that was decided the game could begin. Each player had a pocketknife or other sharp instrument that he would throw beyond the line. If it stuck into the ground after it was thrown, a line would be drawn where the knife landed and the player would take possession of the land.

We felt a sense of safety playing in front of Spitz's house since his father was a high-ranking official who assigned jobs in the labor department of the Jewish Council. He also had a reputation for taking bribes in exchange for assigning an easy job on certain work crews. Spitz was about ten years old and was the smartest one in our group, but he was also the ugliest. He had a narrow, long nose, his chin stuck out, and his head was long and thin; he looked like a witch.

Spitz had a pocketknife that he was always sharpening and he had a strong arm. He usually won the game quickly, but today his opponent had made a perfect throw to the far edge of the rectangle . . . Spitz gave him the game. Moishe, Michael, and I had just arrived when Spitz lost. Michael took his place.

I watched Spitz as he wandered off and went inside his house. Moishe and I stood on the sidelines and cheered quietly for Michael. All of us were careful not to make too much noise and draw attention to ourselves.

I took my turn after Michael lost his land, and negotiated a rocky, rough area for my side of "territory." I did this because it was harder for the knife to stick in a rocky area so I had to give them more land to achieve my goal. Spitz always got mad at me and said it was lousy land and no one would want the land if they did win. He used to tell me that a rich man wants good land and he has to be smart enough to hold onto it. Maybe he was right, but I still thought my method was better and I won more games than he did.

I walked over to a rock and sat down. The wind was blowing and I pulled my coat collar around my face. But I could still feel the wind blowing through the holes in my jacket.

Spitz walked up next to me holding a piece of bread. He took a big bite out of it as I watched with pleading eyes. He glanced at me but ignored my silent plea. He continued to eat his bread. My stomach was even trying to get his attention with its growls. I started to get angry as I watched him eat. I wanted to rip the bread from his hand and gobble the last bite. It wasn't fair, I thought to myself. Spitz always had warm clothing and food because of his father's position.

"You got a lot a' nerve, Spitz! How could you stand here and eat in front of all of us?" I said. The other kids stopped the game and came closer to us. They watched as Spitz put the last bite into his mouth.

He sort of smirked at me. "Yeah, well I did you a favor, I turned the bread over so you didn't have to see the fat I smeared on the other side."

I got up and stood in front of him. I wanted to hit him but then I remembered his powerful father. He controlled the work crew assignments and he could assign my parents to the hardest and most dangerous crews. I held my temper and challenged Spitz to a game of Territory.

I let him win. But I had a plan.

Several days later I went back to play Territory in front of Spitz's house and joined the first game I could. I made no effort to win. I asked Spitz if he wanted to take my place. He gladly accepted.

As the game continued I drifted slowly toward the back of the group. I walked discreetly to Spitz's house. I stood outside of the house and called his name so the neighbors wouldn't be curious. I waited a few moments and acted as if Spitz had called me inside his house.

I opened the door and moved slowly through the rooms looking for hiding places, poking and probing in bags and closets where the food might be hidden. I could feel the sweat in the palm of my hands as I cautiously crept through the house. I kept my ears strained, listening for anyone who approached the house. I walked through the small rooms several times and everywhere I looked, I found nothing. Then I remembered where my father hid our jewelry. I started looking at each of the boards of the floor. Then I went into the bedroom and moved the bed. I checked all of the floorboards. I tapped on the one that had been under the top bedpost. The board moved a little bit. I forced the board up and I found the niche where the food was hidden.

Just like my father's hiding place, a space had been hollowed out and there were about a dozen cans of food concealed. I took four cans of food. Two cans were liverwurst, one can was sauerkraut, and the other was sweet candy. They appeared to be military rations.

When I stepped out the doorway, I saw a neighbor lady peering out the window from next door. I looked at her innocently as I closed the door. I could almost see a small smile on her face as I shoved the cans into the pockets of my coat. I put my head down and ran back to my house. I was elated and felt like a secret agent that had just cracked his first case.

I quietly turned the doorknob when I got home, and tiptoed over to my sleeping area. Grandmother Rochel and Mula were still asleep. I tucked the food under my blanket and sneaked out again. I ran back to the game as though I had never been gone. Spitz was still winning. I reasoned that God had kept the winning streak alive so I could confiscate the illegal food. I stood and cheered for Spitz to keep winning.

My parents came home earlier than usual that night. I pulled the cans out from under my blanket and showed my father what I had confiscated. My father's eyes grew wide when he saw the food.

"Where did you get these things, Schaja?" he asked.

"I found them, Papa," I lied.

"What do you mean you found them . . . Where?" He looked at me with suspicion. He tried to contain his joy about the food until he found out the details.

"I was walking around with Michael and Moishe and I saw the cans," I said.

"Did Michael and Moishe take home some cans?" he asked.

"No, finders keepers," I said. "They said since I found them I should keep them." I looked off into the distance, trying to get my story straight.

"You didn't offer to share?" he asked.

"Yes, but they wouldn't accept," I lied.

"You know these are military rations and they possibly belong to the Germans?"

"It's food . . ." I answered.

My father sat and thought things over. He knew I was lying. My mother listened to my answers as she tidied up the house, not daring to look at me. She knew I was lying, too. Then my father leaned over and opened a can of liverwurst. We all started laughing. Even Mula clapped his hands.

My grandmother smiled when she tasted a bite of bread topped with liverwurst. After we finished devouring the cans of food, my father and I found a spot to bury the tins.

The next day I joined the game in the afternoon as usual.

Spitz came bounding out of his house to join the game. "Someone broke into our house yesterday and took some of my father's important papers . . . any of you guys see anyone?"

We all looked at Spitz with puzzled expressions.

He looked around at the group for any response. "Well, whoever did it is in serious trouble. They took important documents dealing with the labor office."

We all looked even more surprised, especially me!

"I can't believe anyone would be that stupid!" Michael said.

"Maybe they didn't know that it was your dad's house and took things and didn't know how important they were," said one of the kids.

"Why would any sane person want to steal documents?" I asked.

Spitz didn't answer.

We all shook our heads in disbelief at how much trouble the perpetrator would be in if he was caught.

Word spread about the robbery at Spitz's home. But nobody wanted to help find the culprit. Most people just wanted to mind their own business and try to survive another day. No one cared to help Spitz's father; he had made many enemies.

I continued to take food from Spitz's home on more than one occassion. I always shared it with my family. I never confessed my crime to my father, but after a while he figured out where I was getting the food.

"Schaja, you are the little paper document bandit, hmmm?" he said peering at me over his glasses.

"Yes, sir." I looked at him.

He rubbed his chin and said nothing.

"I don't understand why Spitz and his family have more than the rest of us. He always has more food and better clothes than any of us. He's still fat and the rest of us are skinny!" I blurted out.

"They are trying to survive just as we are, Schaja," he said.

"So what!" I said angrily. "I am, too! I suppose you are going to give me a lecture about honesty and integrity?"

He looked softly at me and paused a long moment.

I wish I had held my temper, but I was frustrated. It was a battle between not stealing and starving. I had justified my actions, believing people were supposed to care about one another and Spitz and his family had more than I did, but then again I was taking their supply of food and I wasn't supposed to take what was theirs. It became a mass of confusion as all of these conflicting thoughts circled in my head. I felt bad about taking food from another family. And to make matters worse, I knew about the Jewish Council's vegetable garden. It just wasn't fair; everywhere I looked I saw injustice.

My father saw my frustration and he was at a loss of how to explain the lack of justice in our circumstance. "Erst kommt das Fressen und dan kommt die Moral." He spoke so softly I could barely hear his words.

"Food first and after that morality." He was right.

NINE

I woke up early when I heard shouting coming from the house next door. I was shivering from the icy temperatures of February. It was one of the coldest winters in Lithuania. The shouting got louder. I sat up and looked out toward the house next door. I looked through the exposed window and saw the father talking to his daughter who was crying. He was shaking his finger at her and lecturing as she sat distraught on the bed. I could also see the daughter's boyfriend standing in the recess of the room with his head hanging down. As I shook myself from sleep I realized the conversation was about the daughter being pregnant. Her father's face was turning beet red with anger. He shook his finger repeatedly at the boyfriend.

"Couldn't you keep yourself under control?!!!" he said, turning toward the young man. "You knew the consequences. If they find out that she is pregnant it could mean a trip to Fort IX . . . for both of you!"

"Papa, we didn't mean to." She cried and pleaded with her father. "It was my fault, too, not just his."

The father put his head in his hands and mumbled to himself. Then his voice got loud when he said *abortion*. He wiped away tears when he raised his face. I heard her mother cry loudly when she walked into the room. Her mother came over to the young girl and put her arms around her. She was speaking softly and I couldn't hear what she was saying.

Then the young girl spoke. "No, Mama, please, no. I want this baby. I don't care if they kill me, I want to carry his baby. Please, no abortion," she said crying hysterically.

"They will kill you Kindra . . . you must be sensible," the father said.

She threw herself across the bed and began sobbing. Her boyfriend tried to comfort her. He looked fearfully toward her father as he sat down next to her.

I didn't know our neighbors very well, but I had seen Kindra and her boyfriend kissing when they stood together out of the view of her parents. They looked like they enjoyed it a lot when they kissed. I watched them move their bodies together. It reminded me of the nanny and her boyfriend when he came over and visited her while my mother was not at home when we lived in Kaunas. I used to spy on them. Sometimes she would take her blouse off and they would start breathing like they were running a race.

I never knew my neighbor's name before. Kindra was a pretty name. She was slender, with black shiny hair, and when she smiled her teeth looked very white against her dark complexion. I thought she was very beautiful. Her boyfriend was handsome, too.

I wasn't sure what abortion meant, but I thought it had something to do with not having a baby. I decided that I would ask Michael. He was about thirteen years old and knew about things between men and women.

An older lady entered into the neighbor's room and now there was quiet conversation going on between all of them. I got up and brushed my clothes off. I slept in all of my clothes now because the temperatures were frigid. Firewood for the stove was scarce. I had seen people burn part of the wood from their houses to keep warm. The wooden sides of the outhouses had been torn down and used as firewood to avoid freezing.

When I put on my shoes, I grabbed a small piece of cardboard that I had saved and put it in the bottom of my shoe to cover the hole in my sole. I put on my stocking cap and went outside before my parents were awake. It was a Christian holiday and work crews were at a minimum.

It had snowed during the night and everything outside was covered in a soft cushion of white. I followed the footstep tracks in the street. Some of the tracks were big and I visualized the person that had made them. Some of them were boot tracks. I decided that those were guards. I hid behind the house when I saw someone coming down the street. I pressed myself into a recessed area in the house next to us until they passed by and I moved over to my backyard and drew figures in the snow. I was just beginning to make a snowman when I heard the door open from the house next door. I ran up against the house so I could see who came outside.

I saw the old lady coming out the door with Kindra. As they walked down the street I followed them. I kept out of sight, but I could see that Kindra was still crying. The old lady patted her on the shoulder as they walked. When they had passed several blocks, the old lady stopped and turned to look around before she and Kindra walked into an alleyway. I barely had time to jump inside a doorway before she saw me. After they turned, I moved fast looking down the alleyway. I saw them stop in front of a stone building with no windows. After a few minutes, a large man pushed open a small inconspicuous door. He held the door open until the two women disappeared inside. I watched him as he held onto a grip from the inside of the door and pulled it toward him until it was shut. I was amazed: the entrance now looked like a seamless wall of the building. This was a secret hideaway.

I couldn't wait to tell Michael and Moishe about this adventure later today. I found a place to hide so I could see what was going to happen next. I crawled into a hollowed-out area where I was shielded from the wind. It was so comfortable that I dozed off. I woke up and rubbed my eyes when I heard voices. The sun had broken through the clouds and it was almost noon.

I saw the old lady and Kindra come out of the door. The man was helping the old lady hold her steady. It looked like Kindra was sick. She looked pale and woozy. I watched as both the man and woman walked on each side of her. I followed them all the way home without detection. I slipped inside my own house unnoticed by them.

"Schaja, where have you been? I've been searching all over the neighborhood for you," my mother said angrily.

I jumped nervously when I heard my mother's voice compared to the cushioned quiet outside. "I'm sorry, Ma. I woke up early and went outside and played in the snow."

"Were you out with those older boys you run with, Schaja?" Father asked.

"No sir, I was by myself. I was following the tracks in the snow," I said. I thought this was similar to the truth.

My grandmother was sitting in the corner shivering. I went over and picked up my blanket and wrapped it around her.

She reached for my hand and kissed it. "He's a good boy, Rose. He'll always take care of you." And for one of the few times since Demokratu Square, my grandmother smiled at me.

My mother was so happy that my grandmother seemed content that she forgot her anger and smiled, too.

I looked around and saw that everyone was resting. I was anxious to tell my friends about my morning. "Mother, may I go out and play with Michael and Moishe?"

"Schaja, you just got home. Stay here with us for a while. I've made soup from our vegetables in this week's rations and it would be nice if we could all sit down together."

I shrugged and accepted her wishes. It was almost 4 P.M. before I could go out to play. I stuck two potatoes that I had taken from the vegetable garden a couple of nights ago in my pocket. I went to the street near Spitz's house and saw Michael playing. I stood next to Moishe until the game was finished. I motioned to Michael to follow me.

We had a hangout where we went when we needed to make a plan or have a discussion. The hangout was an overhang that provided a little protection and privacy.

Michael told me that he slept here occasionally. I didn't know where Michael lived and he never talked about having parents. I wondered if he was an orphan.

Moishe followed us. When we were hidden, I handed each of them a potato from my pocket. I was surprised when Micheal pulled something out of his pocket that was wrapped in a white paper and handed it to me. It was a tiny sliver of white cake with sugar icing. I couldn't believe my eyes. I shoved the sweet cake into my mouth and let it melt slowly. Michael and

Moishe both started laughing. I started to laugh, too, but I didn't dare let a single crumb drop to the floor as I laughed.

They started to crunch on the raw potatoes. We were all happy eating our delicacies. Just eating was a treat in the camp.

"Michael," I said after I had finished. "Where did you get the cake?"

"I work with some guys who have a contact on the outside," he said in his cool and nonchalant manner.

"What contact on the outside?" I asked.

"A Lithuanian peasant woman! She's our contact."

"How, how did you get a contact?"

"Well, one of the older kids found a man that arranged with a lady on the outside to smuggle food to us. We have to pay him whatever we make, but there are a few of us who smuggle the food inside."

"Can I work with you?" I asked.

"You'd be the youngest kid in the group," he said reluctantly.

"Yeah, but I can do anything you need. I can run fast," I said.

"You can't be a scaredy-cat," he said and looked at me.

"I'm no scaredy-cat," I said firmly, my eyes meeting his.

"Schaja, why do you want to do this? It's dangerous," said Moishe.

"I'm not afraid," I said standing tall.

Moishe shrugged.

"Okay, kid, meet us where the fence curves at the farthest angle of the camp. We'll have to train you," Michael said, getting up from the ground.

We all started to go back to the games. I pulled Michael back with me. "Michael, what's an abortion?" I whispered discreetly.

He thought for a few moments. "Well, it's when a baby is taken away from a girl that gets pregnant when she's too young."

"But, how does that happen?" I asked.

"The girl has to drink something and then she pees the baby out. I had to have one of my girlfriends do that."

"You had sex with her?" I asked in awe of my friend.

"Sure, lots of times," he said and ran to join the next game.

Michael was really something. He knew how to get food and girls.

TEN

I could barely sleep when I went to bed that night. I wanted morning to come so I could meet Michael and the other boys. I was familiar with the area they used to cross over. But before you reached the fence to the outside there was about twenty feet called the Death Zone. Those twenty feet could mean life or death.

I imagined myself hustling through the Death Zone and under the fence, running as fast as I could to meet the Lithuanian contact on the other side and then running like the wind to bring back a box filled with food. And of course, I was under heavy Nazi gunfire. My desire for food was stronger than the fear I should have been considering. I could already taste the food.

I finally dropped off to sleep only an hour or so before I went on my mission. It seemed like minutes when I opened my eyes and the sun was beginning to rise. I quietly sneaked out of the house while my grandmother slept. It was after seven and my parents were already gone, but there were still a few work crews walking through the front gate on the way to their work sites. Each man now wore a cap. It was a new rule enforced by the Germans. When a worker approached a guard he had to take off his hat as a symbol of respect to a German soldier. I watched the men show their respect to the guards milling around the gate.

There was also a Jewish police officer shouting orders to the workers. He was assigned by the council to help organize workers each morning. There were times that he could save a worker's life by reminding him of all the rules imposed by the Germans. There were new laws enforced every day.

I stayed hidden while I watched the lines form and proceed out of the gate. I was surprised when I heard a scuffle toward the front. Some of the inmates were yelling and then I heard the angry scream of a Lithuanian guard and I saw a man lying on the ground being beaten.

Then I heard the Jewish policeman yell over the crowd's reaction in Yiddish, "Form in lines of four . . . form in lines of four . . . stay calm!" In a very organized fashion the workers formed in lines of four. They continued moving out of the gates.

I saw the guards drag the man off to the side of the gate. Evidently, the rules had changed this morning. The man who had been beaten still had his cap on.

The guard who had beaten him was still angry; he was pointing his finger at the Jewish policeman and lecturing him. I shook my head trying to erase the picture of brutality for no reason from my mind.

I scooted along the ground. When I was in the clear, I ran toward the meeting place by the fence. The picture of the man being beaten and dragged away stayed with me. I wondered if today was the day that I would be met with brutality or possibly death? It almost seemed inevitable. Every day since Jews had been sent here, this silent fear was ever-present. Some were able to joke about it, but most cried about our dilemma with no help in sight. I always thanked God each night when I went to bed that I had lived another day. I didn't believe he was listening, but just in case, I knew it wouldn't hurt. Survival was the focus of my existence and the only motivation.

Michael and his friends arrived a few minutes later. We all talked at once about what happened at the gate. One of the other boys had seen the incident.

"Okay guys, Schaja is going to join us," Michael said, looking at the others. They nodded and smiled in agreement. "He's thin and fast, he can move under the barbed wire after we train him."

I listened carefully as Michael gave us the plan for this morning.

"Schaja, I want you to watch the first time."

I was disappointed, but I knew he was probably right. I needed to know exactly how the plan worked.

"We're going to form two positions for lookout on each side. Tommy and I will go into the Death Zone and move under the fence. Our contact will be about thirty yards beyond the fence. We'll get the food and be back as fast as possible. It takes the guards about thirty minutes once they pass this area to make a round."

"Schaja, when anyone sees trouble, we blow this whistle," he said and handed me a makeshift whistle. "I made an extra one last night for you to use when you're on lookout."

It was a hollowed-out piece of fresh twig with holes on each side to make the wind sound. We all separated and went to our designated posts.

The guard passed by our position and moved out of sight. I watched Tommy and Michael move like darts across the Death Zone and under the barbed wire. They both had material wrapped around one hand so they could lift the sharp barbs without cutting flesh. They disappeared on the other side. It seemed like only seconds when I saw them return. They were each carrying a burlap sack and hustled under the fence and out of the Death Zone.

Michael was out of breath as we all ran back to our hangout with the food. "See Schaja, a perfect operation," he said between gasps. "You just have to be quick."

"I've never seen anyone run as fast as you," I said.

We divided the shares of food. Even though I had only observed the operation they gave me some of the bread and a small piece of butter. It was fresh and still warm, not stale like our rations. As the taste of butter and fresh bread melted in my mouth, I was sure it was worth the risk. Michael took the second sack and delivered it to his customer. He would not give us the name of the customer.

After several days of observing, Michael put me into the plan. This time I was going to meet the contact at a designated area on the outside. I was going with Michael on the mission. As soon as we saw the guard pass out of sight, we both ran as fast as we could across the Death Zone. I hit the ground at the same time as Michael and grabbed the barbed wire with my hand that was wrapped in the material. I lifted it up and was halfway under the fence.

Bam . . . Bam . . . Bam . . . The sound echoed in my ears, and I realized that it was rifle fire. The gunshots continued as I rolled back under the fence.

Michael was already moving and zigzagging his way back to cover. I took out after him, moving in the same zigzag. The dirt was kicking up as the bullets hit the ground near me. My heart was jumping into my throat with each bullet ricochet.

The adrenaline was pumping through my veins as we all ran. We ran to our hangout. After catching our breath we all burst out laughing. Cheating death always brings a strange response.

"Who was shooting?" Ben asked.

"No one was around," one of the others said.

"Do you think they were trying to kill us?" one of the kids said, bringing a somber thought to each of us.

When he said the words, I realized that it was real bullets and we were in real danger. I thought about it for a minute.

"We were lucky," I said.

"What are we going to do with the money now?" Ben asked.

"Do we have to give it back?" Samuel asked. "We risked our lives, that's worth something."

"We have to give the money back," Michael said. "Otherwise, they'll never trust us again."

"Are we going to do this again?"

"We can't," I said. "The person who was shooting may aim better next time. It's not worth it, we can find other ways to get food. There's food right here in the camp. We can go to the garden."

"What garden?" Michael asked.

"It'll have to be just for us," I said.

"Okay, but where is it?" Michael asked.

"Meet me tonight outside my window and I'll show you."

My mother, father, and Uncle Willie were on the same work project for two weeks. They felt safe working together and it gave them an opportunity to further plans for escape. But they were very careful not to stand or walk as a group. The guards would become suspicious.

"I've made contact with a man that I used to do business with and he knows an older sea captain who lives not far from the coast. He would possibly take in Mula . . . at a price," Willie said as he worked near my mother. He stopped talking and kept working when he saw a guard come near the three of them.

They all continued working with their picks and shovels repairing the road as the guard passed. They kept their heads down as they talked and quietly conversed. It was discouraged on work crew to talk to other workers unless it concerned the job.

"Won't they take both of the boys?" my mother whispered after the guard had long passed them.

"My friend says the sea captain and his wife are only willing to care for a young child. Mula would at least be safe, plus the people desperately need money," Willie said as he slammed his pick into the ground. The noise from the pick covered the sound of his voice.

My father walked over to the area and raked the dirt. As he stood close to Uncle Willie, he spoke. "Do we know anything about these people? Mula has no way to defend himself if they try to hurt him. I heard that some of the children that were sneaked out were unknowingly given to officials who turned them over to the Gestapo."

"Mula doesn't have a chance to survive the camp if we don't get him out," Mother said. "You've heard the rumors, Leon. They say that Kovno Camp will be decreased in population before the end of the year."

"I know, Rose," Father answered, shaking his head in disgust. "The bastards say it is taking too much money to feed us our gourmet meals."

Both my mother and Willie chuckled at his small attempt of humor.

"We are willing to pay everything we have to keep our sons safe," he said.

"I'll find out when we can make the exchange," Willie said and motioned that the guard was coming.

ELEVEN

The Jewish Council secretly notified many of the inmates that they had been told about news reports from the United States that were filled with comments from the U.S. president, Franklin D. Roosevelt. It was allegedly said that he wanted to kill one hundred Germans for every Jew that had been killed.

"Why don't we fight back, Papa?" I asked one evening as we sat inside our house during a blackout. We had been instructed to keep the house dark at night when the siren sounded in the camp. I could barely see his face when I asked this question.

"I'd like to son," he answered.

"Then why don't you? I could help."

"It's more complicated, Schaja. If it were just a few men we were fighting maybe it would be possible. But it's an army that has powerful weapons and training. We have no weapons to fight back with. They would sweep us away with the butt end of their rifles."

"I could punch their eyes out with my fingers," I said. These were silly ideas, but I was willing to do anything to keep other Jews from sacrificing their lives.

"And they would kill with their bullets," my father answered.

"But there are many of us, more than the Nazis and Lithuanians," I said, partly a plea and partly a statement of fact. "I watched them beat a man at the gate. He had done nothing wrong and he probably died for no reason," I said.

I heard my mother wince. "Schaja, why do you go to places that are dangerous? Please stay close to the house. I've asked you before to keep yourself safe."

"We are going to escape from here, Schaja. Uncle Willie and I are making plans. Mula will be the first to go," my father said.

"Mula? When? When is he going? Can I help?" I asked, anxious to know more.

"Schaja, we can't talk about this . . . you musn't tell anyone. It will be soon."

"Who will take care of him on the outside?" I asked.

"He will be taken care of by Lithuanians," he answered.

"Is that safe?" I asked. "Are they Partisans?"

"No, they are not Partisans. They are people who need money. They will take care of Mula until the war is over."

"Will I know before so I can tell him good-bye?"

"Of course, Schaja, we will tell you."

"How did you get the money?" I asked.

"I told you, the jewelry, it's for our escape . . ."

I could see in the shadows of the moonlight that my mother was holding my little brother close to her as he slept in her arms.

"I heard the Germans use small children for target practice," I said.

"Schaja, don't say those cruel things," my mother said.

"If he does escape at least he won't have to die from a German bullet," I said and shrugged my shoulders.

"None of us are going to die by a German bullet. We just have to be patient. We will all find our freedom soon," my father promised. He was clinching his pipe, but he had no tobacco. He just kept it in his mouth. He said it relaxed him.

I wondered if I would ever see Mula again after he escaped. I knew if I asked this question it would upset my mother. She started to sing a lullaby and I fell asleep. I dreamed about food again.

Michael and I visited the garden at least once every week or two since I showed him the location. He was in charge of getting carrots or radishes or any other vegetables that were being grown and I was in charge of the potatoes. Since it was late spring the plants were growing in abundance.

It was almost midnight when the first guard went by. Fifteen minutes later, the second guard moved past our hiding place under the bushes. As soon as they passed, we ran to the center of the garden. I was eating my second potato when I heard a noise and quickly rolled into my shallow hole. I covered myself with dirt and held my breath.

I felt the heavy footsteps coming down my row. My whole body started to shake but I did not open my eyes. The footsteps stopped at the top of my head and even though I didn't open my eyes I knew a flashlight was in my face.

"Ge-e-e-t up!" the Jewish police officer shouted.

I heard Michael's running footsteps moving out of the garden.

"There's another one . . . catch him, Ari . . ." the officer shouted.

I opened my eyes a crack. The officer pushed me with his foot.

"Now, you ge-e-e-t up, you're going to jail," he said, as he reached down and grabbed the collar of my shirt. He lifted me in one swoop out of my shallow hole.

He muttered some things in Yiddish about the sins of youth. I looked around to see if Michael had escaped.

"He got away. He was too fast for me," the second guard said as he walked toward the jail with us.

I almost smiled. Michael was ten times faster than the heavy-set officer.

"Who was your friend?" my guard turned and asked me.

I shrugged my shoulders. "What friend?"

"Oh, you're going to take all of the punishment. If you tell us who was helping you we will be lenient."

I looked at him as if I had no idea what he was talking about.

We finally arrived at the police station on Stulginskio Street, several blocks from my house. No one spoke as we walked in the door. The room was a dilapidated makeshift jail with several side rooms used for cells. I was put in one of the empty, drafty rooms. I kept my head down and looked remorseful about my bad deed.

When I heard the cell door open, I looked up. It was the jailer. He called me a thief and said that I was going to be punished severely if I didn't give him the name of my accomplice.

I shrugged again.

"How old are you?" he barked at me.

Knowing that the older you were the better your chance was for survival. I lied to him. "Sixteen," I said.

He peered at me, knowing I was lying.

"What is your name?"

I didn't answer.

"We want to notify your parents."

I still didn't answer him. I didn't want my parents to get in trouble. I didn't trust the Jewish police. I was afraid that they would notify the Gestapo and have my parents murdered.

I sat in the room on a hard bench. Even though it was springtime, the nights were still chilly. I realized they were not going to take me to another room, so I lay down on the uncomfortable cold floor and tried to sleep.

The next morning I was taken to a detention hall. When I got there, I was given a small cup of warm milk and a half a piece of bread. It was a large room with a high ceiling. There were benches lined against the four walls. The benches were filled with other inmates. Most sat wrapped in any kind of clothing they had, staring straight ahead . . . wondering if they had a future.

I spent the next day and night in this detention hall.

When I woke up the following morning on the hard floor, I saw my mother walking toward me with a guard. She looked frazzled. She didn't see me at first. "Mama," I yelled to get her attention.

"This is my son," she pointed toward me and looked up at the officer.

I could hear him telling her where I had been caught and what I was doing.

"Officer," she said smiling at him. "He is only a child. He was hungry and meant no harm. I'm sure that he has never done this before and I am sure that he will never do it again."

"Young boy?" he said. "He says he's sixteen."

My mother shook her head. "He's ten years old."

"He lies and he steals." He shook his head in reprimand and stared at me.

She opened her hand. In her palm was a small velvet sack. "I appreciate you caring for him the last few days and I would like to show you my sincere thanks. I know you must have children also. I want you to have this for your family."

He snatched the velvet bag from her hand and looked inside. A slight smile came across his face. "I have no reason to keep him. You're right, if he had not been hungry this would have never happened. Even my children don't understand the consequences of our grave circumstances."

They walked closer to me and I ran and hugged my mother. "I thought I had lost you, Schaja," she whispered in my ear.

"How did you find me?" I asked after the officer had walked away for a moment.

I saw tears in her eyes. "A boy came to our door last night. He said he knew you. He wouldn't say his name, but he told us where you were. He was a little older and taller than you."

I knew that it was Michael, but just then my thoughts were interrupted.

"Young man," the officer said when he returned. "It is a very terrible thing to steal. A sin before God. In order to survive in this world you must have stronger character so you do not bend in times of dire circumstances . . ."

He droned on for a few more minutes with his lecture. I looked up at him with all the sincerity and regret that I could muster but, I couldn't believe that he was giving me a lecture about morality. I knew what was in the velvet bag he had received. It was jewelry and I knew it was a bribe. It seemed to me that these dire circumstances had made all of us corrupt and morally "bent."

My mother was angry and happy at the same time as we walked home. "Schaja, we thought you were dead. You must, please, be careful and keep yourself safe. We can't be with you all of the time. We have lost too much already," she said, looking at me sternly, yet the moist tears betrayed her anger. "God please let us not lose you," she whispered and bent down to hug me.

I returned to the vegetable garden sometime later, but first I met with Moishe, Ben, and Michael and made an elaborate plan to assure we were never again caught. I didn't want to disobey my mother, but my hunger outweighed my character. While we waited to go to the garden we sang the song the inmates sang in the camp as they traveled with their work crews.

Camp-Jew, Camp-Jew, answer me this—
Who wants to play first fiddle here?
Who of the big shots wants to rule
Over us all just like a king?

Thimbale, thimbale, play, Camp Jew,
Play a song about camp big shots,
About "inspectors," about "chiefs"
Climbing so high in the camp ranks.

Which of the big shots can give you a card,
And maybe a pass to keep you alive,
And how many do you then have to pay,
In order to get in a decent brigade?   (partial lyrics)

"Camp-Jew, Answer Me This"
by Avrom Akselrod, 1942

On March 10, 1942, twenty-four inmates of Kovno Camp were shot to death. The first announcement said they were killed because they were smuggling on the black market and were not wearing the yellow Star of David. The Gestapo insisted that the Jewish Council make this massacre public knowledge with a list recounting the many crimes of the twenty-four Jews. One of the Jews was carrying a gun.

In April 1942, the Gestapo ordered all inmates to turn over any metal item in their possession, door handles and window handles included. If the inmates were found with any item of metal, including silver or gold, they would be severely punished, which meant certain death. They didn't say guns and knives specifically, but we all decided that this was a repercussion for the twenty-four Jews.

We did not turn over our metals of worth. We kept our gold, silver, and platinum. We did turn over any item of value that was visible in our house. We were risking our lives, but we knew it was also the only way we could escape. Uncle Willie did not turn in his knife.

TWELVE

My eyes flew open when I heard my mother. Her voice was shaking and she was crying. "Schaja, please stay at home with your grandmother today. I know you get restless but I don't want you to leave her alone . . . and be home tonight when your father and I return."

"What's wrong, Mama?" I said trying to understand what was happening. I was still half asleep.

"Come with me, Schaja," she said.

I got up and followed her into the other room. I saw my father and grandmother sitting on the bed with Mula. Grandmother was playing with him as he sat on her lap. He was dressed in two layers of clothes. I didn't understand. "Why does Mula have so many clothes on? Is he sick?" I asked.

"Say good-bye to your brother, Schaja," Father said softly.

It dawned on me the moment I saw the sad expressions on Grandmother Rochel and father's face. Mula was escaping today. I went over to the bed and hugged him. "So long, Mula," I said sadly. He started laughing and pulling on my hair, and pushed me away. I teased him and grabbed behind his knee with my thumb and forefinger. It was his ticklish spot and he started to laugh. I laughed, too, but I felt tears stinging my eyes as I tried to stay happy.

My mother paced nervously as she put on an oversized coat that reached to the ground. She then took him from my grandmother's lap with trembling hands and pretended to be playing a game of hide-and-seek with him. She slipped him under the long coat, using her left hand to hold him. She told him that when he was under the coat he couldn't make a sound and he could only peek outside the folds of the coat when she told him the game was over. She explained that he was going to go with her to work and he had to play the game or she would have to leave him at home.

"Why does he have to go? Can't we keep him with us?" I asked. I had always considered my brother a pest, but at this moment I truly believed that if he left I would never see him again. I was going to miss him.

"It's dangerous for him to stay. The Nazis say they are feeding too many people and they will eventually eliminate those who cannot contribute," my father said. "We can't take any chances on when they decide to eliminate babies."

"Where will he live?" I asked.

Uncle Willie came in the door and walked into my parents' room.

"We were just explaining to Schaja our plans for Mula," my father said to Willie.

"He'll be safe, Schaja. He's going to a nice place and will be well taken care of. I've met with them and they are good Lithuanians. They have no children of their own and are very happy to bring Mula into their life."

I looked up at him.

"Schaja, you will be the next one to escape," Willie said.

This didn't do much to change my mood. I didn't have a hope of escaping. I wanted us to stay together. If we died, at least we would be together.

My uncle leaned down next to me and put his arm across my shoulder. "This is a time to be strong and brave. Our future depends on our courage. Mula is a very brave little boy to do what he will do today. We will be separated from him, but it's only for a while."

When he said this I heard Mula laugh. I wondered if he realized what was happening.

"And I know that you are the bravest of all of us, Schaja," Uncle Willie continued talking as he stood up to leave. "I knew that from the first day we came here . . . Remember?"

"Will I go to the place where he's going?" I asked, fighting back the tears, not feeling quite as brave as I felt the day we came here.

"We're not sure where you will go . . ." he said and tried to hold back his own tears.

Several days after my mother had given Mula to the sea captain and his wife, she received a message. The sea captain had become gravely ill and he and his wife would not be able to take care of Mula. Coincidentally, there was a dispute over the amount of money the couple had received. Mother was on work crew outside the camp and quickly arranged to sneak away, risking her own life to speak with the sea captain. The problem was quickly resolved with an offer of more money. We didn't have much more to give, but she had no choice; she gave him what he wanted and prayed for the safety of Mula. Miraculously, the sea captain made a complete and immediate recovery.

When she returned to work that day, walking down the streets of Kaunas, she wondered if she should stay on the outside. It was tempting, but she could never leave us. She could only pray that Mula would be safe in her absence. Despite the difficulties with money, she had faith in the Lithuanian couple that she had just left. Bribery in many forms was just a way of life for us, a means of survival within the prison walls of the camp, as well as the ticket to the outside. My parents were well aware of bribery since they faced it each day on the inside with Jewish police, Jewish officials, and Lithuanian Partisans. It went on with German soldiers taking sexual and monetary favors in exchange for better treatment of some women on the work crews.

After Mula left it was very quiet around the house. I stayed close to my grandmother and slept more than I imagined possible. It was my escape into a world of dreams that had no limits . . . no Nazi soldiers, no sadness, no fear, and no hunger.

When I wasn't sleeping, I tried to be cheerful for Grandmother Rochel. But she was sad and sat all day at the window staring vacantly at the street outside. She had no reason to sing lullabies any longer. At times, I could hear her humming a familiar tune and I encouraged her to sing. I liked to hear her voice.

As the months passed, she became even more withdrawn. Her silent vigil was a sad reminder that her desire to live was slowly slipping into a stronger desire to die. When my parents came home each evening they also tried to lift my grandmother from her depression, but it seemed that nothing could distract her from the misery she felt.

One morning, there was a knock at the door. My grandmother and I both looked warily toward the door. We didn't welcome this surprise. But we immediately knew that it was not a Nazi soldier, otherwise there would have been no knock. Grandmother Rochel rose up from her chair and grabbed her cane.

"I'll answer the door," she said. "You hide in the other room. If you hear any shouting, Schaja, get out of the house and run to a safe place."

I quickly nodded and ran into the other room and slid under the bed. When she opened the door I strained to hear the muffled voices. There were quiet murmurings at first and then I heard my grandmother clap her hands and say, "That's wonderful news. Congratulations!" she said, sounding happy for the first time in months.

I could hear her laughter. I got out from under the bed and walked into the room. I saw Kindra, our neighbor, standing at the door. She was smiling and looked very happy. She and my grandmother were holding hands.

"Schaja," Kindra said, when she saw me standing in the background. I was surprised she knew my name. I immediately thought back to the day when I followed her and the old lady to the mysterious building. I felt embarrassed because Michael and I had since discovered that this place was one of the locations where abortions were performed for pregnant female inmates. I tried to push all of those thoughts out of my head as I smiled at her.

She came into the house and took both of my hands. She was very beautiful as she smiled down at me. "I'm getting married, Schaja! Reuben and I are getting married next Sunday. I asked your grandmother to play the piano for our wedding celebration. The Jewish police officer's orchestra will be playing, too. Do you know how to dance?" she asked.

I was tongue-tied and nodded. I wondered if I would see any of the Jewish police officers I had met during my short detention.

"It will be a wonderful celebration."

"Schaja is a good dancer," my grandmother said, making up for my silence.

"I want all of my friends to come to my wedding," she said and smiled down at me. "And I hope that someday I have a little boy as smart and handsome as you." She leaned down and hugged and kissed me on the cheek.

I could feel my face turning bright red now. "Congratulations," I said, copying what my grandmother had said to her earlier.

She and my grandmother both smiled as though they were amused. I could only hope that I hadn't said the wrong thing.

"I'll see you on Sunday, Schaja," she said and went out the door.

I smiled and wondered if her father was happy now that she was getting married. It had been about a year since she had the abortion.

My grandmother smiled at me. "You're blushing, Schaja."

I was not surprised when I put my hands up to my cheeks and they were warm. We both laughed.

It was the first wedding I had ever attended. My mother and father and grandmother dressed in their finest clothes, even though most of them had holes. I wore a white shirt and a black pair of pants that I had outgrown since our arrival. My ankles showed beneath the cuffs of the pants and my ankles were bare. I was so thin that I couldn't keep the pants up around my waist. My father let me use his suspenders; he pinned them to my shirt. I looked more like a clown than a guest at a wedding.

I asked my mother and father as we were dressing about their own wedding in Kaunas. My grandmother smiled and talked about how beautiful my mother looked on her wedding day. "Rose wore the most beautiful antique white satin dress with pleats and beads and real pearls, with a lace veil that was covered in tiny little pale pink rosebuds, real flowers from her garden."

"It was beautiful, Schaja. We had dozens and dozens of roses that lined the aisle that led to the huppah. The candles were lit at dusk because the wedding was outside in Grandmother Rochel's backyard," Mother said.

"The most beautiful bride ever to walk down the aisle." My father took my mother's hand and started to sweep her around the small room. Everyone smiled. This was the most lighthearted I had seen my parents and grandmother since we came to Kovno.

These tiny rays of hope sprinkled in our lives occasionally, like Kindra's wedding, kept us going through the bad times. We looked forward to any event that would make us smile and renew hope for better times, even if it was only for a moment.

"And when we left for our honeymoon, we boarded a beautiful carriage, drawn by two white stallions," my father continued.

"They had roses in their bridles," my mother spoke wistfully. She paused for a moment remembering.

The wedding guests gathered in a hall that the Jewish police controlled and used for certain occasions in the camp community. The hall had been crudely transformed into a wedding aisle with a makeshift ceremonial huppah at the end of the aisle for the bride to walk to her groom. The hall was dark except for the candles that had been brought by the inmates for the wedding. The soft lighting made the room transform into a dreamy haze.

I wiggled in my seat, anxious to see Kindra walk down the aisle. My mother whispered that someone in the camp was going to smuggle some cake and wine inside for the wedding reception.

That made my mouth water.

I heard a couple of members from the Jewish police orchestra start to play music. I looked to see if I recognized any of the officers. Luckily, I didn't see anyone that I knew. Then I turned and saw Kindra. She took a few steps with her father by her side. They both looked very solemn, but as they proceeded down the aisle Kindra smiled as she met Reuben's gaze. The dress she wore was made with different pieces of material that had been given to her from inmates working in the uniform repair factory.

Her boyfriend, Reuben, was dressed in a dark suit and was standing, nervously with the rabbi. As the ceremony proceeded they stepped under the huppah and repeated their vows, spoken in Hebrew.

As part of the ceremony the rabbi poured two glasses of wine and they drank from them and smashed them on the floor.

"Why did they smash the glasses?" I whispered to my mother.

"They drink the wine for the promise of happiness and when they break the glasses, it seals the promise," she said.

Next, they exchanged their wedding rings. I saw tears in my grandmother's and mother's eyes as the wedding progressed.

Even though it was a long time before I would be of the right age to marry, I had already decided against it. But if I could have two white stallions like my parents and a beautiful bride like Kindra, I might change my mind.

When the wedding ceremony was over and the bride and groom walked back down the aisle and into another part of the building, the men quickly rolled up the aisle carpet and the huppah was cleared away. The musicians moved to the front of the room and began playing music. Happy music. This is when my grandmother, in her faded and wrinkled blue dress, sat down and began to play the piano. Her blue eyes danced with the music. She and the other musicians knew a lot of the same songs and some of the men sang solos during the evening. Most everyone danced.

In the middle of the celebration, two men from the camp arrived carrying a large box. It was a white iced wedding cake! No one could imagine how the cake had been smuggled inside the camp. We all applauded and no one asked any questions. They called it a blessing for the bride and groom.

Immediately, a line formed for a taste of the sweet cake. The music continued to play. I took a piece of cake to my grandmother. But today her food was music and she told me I could have her slice of cake.

I watched as my mother danced with another man while my father admired her. He was not a dancer but always enjoyed watching my mother gracefully glide across the dance floor. Then many of the guests joined a circle dance when the music changed in tempo. I watched as one man was kicking up his feet and laughing.

One of the kids came and grabbed my hand and we formed our own circle dance like the grown-ups. I imitated the grown-ups and kicked up my heels and laughed. Moishe joined the circle and he tried the same dance that I was doing. All the kids laughed when he kicked his foot up too high and fell down.

When the sun started to go down the festivities began to wind down. We didn't want to draw attention to ourselves. We were all aware that the guards could come in at any time.

On the morning of the wedding when the Partisan had smuggled the ingredients for the wedding cake into the camp for the occasion, a German guard noticed the transfer of the large box to a Jewish police officer. He allowed the exchange to take place, but notified his superior. Later in the day the Partisan was detained and taken to the Gestapo headquarters. He was found with a large sum of money in his pockets. The superiors questioned him and demanded an explanation. He quickly told them about the wedding and that he had been paid to bring in the cake. He gave the name of the Jewish police officer.

After his confession he was told to leave and never return to the camp. The Gestapo then took the matter into their hands.

THIRTEEN

Several days later, I was waiting on the corner for Moishe and Michael. It was overcast and misting. The morning was eerie. Maybe it was the overcast weather, but people were walking on the street with their heads down speaking only in quiet and whispered tones. Something was going on, I could feel it.

When Moishe and Michael showed up we went over to Spitz's street to start playing Territory. But, no one was playing any games. We walked over to the Jewish Council building and I saw a few women crying. I told Moishe and Michael that I was going back home to stay with my grandmother. It had been only a few minutes since I had left my block, but when I returned I saw some of the council members standing in front of Kindra's parents' house, next door to us. I slowed as I came closer. The officials were talking among themselves with strained and sad expressions. Some of them were standing in my yard. My grandmother was standing at our doorway with tears in her eyes.

"What's wrong?" I asked. I had a sinking feeling in my stomach. I was afraid something had happened to my parents or my brother.

She looked at me for a long moment. "They took Kindra and Reuben and her parents away."

"Who took them away, Gram?" I asked.

"Nazis," she answered. Her lips pulled back in a thin line.

"When? Why?" I asked. "I didn't hear anything!"

"While we were sleeping they came and took them away," she said.

"How could they . . . I always hear everything . . ." I said, almost questioning myself. I ran outside to the men standing in our yard. "Where did they take them?"

They looked at me and then at each other and turned away.

I grabbed the sleeve of one of the men. "Please, tell me. What happened? Where are they?"

He patted my arm to try and calm me down. "Son," he said softly. "This is a tragedy for all of us. We should thank God that Kindra and Reuben were able to marry."

"Please, sir, I just want to know," I impatiently begged him. I knew they had been killed but I couldn't allow myself to accept this if he didn't say the words.

"I'm sorry, but they were taken to Fort IX," he said quietly.

I felt like someone had kicked me in the stomach. I turned in a circle and felt light-headed. I couldn't comprehend. How could any person, any group of people be so cruel? My mind resisted the truth. How could they be gone forever? Why did they take them?

My grandmother came outside and stood near me. She looked at me wondering if I was going to faint. I felt like I wanted to let go and die; or destroy everything in sight. As I regained my senses, I felt numb. All I could hear was my voice making a painful sound. I went inside and sat down next to the window where my grandmother usually sat. I stared out into the street, wet tears rolled down my face uncontrollably. I wanted time to stop.

My parents came in after dark. They had already heard the story. My mother came and sat next to me, but I still didn't want to talk. They tried to console me. But I had no strength to speak or move. These killings were for no reason. It was another act that was cruel and heartless. I hated the people who had done this even though I would never know their names.

By the middle of the summer in 1943, the Gestapo was trying to undermine and get rid of the Jewish police. The Gestapo officers felt that the Jewish police were protecting the inmates. They were right, the Jewish police tried to protect whenever it was possible. However, one morning a Jewish police officer named Abramson was arrested at the camp gate. The Gestapo claimed they discovered money hidden in the police officer's trousers during a search. The council immediately dispatched a letter to the Gestapo saying that the money belonged to the Council. They had given the money to Abramson. He was released. His life was saved.

No one knew if it was truly the Council's money or bribes paid to the officer. The Gestapo issued orders later in the day for all Jewish police to remain inside the camp.

"My father's in trouble," Spitz said as we were standing in front of his house. I could see tears in his eyes. "Why?"

"Yesterday he was accused of taking bribes," Spitz said, and looked at the ground. "That guy who stole the papers out of our house last year, he was probably a Lithuanian soldier . . . he must have made up lies about the papers."

I felt my face flush.

Spitz looked into the distance, lost in his own thoughts.

I tapped him on the shoulder. "Spitz, that guy was me."

"What're you talking about?" Spitz said and looked at me.

"I was starving and I took your food. I didn't take any papers," I said.

He looked at me for a long time trying to understand.

"I'm really sorry that I stole from you Spitz, but I was starving."

"You didn't take any papers?" he asked. He didn't seem surprised that I had taken the food.

"No," I said.

Spitz just shook his head and walked away. That was the last time I ever saw him.

Uncle Willie came in several nights later, looking angry. "They have assigned me to work at the airfield."

My mother gasped. Working conditions at the airfield were hazardous. It was several miles from the camp and there were rumors of workers being murdered by guards when they were assigned to this work crew.

I wondered if Spitz had told his father about me stealing their food and Willie's reassignment was retribution even though his father was in trouble. He might have used this information to persuade the Germans to let him live.

My mother looked at my father. "We have to talk to someone. What about the man who assigns the workers, Schaja's friend's father . . . He could find a way to change Willie's assignment, Leon," she said. "Don't you know him?"

"I know him, but he has been replaced. The Gestapo took him," Leon answered.

Spitz had not said that his father lost his job. In a way he was lucky, he could have lost his life.

"Don't worry, Rose," Uncle Willie said. "I have someone working for me in the labor department. They said they would get it changed. I'll need to take some of the money with me. I want to be sure I have enough to change their mind about the assignment."

I knew he meant that he would take items to bribe the official.

My father got up and went into the other room. When he came out he had a small velvet sack with him. "I think this will cover it," he said and handed the package to my uncle.

The next time we saw Uncle Willie he had been transferred to another work crew.

The relations between the Jewish Council and the Germans continued to deteriorate and the searches conducted by the Gestapo were pointedly focused on the houses of the Jewish Council members. Bountiful supplies of food and other items were found. The Gestapo seized their belongings and threatened to disband the Council if they did not comply with the rules of all inmates.

The rest of the summer passed by slowly. The heat was stifling in our close quarters and the smell of sewage filled the air. I had very little appetite and slept most of the time. The dragging days were intolerable for me. Tempers were short, people were hungry, and the only thing to look forward to was winter and its frigid temperatures.

During the month of August, the only food we received was bread and rotted sauerkraut. I had to tear away the rotten part, so not much was left to eat. There was no other vegetables or meat. It took more than thirty days to convince the Gestapo to give us more food. The Council had to beg for their mercy.

The entire camp received punishment for the Council's complaints about the food for the inmates. Orders were issued that all healthy inmates must be on work crew. Uncle Willie and my parents felt if I did not go out on a work crew I would be killed.

Colonel Cramer, the city commissioner of the camp, toured through the Jewish workshops one afternoon. I had seen him before, but only from a distance. Later, I was told of an incident that happened on his tour of the camp.

The workshops were responsible for German army laundry and repair. He and his entourage of soldiers walked through one workshop when he noticed a woman that was pregnant. He turned to the accompanying Jewish official and told him that she would have to get rid of the child in her womb or it would be killed at birth. The Jewish official explained that it was too late to get rid of the child. She was almost seven months pregnant. This made no difference to Colonel Cramer.

One of the workers had come outside to smoke a cigarette and he told a group of people what had gone on inside. He cursed Cramer and all the Germans.

"Why didn't all the workers try to help her?" I asked.

His eyes became slits of anger. "If only we could!"

"Why can't you?"

He shook his head, threw down his cigarette, and mashed it out with his foot and walked away.

I went home and told my parents what I had heard. A look of fear crossed their faces. I was angry at the looks of fear. We all knew that every day was just one day closer to death. Like cattle being led to slaughter. This was the atmosphere in the camp.

My father and Uncle Willie bribed an official to assign me to a work brigade. They managed to get me on the roster with an easy job.

"Mamala," my mother said to my grandmother. "You will be alone now during the day."

My grandmother nodded.

"I want you to stay in my room while we are gone. I'll put your chair here in the morning before we leave. If anyone comes to the door you must hide."

My grandmother looked at her quizzically. "But, where, Rose?"

"Under the bed is the best place," Mother said.

"I cannot possibly do that," my grandmother said.

"You must try, Mamala," Mother said.

"I will let them take me, Rose. It will be a *brochah* [blessing]," she said and smiled. She looked at death with relief and my mother was unable to accept this.

"My pain is too much," she said.

"Do the best you can, Mamala. Please, I cannot bear to lose you," my mother said tearfully. "Please, have hope."

My grandmother patted my mother's hand. "I will be fine. Don't worry while you're gone."

FOURTEEN

The temperature had dropped below zero on the first morning I arrived at the gate. I wore my required hat with a bill and was careful to remove it at the right time if I saw a German guard.

I managed to get through the gate without offending anyone. I walked with my group of about forty inmates several miles to our destination. After we arrived at the work site, we were allowed to sit down and rest. I blew on my hands to thaw my frozen fingers. While we rested we were surrounded by a couple of German soldiers and Lithuanian Partisans carrying guns and clubs.

The German officer in charge stepped up and assigned each of us duties. He wore glasses and kept a swagger stick under his arm as he surveyed our group. One by one, he pointed out our designated area where we would work. The crew was here to repair potholes in the road with tar, gravel, and dirt.

I felt my hands starting to sweat despite the frigid temperature when it was my turn to be assigned. I jumped up when the detail leader looked toward me.

"You," he pointed at me as I stood up. "You will be in charge of the tools," he said and nodded toward a small enclosed trailer. It was about ten feet by six feet. The tool trailer was towed by a larger truck and left at the work site each morning. The back of the trailer had a door and a small window.

The job turned out to be one that I liked. I was sheltered inside the trailer, warmer than standing on the road with the wind blowing and sometimes raindrops and snowflakes or sleet hitting my face. My job wasn't as physically demanding as some of the other road jobs. I was convinced my family had arranged for this position through bribes.

My duty included cleaning the tar off of the tools, and oiling the shovels, picks, and rakes. I cleaned dirty tools throughout the day, issuing and reissuing to each worker.

The trailer had only a small window and I left the door open for light while I was cleaning. I noticed that some of the workers on the crew resented the fact that I had this job. I offered to help as often as I could with other jobs, but was soon put to a stop by the work detail leader.

One morning after arriving at the work site the labor guard was especially cruel to many of the workers. I succeeded in avoiding him all day. Rumors started to circulate that another German "action" was being planned because an inmate had been caught trying to escape the camp. Rumors were always bits and pieces of information, never a full account. But every rumor instilled fear in the population. Whoever had tried to escape had a gun and a stash of gold and diamonds that were confiscated. He was armed and had fired at the guards.

When I arrived home I tried to find out more about the rumor but no one had any additional information. It was a day later when Michael and I were standing under an overhang, watching the activity on the street. It was sleeting and there were few people milling around.

"Michael, are you working?" I asked.

"No, I have to be careful," he said.

"Where are your parents?" I asked. "Aren't they on a work crew?"

"Hey, Schaja, look what's coming," Michael said changing the subject, pointed down the street.

We saw the Jewish police coming around the corner.

Michael and I hid and watched the path of the policemen in what could only mean trouble for someone.

We looked at each other and maneuvered from one doorway to the next waiting to see where they would stop. We both felt a shudder of fear in our hearts as we watched their stern-faced and focused resolve. At the end of the street they turned left and abruptly stopped at one of the houses. One of the officers went inside the house.

Michael and I crawled on our bellies across the ground and around the back of the houses and peeked around corners trying to locate the house where they had stopped. Finally, we spotted them about four houses down and across the street from our position.

It felt like an eternity until I saw the door open again. "Wonder who lives there?"

"I don't know . . . wonder if they are in big trouble?" he asked.

A day later the Jewish Council acted on orders from the Gestapo. They posted notice of the public hanging of Meck Nahum, my friend who had helped me to learn to balance on the log. He was sentenced to be hung for crimes against the German authorities. All inmates were required to attend the hanging.

The order also demanded any weapon being held by an inmate inside the camp must be turned over to the Germans. The Germans would not punish you if you handed the weapon over peacefully. They designated an area where the guns could be relinquished, but no one believed that they wouldn't be punished, and no one turned in any guns.

It is documented that the camp guard, Fleischmann, detained Meck Nahum and arrested him for trying to escape. He was trying to crawl under the fence. Another inmate had gone under the fence and into the forest only minutes earlier. Fleischmann stated that Meck had a gun and fired it three to four times in the air. That was his excuse for not catching the other escapee. No one that knew Meck had ever seen him with a gun. He was immediately taken to the camp Gestapo headquarters.

The Gestapo demanded that three Jewish Council members be arrested in reprisal for Meck's attempt to escape. Garfunkel, Goldberg, and Golub from the Jewish Council were brought to the headquarters. Dr. Elkes, the head of the council, would have been arrested, but he was ill and confined to his bed.

While at the headquarters in Kovno, the four men were told they would be killed. Later in the evening, Meck, Garfunkel, Goldberg, and Golub were taken under heavy guard to the Gestapo headquarters in Kaunas. While in Kaunas, Meck suffered endless torture, but he would not reveal the name of his accomplice. Garfunkel, Goldberg, and Golub were threatened again with hanging if they did not force him to reveal the name of the accomplice. The three council members remained silent under threat.

The order was given on November 17 for the Jewish Council to build the gallows and the Jewish police were ordered to hang Meck at noon. The order stated that Meck would hang in view of all for a period of twenty-four hours.

None of the Jewish police officers would build the gallows or participate in the hanging.

When I heard about the notice, I ran to my father. "Isn't there anything we can do?" I asked.

He shook his head. "I know this is hard to understand, but it would do no good for all of us to die."

"We could all stand in front of the jail and block them from taking him to the hanging," I said.

"Schaja, there's nothing we can do," my mother said, to reinforce my father's answer.

I couldn't let Meck die. I ran to Uncle Willie's house. I knocked on the door and a strange man answered. I knew it was one of Willie's roommates; three other families lived in his house.

"Is Uncle Willie at home?" I asked.

The man turned and got my uncle. "Schaja, what are you doing here?" Uncle Willie said after he came to the door.

I pulled him outside. "We've got to help save Meck," I said.

Uncle Willie looked at me and took my hand. We walked across the street to a rock and sat down. "Schaja, we would like to help everyone, wouldn't we?"

"Yes," I answered.

"Well, sometimes it's better not to act in a way that might hurt many others. If we try to do anything it will only hurt more people. We don't have the answers to what we should do right now, but there are many people that are trying to help. Just like you."

"What about your knife, couldn't we use it on a German?" I asked.

Uncle Willie looked at me and didn't answer.

The next morning I began the journey to watch the hanging of my friend Meck. It reminded me of our walk to Demokratu Square. People were streaming from every direction as we gathered directly opposite the council building.

The Jewish police had found two Polish Jews who had been caught stealing in the camp to do the actual hanging in exchange for their release and return to Poland by the Germans.

I stood about sixty feet away from where the hanging would take place. I saw Meck standing on a small platform, like a table, next to the noose of the rope. He was staring straight ahead through one eye, the other was swollen shut from the torture he had endured. He had blood and bruises all over his body. His face had been battered almost beyond recognition. But Meck stood with his head high. I knew the minute I saw him that he was not afraid to die.

The two Polish prisoners moved toward Meck. It looked like they were saying something to each other. I could hear whispers in the crowd.

"What are they saying?" I asked a man standing next to me.

"Meck told the two hangmen that he forgives them, he knows they are being forced to do this," the man said. "Meck doesn't realize that he is their ticket to freedom. At least that's what they think!"

"What do you mean?" I asked.

"The Germans promised them release. But they will never let them go! They are stupid to believe them!" he said angrily.

I dropped my head quickly when I saw the noose go around Meck's neck. I couldn't watch him die. I heard a collective gasp from the crowd as Meck was pushed off the edge of the platform. When I looked up his face was distorted and his feet were dangling, his body twitching as death released his agony.

I felt terrible . . . horrible and helpless. I was sick with sadness.

The area cleared as soon as the event was over. I stood silently, remembering Meck.

"Why did Meck have to die?" I asked my mother later that night.

She stared straight ahead and shook her head.

Again there was no answer.

I returned to where Meck was still hanging early the next morning before work. I could hardly look at him. His body was a grotesquely distorted form now with his eyes bulging and his limbs hanging lifelessly. I remembered how he always smiled and made everybody feel good. I felt a lump in my throat and promised myself that I would never forget what had been done to my friend.

Before Meck was hung some observers reported that he forgave his hangmen and also said to tell his mother and sister that he loved them. Unknown to anyone at the time, including Meck, both his mother and sister had been taken from the camp at 10 A.M. that same day, en route to Fort IX.

They were never seen or heard from again.

Fifteen

I usually talked with the other inmates as we walked to our work site, but everyone was silent today. We walked in rows of three. I looked around and saw a Jewish work leader, a Lithuanian Partisan, and one German officer. The Partisan snapped at me to walk faster.

One of the ladies that I was walking with leaned over and whispered in my ear. "Today is my thirty-third birthday," she said. "My children gave me this necklace."

It was a wire necklace with small rocks used as stones. "That's nice," I smiled. She shared her rations with me occasionally at lunch. "I hope you have a nice day."

She shrugged and rolled her eyes. "What can be nice in our life?"

I wondered if I would live to be her age. I thought about Meck as I did every morning since his death. The picture of him hanging from the rope stayed with me. It was hard to even think about my next birthday or to even wonder about tomorrow. The only future I had was to live through the day.

When we got to the work site, the guard opened the door to the tool trailer. I went inside and saw tools thrown everywhere and some of them were dirty. The tools I had cleaned before we left yesterday had disappeared. The guard stood behind me and reprimanded me for leaving the tools in a disorderly manner and ordered me to clean the place up. I started to speak up in my defense, but then I stopped. I didn't attempt to explain that I had not been the one to leave it in this condition. I couldn't ask him where my clean tools had gone.

He was a large man with a garish face, scarred from his lip to his cheekbone, creating a sinister smile on one side of his face. He wore a black patch over one eye, making him look even more evil. He had probably been sent here from the front lines while his injuries healed. He glared at me before he turned and walked away.

I cleaned and oiled the shovels, working as fast as I could, while the workers waited impatiently for me to hand them their tools. I handed a shovel to one worker and he scolded me for making them late. The workers were laughing at me struggling to get the job done.

At noontime we were given our first break. We were usually allowed to rest after the long walk to the work site, but today had been an exception and the guard had ordered us to work as soon as we arrived. I was exhausted. All of us sat down on the grass trying to regain our strength. The guard and the Partisan walked between the rows of inmates tapping the sticks they carried on their palms.

The sun was shining down, making me feel warm even though the air was cold. I looked up into the sun. I heard some noises a few rows away from me. When I looked back down I had spots in front of my eyes, but I saw the German guard with the black patch standing in front of a young, attractive girl about twenty years old. He and the girl had a short conversation.

A couple of seconds later, he turned and walked over to my tool trailer and the girl got up and followed him. All eyes were watching the unfolding drama as she walked into the shed and closed the door.

People started to whisper and some laughed. One of the men made a joke about which "tool" the guard was using and another about oiling his "tool." One of the men turned around and stared at me. "What do you think is going on in there, Schaja? That's your post over there, maybe the guard is having trouble finding his tool." He laughed as he spoke.

One of the others went along with his joking. "Schaja, he'll be angry with you if he can't find what he needs . . . go help him out . . . it's your job."

Then everyone chimed in and said I needed to go and find out what was going on. I slowly and reluctantly got up against my better judgment, and walked toward the trailer. I noticed that everything suddenly became totally quiet. I could feel everyone staring at my back. When I got to the door and stood to the side of the window. I listened in case they were getting ready to come back outside. I heard no noises. Then I stood up on my tiptoes, cupped my face, and peered through the small dirty window on the door. I couldn't see inside. I knew it was pitch black when the door was closed. What I didn't know was the guard could see me looking in the window.

I turned around and walked back over to my spot on the grass and sat down with my legs crossed.

"What'd you see, kid?" one of the men asked.

"You get a good look?" another spoke up.

I shrugged and shook my head. "It's too dark, I couldn't see anything."

About ten minutes later the shed door swung open. The girl came out first. She walked stone-faced back to her place and sat down next to her friend. The guard came out next. He was glaring at all of us sitting on the ground. He started walking directly toward me. I tried to move, but before I could stand up, his giant hand, clenched tightly in a fist, pummeled the side of my head. My entire body flew sideways. Then he took his fists and pounded both sides of my head over and over and over again.

I heard myself scream as the excruciating pain ripped through my eardrums and into my head. I could taste blood in my mouth. I tried to get up, but I felt nauseous and stumbled into the ground inhaling a mouthful of dirt. He kept beating me until I finally lost consciousness.

When I opened my eyes again I was lying on my back and my vision was blurred. I saw his triplicate, hulking figure walking away from me. I felt like my head was filled with bricks when I tried to lift myself up. Everything was spinning.

He turned to look back at me and screamed. "Get up and go to work!"

I rose as quickly as I could and staggered like I was drunk, reeling from one side to the other, and found my way to the trailer. Through salty tears, blood, and dirt I began to sweep the floor and wish that I hadn't been so stupid to listen to the others when my instincts had told me differently.

By the end of the day my face was swollen and sore. He had knocked out one of my back teeth and I could still taste the blood. When the workers started to return their tools, none of them would look at me. The lady who had told me about her birthday had tears in her eyes when she handed me her rake. The men who had coaxed me into looking through the window had their heads down and avoided my gaze. Some mumbled apologies.

I listened and trusted my instincts in every situation from this day forward. When I returned home that night, my parents were horrified and angry that other inmates had used my naïveté for their own enjoyment. My mother bandaged the wounds with cloth and a small amount of water that Uncle Willie brought from his house.

Adding to my agony were rumors in recent weeks about children's "action." The Nazis did not have enough food to feed the children and the grown-ups. Five thousand Jews allegedly were being transported to Kovno, crowding the camp even more.

Uncle Willie's search for my escape now escalated. The next rumor we heard the following week was horrifying to the camp population. The five thousand Jews being transferred to Kovno never arrived. They were crammed so tightly that some suffocated hours after they boarded. The Nazis stopped the train before the arrival at Kovno and ordered all inmates off the train. The bullets sprayed from the machine guns into the crowd as they massacred every single person. Some inmates carrying makeshift weapons tried to defend themselves, but it was useless.

Documents later proved the Nazis let the bodies lie in the field of bloody massacre while they soothed their own conscience with alcohol. It was several weeks before the inmates' bodies were buried.

Sixteen

Today was the day that I would either escape the camp or ultimately be killed. It was 1944 and I had been here almost three years. For months my parents and Uncle Willie had been devising the plan of escape for me. It took a series of secret meetings on the outside with Lithuanian contacts. Coded messages traveled from one to another to secure a chain of freedom for me to the outside. I was not involved in the details of the arrangements but Uncle Willie explained to me that the less people who knew the exact time, including myself, the better off I would be.

The price of escape from the camp had soared. Hiding an inmate had become an increasing risk with Gestapo searches in Lithuanian houses. The Lithuanians that were going to hide me were only willing to do this for a short time. At the end of the time my parents would have to find another place for me to live. It was not ideal, and very dangerous if they couldn't find me another home. If anything happened to my parents in the camp while I was on the outside, I would be on my own. I was still a kid and they worried about this possibility.

Killings had increased as more and more inmates risked escape. Since the death of Meck over a year ago, the guards were on high alert. The tower outside the fence into the forest was manned twenty-four hours a day. There were rumors that a Jewish resistance army was being formed by those who did escape to the outside.

But regardless of our fears we continued to practice my escape plan night after night for weeks. I would hide under Uncle Willie's coat as we synchronized our walk. He gave me a signal when we got to a designated drop-off point. I would take off on my own to a contact wearing a red kerchief several blocks away from the drop-off point. I knew that if my attempted escape were discovered at any point it would mean certain death for both Uncle Willie and myself.

We all sat on the bed together in my parents' room waiting for Uncle Willie to arrive. Grandmother reached over and pinched my cheeks and smiled at me. When she hugged me, she held me very tight and told me I would be just fine. Her strength on this morning gave me courage.

My mother was crying as she helped me dress in clothing that would not be bulky under Willie's coat. She removed the Star of David from my shirt and jacket. All the time she kept crying and asking, "Where is God?"

Uncle Willie arrived and heard her pleas. "Rose, God is right here and will lead us to safety this morning!" He smiled and began to go over the instructions of my escape one more time.

"This hiding place is temporary, Schaja. We will find a better place soon," my father explained.

"Schaja, you must be a very good boy. Whatever the people tell you to do you must do it with no argument. These Lithuanians are risking their own lives by doing this so you must keep their good will," my mother said between tears.

"Never complain, Schaja. And you must be very quiet. It's not going to be easy but I know that you can do this. And soon we will all be together again." My father spoke bravely, but I could see the emotion welling up in him. I saw his hands tremble as he held me close to him. He finally broke down. "Schaja," he said between sobs. "I am so sorry that you have to go through this terrible time. You are only a child and you have faced so many horrors . . ." He straightened up and tried to compose himself. "All we can do is hope for better times. We love you and we'll miss you."

I was torn between the agony of leaving my family and the fear of imminent death if I stayed or if I failed to escape. I was desperately trying to keep all of the instructions I had practiced straight in my head.

"Just remember everything we practiced. One step at a time," Uncle Willie said. He seemed to be reading my thoughts.

"Yes, sir," I said looking up at him.

"What do you look for once I drop you off?" he asked.

"A lady wearing a red kerchief on her head," I answered.

After we closed the door I could hear both of my parents and grandmother crying. My knees almost buckled with fear and agony. I realized that this could be the last time that I would ever see my family.

It was still dark, a haze of fog surrounded us as we made our way to the camp gate. I walked beside Uncle Willie and he smiled down at me as we neared the area. He saw there were only two guards with the work crew today. There were several hundred people in his crew. "Luck is with us so far," he said and winked at me. We stood quietly as several of his friends gathered around us. They knew our plan and wished me well.

Uncle Willie gave me a signal and I disappeared immediately under his coat. The guards barked their orders as they passed by our line. I could feel the others moving closely around Uncle Willie to protect us. The guards' count of the inmates began. This seemed to go on forever.

The inmates were given body searches each day. This search was done usually on the return in the evening, but occasionally the guards would do a morning search. Uncle Willie signaled me to turn right and start walking. The rehearsals had paid off. I picked up the rhythm quickly and we moved outside the camp gate. I heard Uncle Willie sigh with relief when there were no searches.

After a while, my Uncle squeezed my shoulder again to indicate that we were slowing down. This went on for some time. I had no idea how long it was as we moved through the streets. When I looked down at the pavement I saw light beginning to hit the pavement as the sun rose in the sky.

I had too much time to think as I walked next to my uncle and my thoughts started running wild. I imagined a gun being pointed at me as I suddenly appeared out of the coat at our drop point. I heard my father's sobs ricochet through my thoughts and my mother's questions of where is God? I was so lost in thought I almost missed the alert signal to slow down. I almost tripped over Uncle Willie's feet.

His signal indicated that we were getting close to the drop point. I counted silently until sixty seconds passed and darted out from under his coat. I weaved my way agilely through the inmates marching in the gutter. When I hit the sidewalk, I turned in the opposite direction of the work crew and confidently walked down the street toward my contact.

I was amazed that I was walking on the sidewalk, the forbidden sidewalk for Jews. As the inmate brigade passed me I stared straight ahead, not risking any eye contact. I looked down the street and saw a Partisan guard leaning against the wall of a building midway in the block. He was lighting a cigarette, but kept his head down. My heart skipped a beat as I passed by him. He didn't even raise his head to look at me. At the next corner where I was supposed to turn right and find my contact I felt like a bird flying out of his cage door.

I took a deep breath and kept walking when I didn't see her. I strained to look farther down the street and saw a flash of red as she peeked her head outside of a recessed area. She turned and walked onto the street and I followed her. I stayed ten paces behind her. After a while, she turned into a building and glanced back at me for the first time. I made no recognition as she nodded toward me. I turned the corner and followed her into a dark corridor and through several dark storage areas. Finally, she stopped and put a key into a lock and opened a door into another dark room. I stood behind her quietly waiting for instructions. She made no sound; she just motioned for me to come into the room.

When I walked inside the room she shut the door and turned on a dimly lit bulb hanging in the center of the room. She looked at me closely for the first time. Her red kerchief was drenched with sweat on the edges. I could see perspiration drops on her forehead and above her lip. Her dark brown eyes were wide and fearful. I tried to stay calm.

"You must not make noises! The Germans will kill you if they find you! They will kill me, too," she said in a whispered tone.

"No ma'am," I whispered back. "I won't make a sound."

"We were lucky today, usually there are Nazis on the street." She spat out the words angrily. "It was probably too early for those lazy murderers. All of this horror, it is their fault," she continued, shaking her head ruefully.

I nodded in agreement, but didn't utter a word.

I looked around my new quarters. The walls were white and the ceiling was high. The room was about ten by thirteen.

She pointed at the three flat pillows in a wooden frame. "This is your bed. Your table and chairs," she said pointing at the small desk-size table and two straight-back chairs. "This," she said, pointing at a white pot with a wooden cover. "This is your toilet. I will come by and empty your toilet and bring you food when it is safe to do so."

I nodded in agreement.

She looked at me with her hands on her hips. "Are you hungry?"

"Yes, ma'am."

"I will get food and water to you as soon as possible," she said and sighed.

I heard her turn the key in the lock. I was again a prisoner. I looked around the room after she left. I looked at the small window above the door and pulled a chair over to the door and stood on my toes to look out the window. It was pitch black. I got down and went to my bed. It had been a long day. One of the most extraordinary days of my life. I had escaped from hell! Or had I?

Seventeen

I was lying on the floor of my room when I saw a spider crawl under the door. I watched as it scampered across the floor. The spider had crawled under the door and into my room twice today. I had no way of knowing if it was day or night . . . one day or two days. I wondered if the spider knew. "Hello," I said softly and watched as he maneuvered around the room.

Sometime later, I heard the key in the lock. It was the lady. I stood up to greet her, but just as every other day since I had arrived she never said a word to me. I wanted to talk to someone so badly, but I remembered what my mother had told me about not causing any problems and I kept quiet.

Today she brought a big milk can that was filled with fresh water and an extra bedpan. She also brought me a tiny slice of chicken and a piece of bread smeared with liverwurst and a glass of milk.

I looked at her and whispered. "Can you tell me what year this is?"

She looked at me strangely. "It's 1944," she answered and put the food down on my table and left. I heard the key turn in the lock.

I couldn't believe it. It seemed an eternity since my family had been imprisoned. My birthday had passed and I wasn't sure how old I was. I wondered what day of the week it was and I started to laugh. I could make it any day I liked.

I looked over at the food she had left on the table and decided I would drink the milk since it was still cool from the outdoor air. I would save the rest of my meal for later.

Each day I tried to eat my rations slowly, throughout what I thought was a full day. I slept better if I was not battling hunger pains. But there were many times when I was too hungry and anxious to sleep. But I tried to stay calm.

I learned a lesson that day in Demokratu Square. I stopped thinking about now and thought about something that was happy. I usually thought about my parents and what it would be like when we were together again. I envisioned my grandmother and wondered if she was still sad. I wondered how much Mula had grown. It had been a long time since he had left the camp. I tried to imagine how he would look. I tried to stay lost in my imaginings for as long as possible.

After I drank my milk, I looked around the room to find my spider friend. I had lost track of him when the lady arrived. He was sort of a grayish-brown color and was hard to spot against the stone floor. When I couldn't locate him I lay on the floor again and looked for another bug that might come through the small space under the door. I watched as a few dust balls passed through. But after a while, I got bored and ran in circles around the room. I took off my shoes so I wouldn't make any noise. "One," I counted as I ran the laps. "Two," I continued. When I got to twenty-five I started turning in circles until I was so dizzy that I had to fall into my bed and sleep. Some days I could only do five to ten laps because my energy was low and I had no food.

I realized during this time how important it was to have companionship and conversation with others. To make up for this lack, I talked to myself, but never out loud. I whispered conversations with real and imaginary friends. I pretended that I was talking to Michael or Moishe about Territory and smuggling food into the camp. All of these things were now only memories of the past, but I held onto them.

I sat and watched the doorway for hours just waiting to hear the key turn in the lock. Today was a very slow day for me. I was bored. I tried to figure out how many weeks I had been here. By my count, I thought it was about four weeks.

My boredom was suddenly over when I saw the spider that I had lost track of earlier in what seemed like a week. He was in the corner weaving a web. I sat down close by and watched as he patiently worked at building his home. He drew one string after another from side to side. I felt like hours had passed when he finally reached the edge of his web and stopped. When he finished, I counted eighty-eight threads.

I fell asleep and didn't wake up until I heard the key in the door. When the lady came in, she looked at me and burrowed her eyebrows. She kept looking at me, but didn't say anything. She walked over to my toilet bowl, picked it up, and took it out of the room. I wanted to follow her and see something other than the four white walls, but I knew the rules and I followed my mother's direction.

She came back in with a rag and dust mop. I saw when the dust mop crashed into the spider web and demolished the spider's house. She hit the mop on the floor and out came the spider moving as fast as he could. I could only watch as she took her foot and smashed him. She didn't bother to pick him up. She returned the toilet bowl and wooden top and left without a word. I heard the key turn in the lock.

I walked over to the crumpled spider. His insides had already dried on the stone floor. I tore away a piece of my shirt and picked him up by the leg. I placed him on top of the small square of material and folded the edges carefully around him. I thought for a minute about a name for him. I decided to call him Curly because his legs were now curled up in a ball. I said the only prayer I remembered in Yiddish for Curly and found a small hole between the wall and the floor that would serve as his grave.

The lady's visits became less frequent, it seemed. I didn't receive as much food as before, or at least it felt that way. I was always tired. I woke up one morning and started to rub my eyes. When I reached up to my face I felt a scab on my forehead. I took the straight-backed chair and pulled it up next to the door. I stood on it and tried to see my reflection in the glass window. It was dirty, but I could see the ugly sores on my face.

Several days later when I woke up, I noticed that my fingernails were coming loose from the nail bed. I looked at my hands and the nail from my little finger had disappeared. I was worried but I wasn't sure if I should mention this to the lady. I knew I had worms when I looked at my stools, but I never mentioned it to her. Each time she came I noticed that she looked at me with a very worried expression. I didn't want to cause any problems.

BOOM! BOOM! BOOM!!! I was almost thrown from my pillows by the ear-deafening sounds! I looked around the room and saw the walls shaking. I got up and crouched in the corner, my hands covering my head while the booms continued. My heart was pounding so fast, I could barely breathe. I felt plaster fall on my head from the ceiling. I started shaking so hard I couldn't attempt to stand on the chair and look out the window into the other room. I had no way of knowing if it was day or night, if this was enemy fire or bombs from allies. I thought about my parents and wondered where they were. I wanted to cry but I couldn't because I was so frightened.

After what seemed an eternity the booming stopped. I lay awake for hours waiting for the lady, or anyone to show up. It was impossible for my eyes to shut. I wasn't going to follow the rules any longer.

I finally heard the key slip into the lock and turn. When she opened the door I was already standing and waiting to question her. Before she could shut the door I spoke.

"I know, Mrs. Stravinskas, I am not supposed to impose on you in any way, but, can you tell me what those explosions were?" I asked nervously.

"The Russians, they are dropping bombs. If it was not for those murdering Nazis we would still have a beautiful city. The bombs have destroyed us. They fell close by, they ruined the church. It will never be the same." She walked over and placed my food on the table.

I couldn't bring myself to ask more questions as she ranted about the Germans. But today as she spoke, she put her hands up to my face, examining the sores that I had seen in the glass. She said nothing. Then she bent my head down and twisted my head to one side and then to the other. "Holes!"

"Holes?" I whispered. "What kind of holes?"

"Your hair is falling out and there are sores," she said and looked at me suspiciously. "Is this contagious? Are you sick?"

"I, I never . . . I'm sure it's not. I feel fine."

She said nothing and shook her head. She proceeded with her regular ritual of emptying the toilet. She had also brought a pitcher filled with water to add to my milk can supply.

I felt the back of my head after she left. I realized then that I had bald spots that she called holes. I didn't know why I had the sores and holes in my hair. Maybe it was a disease, I had no way of knowing. I decided that I would act like I was asleep from now on when she came in. I didn't want her to throw me out in the street.

In the following days the blasts and explosions continued. I was no longer frightened and the explosions were music to my ears. I smiled every time the room shook and silently thanked the Russian soldiers for trying to save us from the brutal Lithuanians and Germans.

One day I heard the key in the door lock, I barely opened my eyes. She stuck her head in. I stayed in bed as I had done since she discovered my holes.

"You must turn the light in this room off whenever you hear sirens. We must black out everything!" She slammed the door and locked it.

I didn't understand without a window to the outside in my room how anyone could see a light. But I did as I was told and kept the room dark whenever I heard sirens. At least I would be able to know if it was night or day since most of the bombings I was sure took place at night.

As the days dragged by I became more and more lethargic. I didn't even look forward to my small ration of food. Maybe I did have a disease.

The door opened and I saw the lady come in but she had no food. I closed my eyes.

"Schaja," I heard. It sounded like my mother's voice. I thought I was dreaming. "Schaja," I heard again.

My eyes flew open and I saw my mother standing over me. I practically flew into her arms from the bed. We hugged and kissed.

Mother smiled at me. "Schaja, I am taking you to a new home." She then turned to the lady. "Thank you so much for caring for my son. I know it has been dangerous. Thank God, we are all still safe."

I was so relieved that I was leaving this lonely room that I couldn't stifle my excitement. I started smiling. "Where are we going? Is the war over?"

"Not yet," Mother said and motioned to me that we needed to leave. The lady was getting nervous.

I politely told the lady good-bye and kissed her hand in thanks.

Eighteen

The sunlight hit my eyes as we left the building that day. I squinted and held my hand over my face. It had been some time since I had seen daylight. My mother and I walked happily through the streets toward our new home. We even passed a German army barracks without fear of detection. We casually passed the motor pool with their vehicles neatly parked in perfectly aligned rows. The cars were shiny and clean.

"Mama, are we going to live in a new house?" I asked, thinking that my mother had left the camp for good.

"Schaja, you will be living with a Lithuanian family and they have a nice house," she said.

"You're not coming with me?" I said with surprise.

"No, Schaja, I must return to my work crew and go back to the camp. Your grandmother and father need me there." She stopped and looked concerned.

"But, what about me and Mula?" I asked.

"We will all be together soon, I promise. Willie and your father are sure we will find a way," she said.

"But, I thought we would be together now . . ." My voice trailed off in disappointment. I couldn't stand the thought of having no one to talk to again.

"Schaja, remember we all must be strong, and I know that you have been very strong, but just a little bit longer and we will have happy times again," she said and smiled down at me. "We have been very lucky so far. After you left, the Nazis came and took all the children."

This hit me like a bolt of lightning! "What happened to them?" I asked.

She shook her head sadly. "We don't know," she answered.

"Michael, and Moishe . . . they're gone?"

I thought about my two friends. I couldn't believe they could be dead.

My mother just looked at me silently and we kept walking. Soon we were in front of a house with a large yard. "There are still some children hidden. Michael was older, maybe he made it to the outside. Let's hope that they all survived."

This possibility gave me a ray of hope. When I looked up I saw a warm and friendly, heavy-set lady in a bright flowered dress coming out of the house in front of us. She walked down the sidewalk, talking rapidly even though we couldn't hear her. She had dark hair like my mother, but was turning gray in the front. Her bright smile matched her rosy cheeks.

As she came nearer I heard her saying, "I'm so glad you've arrived . . . you will bring light into our home . . . you and Ignatz will have a grand time . . ." She never stopped to take a breath and never stopped smiling. She reached and patted me on the head and then put her arm around me. We walked together with my mother into her house.

"Bobunia, I can't tell you how grateful I am that you are willing to care for my Schaja," Mother said after we had entered the house.

Bobunia looked at my bald spots, then she looked at my nails. Two nails were completely gone, one on my right hand and one on my left. She lifted my hands to her face and pressed them against her cheek. "We will make all of this better," she said. "It's malnutrition, nothing else, Rose. He will have plenty of food here!"

When we entered the kitchen. I saw her husband, Ignatz. He was an older man with blondish-gray hair. He was not too tall, maybe about five six. He had a scowl on his face as he hunched over the breakfast table reading the newspaper.

"Ignatz," Bobunia almost shouted. "This is Schaja. He looks like his grandfather, yes? We will call you Jonas," she said matter-of-factly. Later, she told me that Schaja was too Jewish sounding.

He stared over at me and nodded. He gave a slight grin and looked back down at the table and continued reading the newspaper.

"Ignatz and Bobunia knew your grandparents," my mother said to me. She took a package from under her jacket and handed it to Ignatz. "This is all we have, but I think you will be satisfied," my mother said to him.

"I'm sure it will be fine, Rose," he said without looking up from his paper or looking into the package.

"Jonas, you may call me Bobunia and you may call my husband, Ignatz."

I nodded and walked over toward Ignatz. "Hello," I said and smiled. I started to extend my hand to him, but he had one hand on his newspapers and with the other he was reaching for his pipe.

He looked up at me as he lit his pipe and nodded. I could see his teeth were yellow from smoking. "How old is he?" he said looking toward my mother. His eyes were squinted and wrinkled, his face lined with years of hard work and hard weather. I would discover that Ignatz was a man of few words.

"He'll be twelve in the fall, Ignatz. He's still a growing boy," she said sweetly.

Ignatz grunted and puffed on his pipe. "You'll make a good gardener, Jonas," he said and smiled at me.

I liked him right away.

My mother held me in her arms and kissed me. "Be a good boy and don't make any trouble for these very kind people."

I nodded in agreement. "I love you, Mama. Tell Father and Grandmother Rochel that I miss them."

"We'll all be together soon," she said and disappeared.

Before I could feel the pain of my mother leaving, Bobunia grabbed my hand and walked with me upstairs to my room. It was a beautiful room with a window that overlooked the front yard. I noticed right away that there was no lock on the door.

"Now, young man, you can go anywhere in the house that you would like, but under no condition can you go outside in the front yard, or even silhouette yourself in the window. You'll go to the garden only when Ignatz and I are with you. It would be very dangerous for you not to obey these rules," she said, still smiling. "But I know that you are a good boy and you are going to do just fine with us."

She patted the bed. "These are fresh, clean sheets and nice soft pillows. If you need more blankets, there are several in your trunk over here." She pointed to the small trunk against the wall that held the items.

"I'm going to make you a hot bath and you can soak in the tub as long as you like. When you're finished you come back to your room and put on fresh clean clothes."

"I'm sorry, ma'am, I have only the ones that I'm wearing," I explained.

"Those are going in the trash. When my son was your age I saved all of his clothes. You'll be wearing his," she said and smiled again at me.

"You have a son?" I asked hoping he was not too much older than me.

"Yes, but he's grown now, almost twenty-four years old. A new husband with a beautiful bride. He only recently married. You'll meet them after they come home from work," she said.

When she talked about her son's beautiful bride, I thought about Kindra. I wondered if her son's bride was as beautiful as Kindra.

"I'll run your bath water," she said.

I didn't tell her that I had not had a bath in three years.

"We'll have dinner at six o'clock," she said leaving the room and closing the door. Soon I could hear the water filling the tub.

After a while I walked into the bathroom and stuck my finger into the water. It was very warm. Bobunia had left me a towel and a washcloth and a bar of white soap. I slowly took off my clothes and wondered what the water would feel like after such a long time of not bathing.

As I stepped in the tub and felt the relaxing warmth of the water, I couldn't believe the good fortune that my mother had provided for me. I sat for a few moments just letting the water swirl around me and then I took the washrag and lathered the soap. I dove under the water and scrubbed the soap into my hair. I was covered in suds from head to toe. Then I started playing games using the bar of soap as a boat. I propelled the imaginary boat around in circles, up the sides of the tub and back onto my body for more scrubbing. The water got darker and darker with every new wash I gave my body and head. I tried to be quiet as I played and blew bubbles under the water.

I was in the tub for a long time. When I got out and dried my skin off I saw tiny white flakes on the towel. When I looked at my fingers they were wrinkled like raisins. There was a dark ring around the tub when the water drained away.

I didn't want to leave the tub dirty. I was sure that Ignatz wouldn't like it. I remembered from a long time ago how my mother used a cleanser and a rag to wash away the dirt in our bathtub at our home in Kaunas. I looked in the bathroom cabinet and I found a rag and a cleaner. I scrubbed the grime away. When I left the bathroom the tub was white again. I hoped Bobunia would allow me to take a bath often.

I went back to my room and saw clothes laid out on the bed. They looked like they were my size. I tried them on and sat quietly on the side of my bed, leaving the door open just a crack. I was so happy with my new freedom, I never wanted to shut the door again.

I heard footsteps on the stairway some time later.

"Jonas, we're waiting for you at the dinner table," Bobunia said peeking her head inside the door. "My son and his wife are home from work."

"I get to sit at the dinner table with the whole family?" I almost shouted I was so excited. I ran and hugged Bobunia.

She held my hand on the way down the stairs and into the dining room. "This is our young friend, Jonas," she smiled as she introduced me to her son and his wife.

"Hello, Jonas, my name is Ignatz, the same as my father," he said and put his hand out to me. "And this is Marlena, my wife."

I shook hands with him and then I bowed and kissed Marlena's hand. "It's very nice to meet you," I said politely.

Bobunia seated me next to Ignatz Sr. He took my plate and filled it full of meats and cheeses, vegetables, and bread.

"I'm going to have to put some muscle on those arms and legs of yours. I want you to eat all of this," he said with a slight smile.

He knew he didn't have to encourage me. I smiled at Ignatz and dove into my plate. I didn't look up until I had cleaned every morsel of the serving.

Ignatz again smiled, even though he had a stern look in his eyes. He filled my plate the second time. When I finished my second plate I could hardly keep my eyes open.

Bobunia led me up the stairs and gave me a pair of pajamas. Before she left the room she gave me a pat on the head and kissed me on the cheek. I felt like the luckiest boy in the world.

Nineteen

We will never be defeated, Papa. We are getting intelligence from the Russians we've captured. We will overcome them. We're moving out another three thousand from Kovno Camp. The status of the camp will change after this," Ignatz Jr. said to his father while we were having dinner one night.

I couldn't believe my ears . . . was Ignatz Jr. working with the Nazis? It was clear from the conversation that he was helping them. I had never seen any Nazi swastikas in the house. How could it be that he was helping people who were killing Jews? I was his enemy and he was now mine. But, no, he wasn't my enemy. I liked him and he was always nice to me. He brought me pastries. He and his wife played with me after dinner almost every night.

He and his father kept on arguing. Ignatz insisted that Hitler was wrong . . . the Lithuanians were wrong . . . the Jews were wrong (he acknowledged that he didn't mean me) . . . the Americans were wrong . . . the Communists were wrong. No one ever asked him who he thought was right.

"Good riddance to all of them," Ignatz said and slammed his napkin down on the table. "If it wasn't for the Jews none of this would be happening! I'm sorry, Jonas, I don't mean you or your family," he said. "I mean those Jews that dress in black and wear those little 'beanie' skullcaps on their head and grow hair on their face," Ignatz growled as he ruminated over the demise of the world around him.

I nodded at Ignatz accepting his apology but my mind was wondering about Ignatz Jr. being a Nazi and the change that would take place in Kovno Camp. Who were the three thousand? But I couldn't ask; they might kill me if they thought I had listened to their conversation.

"I am sorry you joined Hitler and his gang. He is a maniacal tyrant. You should desert the army of murderers and stay at home until this is all over."

"Papa." Ignatz Jr. smiled at his father. "You don't have to worry, it is better to be on the side of power."

"They are all barbarians. The Bolsheviks are no better than the Nazis!"

"This war is ruthless on every side. Thousands have already died."

"There is no doubt in my mind that the Bolsheviks will win this war here in Lithuania," Ignatz concluded. "You are a fool to think otherwise."

Ignatz smiled and shook his head. "That will never happen, Papa!"

"Enough of war talk tonight," Bobunia interrupted. "God doesn't approve of war." She looked at both her son and her husband with a reprising glance.

Marlena rose to help her with the dishes.

"God doesn't have to put up with the Jews and Germans and Communists!" Ignatz retorted.

Ignatz Jr. looked in my direction. "Jonas, I found some very special things for you today. In fact, they were so special I bought two," he teasingly said.

"What is it?" I said smiling.

"You guess," he said.

"Is it from the bakery?" I asked.

"Smart guess since we both have a sweet tooth," he said and smiled.

"Cinnamon bread?" I said, knowing that it was Bobunia's favorite pastry.

We went on for several more guesses. Finally, he opened the package that Marlena handed him. He pulled out two chocolate éclairs. I had never seen this pastry before. It was filled with Bavarian cream encased by a flaky, delicious pastry and topped with a dark chocolate sauce.

Ignatz started laughing. "Jonas, be careful, your eyes are going to pop out!"

Everyone at the table laughed, including me, and we all shared the two pieces of pastry.

Bobunia instructed me to come into the living room and have Bible study one morning. I had never seen the Holy Bible. It was a big book that Bobunia claimed had all the answers in life. I was curious and anxious to finally learn all the answers.

As the weeks went by I enjoyed her lessons about the New Testament and the Catholic interpretation of religion. I looked forward to our early morning sessions. She told stories of Jesus that reminded me of my grandmother telling stories, but not about Jesus. I memorized many of the stories she told me about Jesus changing water into wine, healing blind men and lame men and ladies that had been sick a long time.

"Bobunia, where is Jesus now?" I asked after she closed the Bible, finishing our lesson.

"He's in heaven," she answered. She looked pleased that I was asking questions about her beliefs.

"Why doesn't he stop the war?" I asked. "Does he know about war in heaven?"

"Sometimes, Schaja, we just have to trust," Bobunia answered.

"What do we trust?" I asked.

"God."

This didn't really help me. But I decided that the question was not one that could be answered. My mother, grandmother, father, and uncle had all asked the question and no one had an answer. Trust was something that I didn't understand.

After several weeks of Bible study, Bobunia felt that I was ready to go to church with her and Ignatz on Sunday. She was absolutely thrilled and saw this event as a magnificent milestone in my religious journey. I heard her tell Ignatz that turning me into a Catholic would assure them a place in heaven. I don't think that Ignatz was so sure about that idea.

She explained to me what would take place during the service, called Mass, and what I must do during certain rituals. I would not be sitting with them, but I would stay close by in a pew behind them. Bobunia found a suit that I could wear and on Sunday morning we all rose early, anticipating the big day. Ignatz was irritated at Bobunia's happy singing and did not see the need for all this commotion over a trip to church. He did not find church and religion as entertaining as Bobunia.

When we left for the service I remained behind for several moments until they were ahead of me. As I walked, I saw Bobunia turn around, shade her eyes from the sun with her hand, and look until she spotted me on the sidewalk. I kept my eyes straight ahead and continued walking as though I did not know them.

I had never been inside a Catholic church and I was very impressed by the beauty and the pungent smell of incense. Bobunia had explained to me that the priest was called Father whenever there was an exchange of conversation. I sat on the edge of the pew so I could see the father of the church. I was surprised when I saw a man that was not much older than my own father. I had assumed that he would be very old. He was tall with black hair and blue eyes. He looked at me as he passed by my pew.

Candles were burning everywhere, not just to give light, but they had other meanings. I couldn't remember what Bobunia had told me about this, but I would ask her later. When the service started it was spoken in Latin. I didn't understand Latin, but I realized that most of the people around me didn't understand Latin.

When it came time for Communion I watched as the parishioners lined up and went to the father and he put a wafer in their mouth and gave them a small drink of red wine and said some more words in Latin. I looked over at Bobunia. She got up and stood in line. When she returned she shook her head vigorously, indicating that I should not take communion. I knelt down on the prayer bench and prayed. I prayed about my parents and Mula and my grandmother. I asked God to stop the war. I hoped the Catholic God was more powerful than the Jewish God.

The service came to an end and we walked back to our home.

"Now, Jonas, do you have any questions?" Bobunia said, beaming with joy.

"The wafer at Communion, why does the father give the parishioners this to eat?" I asked.

"This wafer is Christ's body," she answered. "We partake of his body with that wafer and we are filled with the Holy Spirit."

"How can Christ feed so many people with his body?" I asked.

"Because Christ is everywhere," she said.

"His body is everywhere?!" I asked in disbelief.

Ignatz rolled his eyes. "Bobunia, it makes no sense to him. He's not old enough to understand." Bobunia cleared her throat, undisturbed by Ignatz. "You are not ready for this experience. As you develop your faith you will understand. When you understand you can take Communion."

"Are you ready to work in the garden?" Ignatz asked. "A gardener has no rest, he works seven days a week."

"Yes, sir," I said and got up to join him in the yard. I had learned to pull weeds, turn over the soil, and prepare it for planting; trim the flower plants; and dig holes for new seeds. Ignatz boosted my confidence when he complimented my gardening work.

Twenty

By the beginning of the summer, I had decided that I would become a Catholic and my vocation would be gardening. Ignatz told me that I had a "green thumb" and I enjoyed planting and digging, watering, and watching the plants grow. Ignatz had given me a small garden patch of my own where I grew tomatoes. I felt my first tomato should go to Bobunia.

I sat down to wait for Bible study and placed the tomato that was ready to ripen on top of the Bible. It would be the first thing she saw when she came into the room.

She nearly fell over when she walked in. "What is that? Why is that sitting on top of my sacred Bible?!"

"It's my first ripe tomato from my garden, a gift for you," I said smiling.

She grabbed the tomato. "Never, never sit anything on the Bible. This book is an instrument of God," she said picking up the book and brushing it off.

I laughed. "The tomato didn't do anything to the Bible?"

"It's disrespectful, Jonas," she said and gave me a stern look.

"I'm sorry," I said, straightening up in my chair and looking solemn, too. "I didn't mean to disrespect the Bible. I know that it is a very important book."

She relaxed a little bit and smiled as she looked at my gift to her. "Thank you for your lovely tomato. Ignatz says you will make a fine gardener someday."

"I'm going to be a gardener when I grow up, Bobunia, and I'm going to carry around my gardening tools in a wagon drawn by tall white horses," I said.

"A tall white horse? Not a motorized truck?" she asked.

"No, ma'am! I like horses."

She smiled. "Now let's begin our lessons for today. We will begin with the meaning of Communion."

"Yes, I understand Communion . . ."

"No, Jonas, you have never taken Communion. You had a few questions about it the first time that we went to Mass," Bobunia said and thumbed through the Bible.

"Yes, Bobunia, I took Communion last Sunday," I said proudly. "I walked with the rest of the congregation to the priest. He placed a wafer on my tongue. I devoured it and waited to be filled with the body of Christ! Isn't that what you do? I wanted to be filled with the Holy Ghost."

The look of horror that came across Bobunia's face at the moment was one I had never seen. She was so angry that I quickly got up from the chair next to her.

"I was very disappointed, Bobunia. There wasn't much taste. I was very curious how Christ's body could feed and satisfy everyone, and I didn't feel the Holy Ghost," I said.

Bobunia shook her head and put her hand up to her mouth in shock. "I have failed to teach you the proper principles of religion," she shrieked. "You must be punished, Jonas, you have broken a law of the church. I told you that Communion would come as your faith developed. You have broken a rule of sanctity."

She grabbed her whipping cane in the corner of the room and began to hit my backside. It was a thin cane, with knots that had prickly points all the way down the shank with a sharp tip at the bottom. The stinging was excruciating.

"Jesus, please forgive us both," Bobunia wailed as she looked up into the heavens and continued to wallop me. "Jesus, help us, we have sinned! Oh dear God, punish us both."

As far as I could see I was the only one being punished. "Jesus, please help me," I cried. "Bobunia is hurting me."

Ignatz came running into the room when he heard the commotion. He quickly pulled Bobunia away from me. He took the cane and tossed it away. "What are you doing?"

Bobunia took a breath and ran to me. She held me closely to her now. "Jesus, forgive me, please, forgive me," she pled.

I assumed that she was asking Jesus to forgive her for hitting me so hard. I felt bad that she was so upset. "Don't worry," I said, still feeling the stinging on my backside. "I won't take Communion again, ever, without your permission." This seemed to satisfy her.

I decided that I was better at gardening than at becoming a Catholic.

TWENTY-ONE

Ignatz and I were working outside when we heard the air-raid siren. It meant that the Russians were about to fly over and drop their load of bombs. I was always happy when I heard the siren, even though the explosions were frightening. We went inside the house and grabbed a few pieces of clothing and went into the cellar. It was the second bombing of the day; the bombings were no longer confined to the night.

We sat down and listened for the first explosion. Before anything hit, Ignatz began to curse the Russians, the Germans, and anyone else that came to mind. I started laughing until the first impact shook the ground around us. The louder the explosions got, the louder Ignatz was yelling. The three of us cowered in the corner of the cellar. Bobunia was frantically praying while she held her rosary beads. Her prayers got louder as the bombings progressed. The bombing went on for about twenty minutes. Finally we heard the "all clear" signal and cautiously crept up the stairs to see what damage had been done to the house. There were broken windows and glass everywhere. Some of Bobunia's dishes had crashed to the floor. But Bobunia crossed herself and gave thanks to God that the house was still standing and we were safe.

Ignatz and I cleaned the glass off of the floor and placed pieces of cardboard in the windows that were broken.

"Who's going to pay for all of this?" Ignatz muttered to himself. "Glass costs money, but the bombs, they do not care. I suppose that I should ask the führer for a few of his coins to pay or perhaps Stalin. The bombs . . . the leaders . . . they do not care for the poor common man." Ignatz kept mumbling as we took the last of the glass shards to the trash can. He shook his head when we heard secondary explosions in the distance. We looked up and saw billowing clouds of dark smoke overhead.

"The barracks are hit," Ignatz said as he looked down the road. "That's where all of the smoke is coming from."

We went back into the house with Bobunia. Ignatz couldn't sit still and kept peering out of the remaining windows toward the German barracks. "I think we better go have a look at the damage," he finally said.

"Ignatz, you have no business down there. You stay here where you are safe," Bobunia said.

"No," Ignatz said. "Jonas and I need to go. They may need help."

"You are going to take Jonas to the German barracks!" Bobunia almost screamed. "Have you lost your mind?"

He gave her a look that only married couples have when there is no need for further discussion.

"His brain power leaves much to be desired . . ." she said to herself and turned to leave the room.

Ignatz and I walked outside and down toward the German camp. We saw fire leaping in the air and large plumes of smoke. People were running in every direction. A German soldier ran toward us screaming for help. Part of his clothing was burned off; only his blackened skin was visible. We tried to help him but he was in shock and just kept walking and screaming.

The fence that normally surrounded the camp had large gaps. Another soldier, drenched in blood, came toward us. He fell to the ground. Ignatz caught him as he went down and I tried to help get the soldier flat on the ground. Ignatz and I started yelling for medical help and someone came running with an already bloodied gurney. The medic had an aid kit and began to work on the wounded man.

When we entered the compound we saw buildings had been partially demolished. A soldier asked us to help drag soldiers out of barracks that were not still burning. This was the first time that I had ever seen this kind of devastation. Ignatz and I drug out soldiers that were already dead. Others that we helped were critically wounded and in shock. We saw many wounded soldiers.

A soldier grabbed my hand as we pulled him out of the barracks. He was screaming and obviously in extreme pain. I looked at him for a moment. There was nothing I could do to help with his pain, and I wasn't sure that I would if I could. Somehow, I saw this event as justice for what the Germans had inflicted on my family and all Jews. I wondered how he would feel if I told him I was a Jew.

Ignatz nudged me after a while and motioned for me to follow him. "We have to go home now," he said. "I don't want Bobunia's assessment in coming over here and bringing a Jew to be correct!"

As we walked home I noticed that I had blood on the front of my shirt. German blood.

Twenty-two

Throughout the early summer of 1944 it was apparent that the war was not going well for the Nazis. Every day we heard artillery fights and bombs being dropped by the Soviets. I could see defeat on the faces of the German soldiers. Their former arrogance, confidence, and pride withered in the face of defeat and disillusionment.

"The camp was burned to the ground yesterday. All the Jews were taken away," Ignatz announced one warm morning after he had been downtown.

His message hit me like a ton of bricks. "Where have they taken them . . . the Jews?" I asked.

"To hell, where they belong!" Ignatz said and quickly glanced at me. "Of course, Jonas, I don't mean you or your family. The good Jews I pray always for their safety, but you know the ones I mean."

"Jonas, try not to worry. Your mother and father and grandmother are very smart and courageous. I'm sure they are alive," Bobunia interrupted. She looked angrily at Ignatz.

Ignatz went outside and called me to come with him. I wondered how many people had been killed in the camp when it was burned. All I could do was hope that my parents were still alive. I thought about my grandmother and how frail she was when I left . . . and Uncle Willie. I couldn't think about them being dead. I just had to pray that they were alive. Maybe this was what Bobunia meant about faith and trust.

Ignatz complained all day about the lesser of one evil was taking over another evil. Replacing the Nazis would be the Bolsheviks and Communism. Most of what Ignatz was talking about made no sense to me. He didn't like any government. I decided that Communism was better than Hitler's regime, especially if you were a Jew.

Several weeks later, as I did each morning, I started filling my water cans. I had two of them that I filled and carried across the garden. After I poured them on a section I would repeat the process until I had covered the entire area. It usually took me half the day to water the garden.

Ignatz walked toward me as I finished filling the cans. He was carrying a pole with two pieces of rope hanging from each end with a hook. He put his hands on my shoulders and turned me around with my back to him. He hooked the ropes onto the handles of the two water cans sitting on the ground. He placed the pole across my back. This new efficient toy he had created would cut my workload in half. Ignatz was very pleased with his new invention. Of course, this device had been used in service from biblical times, but as far as Ignatz was concerned, he was the inventor.

I saw the priest walking toward us before he did. "It's the father, Ignatz."

Ignatz immediately turned his attention to the priest, dressed in his black robes and red cap. He was very friendly to both of us and he patted me on the back.

Ignatz happily showed our new water transport system to him. After a few moments of conversation, Ignatz asked me to go pull weeds at the far corner of the garden. I kept my eye on them while they talked. From their expressions it looked like a serious conversation. Occasionally they would glance in my direction. I was sure it must be a conversation concerning my parents. I waited for them to approach me and give me the bad news. But to my surprise, I saw them walk toward the house. Ignatz and the priest both had their heads down when they went inside.

I waited until I saw the priest leave before going into the house. Both Ignatz and Bobunia sat at the table in the kitchen. Neither acknowledged me when I walked in the door. They both had very sad expressions on their face. I knew better than to ask questions. I did know that if it concerned me that they would have told me.

The next morning, I woke up very early and went downstairs. Ignatz and Bobunia were already sitting at the kitchen table. Bobunia's eyes were red. It looked as if she had been crying all night.

"Our son and daughter-in-law will be here with us for dinner tonight. They will come after dark. If anyone asks any questions it's very important that no one knows they are coming here," Bobunia said and looked at me sadly.

"Yes, ma'am," I answered. "I will look forward to seeing them. I've missed them since they moved to their own house." Usually this would be a festive occasion but I could see and feel that this was going to be a sad event.

Ignatz got up from the table. "Jonas, after you have some breakfast come outside and we'll pick some ripe vegetables for the church."

"I will, sir," I said and turned my attention back to Bobunia.

"Tonight is a very special occasion and I'm preparing a very extraordinary meal for them," she looked wistfully out of the window as she spoke. "All of my son's favorite dishes."

"Yes, ma'am," I said.

She sat a bowl of cereal and milk in front of me. I quickly ate and joined Ignatz in the garden. Throughout the day Ignatz did not speak a word. I saw him take his white handkerchief out of his pocket and blow his nose and wipe his eyes several times. It always made me laugh when he blew his nose. He only used the handkerchief to hold one side of his nose and blow the other side's contents to the ground. I tried not to laugh this time.

After we had picked the best vegetables I put them in a sack. At the end of the day Ignatz carried them to the church. When he returned he was angrily cursing the Russians.

When we went into the house it was silent. A heavy silence. It reminded me of my house when there was so much sadness and death. I wasn't sure what was wrong but I knew it wasn't good.

After dark when Ignatz and Marlena arrived I was standing in the door of the living room. The moment they walked in the front door I knew there was something terribly wrong. They both looked worn and haggard. Ignatz had lost weight and looked as though he had not slept in days. Marlena was sobbing as Bobunia held her and tried to comfort her. Ignatz Jr. nodded at me but his expression was tense. He was immediately in deep conversation with his father. I could hear Ignatz cursing the Germans, the Russians, and the Jews again.

There was a knock at the door and Bobunia rushed to answer it. It was the priest from the parish who had stopped in the yard yesterday. He whispered to Ignatz Jr. and his father. Then he turned to leave as quickly as he came.

"He must leave as soon as possible," Ignatz said to Bobunia.

During dinner I tried to pick up bits and pieces of conversation. Ignatz looked vacantly at his plate of favorite foods. He was very worried, a stark contrast from his usual relaxed and playful self. Marlena could barely take her eyes from him. She and Ignatz held hands.

"The NKVD [later known as KGB] is as ruthless as the Gestapo. If they find me they will kill me," Ignatz Jr. said, looking down to hide his tears.

"Who told them?" Ignatz asked.

He shrugged. "I don't know."

"The bastards. You stay here with us and if they come to take you I will kill every one of them!" Ignatz exclaimed. "You were acting on their orders. Tell them to find Hitler and kill him."

"Papa, if they find me here they would kill you and Mama. I can't bring this battle to you. I would like for Marlena to stay with you until I can return to Lithuania."

"The Russians will look at us favorably, son. We saved Jonas from the Germans," Ignatz said proudly.

"Papa, they will act now and ask questions later," he answered.

"Ignatz," Marlena said, turning to her husband. "I am going with you. We are together. We've only been married a year and I have no desire to be a widow. Our destiny is together. The father will help us."

I could see that Ignatz Jr. was touched by her words to him.

"I can't let you sacrifice more than you already have," he said softly.

She put her fingers to his lips. "Shhh . . . together."

I thought it would probably be safer if she stayed with us. I didn't think the Russians would kill her. She had nothing to do with the war. But she loved Ignatz and wanted to stay with her husband.

"We will give you money. You will need it to pay off those who smuggle you out of the country," Bobunia said.

After we finished dinner, Ignatz turned to me. "Come with me, Jonas."

He told me to go to the shed and get the shovel. Then he and I walked to the yard near the back of the house. "You dig about two feet down. There will be a box there."

I started to dig. He hid his money like Uncle Jacob. After a while I heard the sound of hitting metal. I leaned down and scraped the dirt away and brought a small metal suitcase with a handle and a lock on it out of the ground. I handed it to Ignatz.

He brushed off some remaining dirt and carried the metal box inside. He placed it on the table where the dinner dishes had been cleared and handed me a key from his pocket. "Open the box, Jonas."

I opened the box. Inside was money, gold coins, silver, jewelry. I saw the things that my mother had given him.

"Put it all on the table," he said, sadly.

I did as he ordered and poured the items on the table. He looked at each item. "This is all we have . . . our savings from the time we were married." He shook his head sadly. "I only wish I had more . . . I don't know if this is enough to protect him. I don't know if there is enough money in the world to protect him."

He looked at me so sadly that I thought he probably knew this was the last time he would see his son. "You're a good father, Ignatz."

He looked at me and I saw water gather in his eyes. He nodded and went into the room with the others.

Soon the priest came back and Ignatz and Marlena left with him.

Twenty-three

On August 1, 1944 the Russians troops entered Kaunas. They arrested or killed any German soldier they caught. Several weeks later two NKVD agents came to the door. Ignatz answered the door and invited them inside.

"We have some information that your son was here several weeks ago," one agent said to Ignatz.

"Son, what son? We have only this boy, Jonas. He is not our son, but we have provided him a hiding place since he escaped from Kovno and the Gestapo animals! We have lived in Lithuania all of our lives . . . my country has been turned upside down by the maniac Hitler!" Ignatz expounded. "Thank God you Russians have come to give us some order and safety in our town. This boy suffered tremendously at the hand of the Germans," Ignatz said turning a sympathetic eye toward me.

The two men watched silently as Ignatz continued to rant and rave about the Germans. After a few more minutes of conversation the agents got up and started to leave.

"Do you know if there are any survivors from Kovno Camp?" I asked. "Do you know where they were taken?"

They looked at me and then over to Ignatz and back to me. "We've not been given any information." I was sure my parents were dead.

"Can I offer you a few tomatoes that Jonas and I have grown?" Ignatz asked. They gladly took the tomatoes and left Ignatz and me standing in the garden.

"Those sorry, rotten bastards. May they choke on my tomatoes. They touch my son and God will strike them dead! God will someday take all the Nazis and Communists and any other predator and burn them in Hell, Jonas," Ignatz said. "You mark my word!" He stomped back to his house and went inside.

I followed him. I watched as he took a bottle of vodka off of the shelf and poured a good amount into the glass. Ignatz had started to drink more since his son had left. He and Bobunia were both very sad since there had been no word since they departed.

I wondered if I should ask Bobunia and Ignatz to help search for my parents. No one had said a word. I assumed they were dead, but I needed to know for sure. Then I thought about Mula. How could I support him and provide a home for him? He was probably better off with the sea captain and his wife. I wondered how long Bobunia and Ignatz would let me stay with them. These thoughts were with me daily as I worked in the garden.

I was deep in thought one day, thinking about the future, when I looked up and saw a woman walking down the path. My mother had a very distinctive walk, and as I watched in the distance I thought the walk looked familiar. It looked like my mother's walk. But then I thought I wanted so badly for my parents to be alive that I might be imagining. I kept an eye on the woman as she walked toward me. Then I saw my mother push her hair out of the corner of her eye like I had seen her do a thousand times and I knew it was her.

"Ma . . . Ma," I shouted. I saw her smile and run toward me. I dropped my rake and ran to her and jumped into her arms. She held me and we hugged and kissed. "Mama, I was so worried . . . they said everyone was killed . . . How did you get out? How did you escape?"

She looked at me and I saw the anguish between her smile and tears of sorrow.

Before she could answer me Ignatz and Bobunia were standing with us. They hugged my mother and we all started talking at once. We walked hand in hand to the house and sat down at the kitchen table. My mother and Bobunia prepared a feast that night. It was a happy time for all of us.

Later, when my mother came to say good night to me, I asked her about Papa and Grandmother Rochel. She sighed. "It's late, honey."

"I know," I said. "But I'm not sleepy."

She sat down on the bed and began with the day that she had returned to work crew after leaving me with Ignatz and Bobunia.

ROSE'S ESCAPE

I hurried back to work crew. I felt elated about your new home. Your father had found Bobunia and Ignatz through former friends of his parents on the outside. They were sympathetic to our plight. I had once met Ignatz and Bobunia and I knew you would be happy living with them. It was a great relief for me. I had received many notes from the other Lithuanian telling me about your physical problems. I worried every night. Your father and Uncle Willie searched desperately for a new location. We were all concerned that the Lithuanian would abandon you if you were ill.

When I returned to the hospital that day I saw guards standing at some of the entrances. My heart leaped into my throat. I started shaking and wondered if they had discovered I was missing. I didn't know if they were waiting for me. Should I go back to the camp and claim that I got sick while I was working? My mind raced frantically. I didn't know what to do.

I saw a group of nurses getting ready to report to work, walking and chattering as they approached the hospital. I put on my jacket the hospital had supplied me for the day and fell into line with the group. I spoke Lithuanian with the girls as we walked down the sidewalk.

"You were almost late today," one of the girls said to me.

It took me a few minutes to catch on.

"I walked out on the Professor's lecture. You should have, too," the girl continued.

"Yes," I answered.

"He was so boring talking about hemoglobin and platelets, since we have been over this time and time again." She kept chatting in a light-hearted way as we neared the entrance of the hospital. This "saint" was my only hope. We stood together waiting as the others crowded through the door.

She leaned over and whispered in my ear. "I know that you are from the work crew from Kovno, but we all hate the Nazis. I saw you come into line and I know you need to get back. My name is Mary, I will help you get inside," she whispered to me.

We walked into the hospital without the guards noticing.

"Mary, you've saved my life, I don't know how to thank you," I said after we were away from the soldiers. "I had to take my young son to a place to hide."

"What has been done to the Jews in the camp is deplorable! We are all defenseless against Hitler. Lithuanians have been stupid for centuries and we were stupid to listen to the madman's promises. My brother convinced all of us to support the führer against the Soviets long ago. Today he is dead at the hand of a Nazi soldier," she said, shaking her head in disgust. "You can always find me here. I will help you in any way I can."

I couldn't believe her generous words. I was so relieved. When I went back to the crew, they told me that the guard had counted after I left. They told him that I was in the restroom and they didn't know if he had checked.

I was frightened all the way home. I thought I might be arrested at the gate, but no one said a word.

A week after you left, the Jewish Council announced another "action." The Gestapo again ordered all guns to be turned in after they confiscated from twenty-four Jews who tried to escape. At the end of thirty days there was only one gun turned in. This made them furious.

Early one morning we heard heavy trucks moving into the neighborhoods. They were taking everyone that didn't have work. Last fall your father and Uncle Willie had built a cubbyhole in our attic for us to hide, in case this happened. I ran to your grandmother and told her we had to hide. She wouldn't go, and began to cry.

I reached out and held her hand. I started to cry, too, when I thought about my grandmother. I wanted to stay with her, but your father made me go with him to the attic.

[Then her face turned hard and angry, but I didn't understand why.]

He did nothing to try to save her. I had to listen to the footsteps of the guard when he walked in the door. He took her, Schaja . . . he took her to Fort IX. (She paused and just looked into space for a while.) I know she wanted to end her life . . . but it was horrible.

[I didn't interrupt my mother's thoughts. It seemed she had gone over this scene in her mind, again and again and again. I kept listening.]

Rochel Schuster, Schaja's grandmother, was taken to Fort IX and brutally murdered that day. She was pushed into a dirt pit along with hundreds of other inmates that had been put in the trucks and transported to Fort IX. The killers aimed their machine guns and riddled the stacks of bodies with bullets.

I was angry and heartbroken after this. I was angry with your father. I tried to get over it but it just was impossible to forgive him. He didn't understand why I blamed him for her death. But it wasn't just her death; I blamed him for a many things.

[My mother was talking to me very candidly. Like I was a grown-up. She continued her story.]

Uncle Willie tried to convince me that I was wrong to be angry. He said he mourned our mother also, and it was no one's fault but the Germans. It was the Germans who made her last years miserable. I felt so helpless and alone. I know your father and I aged twenty years after Mother's death.

All I could think about was that I should have stayed with her. I should have protected her. I could have talked to the Germans. It was my fault she died.

Then one night I came home before your father. He was on a different work crew. I sat down in my chair next to the window and waited for him. I finally fell asleep and when I woke up I called for your father and there was no answer. I went into the bedroom to see if he was asleep. He wasn't there.

I sat up all night waiting for him. I got up and looked outside every hour. Finally, the sun rose and I joined my work crew. I managed to work through the day. I found Uncle Willie after work and told him that your father hadn't come home. He didn't know what had happened to him.

Three days later a lady at work crew approached me and told me that your father had gone to join the resistance fighters. But she heard that the group he escaped with had been caught and murdered. She also said it was only a rumor. I didn't know what to believe. I don't know where he is . . . if he is alive or if he is dead.

[I knew that my father must be dead. He would never leave my mother alone. But, I felt numb inside. This was just one more casualty of war. My mother went on with her story.]

Then one night, very late after I had gone to bed I heard the door open and the sound of heavy boots. I rushed into the other room. A Jewish policeman stood in front of me and I heard others outside the front door.

"Can I help you, Officer?" I asked.

"I am looking for Leon Shachnowski," he said.

"My husband is dead," I said. It was the only answer I could give him.

"There is no record of his death," he said.

"Then you know more than I do," she said. "I was told he was killed on his work crew, according to the workers that saw him die."

The officer looked at me. He didn't believe me.

"Can you tell me how long he's been dead?" he asked.

"Over two months now," I answered.

"It is my job to investigate all escape attempts whether they are successful or not. We have no evidence of the body of your husband being returned by a work crew," he said.

[I almost laughed when my mother imitated the policeman, but I also imagined her fear when he came into her house. She probably thought he was going to rape her like the Partisan.]

I stayed quiet. There was nothing I could do but let him draw his own conclusions.

He walked over and sat down in the chair next to the window and looked at me. It scared me when he did this.

"Why would he leave you here alone?" he asked.

"He would not leave me alone if he were alive . . ."

He got up and walked toward the door. "We will continue searching for him."

I knew after he said this that he would be back. I was awake the rest of the night trying to decide what I needed to do.

The next day when I sat on the ground with the rest of the work crew during our break I knew this was my chance. I stopped the guard. "May I go to the restroom, sir?"

The guard passed me but he didn't even look at me. "No!"

I just shrugged nonchalantly. "Yes, sir," I smiled. I was used to this kind of intimidation.

The guard walked back toward me later and motioned permission to go to the toilet. I gritted my teeth and smiled at him.

"Make it quick," he said.

I went into the tiny restroom. I stood and thought for a moment. I was so frightened I wasn't sure I could go through with my plan. My hands started to sweat. I looked up at the small window and thought about that policeman's visit last night. I took off my Star of David. It had left an imprint on my jacket. I wrapped the jacket and the Star of David into a tiny bundle and shoved it behind the toilet. I stepped up on the sides of the toilet. When I looked at the window I wasn't sure I could slide through, it was so small. I opened the window as wide as it would go and hoisted myself halfway through the window. I struggled and moved my hips at an angle to slide the rest of my body outside. After I hit the ground, I kept my eyes straight ahead and ran as fast as I could away from the work crew.

When I got to the street I slowed down and calmed myself. I tried to look as casual as possible, even though my heart was racing with fear. I looked around the street to get my bearings. I wasn't sure what I was going to do. I had to find a place to hide and think.

I decided my only choice was Mary, at the hospital. I didn't know who else to trust. I walked around for a while waiting until I knew her shift started. When I got to the hospital I went through the lobby with no questions asked. I climbed the stairs to the fourth floor and found Mary.

The minute she saw me, she knew I had escaped. She took my hand and led me to a supply room and told me to stay there until she could make some contacts. Several people came in to get supplies, but I hid in a corner behind a stack of towels.

The door opened slightly after a while and I heard Mary call my name. I got up and she handed me a piece of paper with directions written down and a name at the top. She told me that her network of friends would hide me. Sometimes only for a day or two at a time. It was still very dangerous to hide an escapee.

"I am so grateful, Mary. What can I ever do to repay you?" I asked her before I left.

"Survive." Mary said and turned to go back to hospital.

One word Schaja, *survive*. She let that word hang in the air. I stayed away for a month before I came here today.

"Is Uncle Willie alive?" I asked.

She shook her head. "I don't know."

She leaned down and kissed me good night. "It's almost three o'clock in the morning. Time to go to sleep. Just remember, survive. We will survive."

I was awake the rest of the night thinking about all that had happened after I left. I tossed and turned. Questions were racing through my mind about the past and the future.

In the next several days my mother and Bobunia talked for hours. They reminisced about the past and recalled friends of long ago. I watched them laugh and cry together about their lives. Some of their conversations were whispered secrets.

I spent most of the time outside with Ignatz. "Ignatz, I'm going to miss working in the garden. You've taught me a lot and I hope that I can be as good at gardening someday as you are," I said to him one afternoon.

He didn't answer me for a few minutes. When he turned to look at me I saw tears in his crinkled eyes. "I will miss you also, Jonas. You are like my own little boy," he said as his voice broke.

I walked up next to him and held his hand. There was nothing I could say. I could feel tears welling up in my own eyes. My mother and I embarked on our search for Mula. As I left Bobunia and Ignatz, I also left my name, Jonas, and became Schaja once again.

Twenty-four

As we walked we saw the destruction of war throughout the country-side. Houses on either side of the road were shells. Barns were standing empty of animals. There were German vehicles with swaztikas on the hood left on the roadside partially destroyed by mortar shells. There were deep gashes in the road where bombs had hit. Very few houses were still inhabited.

"Do you think Mula will remember us?" I asked my mother after a while. We had started our journey at midmorning but now the sun was warm and beaming down on us. We didn't have a watch but I looked up in the sky at the sun and determined it was about 3 P.M.

My mother looked down and smiled at me. "He'll know us . . . he will know us when he sees us," she said.

"But I've grown and I'm older," I said.

As dusk approached we found a barn that was empty and gathered some hay and made our beds. It wasn't as comfortable as the bed that I had slept in for the last few months, but I was so happy to be with my mother that I could have been sleeping on hard rocks.

It took us a few days to walk to the town where the sea captain and his wife lived. Mother asked people on the streets of the small village if they knew the captain. It took us most of the day to find the directions to the home. It was dark when we finally arrived at their doorstep. My mother knocked on the door and the captain recognized her immediately.

I had never seen these people before. They were very formal. After a few moments they invited us to come in. Mula recognized my mother and me when he saw us. He ran to my mother's open arms. When he saw me he started laughing and playing. My mother was right, he remembered us. He had grown several inches and was talking.

The three of us slept in the captain's barn that night together since there was not enough room in their small house.

The next morning we left to return to Kaunas. We took our time. We stopped and played in the countryside and swam in the streams. Mula and I climbed trees and played hide-and-seek. My mother was relaxed and we all were happy to be together. It felt like a vacation.

As we were crossing a field toward the next road on our fourth day, I saw a horse. I ran to see him. Mula and my mother followed me. I petted the horse on the nose. He seemed to like it. I stroked his mane and patted the side of his neck.

"I wonder if he belongs to anyone?" I asked.

"I'm sure, he does," she said and looked around the fields.

"I'm hungry, Mama," Mula said.

"We need some food," Mother said. "It's been a day since we've eaten." She looked across the field again and saw some people near a farmhouse in the distance. "I'll go over and ask them for some scraps."

"Ask them if I can have a carrot or an apple for the horse," I yelled after her. I could see her shaking her head and laughing. I continued to pet the horse down his back. I started to grab his mane and wondered if he would let me ride him. I felt he trusted me, but, I just walked beside him. I saw my mother walking across the field.

"They had nothing to give me," she said, looking at the horse. "I see you've made friends."

"He's a nice horse, really tame."

My mother looked over to the ground where we had been standing before. "Where's Mula?"

"I don't know, he was right over there when I started petting the horse," I said.

"Mula, Mula," she cried. He was nowhere to be seen. "You were supposed to watch him, Schaja! He's still a baby!"

I ran toward a wooded area about twenty yards from us. I was shouting his name and looking behind each tree and under the brush. I heard him say my name, and I looked behind a tall shrub and saw him. I brushed the leaves from his hand and mouth and brought him to my mother.

"Where did you find him?" she asked and I saw that look of stress on her face.

"In the woods, he was eating some green leaves," I said.

"You have to watch him, Schaja. You're his older brother and the only one I can turn to for help!" she scolded.

I realized at that moment that I was the only one she could turn to with my Pa and Uncle Willie gone. I had to be responsible. I felt very bad about my negligence.

"From now on, Mama, I'll go ask for food," I said. I knew I could get someone to give us food.

I stopped at every farmhouse along the way where we saw people. I gave them very sorrowful looks and begged for food. They could see that I was very skinny. Each time I returned to Mula and my mother I had food in my hand. Some gave me fresh vegetables that they had grown themselves. Some gave me a small portion of bread or a sliver of fat. I stopped at one farmhouse where I was given a full roasted chicken. I offered to work in their garden and plant seeds for vegetables.

Five days later, we arrived home to our neighborhood. I was so happy when we turned the corner and walked down our old street. I was looking forward to watching the Lithuanians vacate our house. I would stand on the corner and watch. They would know we had survived.

PART II

The Road to Freedom

1945–1955

TWENTY-FIVE

Two soldiers came out of the front door of our house carrying guns. There were Russian army vehicles parked along the street and soldiers in almost every yard on our block.

My mother looked down at me with concern on her face. She told Mula and me to wait on the corner. She walked up the sidewalk toward our house and stopped the officers we had seen coming out the door.

One of the officers was round and short, with no hair on top of his head; only a five o'clock shadow of beard on his face. He carried his helmet by his side. I laughed when I saw his boots make his pant legs balloon over the edge.

The other officer was medium size, lean and muscular with a chiseled handsome face and a quick smile. Both looked as though they had not shaved in a couple of days. My mother smelled the vodka and cigarettes from the night before. Both men were laughing as she approached them.

"Good afternoon, Officers," she said, speaking to them in Russian. I wasn't far away and could hear their conversation.

"May we help you?" the short, round officer asked courteously, still smiling.

Mother paused for a moment, not quite certain how to tell them that this was our house. "Do you live here?" she asked.

"This neighborhood"—he waved his hand toward the other houses— "we are using for barracks. Six of us live here now. Do you know this house?" the other officer asked.

"Yes," she smiled and paused. "This was my . . . our home . . . my husband and children, we lived here before the Nazis moved us to Kovno Camp."

"You escaped?" the handsome, muscular officer asked. He looked at her as though he had seen a ghost. "You escaped from that camp?"

"Not long before they burned it," she answered.

The officer looked across to the corner where we were standing. "And are those your children?" he asked.

"Yes, my two sons, Mula and Schaja."

"I am Captain Uri Malvich," he said and then turned to the other soldier. "And this is Lieutenant Kaluzny."

A Lithuanian policeman came barreling down the sidewalk after he saw the soldiers being bothered by a local. But he realized it was my mother and stopped abruptly. He looked closely to make sure. He glanced across the street and saw Mula and me. By the time he reached the soldiers, he had recalled the afternoon that Willie, my mother, father, grandmother, Mula, and I had been boarded on a wagon to Kovno.

"This was your home? We removed a family that said it was their home," Captain Malvich said. He turned and saw the policeman running up the sidewalk toward him.

"This is Mrs. Shachnowski," the policeman said breathlessly, as he approached the group.

Mother turned and smiled at the officer. "Officer Mikitis, so nice to see you."

Mikitis almost embraced her, but hesitated. My mother put her hand out to him. He warmly grabbed her hand and held it. "I know Mrs. Schacknowski and her brother. This is her home."

"Yes, Officer Mikitis was here when they took . . . he's been a friend for a long time—" She stopped short. She was afraid if the Russians knew that he was there when the Nazis took us away it might cause trouble for him. The Russians were known to kill many Lithuanian Partisans that had assisted the Germans. She knew that Mikitis was just doing what the Nazis told him. Uncle Willie had always spoken well of the officer.

"You survived! And Willie Schuster?" he asked.

Mother shrugged and fought the emotion in her voice. "I am not sure . . ." Her voice trailed off.

Malvich spoke up quickly. "Lieutenant, get our commander . . ." He turned to the other soldier.

"All I need is a small room for the three of us," she said. "And perhaps if you could give us some of your food ration. We could clean the house in exchange."

He turned and smiled at her. "I am sure that we can make arrangements."

"Thank you . . . thank you so much," my mother said.

The captain's eyes and voice softened. "The Germans are animals. My own brother was captured and killed by the Nazis."

Officer Malvich walked with mother over to where Mula and I were standing.

Mother introduced us to the captain. "Everything is fine, the soldiers have agreed to give us a room."

Officer Uri Malvich took Mula's hand and helped him across the street as my mother and I followed.

————

When I walked into our house, it looked very different. There was none of the familiar furniture. The draperies had been taken from the windows. The dark wooden floors were scratched and dirty. The only remaining item from our former home was my grandmother's piano. Lying on top of the piano were guns and ammunition. Rifles and more ammunition littered the floor. There were four or five tables with red tablecloths and four chairs at each table in the middle of the living room. There was a candle and several ashtrays on top of the tables. A sofa was lined up against the wall.

My mother went into the kitchen area and spoke to a man that was the commander of the troops on our street. He agreed to let us live in our house. Mula and I followed her to the back of the house to a room that we had formerly used for storage. It was a square room with a private entry into the bathroom. The room was furnished with three cots. Each had a small pillow and a dark green blanket folded up neatly at the bottom. There was a soldier putting one of the red cloth table covers from the living room as a partition between where my brother and I would sleep and where my mother would sleep.

Soldiers walked in and out of the room as they removed their belongings. They finished very quickly and the three of us were alone.

The three of us sat on our cots and looked at each other. I started to smile. I never thought that I would ever see my grandmother's house again. I knew that she would be happy that we had returned to her home.

I looked over at my mother and she looked around the room and began to smile. Then Mula started to laugh. An electrical current of joy ignited in the room. We all began to laugh and jump and dance in a circle. It had been a long time since we had been this happy. We tried to stay quiet, but we knew the soldiers could probably hear us. After a few minutes there was a knock at the door.

"Is everything all right?" a deep voice asked.

It was Captain Malvich.

"Yes," my mother kept smiling and opened the door. "Please come in."

He stepped into the room.

"We didn't mean to make so much noise, but we never thought while we were in the camp that we would ever be here again. Even living from one day to the next, we were never sure," mother explained, laughing and crying at the same time.

He smiled with us and watched as we danced. After a few moments, Mula and I sat down on our cots. Captain Malvich and my mother sat next to each other.

"We came to this neighborhood after we took over Kaunas," Captain Malvich said. "Lithuanians were living in your house."

"What happened to our furniture?" my mother asked.

"Only the piano was here after the Lithuanians left. They took all of the furniture," he explained.

My mother shrugged as she looked up at the captain. "The piano was my mother's," she said. "She was killed."

"I'm so sorry," Captain Malvich said.

My mother nodded. "But in a way I feel close to her here. I haven't laughed like this in a long time. It feels good to be home."

Mula was still jumping and playing with me. The captain smiled as he watched us.

He cleared his throat and looked a little nervous. "In the evening we usually gather in the living room . . . we sing and we talk," the captain said, looking at my mother. "Please join us tonight." He then pulled out some rations from his pocket and gave them to my mother. He handed candies to Mula and me.

Later that night, I sneaked down the hallway and stood under the recess of the stairway to watch the party later that night. Our living room was like a cabaret. The lights were dimmed and a heavy smell of cigarette smoke filled the air. Several women I had never seen before were standing, smoking cigarettes and holding a glass of vodka. They were laughing with a few of the soldiers. I saw my mother in the shadows at the back of the living room sitting on a sofa next to Captain Malvich.

I went back to my room to check on Mula and he was still fast asleep. I returned to my spot under the stairway and watched more people drift into our house. There were a couple of soldiers sitting in a circle in the middle of the room. One was playing a balalaika (a three-stringed instrument, similar to a guitar, but with a triangular body) and the other two were singing rowdily. They filled their glasses with more vodka and then sung even louder. They started laughing and making jokes. Then they would drink another shot of vodka. Pretty soon, they reeled and slurred their words.

I started to laugh when one soldier fell over the sofa. Everybody started laughing when the soldier got up angrily.

"I'll kill the son of bitch who pushed me." He looked around the room glaring from one person to the next. He swung his arm in midair, turned in a circle, and fell down on top of the sofa where he passed out.

One of the other soldiers who played the balalaika walked over to the sofa and played a lullaby. Everyone burst out laughing and joined in on the song. The passed-out soldier didn't move.

After that, things got quiet and I went to my bed. I didn't hear my mother when she came in that night.

————

As the weeks passed the soldiers taught me about the guns they carried. They let me take a gun apart and showed me how to put it back together. They told me stories about the battles they had fought against the Nazis. They all hated the Nazis and the Germans, and claimed they were usually unwilling to take prisoners. They wanted total destruction to come to all of Germany.

They asked me to run errands for them and shine their boots and organize the boxes of ammunition. I spent each morning arranging the ammunition closet. In return, they gave me a few coins. They called me Lucky.

One evening, late, after my mother had gone to bed, I was still lurking in the shadows under the stairway watching the party. One of the soldiers spotted me. He had been drinking vodka all evening and was feeling happy.

"Lucky . . ." he tottered slightly as he came up to me. His words were slurred. "I have a little something for you."

I thought maybe he would give me a coin or something to eat from his rations. Instead he handed me a pouch of *Machorka*, a potent Russian tobacco. I took it from him. "Thanks, Gaspadin Polkovnik."

He wandered off to the bathroom.

I never smoked a cigarette. I had watched the soldiers as they rolled their tobacco in a newspaper, glued it together by moistening the paper with their tongue, and lit up. I opened the pouch and took a whiff of the tobacco. It had a strong but sweet smell and reminded me of my father's tobacco he used in his pipe.

The soldier came back down the hall and I stopped him. "How do you roll these?"

"Come with me, I will teach . . ." he said. He staggered over to a table and took a small square of the newspaper out of his pocket and spread it flat. He reached for the pouch from my hand and sprinkled a healthy portion of tobacco on the small square and wet the paper with his tongue and pressed it on the rolled side. He then handed me the completed cigarette. "See . . . very easy . . ."

I put the cigarette in my mouth and he held a lighted match to the tip. I sucked on the cigarette, just as I had seen the soldiers do. But I had no idea that my mouth and lungs would suddenly be filled with such acrid, strong smoke. A taste that was repulsive. I started coughing. I couldn't get the smoke out of my lungs or the taste out of my mouth. I gasped for air, but the burning sensation stayed in my throat. The soldier that had given me the cigarette patted me on the back as I doubled over and coughed.

The others in the room started laughing.

I felt dizzy and my eyes watered. One of the ladies in the room handed me a glass of water. I was finally able to wash the terrible taste of smoke out of my mouth and throat. It would be the first and last time that I tried cigarettes.

———

After the soldiers had left for their duties early one morning, there was a knock at our door. I looked through the glass of the door and I saw Uncle Willie. I jumped up to open the door. "Uncle Willie," I yelled and hugged him. "You're alive! Where have you been?"

My mother came running into the room. "Willie," my mother hugged and kissed him on the cheek. "I was so frightened. I thought they had killed you!"

"No, Rose. I told you not to worry about me," he said, grinning. "I joined with the Resistance and I am now a fighter!" He leaned over and showed us his insignia.

When he bent toward me, his jacket fell open. I saw his knife. It was the same one that he had when we entered Kovno Camp.

We all sat down in the dining room. Willie looked around the room. "I heard the houses in the neighborhood were now Russian barracks. I didn't know if I would find you here."

"The soldiers have given us a room," Mother answered.

Mula came into the room rubbing his eyes. He looked at Willie. Mula had no memory of him.

"Mula, this is your Uncle Willie," Mother said.

Mula looked at him. Willie went over and spoke to him. Mula hugged Willie and I could see tears form in my uncle's eyes. He shook his head. "I never thought I would see this moment. So much has been lost, Rose," Willie said sadly.

"Mama's piano is here," my mother said softly.

Willie and mother walked over and sat down on the piano bench. Willie looked sad for a few moments. Later, he told us stories about his Resistance group.

"I watched a German soldier die," I said.

Both Willie and my mother looked at me. "When?" Mother asked.

"Ignatz and I went to the barracks after the Russians bombed them," I said quietly.

"Why would Ignatz take you there?" Mother asked.

"Bobunia didn't want him to. But it made me feel like there was some justice in the world."

"Well, they are gone now," Willie said. "Your father . . ."

"What about my father?" I asked.

"I was going to say that I'm sure . . . well, if your father made it out of the Kovno Camp that he joined a resistance group," Willie said. He looked at my mother and she wouldn't meet his gaze. My mother seemed upset.

TWENTY-SIX

I opened the door to the closet where the ammunition was stored and took some bullets out of a box. I shoved them into my pocket before anyone could see me and went outside to meet my friend Linas. He lived a couple of blocks away and we met on the corner. As we walked down the street, we passed by a few soldiers. Some of them called me by my nickname, Lucky. Linas was always impressed when they called me by that name. He looked up to the Russian soldiers and someday wanted to join their army. I let him help me shine the soldiers' boots whenever I had more than I could finish. I paid him half my tips when he helped.

We turned into an empty alleyway and I pulled the bullets out of my pocket. I removed the casing from each one of them and sprinkled the gunpowder in a line about six inches long.

Linas pulled out the matches and handed them to me. I struck the match and placed it against the gunpowder. I watched the line of fire, smoke, and flare. I always put an extra amount of gunpowder at the end of the line of fire when it faced the sidewalk. It flared suddenly in a big flame as a man and woman passed by. Linas and I started laughing when the lady jumped.

There was a haze of smoke where they were standing. When it cleared, her husband started down the alley after us. We ran and hid behind a nearby building before he could catch us. When the coast was clear, we came back out to the alley and Linas handed me some heavy paper. We tore it in strips about two inches wide. And just like I had learned to roll the cigarette, I rolled the gunpowder into the paper in the same way. I twirled the end and made a fuse at the end with the paper. We made about six of these firecrackers. I lit them, one by one, and threw them into the street. They started popping, one after the other. It was a loud sound that echoed down the alley.

"You boys get out of here or I'll come down . . . you're nothing but hoodlums. We've had too many explosions in Kaunas. Enough to last a lifetime! Some of us are trying to rest!" a man yelled out the window above us. He slammed the window down so hard I thought the glass would break.

Linas and I ran out of the alley. We didn't want any trouble. Linus went home, so I decided to walk down to the bakery on the main street of Kaunas. The bakery was one of the first businesses to reopen since the war ended. I went to the bakery at least twice a week and spent the extra money I earned from the soldiers on a pastry.

I could smell the aroma of fresh-baked bread when I got near the bakery. It made my mouth water. I could already see the pat of butter melting on the fresh, hot steaming bread that Mrs. Javitz would hand me.

"Can I help you, young man?" Mrs. Javitz asked as I came in the door.

"Yes, ma'am," I answered.

I saw a baker bring out a fresh loaf of bread from the oven. "I'd like to have a piece of that warm bread."

She smiled at me. "You always know when it's fresh! We need a couple of minutes before we cut the loaf."

"Sure," I said and smiled back. I looked on the shelves at the pastries. I could have eaten all of them. I watched Mrs. Javitz slice the fresh loaf. She smiled as she handed me the warm slice with butter on top.

"Thank you," I said to her. The bread was warm in my hands. I tossed it from side to side until it cooled. Then I took a big bite. It was just the way I liked it.

I went out the door and started to head home. It didn't take me long to eat the bread. I wiped my face and hands with my sleeve and looked across the street. I blinked twice when I saw a man that looked like my father. I watched him walk down the street for a moment. He even walked like my father. I shook my head and rubbed my eyes again. It looked so much like my father. I ran and got in front of him. We met face to face. When we made eye contact I knew it was my father and he knew I was his son. We ran to each other and hugged and kissed. We both were shocked to see each other. "Pa," I said. "We thought you were dead!"

He smiled and hugged me. "I'm here, Schaja," he pinched himself. "Alive!"

"We've been back at Grandmother's house for six months. Why didn't you come home?" I asked.

He looked at me. "I had no idea, Schaja," he said, evasively. "Come around the corner with me to my apartment. I'll show you where I live."

He looked down at me. "You've grown. You're getting tall, Schaja."

"I've grown out of all my clothes," I said and pointed at my trousers that were too short for me. "Ma will be so happy when she sees you!"

He looked straight ahead and didn't say anything.

"I joined the Resistance after your mother escaped," he said after we sat down in the living room of his small apartment.

"I thought you left before she did," I said.

He looked at me and just shook his head. "There were several of us who escaped. We hid out in the forest for a while and then joined with some

Lithuanian and Russian Partisans who were fighting the Germans. When I first arrived, some of the men didn't want to let me join. They had known my parents and thought I was a capitalist. They knew we owned property and felt that I did not believe in the doctrine of the Soviets."

I had a hard time seeing my father as a fighting soldier. I was amazed as he told his story.

"They accepted me on a trial basis. I went with them on their next mission and I convinced them that I could fight against the Germans. After being in Kovno Camp I would have killed any German."

"Did you kill a Nazi, Pa?"

"Many," he said.

"Uncle Willie was a fighter for the Resistance," I said.

My father nodded as though he knew. He walked over and looked out the window. "It'll be dark soon. Your mother will worry about you."

The front door opened behind me and I turned around. It was a lady, a young lady. She was very attractive. She looked at me as though she knew me. "Hello, Schaja." She smiled and walked over near my father.

"I recognized you from your father's description," she said and smiled again.

My father cleared his throat. "Schaja, this is Eve. She lives here with me."

I was sure that I looked puzzled. I didn't understand why she was living here with my father.

"It's nice to meet you," I said politely.

My father then told her how we had found each other.

"Schaja, I have heard all about you and your brother," she said.

I didn't say anything. All I could do was smile. I wondered, after she said that, if she had heard of my mother.

My father walked me home that night. I pleaded with him to come inside and let Ma know he was alive. He avoided answering me. When we got near our house, I turned to him. "Pa, please come inside. Ma will be so happy. We've all missed you. I've thought about you so much and every time I start to talk to Ma about you I see the pain on her face."

He said maybe it would be better for him to wait and make plans with my mother for a later date.

I thought this was all very strange. I assumed that they would be overjoyed to see each other. We walked the rest of the block in silence as I thought things over. When we got in front of the house, I looked through the window. I saw silhouettes of the soldiers. My mother was sitting in Captain Malvich's lap. It dawned on me that I had put my father and my mother in a very difficult position. Then I put two and two together and realized that my parents knew all along where the other one was living. "You knew, didn't you?" I asked.

"There are many things that you don't understand yet . . ." Pa said hesitantly.

"Why didn't somebody tell me?" I asked. I couldn't believe that my parents would deceive me.

"I left it up to your mother, Schaja."

"Well, you're both my parents and somebody should have told me," I said. I was angry, hurt, and embarrassed.

He tried to make me feel better as we both stood watching my mother and the captain. My mother had been discreet in her relationship with the captain until I saw them at that very moment.

"Schaja, the war caused many problems in many ways. Now don't worry. I'll contact your mother."

I said good night to my father and made plans to come see him the next day. When I got to the doorway of the living room, I stared at my mother. After a while, still sitting on the captain's lap, she noticed me.

I motioned for her to come over to where I was standing. When she walked up to me, I could hardly control my feelings. I looked at her accusingly. "I went to the bakery this afternoon and you'll never guess what happened, Ma."

"What is it, Schaja?" she said laughing at me.

"I saw my father. He is alive," I looked at her reaction.

She gasped and put her hand over her mouth, trying to act surprised, but I knew better. I turned and walked away from her.

"I hope that you and my father will try to talk to each other. I know now that you lied to me about him being killed," I said, looking over my shoulder at her.

"Schaja, there are many things that you don't understand. Someday I will explain," she said.

"He has a lady living with him," I said and stared at her.

Again she looked surprised, but this time it was real.

I went to bed that night unable to sleep. All I could think of was how I had botched up my parents' relationship when I brought my father to our house. I knew that many things had happened after I left Kovno Camp. Now I wished I had stayed. The war did more damage than bullets or body counts would ever show.

TWENTY-SEVEN

When my mother walked in the door that night, I couldn't believe my eyes. I hardly recognized her. She had dyed her hair blonde. She had on a new dress and she had painted her fingernails bright red. All of the soldiers started whistling and clapping. She laughed and walked around the room, acting like a model. She was happy and I was glad. I thought it must be because she had seen my father that she was this happy, but I was wrong.

Later that night, for the first time, the captain slept in the room with my mother.

I opened the door and went into the bedroom one afternoon. It had been weeks and my parents had made no contact with each other. I went by my father's apartment often and encouraged him to talk to my mother. He told me that she was angry with him. When I tried to approach my mother, she would just get angry with me. She said she was happy with her Russian boyfriend. I didn't like him.

One afternoon my mother and Mula had gone downtown and I stayed home. I walked into my room and started whittling a stick with a pocketknife that one of the soldiers had given me.

I saw Uri's boots on my side of the curtain, just at the edge. This made me mad and I threw them under the curtain to his side of the room that he shared with my mother now. I heard a thud and then a voice.

"Good shot, Schaja," Uri said groggily.

I was silent for a moment. I hoped I had hit him in the head. "I'm sorry, I didn't think anyone was in here," I said, lying to him.

I kept whittling but I felt his stare. When I looked up, Uri was standing in his dirty white undershirt and dark tan slacks. His beard was unshaven.

"I heard the Machorka was a little strong for you," he chuckled.

"It was okay," I shrugged and kept honing the wood with my knife.

He looked at me as I continued to whittle. I could feel his eyes on me.

"You don't like me, Schaja," he said.

I shrugged.

"I know you wish your father were here. I'm sure if he were still alive that he would want to be here." He sucked on the cigarette and thought for a moment.

I couldn't believe he thought my father was dead. "You're wrong."

"What do you mean?" he asked.

"My father is alive. He lives here in Kaunas. If it weren't for you, he would be living with us." I stared at him.

He looked surprised. "I didn't know."

I heard Mula's voice coming down the hall. "Ask my mother," I said, egging him on.

My mother and Mula came into the room.

"Tell him, Ma. Tell him that my father is alive and lives here in Kaunas," I shouted. All the anger that had been pent up inside of me came out in a torrid of words. "He said my father was dead and he's a liar. Both of you are liars if you told him that! All I want is you and Pa to be together. He's not my father," I said pointing at the captain.

I went outside and started to walk toward my father's apartment. But before I got there, I turned around. I regretted my angry words. I knew my mother was struggling to survive. She had done her best to provide for my brother and me. Her boyfriend kept us from starving. Captain Malvich had tried to be nice to me. He always gave me coin change from his pocket. When he saw me go through the wallets of soldiers when they passed out in the living room, he never told my mother. He just smiled and winked at me.

I stayed out until after dark that evening. When I came home no one said anything about the incident. Later I apologized to my mother and to Uri.

It was months later when Uri received his orders to move to the front line. The Germans were facing defeat in Berlin and the Russian army needed soldiers. My mother and he said good-bye. I had renewed hope that she and my father would get back together.

I didn't know it at the time but the front where Uri was going would be the final defeat for Hitler. Over 2.5 million Russian soldiers descended on Berlin along with 8,000 aircraft. At the end of the battle 102,000 Russian soldiers were killed. We never knew if Captain Malvich survived.

A few days after Uri left, I went over to my father's apartment determined to persuade him to come home with me. When I knocked on the door Uncle Willie answered. I was surprised to see him. The three of us sat down at the table with my father.

"I'm telling you, Leon," Willie looked seriously at my father. "We cannot make the same mistake twice. We cannot wait until the Communists seal the borders. We must go now."

"But where? It's always the same question," my father looked dejected. "Where can we be safe? Israel, Mexico, Venenzula, America?"

"Once the war is over, the Americans will occupy Germany . . . you can speak German . . . the country is familiar," Willie suggested.

"Why can't we stay here?" I asked. "Why will Communists seal the border?"

"It's politics, Schaja," Papa answered. "We thought we found freedom when we left the camp, but only a small degree of freedom."

"We must find a place that will protect the Jews," Uncle Willie reiterated.

"Where will Rose go?" Papa asked.

"She wants to go to America. Our brothers Max and David are there. Your Uncle Max is in a place called Masktuzet," Uncle Willie said, unsure of the pronunciation of Massachusetts.

"What can I do in America? I can't speak English. My degree may be worthless," Papa said to Willie.

"Max has done very well there. He owns a petrol company. He fills gas tanks for American cars," Willie said.

My ears perked up. Automobiles. All I saw now were beat-up Russian vehicles and horse-drawn wagons on the streets of Kaunas, but I had heard about the shiny, new American cars.

"You have responsibilities, Leon. You must try to smooth out your problems with Rose," Willie said.

"Captain Malvich left, Papa. That is why I am here today. I want you to come home and be with us."

"It's not that simple, Schaja," my father shook his head sadly. He lit his pipe and thought for a moment. "I think, Willie, that Rose, Schaja, and Mula should go first. I have to resolve some issues."

"If you are thinking of getting your father's property, your head is in the clouds, Leon. The Communists will never allow ownership of anything! They are only the lesser of two evils, Leon. You have proof of ownership but you will not have possession as long as the Communists are in power," Willie said.

My father sighed heavily. "There are many reasons, Willie."

Willie looked at him and shook his head. "We had these same arguments before the Germans came," Willie said.

My father looked at him. "How could we have known what was before us? Besides, things are very different now."

"Nothing is different. We can't take any more chances. I have contacted a Zionist group that will help us escape."

"I will stay and Rose and the boys will go," Pa said and shook his head. He looked very depressed.

"Leon, you will never learn . . ." Willie said, annoyed.

My father went to the shelf and pulled out a bottle of schnapps.

He poured a glass for himself and one for Willie. Then he took another small glass and poured a few drops into it. He handed it to me.

They raised a glass in a toast. I followed what they did.

"*L'chaim.*"

My father and Uncle Willie tossed the liquor into the back of their throats. I tasted the schnapps with my tongue. It burned as it went down my throat.

"Uncle Willie, when will we go to America?" I asked.

"Soon, Schaja," he answered.

Willie and my father exchanged war stories for the rest of the afternoon. They had not been in the same resistance group, but their battles with the Germans were filled with drama and exaggeration. Maybe not on Willie's part, but I doubted my father's stories of danger and risk. I remembered him standing in front of the Nazi officer, shaking and trembling. If it had not been for my mother we would have been sent to Fort IX.

Twenty-eight

I was standing outside one morning when a farmer drove past our house in a carriage drawn by the most beautiful horse I had ever seen. He was elegant and spirited and he captured my attention as he passed by. He was a tall horse, maybe seventeen hands. He was shiny black and I saw his magnificent power as he pranced down the street with such assurance and purpose. I had never seen a horse like this. The taxi wagons usually had swaybacked horses that kept their heads down as they trudged along. They only moved quickly when the driver cracked his whip.

He unhitched his horse in our backyard. Many people would leave their horses near our barn or in the backyard when they came to town. "That's some horse," I said to Linas and Mula, who were standing in the street with me.

"Yeah, wouldn't you like to ride him around town," Mula said, nonchalantly.

I looked at both of them. "Let's go for a ride."

"No," Linas said. "It's not your horse . . . or carriage."

"The owner's gone downtown and he won't be back for a while. He'll never know. We'll be back before he returns. Don't worry."

I ran and hitched the horse onto the carriage. I stroked his mane and patted his muscles that were strong and taut. "Get in," I said. I mounted the seat. Mula and Linas climbed onto the carriage. The horse smoothly made his way into the street.

We traveled all over Kaunas. We were all laughing and having a great time until we turned the corner to go back home. I swallowed hard when I saw my mother as she caught a glimpse of us coming down the street. I smiled and waved, hoping to make things better, but it just made things worse. I could see that she was steaming mad.

We pulled up the horse and carriage and I saw the owner coming toward us. His face was beet red. "Who told you that you could take my horse and buggy out for a ride? You had no business taking my property!"

"I wasn't going to steal your horse and carriage," I said innocently.

"You are nothing but a common thief, young man!" he sputtered as he spoke.

My mother was at my side before my feet touched the ground. She grabbed me by the arm. "Schaja, you have done some terrible things but this is criminal. Why would you do a thing like this?! This man was getting ready to call the officials. You could go to jail!" She started swatting my backside with a stick. "I want you to go inside right this moment!" She then turned to Linas and Mula. "You go home," she said, pointing at Linas. "And Mula, go inside!"

I could hear my mother apologizing profusely as I walked toward my house with Mula running after me. I turned and looked back at the horse. I hoped that one day I would have a horse like him.

My mother came into the house later and started screaming at me. I couldn't even understand her words she talked so fast. She had a thin stick in her hand and started hitting me. After she was finished she ordered me to go to the attic and spend the next two days thinking about my bad behavior with no food, no water, nothing!

After I had spent a couple of hours in the attic I heard Mula sneak up the stairs. He was carrying some food he had saved from his dinner plate.

"Did you get into trouble?" I asked him.

He nodded his head. "But not like you're in trouble."

He continued during my punishment period to sneak food up to me. I spent my two-day imprisonment watching the street from the attic window trying to catch a glimpse of that horse again. I swore I would take him for another ride if I had the chance. I was only sorry that I had gotten caught.

My mother and father had two different ideas of discipline and punishment.

I heard someone plodding up the stairs to the attic. The footsteps were too heavy to be Mula.

"Schaja?" a voice called out.

It was my father.

"Papa, I'm up here!" I said and ran to meet him.

"I hear you got yourself into trouble. Your mother told me that you took a pony and buggy," he said looking concerned.

"Yeah," I nodded solemnly.

"What kind of pony was it?" he asked.

"Papa, it was not a pony. It was the most beautiful solid black horse I have ever seen. He was so elegant and confident the way he pranced."

"You love horses don't you?" he asked, smiling.

"Yes, I do," I answered.

"You know it was wrong to take the horse?" He looked at me.

I shrugged. "I wasn't trying to steal the horse. I just wanted to take him for a ride. It didn't seem like it would harm anyone. I'm very careful with horses."

"Well, the man didn't know what had happened to his horse. Would you have been worried if your animal was gone when you returned?" he said, looking at me to answer.

"Well, I guess so . . ." I reluctantly agreed.

"It's hard to be angry, Schaja. I know you weren't going to steal the horse. But, it's important to respect others and their possessions. Someday you'll have your own pony! But in the meantime no more borrowing someone else's pony," he said and patted me on the shoulder.

Rose was standing at the bottom of the stairs listening to Leon and Schaja. She shook her head. She had asked Leon to come see Schaja. He needed some direction. But she should have known that Leon wouldn't be hard on him. Leon was always a man of words . . . and promises, and he was also a man of hope. A man of hope; this was what she missed the most about him.

She could already feel her heart softening. She wanted him in her life again; it would take time before the wounds would heal, but she loved him and knew they would be together always.

Twenty-nine

My parents had been communicating ever since I had taken the horse. It was a gradual process. My father came to dinner several times a week now. After dinner one night, my father pulled me aside and we went into the living room. "Schaja, you and Mula and your mother will be leaving Lithuania pretty soon."

"When will we leave, Pa?" I asked. I knew the Zionist group had contacted Willie last week.

"We won't know the exact day until a few hours before you leave," he said. "We still must be very careful."

"Where are we going?" I asked.

"Germany," he said. "U.S.-occupied Germany, and then we'll apply for a visa to go to the United States. But the Zionist group thinks your destination is Israel."

I didn't understand why we had to tell them this but I accepted it without question. "Pa, are you going with us?" I asked. I was excited about going to America.

"I will join you in Germany, Schaja. I still have a few things to take care of here in Kaunas," he said, as he shook his head.

I was disappointed. I thought we would be a family again.

He looked at my downcast expression and continued. "This is why it is important for you to help your mother. You'll be responsible for her, making sure you're little brother doesn't get lost."

I nodded with each of his comments.

"It will be a long trip," he said.

"How long will it take us?" I asked.

"I'm sure it will take several months. No one can know that you are traveling from one country to the next. There will be people that will help you."

"When will you come to Germany?" I asked.

"I will come later. I'm not sure of the date," he said. "I have things I need to take care of before I leave Lithuania."

I wondered if he still had his girlfriend.

In the summer of 1945 we would begin our two-thousand-mile journey to Germany. The Nazis had been defeated and Hitler had committed suicide. At least, that's what we were told. Uncle Willie wanted to make sure that we didn't stay in Lithuania until it was too late. I wondered why the Russians wouldn't let us live the way we had before the war. I remembered Ignatz had once called the comparison between the two countries "the lesser of two evils." Was Ignatz right?

Germany was chosen as our destination because it was now occupied by U.S. troops. We felt that it was the safest place for us. Others in the group were going to Israel, and in fact this was the destination that the Zionist planned for the whole group. We had not informed them that we would be staying in Germany. But I was glad that Germany was not going to be our final destination. We hoped that our relatives would help us get to the United States. Our dream was that one day we would become Americans.

It was midnight when Uncle Willie knocked at our door several weeks later. We were standing in the hallway ready with our makeshift backpacks. We had devised a strap made of heavy twine and heavy material that my mother had sewn to carry our belongings. We all dressed warmly in layers of clothing for our nighttime excursions. But we left enough room to pack the extra clothing when the day became warmer.

Willie took us to our meeting point. I was surprised that my father did not come with him. "Where's Pa?"

"It's safer this way, Schaja" Willie answered.

I didn't understand why, but I took his word for it.

We had to be very quiet and walk quickly. Mula was now seven years old and didn't quite understand why he had to walk so far in the middle of the night.

When we arrived at our meeting point, we joined nine other people standing in the area. Most of them were adults.

Our guide stood up in front of the group and began to explain what our journey would entail. He introduced himself only as Isaac. He did not ask our names. All identities remained vague because the consequences would be grave if we were caught.

He explained that the government did not sanction our travel, and he wanted to pass the Lithuanian border as soon as possible. At this point in Lithuania the borders were very loosely controlled due to the lack of governmental structure. But still, he warned us, it was always more dangerous for Jews.

He said that many Jews were fleeing eastern Europe. We would be traveling and crossing borders, legally, semilegally, or illegally. The means would not matter, but somehow the borders would be crossed. We must follow instructions from our guides, work as a team, and be strong. This would be a demanding trip . . . by foot, train, and other types of transportation . . . sometimes at night . . . other times during the day. Our ultimate destination would be Israel.

We followed the others and walked several miles until we were outside of Kaunas. We then boarded horse-drawn carriages that took us close to the border. We crossed the border of Lithuania into Poland by foot.

Several days later when the sun rose, I looked around at the beautiful hills and lush green fields and flowers. I had never been outside of Lithuania and I felt very glad to be leaving. I had escaped from hell. I hoped that I would never have to go back to Lithuania.

At our first stop, we stayed with a Polish family who had two children about the same age as Mula and me. It rained the first day we were there and we stayed inside all day. The kids shared their toys with Mula and me. I looked at the boy that was the same age as I was and felt like I lived in a different world than he inhabited. I felt much older than him even though we were both twelve years old. I realized I had left my toys and games behind the day I entered Kovno Camp. Survival was the only game we could afford to play. Even when we played Territory we were like grown-ups, not kids.

I knew this journey to another country would not lead me to the end of the rainbow and a pot of gold. I was no longer naïve. It was just another step toward survival. And I knew with the Nazis' defeat, it didn't mean that Jews were safe.

As we continued on foot through Poland there were many nights we had to sleep in barns with animals. The rain slowed us down and it seemed like it was raining almost every day. All of our shoes were damaged as we walked through the mud for miles.

There were many occasions when our route was abruptly changed because of borders that were considered too dangerous to cross. We had no papers and the Zionists helping us could have been jailed and we would have been sent back to Lithuania, or worse, if we had been discovered.

When we finally reached the border crossing in Czechoslovakia, our guide asked us to sit down on the side of the road.

"We have made the arrangements for your passage, but you will be checked carefully for any contraband in your luggage or on your person. It could be as detailed as a strip search. So please be careful," he said.

My mother pulled me aside after everyone had continued down the road.

"I have some gold and diamonds, Schaja," she said, fumbling through her pockets as she spoke. "If they search me and find the jewels they will take them and it is all we have to live on once we arrive in Germany," she whispered in my ear. She then handed me a small package wrapped in white cotton cloth. "Hide these the best you can, Schaja," her voice sounded a little frantic. "I'll hide the rest."

I figured that my mother gave me the diamonds thinking that a child is less suspicious than a grown-up carrying these valuables. I watched the line of people going through the checkpoint. I saw each person being escorted into a building at the perimeter of the checkpoint. The thought of a strip search hit me, so I decided I had to take dramatic steps to hide the jewels.

I stepped off the road to a secluded area. This cache of savings had to be hidden in the most private and undisclosed area of my body. I pushed the packet of diamonds carefully into my rectum. I took a few steps to make sure that there was no chance of them falling out. I was sure that I was walking very strangely when I returned to my mother and Mula.

As we approached the officials at the inspection point, all of the horrors of the past were racing through my imagination and I was frightened. By the time we stepped up to the official, my knees were shaking so badly I was afraid I might fall down.

The officer looked bored as we stepped up. My mother smiled at him and he returned the smile. He then patted us down lightly around our pockets and waved us through the line. I turned and watched to see how he would treat the next person and he pointed for them to go to the building where the searches were being done.

I let out a sigh of relief when we passed the borderline into Czechoslovakia. I ran into the bushes and removed the jewels from my body. When I handed them to my mother and she realized what I had done, we both began to laugh.

When we crossed the bridge our new guides were waiting for us. They were very helpful and kind people. They gave us food and water. It seemed the farther we got away from Lithuania the happier and more relaxed we became.

We continued to walk, ride trains, and board wagons. I was always amazed at how organized the smuggling operation was, considering the chaos in every country. Everything was synchronized down to minute. There was an incredible sense of cooperation with our contacts in every country.

One morning we crossed the bridge over the Danube River that separated "Buda" and "Pest" in Hungary. I was exhausted and walking with my head down. It had been a couple of months since we left Lithuania and a hard trip, mostly by foot. It seemed like an eternity to me. We had only the clothes on our back and I questioned how we would survive once we arrived in Germany. I noticed a shadow on the ground in front of me and looked up.

Standing in front of me was a very beautiful and gracious lady.

I smiled at her. She smiled and held a bunch of grapes toward me.

"For me?" I asked.

She smiled and bowed toward me and placed the grapes in my hands. It seemed almost magical, and without saying a word she continued across the road.

I had never before eaten a grape. I popped one in my mouth and bit into it. It was the most juicy, delicious taste I had ever tasted. I ran to my mother and Mula and shared the grapes. To this day I couldn't tell you why this woman chose me to extend this kindness, but I vividly remember this gracious act of generosity. It changed my attitude in a split second from being downhearted to looking forward to the future.

By the end of our passage through Hungary the weather had become extremely hot. We were in Austria and had walked ten miles to meet the train that would carry us to our next destination. The Zionist contact had made a deal for our passage by paying off the train engineer to smuggle us into the cattle car. But, if we were caught, it was up to us, not him, to explain our presence.

My feet felt like two huge blisters when we reached the rail yard where the train was halted. I had not dressed appropriately to protect my skin from the sun.

I looked down at my arms and shoulders and legs, my skin was burned and blistered. It was so uncomfortable I couldn't find a position to sit or stand when we jumped onto the cattle car of the train.

"Ma, I need some water," I said weakly after we boarded. She could barely understand what I was saying because my tongue was stuck to the roof of my mouth from dehydration.

She looked carefully at my reddened skin and saw the blisters on the top of the burned flesh. She knew I was in serious trouble. Since we were stowaways, we had to keep our presence hidden making it dangerous to ask anyone for water.

"I'm going to go get you some water. Just stay here and take care of Mula," she said and jumped off the train.

Mula and I sat quietly, waiting for her return. Suddenly, I felt the train jerk forward and start to move. I jumped up and looked outside for my mother. My throat began to close in panic. I looked at my little brother and tried to stay calm.

The train suddenly stopped again. We had moved about a hundred yards. I stuck my head out of the door looking for my mother.

I was jerked forward when the train suddenly moved again! I jumped off the train. Then I remembered that Mula was on the train and was to small to jump off. I just as quickly hoisted myself back onto the train. I was in excruciating pain with every move I made. After the train traveled about a quarter of a mile it stopped again.

I started wondering what I would do if my mother never returned. Again, I started to panic. I realized I didn't even know where we were. The towns and countries had begun to all run together. I started getting dizzy just thinking about this prospect and I started feeling worse from the burning of my skin and dryness of my mouth. I closed my eyes and thought I was going to pass out.

When I opened my eyes again, my mother was leaning over me coaxing me to take a drink of water. I was unconscious when she returned. She had poured water on my face to revive me.

We finally arrived in Nuremberg, Germany, in the fall of 1945. We were now considered DPs (displaced persons). Most of us were destitute and often sick. We had a choice to live in one of the displaced persons camps. Although many in the camps were Jews, they also housed those who hated Jews. Rumors were that morale in the camps was low and living conditions were unpleasant, overcrowded, and filthy beyond description. And even though no one was starving, there were food shortages.

THIRTY

Mula and I walked beside my mother and looked at the devastation of the buildings in Nuremberg. We were all in awe when we saw the towering remnants that were now reduced to rubble and ashes. My mother was shocked. She had seen pictures of this city that was called the "gem of medieval magnificence," but those pictures were shattered with each block we passed. The buildings that were left standing had blackened exteriors. The bombings had been horrific in this center of power of the Third Reich.

"What are we going to do now, Ma?" I asked several hours later, wondering where we would sleep tonight.

"We must prove, Schaja, that we can be independent and support ourselves. That's the most important thing to do now. If we show that we are self-sufficient it will help us when we apply for a visa to the United States," she said firmly.

I looked at her. She was talking about our future; I was talking about our immediate needs. "I mean where are we going to stay tonight?" I said, laughing even though my feet ached and I was exhausted.

She laughed and shrugged. "There will be a place," she said.

As we walked down the street, the sidewalks were filled with people. Some were begging for food or a cigarette. Most of the homeless sitting on the street were women, usually the wives of the soldiers who were still away, dead, or in prisoner-of-war camps.

My mother spotted a building that looked like it was inhabited. She approached a lady as she came outside.

"Can you tell me where my children and I can find a small room to sleep in tonight?" my mother asked.

The woman looked at her irritably, but gave us directions to a building with rooms for rent.

It was an old structure, but at least it was still standing. I looked at the tall ceilings with carvings at the corners as a tall German man led us up three flights of stairs to our room. When he opened the door, the smell of ashes and dust made me sneeze.

"This is the only room we have. Only one bed, but we can give you some blankets for your boys to sleep on," he said loudly.

"This will be fine," my mother said.

"I'm sorry," he spoke loudly, cupped his ear and leaned toward my mother. "I don't hear you."

I started to laugh and so did Mula.

My mother shushed and scolded us. "This room will be just fine, sir," she said politely to the man.

The next morning we left our one-night accommodation and began to search for an apartment. There was very little housing available. Mother stopped in shops and spoke to many people asking about an available apartment. Most just shook their heads and rushed past us.

"Sir?" my mother stopped a tall, nicely dressed gentlemen who was walking down the street next to us. "Do you know of any available housing?"

He stopped and looked at her for a moment. "I heard of one early this morning, but it may not still be available . . . they go fast," he said. He took out a paper from his wallet. "A family is renting some rooms at 10 Banhofstrasse in Furth," he said.

"Furth?" my mother asked.

"It's just a few miles from here outside Nuremberg. It's very nice," he said and walked away.

We started walking immediately to Furth. We knew that if we didn't hurry, the apartment would be gone. We stopped and stood in front of a glass window and my mother combed her hair, applied some lipstick, and straightened her clothing. She looked very nice, even though she was wearing tattered clothing. My mother had a way of carrying herself that always gave her a look of confidence and authority.

Mula and I straightened our clothing and hair. I smoothed my hair back and combed it flat. When my hair was combed back I looked older. Mula started laughing when my stomach started growling. We had not eaten since the night before.

When my mother knocked on the door at 10 Banhofstrasse, a very distinguished German gentleman answered.

"Sir," my mother said. "We heard there might be a room to let here."

He had a pleasant face and looked us over. "Yes," he finally said. "I live here with my wife and daughter and we have two vacant rooms." His name was Babel and he seemed to fit his name. He talked very quickly. "We need the money, otherwise we would have no reason to rent. Do you have money?"

"Yes, I have money, I can pay you today. May we see the rooms?" she said.

"You understand, everyone wants the rooms, but few can pay," he continued.

My mother nodded.

He took us to two small, sparsely furnished rooms that were adjoining. He said we could share the kitchen as well.

"We'll take it," my mother said and handed him enough cash for our rent. "May we move in this afternoon?" she asked.

"Yes, that will be fine," he said. "If you need any help with boxes I'll be glad to help you . . . and I guess you realize we will all share the bathroom."

My mother nodded. "We have only what you see us wearing so we won't need any help to move."

He wrinkled his brow. "Are you from here?" he asked.

"No, we have come from Lithuania," she said.

"That's a very long trip. Why would you leave Lithuania and come all this way?" he asked.

"We were in a Nazi concentration camp for three years and have no desire to be under the rule of the Communists!" she answered honestly.

I watched as his face fell from a polite smile to a dour expression of disappointment. "You're Jewish?" he almost gasped.

My mother smiled and nodded.

"Oh, my," he said. "You know, you probably would prefer to be close to the Jewish community . . . but you know, it . . . ahh . . . it makes no difference to me if you're Jewish . . . I just think that it would be more convenient."

My mother smiled at him. "Oh no, this is just perfect for us."

Mr. Babel evidently reconsidered his obvious bigotry. He needed the money and he was well aware of the War Crimes Trial being held at the Justice Palace. This was no time to show his prejudice.

After my mother gave Mr. Babel the money for the apartment, he introduced us to Mrs. Babel. Within two hours, Mr. Babel had three Jews living under his roof.

"Schaja, it's time for you to enroll in school," my mother announced one morning. "Mula, too."

"But, Ma, I need to earn money. Wouldn't it be better if I worked?" I answered.

"You can work after school," she said. "Both of you get dressed and we'll go to the neighborhood school."

I had never had formal schooling. My parents had taught me basic math and how to read. I could add, subtract, and divide. Multiplication was a little foreign to me. I could barely read Lithuanian, but was fluent in Yiddish, making it easier to learn German since the two languages were similar.

When we got to the school and talked with the schoolmistress, she was dumbfounded that at thirteen years old I had no formal education and no apprentice skills. Postwar Germany had no educational programs to deal with Mula or me. The school system was very rigid and the teachers had no desire to adjust their curriculum. The lady politely informed my mother that it would be impossible for me to become a normal student at their school.

She offered to let Mula begin, and my mother reluctantly agreed. She was not anxious to leave Mula alone at school with other German children.

"Ma," I said as we were walking home. "I'll find work. School is just a waste of time, don't you think?"

She looked at me with a worried expression. "There are no jobs, Schaja, especially for immigrants. I've tried every day since we moved here to get a job and I speak the language. Your education is very important and you will need this when we get to America."

"I'll go to school when we get there," I said impatiently. The most important thing right now was to make enough money to survive. "I'll find a job."

"I am worried, we've had to spend a lot of money since we've been here . . . we bought clothes and shoes . . . and food is so expensive."

We had bought most of these items on the black market. It was the only thriving economy in Germany. Items were sometimes stolen property from houses that Nazis had fled, or department stores that had shut down or contraband from American GIs.

Thousands of goods and items were quickly gathered by entrepreneurs and sold on the sly. Confiscated Nazi uniforms were retailored into coats, skirts, and other necessities. There were no retail stores open; if you needed something you had to buy it at a premium from the black market.

My mother bartered with one particular black market dealer for the items we needed. She traded jewelry and some money we still had from Lithuania. Mula and I went with her on one of her bartering excursions. I stood by listening while my mother and the dealer discussed some items that she needed. She made an offer and he countered the offer. She was very good at negotiating and ended up getting a better price.

I watched as a lady opened the door from outside and came into the room carrying some items of clothing. She went to the dealer's helper and handed the items across the counter. He, in return, handed her some money.

Several days later, I returned to the block where the black market dealer was located. I stood across the street and saw a kid about my age ride up to the door on his bicycle and go inside.

I walked across the street to look at his bike. It was one of the nicest bikes I had ever seen. On the back of the bike was a rack attached to the bottom of the seat and laid flat over the back wheel. The front of the bike had a headlight, with a small generator attached to the wheel. When he came back outside, he saw me looking at the bike.

"You got a bike?" he asked.

"No, I wish I did," I said and looked up at him. He was about two inches taller than I was and had brown, curly hair. "If ya ever want one I can get you one cheap." He swung his leg over his seat and started to take off. "Hey, my name's Hans." He stuck out his hand to me.

"Hi, Hans. I'm Schaja," I said, shaking hands with him.

"That's a funny name . . . where are you from?" he asked.

"Lithuania," I answered.

He whistled out loud. "That's pretty far away. How long you here?"

"A couple of weeks," I said.

"I'm always around here, so when you need that bike look me up," he said and arranged some items in his basket.

"Do you know of any jobs?" I asked before he left.

He looked me over for a few seconds. "How hard you wanna work?"

"As hard as I need to," I said.

"My dad runs this place."

"He sells all this stuff?" I asked.

"You know it's illegal don't you? If I get caught I could go to jail," he said.

"Where do you get the stuff to sell?" I asked.

"Trade secrets," he said. "You want to go to work?"

"Yeah, I'm looking for a job . . . but, I don't have a bike," I said.

Hans shrugged.

"I'm a pretty fast runner . . . could I make deliveries by foot?" I asked.

He looked at me and nodded. "Sure, but you got to get a bike to make 'real' money."

The next morning I started working in the black market. Mr. Schmidt, Hans's father sent me on errands to pick up merchandise. He gave me envelopes with names on them. On the outside, in code, were the addresses and amount of merchandise to be picked up. He made it clear to me that I could not use the main streets, only the alleys and side streets to bring back merchandise. He said if I got caught it was my problem and not his.

On my first courier stop, I delivered cartons of cigarettes. I had a rucksack that was normally used to carry books. I filled it with the cartons and quickly walked to the address I had been given. When I handed the man the items, he gave me an envelope. I stuffed it into my pocket and quickly returned the envelope to Mr. Schmidt. I made a number of trips back and forth that day.

He told me to come back the next day and then handed me some cash. It was the first time I had ever earned any money. I was exhausted but I had renewed energy when I went home and handed my mother the money I had earned.

THIRTY-ONE

My mother stood in front of the table where Mr. Schmidt was sitting. "How much are you selling nylons for today?" she asked.

"Mrs. Shachnowski, for you we always have a special price!" He handed the slim package to her and waved his hand. "It is my pleasure to give you these at no charge."

She thought for a moment. If he was willing to give her the nylons free, and she knew they cost quite a bit, he must be making a lot of money. This was a thriving business. A light went on in her head.

"Mr. Schmidt, I would like to make you a business proposition that could make both of us money."

I could see his eyes grow wide . . . he was interested in what she had to say. She proposed to him that she start her own black market business. He could give her some cash to begin her business and she would pay him back with interest. Of course, I would work for her and each month she would pay him a percentage of her profits.

Mr. Schmidt said that he would consider her proposal. He handed me a stack of items to be delivered and I went out the door. My mother remained behind.

When I arrived back at Mr. Schmidt's at the end of the workday he looked at me very seriously.

"Schaja, you can stay home tomorrow," he said, looking at me over his wire-rimmed glasses.

"But, Mr. Schmidt, why?" I asked. I thought he and my mother must have gotten into a fight.

"I won't be needing you any longer," he said nonchalantly.

"Did I do a bad job for you?" I asked as I felt my heart sink.

"No, you've been very good."

"Did you get angry with my mother? Is that why you are firing me?"

"Did I say I was firing you?" he asked.

"Well, isn't . . . well, I'm sorry . . . maybe I misunderstood." I could feel my face burning with embarrassment.

Mr. Schmidt burst out laughing. He then told me that he and my mother had agreed on arrangements for us to have our own business. "Schaja, if you have only half the will of your mother you will be a success in life. She's a very strong woman."

Things got even better when I arrived home. There was a brand-new bicycle sitting out on the sidewalk. My mother stood at the door and smiled at me.

"It's yours, Schaja . . . but you must pay me back from your earnings," she said.

I ran to her and gave her a hug and went back to the bike.

"Sure, Mama. I'll pay you back." I would have paid double. I was so happy to have a bicycle that I could ride from morning until night.

I stood at the end of the hallway and stared at the closed door. I was alone in Mr. Babel's house and I had always been curious about this closed door at the end of the hall since we moved in. I walked down the hall to test the handle. I was surprised; it wasn't locked. Mr. Babel was the only person I had ever seen go into the room and he always opened it with his key.

When I opened the door, the room had a musty smell. I walked inside and turned on a light switch that lit up a dangling lightbulb. There were boxes stacked in rows. I walked back over to the door and closed it.

I opened one of the boxes and found some very interesting looking knickknacks. The next box I opened was filled with toy soldiers made out of lead. They were the most extraordinary toy soldiers I had ever seen. There were several hundred of these fighting soldiers in all different positions, some riding, some shooting, others stretched out, lying on the ground. I took a few of them out of the box and played some battle games with them.

After a while I went to another box. It was filled with certificates . . . certificates of acknowledgement to the outstanding achievements and contributions made by Mr. Babel to the Nazi Party! I dug into the box and found pictures. I gasped out loud when I saw him in a picture with Field Marshal Hermann Göring. There were stacks of more pictures with high-ranking Nazi soldiers and Mr. Babel. I couldn't believe we were living with a Nazi.

When I left the room and closed the door, I started to laugh. I wondered if only months ago Mr. Babel would've believed that he would be down on his luck and forced to take a Jew as his tenant to supplement his income. I'm sure that he would have thought that was crazy. But then, I had learned a long time ago that life was filled with these little ironies.

"Rabbi, my name is Schaja Shachnowski and I would like to start preparing myself for my bar mitzvah," I said. I had just arrived at the synagogue on my new bicycle. I was out of breath since I had pedaled for some distance.

He smiled down at me. "And how old are you, young man?"

"I'm thirteen years old and fourteen years old on November 23," I answered.

"I haven't seen you here before . . . who is your father?" he asked.

"My father is still in Lithuania, but he will be here I hope by my bar mitzvah," I said. I didn't think it would hurt to say that. My father *might* be here, even though we had not heard from him.

He nodded knowingly, realizing that family stability was one of the many casualties of war. "There is a great deal of study involved when you prepare," he said. "Are you willing to put in all of that work?"

"Yes, Rabbi, that's why I'm here, I want to start studying. I just got my own bike, otherwise I would have been here before. We live across town and it's a long walk, Rabbi."

"Where do you go to school? Here in Furth?" he asked.

"I don't, Rabbi. I don't write or understand German well and there are only German teachers in the school near us and they wouldn't allow me to come to school."

"Have you ever read any Hebrew?" he asked.

"A long time ago in Kaunas. My grandmother, mother, and father taught me some Hebrew and they made me say my prayers in Hebrew. I know Yiddish. I remember some of the things they taught me," I said. "I want to be a good Jew, Rabbi. I want to know everything. I have a lot of questions."

He chuckled as I streamed on in my conversation.

We decided on a schedule that I could follow in taking the instruction for preparation of my bar mitzvah. I could tell the rabbi liked me and I enjoyed talking to him. Maybe he could finally answer some of my questions about God.

"Now, Schaja, let's see that new bicycle of yours," he said.

We went outside and he admired my prized possession.

In the next months I arrived at the Jewish Center at 6 A.M. each morning. I took classes and studied until 9 A.M. I rode back home and started my deliveries and pickups of cigarettes, alcohol, candy, clothing, nylons, and any other request that our customers made. Then I studied for two more hours at night. On Sundays, the only day off I had, I got on my bike and sped through the streets of Furth and Nuremberg with Hans.

I was always glad to attend synagogue. When I prayed I felt very good. The rabbi and I had a special relationship. I enjoyed the attention and spiritual guidance that he provided.

"Schaja," Rabbi said, after several months. "I think you have a great deal of potential as a human being. I admire your courage and persistence. I also think you have a great deal of humanity within your heart."

I could feel my face turning hot and flushed. No one had ever given me this kind of encouragement. It inspired me to work twice as hard to live up to the rabbi's expectations. I worked very diligently in my studies and continued to enjoy the serenity of praying. I don't know if I prayed properly or not; the rabbi never asked me about what I prayed for in detail. I always felt it would be selfish to ask for things. My prayers were thanks and gratitude to God for giving me good health and for my general sense of well-being.

"Why did God let the Germans kill so many people?" I asked Rabbi during one of our sessions.

"Schaja, God always tests our faith," Rabbi answered.

"The war was a test?" I asked.

"All challenges to our faith are tests," he said.

"How do we prepare for tests?"

"We study to understand God so that we can lean on him in times of trouble," Rabbi said.

"Did God know that I might get killed? Did I pass the test because I lived?" I asked.

"We pass the test by acquiring deeper faith. You are proving your faith by studying and being such a good student, Schaja."

"Does that mean I won't have to go through any more wars?"

"Perhaps," Rabbi answered and looked at his watch. "Do you know yet if your father can attend your bar mitzvah?"

"I am concerned, Rabbi," I said. "We haven't heard from him."

"Don't worry, there's power and value in prayer and faith in God," Rabbi said with a smile on his face.

I still would like to have known where God was when we were being slaughtered . . . why did he not help us? What had we done to be punished like that? Where was my father? I was never quite satisfied with Rabbi's answers about God. I hoped that if I studied the Torah more, I would find my own answers. I frequently posed these questions to God directly, but he never answered me. The one thing that I did know was when an enemy of the Jews said he wants to destroy us . . . believe him . . . take him seriously.

Thirty-two

We heard music when we turned the corner of the street on our bicycles. A U.S. Army jeep was barreling down the street toward us. There were about six GI Joe's hollering and singing. Hans and I saw them before they saw us. Our tires skidded as we slammed the brakes on the handles of our bikes and stopped just in front of the jeep that had also come to a screeching halt.

"What kind of a driver are you, Mitchell?" one of the soldiers yelled.

"The best damn driver, this side of the Mississippi!" Mitchell shouted back and got out of the car and walked over to us.

He was about six two. His black hair was cut in an army buzz cut. He took off his soft army cap and looked at Hans and me. "You boys okay?" he asked and smiled at us.

I understood only bits and pieces of English. But I understood okay. I nodded my head and smiled.

Hans nodded also.

The soldier broke into a smile and hollered. "I can stop that machine on a dime. I learned to drive on the back roads of Kentucky."

We looked at him blankly.

He realized that we didn't understand English. He did his best to repeat everything in broken German. I had gotten reasonably good at understanding German.

The MPs drove up and stopped. "You got a problem here, Sergeant?" one of the MPs asked.

"No, sir," Mitchell turned and smiled. "I'm just givin' these kids some candy," he reached into his pocket and handed me a chocolate bar.

I looked at it and smelled it. These were prime products on the black market. I unwrapped the candy and took a bite. I smiled at Sergeant Mitchell. "Danke schön."

"Take it easy tonight. We don't want to have any problems," the MP said and drove off.

"Are you from America?" Hans asked in part German and part English.

"Shore am!" Mitchell replied.

Hans translated for me.

"Salem, Massachusetts?" I asked, trying to pronounce it properly. This was the only place in America that I had heard about and had learned to pronounce.

"Naw," he said and shook his head in case I didn't understand. "Cain-tucky!"

"Cain-tucky," I repeated, just like he had said it.

He leaned down and crouched on his knees and smiled. "The Bluegrass State!" he said.

"Blue grass?" I said and laughed, copying him in bad enunciation.

The soldiers started to laugh.

"Here kid, anybody that can pronounce Cain-tucky that way deserves my good luck piece. He took a chain from around his neck and handed it to me.

I looked at it carefully after he handed it to me.

"It's a rabbit's foot. First jackrabbit I ever shot on the farm. It'll bring you good luck, kid!" he said.

"Thanks," I said. "Thanks a lot." I put the chain around my neck.

He got back into the jeep and drove off. I could hear him singing some song about Cain-tucky.

When I went to see the rabbi the next morning, I showed him the souvenir that the soldier had given me. He explained to me in Yiddish that a rabbit's foot in America was a good luck piece. If I wore it I would always have good luck. He said we all needed it.

The day of my bar mitzvah finally arrived. It had been almost a year since we arrived in Germany and I was proud of my accomplishments in the study of Judaism and the experience of this rite of passage. My father had not yet arrived in Germany.

Rabbi Bronstein had taken me under his wing in the absence of my father. He invited me to a small dinner after the ceremony. This was a traditional dinner with prayers between each course of fruit as an appetizer and kosher meats as the entree. My mother and Mula were not invited to this dinner. Mr. Schmidt and Hans were invited to attend. I was presented with a beautiful prayer scarf at the end of the dinner. I felt very privileged to reach this point in my spiritual studies.

I continued to attend synagogue almost every day. I was on the road to becoming a very religious Jew. I admired Rabbi Bronstein. He was a very kind man and always listened patiently to my many questions. I spent every free moment I had with the rabbi and always tried to ask him in many different ways the question about God's whereabouts during the killing of Jews. Why were we called the "chosen people" if we were almost annihilated by Hitler? I still did not get a satisfying answer. But I continued to study about "miracles." Why didn't He perform one for us?

Hans and I usually crossed paths at least once a day while we were making deliveries. If one of us was behind on our deliveries or pickups and the other wasn't busy we helped each other.

Today was a slow day and I had stopped at a bakery to get a sweet pastry. I enjoyed the break and was slowly eating the pastry. I ate the icing on top first and then I tore a little piece of the dough away toward the center area that usually held some type of warm cream. I had finally reached the center and put the warm cream in my mouth. When I looked up and saw Hans speeding down the street so fast I almost didn't recognize him. Then a German policeman on a bicycle sped by trailing a good distance behind Hans.

I knew the route that Hans would take and I took a shortcut to get to the alley before he arrived. He turned the corner and saw me.

"Hans," I yelled before he got to where I was sitting. "Give me your stuff."

He hit his brakes and handed me his sack that held a carton of Lucky Strike cigarettes and other goods. I shoved his smaller sack inside my rucksack and put it on my back. I headed in the direction that the policeman was coming and looked away as I passed him. He continued in hot pursuit of Hans. I pedaled as fast as I could to my house and hid the items under my bed.

When mother got home I told her the story.

"Have you talked to Hans? What happened?" she asked.

I shrugged my shoulders.

"Schaja, I think you better stay home for a few days," she said, looking worried.

"Who'll make the deliveries?" I asked.

"I'll take care of them," she said. "I don't want you to end up in jail."

The next morning, I went to the synagogue. I decided that I would spend the morning there since I had no deliveries or pickups. I left the synagogue about noon. I bounded up the stairs and out the door and around the corner to my bike. When I turned the corner, I couldn't believe my eyes. My bike was gone!

I turned in circles looking down the street, across the street. I ran to the next block. I stopped people on the street and described my bike to them. No one had seen it and there was no trace of my bike. I walked back to the spot where it was stolen and sat down on the curb. How could this happen? How could God allow this to happen? This was my prized possession that I had paid for myself. It was how I earned money. I stood up and walked over to the wooden stair post. I punched the post. I was so mad it didn't even hurt me. I punched it again. I saw the blood on my knuckles. I picked up a rock and threw it down the street. I looked around and saw the blackened buildings . . . the sad expression on those faces passing by me. The crying child I heard in the background. I shook my fist at God. How could he watch millions suffer, be tortured, go hungry, live in poverty, and now my bike. It was the last straw. I shook my head and started the long walk home. I did not return to that synagogue.

I visited Sgt. Pete Mitchell almost every Friday night. Hans and I watched he and his buddies caroused around the bars. We watched a few brawls that the MPs broke up, and were fascinated with the life of the American GI Joe. They were always happy and they always had money to spend or something to give away. These military men were vastly different from the Nazi soldiers I had known in Kovno.

Frequently the sergeant brought Hans and me a surprise. He brought us candy or patches that we could sew on our shirts and when he had time he always told us stories about the United States. I admired the soldiers. Hans and I talked about them daily.

Hans and I decided to save our money and bring Sergeant Mitchell a bottle of schnapps that we sold on the market. We arrived one night with the bottle of schnapps in a paper sack so no one knew what we were carrying. I spotted Sergeant Mitchell about a half a block away. He was surprised when we handed him the paper sack.

"Well," he said taking off his cap. "I just don' know wha' ta say. You boys shun'da done this . . . spendin' all yur money."

"Thank you, Sergeant Mitchell," I said.

"Don' thank me . . . shoot, I need to be thankin' you," he said and opened the seal on the cap and took a swig.

Both Hans and I smiled. His big muscular body swayed a little bit as he tipped his head backward.

After he had put the cap back on the bottle he looked at us with one eyebrow raised. "Where'd you young'uns get this kind of stuff . . . n' don' tell me you jis' bought it somewhere!"

Hans and I looked at each other. "Our parents . . ." Hans said.

I stopped him and spoke in German. "Hans and I make deliveries for a wholesaler and he gets all kinds of stuff. We bought it from him," Hans translated.

Sergeant Mitchell laughed. "You boys are black market couriers?" He looked down at us.

"Yes, sir." I said.

He looked off into the distance and took another shot of schnapps. "Y'all ever tasted this stuff?"

"No, sir," Hans said.

I shrugged.

"Hans run over there to the jeep and there's a couple of paper cups in the floor of the backseat," he said.

When he got back Sergeant Mitchell poured a small shot into both paper cups. He then held his bottle up in a toast. "Up to yur lips . . . over yur gums . . . look out, Mamaaaa . . . here it comes!" We all downed the schnapps. I remembered having schnapps with Uncle Willie and my father. It still had a terrible taste, worse than cigarettes. I swallowed the stinging liquid but I felt like my throat and stomach were on fire! I started to cough. Hans was even worse. He had spit the schnapps out when he first tasted it.

"Mighty fine," Mitchell roared. "Warms your soul." He dismissed our reactions and acted like we must have enjoyed it along with him.

We sat down on the curb with Sergeant Mitchell between us. He lit up a cigarette. "Well, if I were workin' the underground market, I'd think that gasoline might be a pretty good seller," he said and paused. He spoke to a soldier passing by with a girl who was hanging on his arm.

"There's some mighty fine 'beaver' in Germany, boys," he said, his eyes lingering on the tall blonde woman.

Hans and I both agreed.

"About that gasoline. You know there are jeeps parked down at the motor pool at night. When I was a kid, when we needed gas for the car we took a little tube about three or four feet long. Ummmm . . . Maybe from a garden hose. Then we'd dip down into the tank of the tractor, suck on it until it we could almost taste it, and then we'd drop the gasoline into an empty bottle. We'd always have to take jis a li'l bit, then we'd do the same thing over again at the next tractor til' we got 'nuff to get the car started." He looked around at us and winked. "I gotta be goin' boys, see ya next Friday."

Hans and I took Sergeant Mitchells' veiled advice about stealing gasoline from the jeeps. Gasoline was a very expensive item on the black market and it sold as fast as we could supply. I figured that with this new item I could make up the loss of not having a bicycle.

"Hey, Schaja, what's a beaver?" Hans asked after we left the sergeant.

I laughed. "You don't know what a beaver is?" I said teasing him. I sure didn't know what a beaver was, but I wasn't going to let him know that I didn't.

THIRTY-THREE

"How would you like to take a vacation?" my mother asked at breakfast one morning.

"We've never taken a vacation before," I answered and looked at her. "I think it would be great. But where would we go?"

"We've been invited to a little rural town about an hour from here, called Zirndorf. It's out in the country where it's beautiful and quiet," my mother said. "I have a friend, Franz Wilhelm. He has a home there and would like to take us."

Another boyfriend, I thought to myself. I thought about my father and realized it had been over a year since he had promised to join us. There wasn't much I could say since my mother was caring for us without his help. But I still wished that we could be a family again. I didn't understand my parents.

That morning we packed up our clothes and met Mr. Wilhelm at the train station. We sat in a compartment in the train that held the four of us. Mr. Wilhelm smoked a cigar and talked the entire time. I thought it was funny because he was the kind of person that would ask a question and answer it himself, before you had a chance to say a word.

After we got off the train, Mr. Wilhelm took us to his house. It was a nice cottage that overlooked the valley below. He had bicycles and told Mula and me that we could ride them.

Mula and I went off on our bicycles and were gone for the rest of the day. When we got back my mother had prepared a nice dinner of veal and spaetzle. This was a dish that I had not eaten since before the war. My grandmother had made it for us at her house, long ago. I decided that Mr. Wilhelm must be very wealthy to afford this kind of food.

The next morning Mula and I sped off on our bicycles again. We had been riding for about an hour when we found a path that went almost vertically down into the valley. I was riding very fast and showing off to Mula since he was going very slow and was impressed with my agility on my bicycle. I looked around at the green, lush hills, the blue sky, and felt the warm sunshine and the wind blowing through my hair. Within a second, I felt myself flying across my handlebars and across the road, landing hard on my hands and knees.

I heard Mula scream as I hit the ground. When he came running up next to me, he was holding the rock that caused my accident. It was large enough that I had been thrown off balance. I was angry with myself for showing off. I should have kept my eyes on the road.

I felt something warm and gooey on my knee. I pulled the leg up and saw I had a deep gash across my right kneecap. I searched in the grass to see what I had hit. It was a piece of jagged, broken glass.

I tried to walk, but it was painful. I dragged myself up to the top of the hill and asked Mula to go to Mr. Wilhelm's house and tell him and Mother that I was hurt. The house was only about a kilometer away.

It wasn't long before all three came to help. My mother quickly bandaged my knee and tried to stop the bleeding. But it was still pouring blood.

"Rose, I think we need a nurse to sew up that wound," Mr. Wilhelm said. "It's pretty deep."

Mr. Wilhelm knew of a small clinic in the town. I leaned on him and my mother as we walked to the clinic that was twenty minutes away. The nurse cleaned the wound and sewed up the gash.

When I woke up the following morning, the gash was sore, red, and swollen. We had to cut the bandage off of my leg because it was so tight. My knee was infected.

Mr. Wilhelm called for a doctor, who recleaned the wound and used a stronger antibiotic. He told me to stay off my leg until the infection had cleared. I spent the rest of our vacation lying on the sofa.

Since I was lying on the couch all day, I was a victim to Mr. Wilhelm's constant conversation. He talked to me daily about learning a trade. He told me I needed a trade to always fall back on. He knew I had no education.

"When you meet people," he said, "and they ask who you are, they're not interested in your religion or politics, they want to know what your occupation is, Schaja. It is your identity, a doctor, a lawyer, or a watch repairman." He seemed pleased with himself each time he went over this with me.

Almost a month after we returned from our vacation, Mr. Wilhelm told me there was a job opening for a watch repair apprentice. He persuaded me to apply for the job in Nuremberg.

The next morning I dressed in my only white shirt and black pants. As usual, the pants were a little short because I had grown at least an inch since I wore them last. Mr. Wilhelm helped tie my black tie and I was off on my bicycle to become an apprentice.

My heart sank when I saw the line of boys standing in front of the watch repair shop waiting to interview for the job. I would never be able to compete with all these applicants. I was sure that they had the education that I had missed. I almost turned around and went back home, but I decided to stay.

After almost an hour of standing in line I had my interview. Mr. Steinham, the master watchmaker, asked me questions. I was nervous, but after a few minutes, I was okay and let Mr. Steinham know that I was anxious to learn.

Several more hours passed until he finished all of his interviews. He came outside and announced the three people that he had chosen to work as his apprentices. I nearly fell over when I heard him call my name. He told me to report on Monday at 7:00 A.M.

On Sunday, I met Hans and a group of our friends. I saw Nicholas, one of our buddies, speeding toward us on his bike.

"What's the plan today?" he asked as he curved his bike fancily in front of us. Nicholas was about three years older than the rest of us.

We all shrugged.

"We could go to the park and have an ice cream," Hans suggested.

Nobody was very enthusiastic.

"I found something yesterday that you might want to see," he said. "We'd have to wait till dark to go in."

"What is it?" one of the kids asked.

"The underground tunnel below the castle," he said. "I know where there is an entrance under the building."

"You mean, the Nuremberg Castle?" I asked.

"That's it," he said confidently.

"I thought that underground was condemned after the war," Hans said.

"Yeah, sure, but I found an entrance," Nicholas said.

"What if it caves in when we're down there?" Hans asked.

Nicholas shrugged.

"Yeah, let's go," I said.

We all got on our bikes and rode to the castle. Once we arrived, our imaginations went into overdrive. When it grew dark, we each took our flashlights and sticks to battle any predators that might be lurking underground.

"I heard that some people hid underground until the war was over. What are we gonna do if they are still there and try to hurt us?" Hans asked.

"If there is anyone underground, they're nothing but corpses by now," Nicholas, the ringleader answered. "I wonder if they murdered anyone down here during the war? We may find thousands of missing people."

"There's going to be rats in here," I said.

"Jeez, I heard that there are rats underground that have teeth two inches long. They probably have rabies, too," one of the others chimed in.

"I'm taking no chances," Nicholas said and put on a pair of gloves he had in his jeans pocket.

By the time we had traveled through several of the paths in the maze of twists and turns, we had worked ourselves into a frenzy. We began to run through the damp, smelly tunnels and passages like wild men. After we had been inside for about thirty minutes one of the boys screamed.

"You guys, it's a skeleton . . . I think it's a human skeleton," he said.

We all ran toward him. One of the boys leaned down and touched one of the bones.

"Don't touch it, you'll get a disease," Hans shouted when he saw this.

I walked over and knelt down. I shined my flashlight on the pieces of bones. When I got down to the feet of the skeleton, we decided that it must have been an animal. We considered the size of the bones and decided that it had been a wolf.

This discovery heightened our fears even more. What if it had been a female and she had baby wolves and they had grown up in total darkness and were starving? I could almost see saliva dripping from the wolves' fangs as they got ready to take a bite out of my arm.

We continued exploring the black tunnels. At every turn we made new discoveries. German weapons. Gas masks. Papers with German writing scribbled, but now ruined by the water and condensation. Tire rims and the hood of one of the Nazi vehicles with a swastika on the top.

"How do we get out of here?" Hans asked Nicholas after we had been in the tunnels for more than an hour.

We all looked at each other. None of us had a clue at this point how we had entered.

"Let's go this way," Nicholas said.

We walked and walked. We were lost. I was kicking myself for coming into the tunnels. I knew we would never be found. Some kids fifty years from now would find a skeleton and it would be mine. I thought about my job that I was supposed to start tomorrow.

I took over the search for the entrance after a while and started leading the pack in another direction. I flashed my light ahead of me as I walked. I had been leading for about thirty minutes. I looked ahead of me and saw a giant pack of rats. It must have been their nest because I saw so many of them. I turned around abruptly.

"What's wrong?" Nicholas asked. He could see by my expression that it was not good.

"Let's go the other direction," I said, holding my breath to keep the panic from rising in my throat.

He took his light and flashed it down the tunnel. He saw what I had seen. "Jeez," he said and we all took off running. After several more hours of roaming, we accidentally discovered the entrance.

THIRTY-FOUR

I looked at the sign above the door when I rode up to the repair shop on my first day of employment: "Uhren Haus Gehlen." It was 7:02 A.M. and the workers were already busy when I stepped behind the counter. "Ah, Mr. Shachnowski, come over here," Mr. Steinham said.

I peered over his shoulder.

He had the back of a wristwatch open. He put a magnifying glass on top of his wire-rimmed glasses. "Watch, for a moment," he said, picking up a tiny tool.

I leaned down to get a closer look. He moved the tool just a bit, then he stopped and then moved a bit, then stopped, then moved.

"This is an art. The movement of the tool . . . a little bit too much," he mimicked a motion. "And it is ruined. Just enough . . ." again he mimicked a motion. "Just right," he looked at me and smiled.

He sat me down at a table and handed me a big watch. He then handed me a set of tools.

"This clock has one movement and will be easy for you to work with," he said and handed me an apron and a jeweler's magnifying glass. "Take it apart and when you get stuck I will show you what you have done wrong . . . and then you will take it apart again."

Mr. Steinham rang a bell in what seemed only minutes to me. I jumped because I was so deep in concentration. This was evidently his signal each day that it was time for lunch. It was the first time I had looked up from my work all morning. I saw everyone rise and go to a back room. I followed them.

The lunchroom had a table and several straight-back wooden chairs. There were cabinets lined up against the wall. On each door of the cabinet was the name of each employee.

I watched as Erwin Knauer, the master's understudy, took out his briefcase and placed a piece of fruit, a sandwich, and a thermos in front of him. He opened the thermos and poured some hot soup into the top.

I had not even thought about lunch at work. I don't know why but it had never occurred to me to bring food. I sat and watched as everyone began to eat and chat. Erwin nudged me. "You want part of my sandwich?" he asked.

"You sure?" I asked. "I'll bring some extra tomorrow."

Erwin and I became good friends. As I learned and progressed with my work, I chatted with the others as I cleaned and repaired the work that Mr. Steinham gave me. I enjoyed my job very much and even though I knew I would never be a master, I was quick and efficient at the work I did. Mr. Steinham appreciated my labor and encouraged me in my progress.

One afternoon a customer came in carrying a very old, ornate, delicate grandfather clock. He explained to Mr. Steinham that it was running a little bit slow. It had been handed down for several generations. He wanted Mr. Steinham's assurance that the clock would be treated with "kid gloves" because it was a priceless antique and also had great sentimental value for him and his family.

After the customer left, Mr. Steinham ceremoniously brought the clock over to me and set it on my table. "I think this would be a good job for you, Mr. Shachnowski. You know how to do the repairs. And I'm certain you will be very careful."

He explained the repairs to me and I was sure that I could handle the job. The next morning I began working on the clock, and before the end of the day I had completed the repairs.

I walked over to the wall and very carefully found a hook to hang the clock. This procedure was always done to make sure the clock ran properly when it was repaired and on the wall. As I started to step back from the clock to see that everything was right, I saw the clock careen to the ground with an awful crash. I tried to catch the clock before it hit the ground but it was too late. The prized possession was in a heap of broken pieces scattered all over the floor.

Everyone in the shop sat in stunned silence. Mr. Steinham leaned down and started to pick up the pieces. He waved at me to go sit down. I could see his expression of shock, disgust, anger, and horror.

I felt numb. I couldn't believe this had happened. If only . . . if only . . . if only . . . Why did this happen to me?

The next day the customer arrived to pick up the clock. Mr. Steinham explained what happened and apologized profusely. The man became enraged. From his conversation I realized he was from a very prominent family in the neighborhood.

"Not even the war could destroy this clock!" the man ranted. "How could one stupid, little apprentice destroy this treasure! What good is an apology, Mr. Steinham," he continued to shout. "This is a travesty! I want the person responsible fired!"

"That's very harsh, sir. He didn't do this on purpose," Mr. Steinham tried to persuade him.

"He has no business working here and if he is not fired I will let everyone in the neighborhood know what has happened!" The man turned and marched arrogantly out of the store.

Mr. Steinham turned and looked at me with a very sad expression. "I'm sorry, Mr. Shachnowski," he said.

I took off my apron and looked at my coworkers and then at Mr. Steinham. "I'm sorry about the clock, Mr. Steinham." I was very embarrassed that I had made such a problem.

"Come by on Friday for your final check."

I returned on Friday and I received my final pay. I stayed for a while and chatted with my coworkers. We had become good friends and I was sorry to leave them. Before I left, Erwin invited me to come to his home on Sunday afternoon and have dinner with him and his family to celebrate his birthday. He handed me an address with 2:00 P.M. written on it.

Hans and I went to see Sergeant Mitchell later that night. When we got to the street where the bars were, we heard people yelling and bottles breaking. We hid in the recess of one of the buildings and watched as soldiers and local German men slugged each other. I saw some German kids throwing bottles into the fighting area in the middle of the street.

I watched two groups of men walking toward one another in confrontation. There were three soldiers being taunted by four local German men. "If I ever see you with one of our women again I'll beat you till you're blind . . . and . . ." The German glared at the soldier.

The soldier landed an uppercut on his chin before the German could finish his sentence. The other two soldiers piled on, and pretty soon there was another fight going on. But the three soldiers took care of the Germans in a matter of minutes.

Just as they had the Germans on the ground, I heard the MPs' siren. Everybody on the street scattered.

"What was all the fighting about tonight?" we asked as soon as we found Sergeant Mitchell.

"Race," he answered succinctly.

"What does that mean?" I asked.

"Stupidity. Some of these white ya-hoos think a black man don't have no business with a white woman. That's how it started anyway and then the Germans got into it."

"Why don't the white men like the black men? They're on the same side aren't they?" I asked.

"It's been goin' on since time began," he said. "You'll learn about it someday, it's something that's taught."

———

On Sunday, I rode my bike to Erwin's house. I was impressed when I saw the large and elegant house where he lived. I hadn't realized that Erwin's family was so prominent. His mother answered the door when I knocked.

Mrs. Knauer was very friendly, and I was relieved. I knew that Erwin had told them I was Jewish and I wasn't sure how I would be received, since his family was not Jewish.

"We've heard so much about you from Erwin," she said smiling and patting me on the shoulder.

Erwin came downstairs as I walked inside. He introduced me to several more couples that were relatives. We soon went into the dining room and sat down to have lunch. Everyone was chatting and happy at the dinner table.

"What do you think of the latest developments in the trial?" Mr. Knauer, Erwin's father, turned and asked me.

I knew he was referring to the international tribunal that was trying twenty-four Nazi officers for war crimes. It was taking place about two miles from where we were sitting. The senior officer being tried was Hermann Göring, who was believed to be the number-two man in the hierarchy of the Third Reich. I knew the evidence being presented was damning up to this point. The accused claimed that as an officer he had never been a part of any actions; however, the evidence showed his signatures on the orders. Mr. Knauer's question made me uncomfortable, as I was not sure if he sympathized with the Nazis. I didn't want to stir up a problem as an invited guest. I thought for a moment and looked at him. "I hope that justice will be served."

"I'm just unwilling to accept these horrible accusations," a woman at the end of the table said. "How could anyone be so inhumane . . . It's impossible."

I could hardly breathe.

The man next to her harshly interrupted her. He was tall and slender with a sharp nose and ridged cheekbones. His voice was commanding, loud, and deep. What he said caught me by surprise. "They are guilty and they knew as did most Germans. Our behavior is unforgivable. Most Germans have no active hatred for the Allies and they did not want this war, and there is very little real hatred for minority groups whose persecution they condoned. I know many whose best friends were Jews. But the frightening thing is that it was not hate, but our moral psyche. Those responsible for molding our ethical sense of right and wrong are to blame: parents, youth leaders, teachers, society standards . . . in other words, my friends, the blame lies with the education we were given. It's taught . . . not inborn."

The table was in stunned silence. I looked at the expressions on each guest's face. I could tell some others were not in agreement with him. I remembered what Captain Mitchell had said about hatred being taught.

Mrs. Knauer asked the servers to bring in the birthday cake.

Thirty-five

I searched for a job to replace the one I had lost. With no education and lack of language skills I was out of luck. I had blown my opportunity to learn a trade and I knew it. Each day the bills piled up. The rent was due, we needed groceries, and we had little money.

The authorities had cracked down on the black market trade and my mother had cut down on deliveries and purchases since it had become dangerous. There were checkpoints set up randomly to catch couriers and even the customers were suspect for turning a dealers into the police.

I saw Hans on the street one afternoon and told him about my mother's concerns and our problems. He offered to loan me some money until I got a job. I told him I would rather have my old job back.

"What about your mother, she'll be angry," he said.

"Not if I bring home cash," I said.

"I've never gotten caught and you won't either," he said and we took off on our bikes. Within an hour I was earning money again. Hans told me where the checkpoints were usually located and I learned ways around them. There were a few times when I got stopped, but my innocent face and friendly smile saved me. I was glad to be earning money again.

I was at home babysitting Mula one night while my mother was out with Mr. Wilhelm. We were listening to radio and playing games when Mr. Babel, our landlord, knocked on our door.

"There is a man at the front door asking for your mother," he said. "Would you like to talk to him?"

I had no idea who it might be but I decided that it would be best for me to talk to the person and not disturb Mr. Babel. "Sure, Mr. Babel," I said and turned to Mula. "You stay here, I'll be right back."

"I told him I would see if anyone was here," he said. "He said he would just wait outside."

I went outside and saw the form of a man on the landing of the stairway. He had his back to me but I recognized him. My father was finally here.

I ran to him as he turned around he had his arms opened, waiting for me. "Pa, I knew you would come! I knew you wouldn't leave us!"

"We are together again," he said smiling and looking at me. "Wait, I must look at you." He stepped back. I had grown several inches since we had left Lithuania three years ago. "You are no longer my little boy," he said, tousling my hair. "You are a handsome grown man!"

I laughed and shook my head. "We have two rooms here at Mr. Babel's. Mula is inside. Come on, Pa," I said and took him by the hand.

Mula was still playing with his clay on the floor. He looked up when he heard the door open. He looked at me as I walked in. My father was behind me and quickly ran over and hugged him. "Mula, Mula, my baby has grown into a boy!" he laughed and tickled Mula's ribs.

"Pa, where have you been for so long?"

"I almost got stuck again. The Soviets sealed the borders and I couldn't get a visa. I ended up making the same trip that you made. It has taken so many months."

As we talked my father kept looking around the room. I knew he wondered where my mother was tonight. "Where is your mother, Schaja?" he finally asked.

"She's out with friends, Pa," I said. I couldn't meet his questioning gaze.

"Out?" he said and pondered this for a moment.

"I think I should leave, Schaja. Hmm . . . you will let her know that I came here tonight and I will come back tomorrow."

"No, sir," I said.

"No?" he asked and looked at me.

"Pa, she will be home later. You can't leave, I have prayed and hoped for you to come here . . . and I won't let you leave until you see her."

He looked at me for a long time. "Okay, son, I will stay. And I will make you a promise: I will never leave you again."

"A promise is forever, Pa?" I said and looked at him wanting some assurance.

"Our family has gone through terrible times," he said. "Your mother was very angry before and I am here to try and heal wounds."

"Why did you leave her alone in Kovno?" I asked.

He looked shocked. "Is that what she told you?"

"Yes, sir," I answered.

He looked at his watch. "It's late Schaja, you better go to bed. What time is your school tomorrow?"

I looked at him now a little shocked. "Pa, we're not in school."

He shook his head. "You haven't gone to school for the last three years?

"No, Pa, they wouldn't take us," I said.

"You must get your education, Schaja. You've already missed so much."

"But I have to earn money," I answered.

"I'm here now and I'm going to take care of earning money," he said. "I'll talk to your mother when she comes in."

I couldn't sleep. I heard my mother come in around midnight. I listened to my parents' muffled voices for a long time, until I drifted off to sleep. I knew that Pa was here to stay and I never saw my mother's boyfriend, Mr. Wilhelm, again.

My father's presence had a very positive influence in our lives. He and my mother seemed to get along very well and they were both relaxed and happy. Ma didn't have to worry about where the next meal was coming from or how the rent would be paid. Life for us as a family had finally settled into reality.

My father made friends in Germany very quickly. He and Mr. Babel even became friends. They chatted for hours. I told Pa the story of Mr. Babel's Nazi certificates I had seen in the attic. My father and I always laughed about how he and the Nazi shared a cup of coffee and reminisced about the old days.

My father insisted that my brother and I be enrolled in school. He would not allow me to continue to work on the black market.

The German school system was more receptive to Mula and me enrolling this time. I thought it was senseless for me to start with my age group, but that's where they put me. I sat in class feeling like a dummy the entire semester.

The teacher spoke in German rapidly. I could make out some of the words but not all of them. I probably should have started in the first grade but I was too old as a teenager. The school system still had no programs to handle an immigrant that could not speak or write the language. I was totally lost in the learning process. I left school each day feeling frustrated without a clue about how to learn what I was being taught. I tried to convince my parents that my time would be much better spent if I worked on the black market. But, my father was adamant about an education for both Mula and me.

My father found a job at the American Post Exchange Warehouse. It supplied the military PXs with goods. The military required employees who had no connection to the Nazi Party. My father was easily able to prove that he had no part of the Nazi Party, which assured him a job despite the high unemployment rate in Germany. He also spoke the German language and understood some English. He was promoted quickly and was able to earn a good living.

With the help of my father's acquaintances from work, he began the process of applying for a visa to enter the United States. He discovered that it would be a long process of filling out applications, taking interviews, and answering questionnaires. At the end of the paperwork, he would be given a number and told to wait. At the end of that wait for approval, we would have to wait even more time for an actual date to immigrate. He was told that it sometimes took years.

When my father brought the paperwork home to fill out, he contacted my uncle to make sure he would be our sponsor to come to the United States. Max and Sara Shuman, my mother's brother and his wife, who lived in Salem, Massachusetts agreed enthusiastically, and offered to do anything they could to help the process.

"Rosala, I think I should put my birthplace as Russia," he said, peering at the forms.

"You were born in Kaunas," she answered.

"My friends told me that my application might be considered more quickly if I said I was born in Russia . . . they are allies," he said.

Little did we know that the Cold War was already developing between the United States and Russia.

"There were not many records kept at that time of your birth, Leon. They may not even notice. So many things were destroyed during the war," she said as she dried the last supper dish.

"Yes, I will tell them that records were destroyed and I have no proof."

The next morning after the papers were finished we all were filled with anticipation of going to the United States in six months to a year. I was able to face my grueling misery in the German school more easily with the hope of going to America.

"We have been turned down," my father said after receiving a notice from the U.S. Immigration Bureau months later. He shook his head sadly. His words hit us all with surprise.

"Why? What reason? We have a sponsor . . . I don't understand." My mother's face was filled with concern.

My dreams felt like they were slipping away again when he gave us the bad news. I wanted to live in America.

"I have heard that South America is not so strict for refugees. Venezuela, I have heard, is a nice country and safe for Jews," she said one afternoon as she and my father were discussing other possibilities for relocation.

"Rose, the best place in the world is the United States. Maybe there is another way to get there," he said. "I was stupid to lie about my birthplace. It made me look like a phony. I'll reapply and tell them the truth. I'll explain why I lied. Perhaps they will understand."

"It's going to take time, Leon," my mother said. "The boys might be grown by the time we are reconsidered. My friends told me a story about this . . ." She thought for a moment. "There are two displaced people and they meet. One asks the other where he plans to immigrate . . . 'Oh,' he says, 'Canada or Australia.' He asks, 'Why not the U.S.? The other rolls his eyes and answers, 'The Americans put you on a scale and start adding papers to the other side. When the papers equal your weight, they render a decision.'"

My father chuckled. "It won't take that long, Rose," he said optimistically, not knowing himself if the application would even be reconsidered.

Months later, without notice, we received word that our application had been approved. I will never forget the date we were told this news. It was November 23! My birthday. We would depart in a matter of weeks.

THIRTY-SIX

"I heard the ship is a luxurious, very special cruise liner," a lady standing behind me said and giggled excitedly.

"The rooms are supposed to be as big as our living room," another person said. "It's all American-style food. I hear it's delicious."

"Yeah, as long as you're not seasick," a man said and laughed.

I stood listening to all the conversations going on around me, while we stood in line to board the ship. I was anxious to board and arrive at the place I had dreamed of for so long. America. I had to pinch myself to believe that this wasn't a dream. My father and mother and Mula stood in front of me as we went through customs inside a large building. After we had passed through this area we walked out a door and onto a dock. The ship was named the USS *Sturgis*.

"I don't think this is a luxury cruise liner," my father said and laughed. "It's a troop ship."

"Some of our fellow passengers are going to be disappointed," my mother said and laughed with my father.

Nothing could dampen my spirits. I didn't care if it was a rowboat. Sergeant Mitchell had told Hans and me many stories about America. Before I left, he encouraged me to memorize every state in the union. I knew all forty-eight of them and how to spell their names. Massachusetts was actually the hardest one to spell . . . or was it Mississippi?!

As I boarded the ship I rubbed my rabbit's foot from Sergeant Mitchell for good luck.

The first afternoon at sea, Mula and I explored every area of the ship that we were allowed to enter. I was lying wide awake that night in my cot when I began to feel the ship toss and turn. The winter seas were icy, rough, and turbulent. The tossing and turning kept getting worse. I clenched my teeth to keep the nausea from rising into my throat. I tried to lay still and stiff to keep myself balanced on the bed. Pretty soon, I realized that the entire family was suffering from the turbulence. We were all differing shades of green, and not alone; everyone on the ship was sick.

This turbulent, rocking motion continued throughout the journey. We were all retching with every giant blow the waves made to the ship. None of us could eat anything other than the clear soup that the ship offered to those who were sick. We took turns bringing the liquid dinners offered by the ship to our bay that we shared with hundreds of other passengers.

Tonight it was my turn to go with my father. We got off of our cots and went into the hallway. We both lurched as the boat rolled from side to side. Before we reached the dining area, we decided we would try standing on the deck to get some fresh air. When we walked outside the wind was icy and bitter. The rain was blowing horizontally against our face. The fresh air didn't help and we went back inside and completed our journey.

When we returned, the soup was already cool and the cartons were only half full. But no one felt like even sipping the soup. It felt like this nauseous feeling would never end.

On the fourth day of our seven-day journey, there was an announcement over the loudspeaker that went throughout the ship. "There is a limited amount of candy available. If you would like candy please report to the third deck." Even though I could not eat anything and keep it down, I couldn't resist this treat that was offered. This opportunity might never come again. I got off my cot and weaved my way to the designated area. I was given two Clark bars. I hid them in my knapsack until I was able to eat them. I knew it was only a matter of time before I felt better.

On the seventh and final day, the waves finally calmed. Our nausea subsided, and we were very anxious to arrive in Boston Harbor. The USS *Sturgis* was one of the few ships that docked in Boston carrying immigrants. In the past, most ships carrying immigrants arrived in New York at Ellis Island. We packed our belongings the night before and we were standing on the deck watching the sun rise on the day of arrival.

Sergeant Mitchell had given me one of his old army coats before I left Germany. It was big on me and hung to my knees. The shoulders reached almost to my elbows. My trousers were secondhand and worn and I had army boots on my feet. I had taken great pains to assemble this outfit to wear for my first step onto American soil. I had imagined that soldiers in America were the wealthiest most important men in the country since they were always carefree and happy. Most of my life I had been in circumstances of worry. I wanted to be like them.

It was several hours before we could be taken to the dock. Mula and I passed the time playing a button game when we returned to the bay. I later found out in America it was called tiddledywinks. Finally our names were called and we went to the deck and were led to a large building where there were hundreds of people waiting in line. There were people in red jackets assisting immigrants to find transportation and their waiting sponsors.

Our eyes met before I knew it was Uncle Max. But I knew that the man looked familiar. He and my mother resembled each other. "Mama, it's Uncle Max." I pointed in the direction where he was standing. People had stepped in front of me and I lost sight of him.

"Max, Max . . . we're over here," my mother shouted, trying to be heard above the echoing buzz in the hall. "Over here," she held her hand up and waved.

Max heard her voice and ran toward the waving hand. "Rosela, Rosela," he said over and over again. I liked him immediately. He turned and saw my father. "Leon," he grabbed and hugged my father.

Max was very tall, almost six two, with gray curly hair and metal wire-rimmed glasses. He wore a nice wool tweed overcoat with a wool muffler wrapped around the collar. His white shirt was starched and pressed and he wore a bow tie.

I put my hand out to shake his hand when my parents introduced me. Sergeant Mitchell had told me that in America, most of the time men shook hands when they met each other. "I'm Schaja, Uncle Max."

"You are a grown boy, Schaja," he held my hand and leaned down and hugged me. He hugged my brother and kissed him. He led us out of the building and I admired how he walked with assurance in the midst of all of the chaos.

I could hardly believe we were finally here. I thought about the many horrors we had left across the ocean. It seemed far away now. This was a new life.

When we walked out the door of the building it was snowing. Even the snowflakes were more magnificent in America. The soft glow of the street lamps gave a surreal look to the streets as we walked to my uncle's car. It was a brand-new Buick that was immaculate. Even with the soft dusting of snow on the car it looked like a picture out of a magazine.

The drive to Salem, Massachusetts, was like a dream for me. When we got into the car, he turned on the headlamps of the car that gave a soft glow onto the street ahead of him. I had never seen or been in a car like his before. As we drove through the streets there were colored lights strung everywhere, evergreen trees decorated with colored balls and more lights. It was the most dazzling display of lights and colors that I had ever seen.

"Uncle Max, what is that blinking colored sign in that window?" I asked as we passed by an eating establishment.

"That's a neon sign, Schaja," he said in Yiddish.

"What's neon?" I asked.

"It's a gas that gives light. I don't know how but it's the newest thing in advertising. The town is especially beautiful right now with all the decorations for the Christmas season."

When we drove up to my uncle's apartment building, I saw a big sign draped across the yard above the entrance. My uncle started laughing. "You see the sign? It says in English, "Welcome to America!" He translated to us in Yiddish. We all felt very special because everyone in my uncle's apartment building was waiting to welcome us to our new home.

As soon as we walked in the door and hugged Aunt Sara, she told us to take our shoes off. None of us understood exactly the reason until we walked into the living room and saw the plush three-inch-thick white carpeting. The slightest speck of dirt would show on this luxurious floor. I started laughing when I saw that everyone else was in their stocking feet also. The house was immaculate; some of the furnishings were covered in plastic.

Mula and I sat down on the sofa and started to slide on the plastic. We thought it was a good game until my father told us to sit still.

Aunt Sara was an excellent cook and she had prepared what looked like more food than we had eaten during our entire life in Lithuania. The dining room table was covered with huge platters of food. There was roast chicken, roast turkey, a brisket of beef, freshly baked rye bread, latkes, applesauce, sour cream, a dish with carrots and raisins, pickles, puddings, pies, and cakes. We sat around the room in the dining room chairs that were placed against the wall to allow people to fill their plates from the table.

After I finished feasting, I went into the living room area. My parents were chatting with Uncle Max and Aunt Sara. After a while Uncle Max went over to a mahogany box sitting against the wall and turned some buttons on the front of the box. To my amazement, a picture came across the screen at the front of the box. It was a man's face and he was talking. My uncle adjusted the volume with another knob and we could suddenly hear the man's voice as if he were in the room with us. In fact, he seemed to be talking directly to me. My mouth dropped open and my uncle started laughing at my confused shock.

"It's called television, Schaja. The program is called *John Cameron Swayze and the News*. It comes on every night at this time."

No one in my family uttered a word and everyone in the room glued their eyes on the box. Even though Mula, my mother and father, and I didn't understand what the man was saying, we watched as raptly as the others. John Cameron Swayze was talking very rapidly and then suddenly his face left the picture and a pack of cigarettes appeared on the screen with a lady standing in the picture. I was completely mesmerized by now.

"This is a commercial. It's for Lucky Strike cigarettes."

This country had one delightful surprise after another for me. I could not believe that we had landed in such a paradise. I reached into my pocket and rubbed my rabbit's foot. I wanted this good luck to continue. After the news everyone got up and went back to the dining room for coffee and pastries. I stayed behind. My curiosity had gotten the best of me. I walked over to this puzzling box with the magic pictures and looked behind the box at the wires that plugged into the wall and another that attached itself to a V-shaped apparatus on top of the TV. I leaned down and looked to see if there was an opening on the floor for the pictures to somehow jump onto the screen. I was mystified about this box and couldn't begin to comprehend how it worked.

After the neighbors left we all stayed up until the wee hours of the morning. My parents had countless stories to tell. Then Uncle Max made many phone calls to other relatives in the United States. My parents chatted to each of them.

Finally, Aunt Sara took Mula and me to the bedroom where we would sleep. When I fell into bed it was a soft and comfortable mattress and felt like a cloud. Somehow it seemed right that America would have beds that felt like a soft and comfortable cloud. When she left the room and started to close the door, I asked her to leave it open just a little crack. I fell asleep with a smile on my face.

THIRTY-SEVEN

The next morning when I opened my eyes, I smelled the aroma of coffee and I heard chattering going on in the kitchen. I jumped out of bed and quickly dressed to join everyone in the kitchen. I tiptoed out of the room since Mula was still sleeping.

"Good morning, young man," Uncle Max said, smiling. "Sit down and have some breakfast."

Aunt Sara already had a place set for me. She had prepared another feast. Orange juice, milk, a cereal called Shredded Wheat, bagels, lox, cream cheese, scrambled eggs, and pancakes. I tried everything. I had never seen anything like this before.

Uncle Max showed me how to eat pancakes. He piled three of the thin cakes on my plate. Then he took ample slices of butter and placed them between each warm cake and poured syrup over the top. I ate every single bite and wiped the sweet syrup off the plate with each warm and scrumptious bite.

He then placed a biscuitlike item in a bowl. Shredded Wheat. I started to pick it up and eat it like a cookie.

"No, no, Schaja, you pour milk over it and sprinkle sugar on the top."

I did as he said. This was different from anything I had ever tasted. Then I had a bagel with cream cheese. It was the first bagel I had ever tasted.

"All of this food is from Schussels," he said proudly.

We all looked at him; we had no idea what a Schussels was.

"Schussels is the finest gourmet deli in Salem," he said. "We will go there and you will see."

Mula came in and sat down next to me. Uncle Max went through the same demonstration he had done for me.

When I finished my breakfast, Aunt Sara handed me a paper sack. "Schaja, go to your luggage and throw your clothes into this sack. We will buy you some new things today."

I was very attached to my clothing and I hesitated to throw most of them away. These tattered and frayed clothes were very much a part of me. I couldn't quite let go of my past so quickly. I folded the clothes and placed them in that sack but I kept them in the closet. I insisted that I wear the jacket that Sergeant Mitchell had given me even though it was too big.

The phone began ringing early that morning. Relatives were inviting us to dinners, lunches, and arranging for cousins to meet Mula and me. Everyone wanted to come and meet us.

Uncle Max came into the room after one of the phone calls. "The newspaper wants to interview you and take some pictures. You are Salem's first refugees from the war."

This was a mysterious thing to me. Why would they want to talk to people that didn't even speak English? It hadn't dawned on me that we would become a subject of curiosity. I didn't realize how much America was removed from life in the camp and that people were only just now finding out about the cruelties of Hitler.

The thought of having a photograph taken was a painful experience for me. I was very shy and had learned that being the focal point in any instance was dangerous. But arrangements were made for the reporter to come to Uncle Max's house for the interview.

"Time for everyone to get a haircut," Uncle Max ordered after he hung up the phone with the reporter. We all went out to his car and I was lucky enough to ride in the front seat next to my Uncle Max. I had never ridden in the front seat of an automobile. I watched as Uncle Max turned the knobs and pulled on the choke as he started up the car. I saw the lights on the dashboard indicating different information to Uncle Max. With little effort Max moved the gearshift, and backed the car up and made it dart smoothly in and out of traffic. At the same time he was operating this intricate machine, he was laughing and talking with us. I thought he must be a genius.

We stopped in front of one store and my mother and Aunt Sara got out of the car. They were going to visit the beauty shop.

Our next stop was the barbershop. My uncle pulled up in front of a store that had a glass window and a red, white, and blue post next to the door that turned in circles. There were two men standing in the shop. They were standing in front of chairs that were high and leaned back to a bowl that was deep; water came out of a long hose with a funny nozzle on the end. They had a variety of shears and scissors and creams. The two men greeted us like we were royalty. They had a long conversation with Max about the type of haircuts we should be given.

The barber then threw a long, white, sheet-type material around me and leaned the chair back and used the water in the hose and nozzle to wash my hair. He lathered my head and scrubbed my scalp. He rinsed the soap off and dried my hair. With a comb, electric clippers, and scissors he gave me an American-style haircut. It was short and neat, close to my ears with a little length at the top so I could comb it to the side. After he had clipped and combed my hair, he took the white sheet off of me and with a large brush cleaned the hair off of my neck. He then showed me how to wet my hair every morning and how it should be combed the proper way. When I looked at myself in the mirror I looked more like the kids I had seen on the streets in Salem. Mula, my father, and I became Americanized that afternoon.

After everyone was given their haircut, we got back into the car and drove to Schussels, the deli. It seemed to be a big event when we walked in the door. The store was very busy, but many of the people began to stare at us when the owner announced who we were. I kept my eyes to the floor not understanding what was going on, but I was completely swallowed by the enticing aroma of fresh pastries and warm coffee. After our welcoming applause died down, I cast my eyes toward the glass-paneled shelves filled with food. It was more food than I had ever seen in my life. No matter where I looked there was another platter of items to choose from. Everything looked delicious, but I was still full from my marathon breakfast.

"I will order you a Coca-Cola, Schaja. This is America's most celebrated beverage. It's sweet and it tastes the best right out of an ice-cold bottle."

A lady came over with four bottles of Coca-Cola on a tray. The bottles were sleek and wavy with a light green tint. My uncle took each bottle and popped the top off. I watched a few bubbles rise to the top and then dissipate. I wrapped my lips around the top of the bottle, anxious to take a nice, big gulp of this dark, sweet potion. I was startled as the sweet fizzy taste. It burned my throat on the way down. I thought it was disgusting, and it tasted like medicine. I wondered what all the fuss was about Coca-Cola. Maybe you had to get used to this burning sensation that the bubbles have when you swallow. I couldn't imagine how anyone could drink Coca-Cola if they don't have to. But I didn't want to disappoint my uncle and I continued to drink the stuff. He, Mula, and my father all looked like they were enjoying the drink.

Our next stop was the men's store near my uncle's gasoline station. It was called Sylvan's and they had all sizes, from Mula's size to my father's size. My uncle bought us suits, shirts, ties, denim jeans and khaki pants, and shoes that were reddish brown in color.

The following day the reporter came to interview us and take a picture for the newspaper. My uncle translated the questions and answers. It took more than an hour to conduct the interview. I was praying that they didn't ask me any questions.

The next morning I heard everyone in the kitchen oohing and aahing. I got out of bed to join them and they were all looking at the newspaper. Our photographs were in the paper and we all looked very distinguished. The headline across the page was about us being survivors of the German concentration camp in Lithuania. It was a lengthy article that my uncle read and translated for us.

Now when we walked down the streets in Salem people would turn and look at us. Some would point their fingers and whisper. Someone said we were "local celebrities." I wasn't sure if I liked the attention.

Thirty-eight

On Sunday morning we all piled into Uncle Max's car again and headed out to a suburb called Newton. We were going to visit our relatives, the Shaffers. When we pulled up to the house I knew immediately that they were wealthy. This was a very upscale neighborhood. I gawked at the sweeping, well-manicured lawn in front of their home. When I walked into the spacious and stately manor, I realized that Mr. Shaffer must be a very successful man in America. The Shaffers had never met Mula and me before but they were warm and friendly and embraced us as though we were their immediate family.

My parents talked to them about Lithuania and where the Shaffer family had once lived. They listened intently to every detail of our experiences during the war. After several hours of conversation we were taken into a room with high ceilings and large oil paintings hanging on the walls. One wall was a massive fireplace that you could almost walk into. The table, even though it was very large, was dwarfed by the massive size of the room. By the time we ate dinner there were about twenty of our relatives sitting at the table.

We were served lunch by people in black-and-white uniforms that worked for the Shaffers. There were many courses served during the meal, one more delectable than the last. Everyone was talking at once. I was seated next to a distant cousin, Jack, who was several years older than I was and he did not speak Lithuanian. However, I could hear others speaking my language and I joined in occasionally.

For dessert we had fresh, warm chocolate éclairs that were passed around the table. As I sunk my teeth into the warm custard and melting chocolate, I thought about Ignatz and the first éclair that I had ever eaten. For the second time since we arrived, I thought how far away the past already seemed now that we were in America.

"What about Isaiah?" someone asked.

"Too biblical," another answered.

"What about Samuel?" another said.

"We need American names," Uncle Max answered. "Bob, Ted, Johnny."

"No, more sophisticated," someone piped in.

"How about Sidney or Stanley?" one of my reletives said.

"That's it! They'll sound like bankers," Uncle Max said and laughed. "Schaja will be called Sidney, and Mula will be called Stanley. And we'll shorten your last name to Shachnow. Shachnowski is too many letters. Americans don't like that."

He then took a piece of paper and wrote out the names, Sidney and Stanley Shachnow. He looked up at my parents. "And you are Rose and Leon Shachnow, father and mother of Sidney and Stanley Shachnow!" Everyone at the table broke out in laughter. Then suddenly everyone lifted their wineglasses and made a toast. I assumed this was the ritual to seal our Americanization.

I looked over at my mother questioningly. "Schnidnay," I said my name for the first time.

"Sidney," my mother pronounced succinctly.

"My name is Sidney," I said. It was easy the second time.

"My name is Stanley," my brother said, copying me.

"The kids at school will probably call you Stan and Sid," Uncle Max said.

The thought of school abruptly shattered my euphoria. But later, after a family discussion, it was decided that Mula and I should wait to enroll in school at least a couple of months. They said we needed time to adjust. I didn't care what the reason was, I was glad I didn't have to go to school.

I went to work the next week in my uncle's Texaco gasoline service station and garage. I worked with his mechanic, Benny. Benny was a veteran of World War II. He learned his trade as a mechanic in the U.S. Army. Benny was not highly educated, but he had a great deal of common sense. He liked me from the start and took me under his wing. He painstakingly taught me phrases in English I needed to know when I waited on customers and taught me how to pump gas and make change in American money.

Uncle Max's station was a booming business. It had increased since the article in the newspaper about our escape from the concentration camp. Customers recognized my face from the picture in the newspaper and gawked at me when I filled their gas tanks and washed their windows. But it could have been about the way I wore my hat, pulled down over my head with my ears sticking out horizontally. This was the only way I could hear the customers clearly and stay warm.

One day a man pulled up in a station wagon. He told me to check the oil. While I was standing at the window looking at him trying to determine what he had said, he politely repeated his request. Sitting in the backseat was a young girl who looked at me and smiled. I thought she was laughing because I didn't understand English, so I smiled back. I went inside the station and asked my uncle about the oil question. He explained what the man needed and I went back outside and checked the dipstick. This girl in the backseat smiled even more when I came to the window and told the man that I had looked at the dipstick and he didn't need any oil. Now he had a hard time understanding my broken English. The girl laughed again. When they drove off I could see that she was still laughing. I had no idea at the time that this happy girl, Arlene, would become my future wife. She explained to me many years later that she wasn't laughing at my English, she was laughing at the way I wore my cap and the way it made me look. When I asked how it made me look, she answered, "Stupid."

During my spare time, Benny taught me about an internal combustion engine. I helped him on minor repairs in between gasoline fill-ups. My uncle spent all day long in the station office listening to his favorite radio programs. Benny and I both knew never to interrupt Uncle Max when *The Lone Ranger* was playing. He did not want to be disturbed.

Sometimes when business was slow, we would all sit and listen as the Lone Ranger and his sidekick, Tonto, saved the day. Then my uncle would rave about the Lone Ranger being a hero like no other in the world. Uncle Max was so convincing, it seemed like he knew the Lone Ranger personally. I sometimes wondered if the Lone Ranger lived in Salem.

Four months after being in the United States, Uncle Max and my father took Stanley and me to a local school. The principal and my uncle discussed how we should begin our education. I was a seventeen-year-old boy who needed to start learning at the second-grade level. Stanley was now eleven and he could begin in the lower grades without a problem. The principal explained that there was a system in the United States that required credits and courses to be taken in order to graduate. I had none of these needed requirements and yet I was almost at an age to graduate.

Finally it was decided that I would begin my education in the eighth grade, after the principal consulted with the school superintendent of Salem and the other school staff members. A test program was put in place at the school for Stanley and me. We would spend half of the day at school being privately tutored in mathematics, English, and U.S. history by teachers who volunteered to help us. The other half of the day would be spent in the classroom with other students, in my case eighth-grade students. Stanley was placed in the fourth grade.

Since I was not accustomed to formal schooling other than the short time I was in the German school, I realized that what came naturally to the students at Staltonstall Elementary was foreign to me. My lack of understanding when trying to accomplish the simplest tasks in school turned out to be a trying event for me. Learning English, social skills, math, history, playground etiquette, civics, and social studies became a mass of confusion. I had homework every night that took me three times the amount of time and effort that it would require of a normal student. However, I was learning English rapidly because I was forced to speak it daily. Stanley progressed much more rapidly academically and socially.

Stanley and I ate our lunch together in the school cafeteria, usually by ourselves, since we didn't fit in socially with the other children. It was a relief to speak to someone I knew.

At recess one day during the spring, I was crouched down against the red brick wall, watching the eighth graders play games. It was a game where the ball was thrown in the air and someone caught it when another person shouted out a name.

"Hey, I'm Bernard," he said and looked at me. "You wanna play?"

"Yeah," I answered and walked over to the circle of kids. "I'm Sidney."

The others looked at me as though they were trying to keep from laughing. Then a guy threw the ball in the air and yelled "Bill" and another kid ran and caught the ball before it hit the ground. I had no idea what the rules were or who was supposed to catch the ball. I didn't understand what shouting out a name meant. I found out much later if your name was called then you were supposed to catch the ball.

"Sid," one of the players called out. I turned around and looked and I didn't know who had said my name. The ball in the air hit the ground. Everyone started laughing. I smiled, too, going along with the crowd. I had discovered that if you smiled in America when you didn't understand something it made things easier.

The ball was tossed again. "Sid," a voice said. I still didn't catch on and watched the ball fall to the ground. Everyone started laughing. Next thing I knew they were calling Sid each time and broke into peals of laughter when the ball hit the ground. Finally it dawned on me that I was supposed to catch the ball! I was so embarrassed, I could feel my cheeks burning and my anger rising and quickly turn to fury.

Bernard was making fun of me and pointing at me. "What a retard," he said. "He's stupid!"

I didn't understand what he had called me until later, but I knew I was being ridiculed. I walked up to him and punched him in the nose. I was bigger than he was and the power of the punch did some damage. I saw blood streaming from his nose.

"What happened here?" a teacher asked appearing in seconds.

I stood silently. The other kids said I had beat up Bernard. The teacher jerked me by the arm and took me to the principal's office. I knew that I was in big trouble. I sat in a state of anxiety while I waited for the principal. When he arrived in his office we couldn't communicate because of the language barrier. He picked up the phone and called Uncle Max. I felt the heat creeping up my neck, embarrassed that my uncle had to be involved.

Within minutes, my uncle walked in the door of the principal's office.

He gave me a harsh look. He and the principal walked out of the office together to discuss the playground incident.

"The principal is very concerned about your behavior. It is not acceptable in this school. I want you to apologize to the young man you hit and you must never, never do that again to anyone," my uncle said sternly after they returned. He was leaning down and peering into my face. "And if this behavior is ever repeated at this school, the principal will kick you out and have you sent back to Lithuania."

Those last words put the fear of God into me. The thought of returning to Lithuania and the Communists, alone, without my family, was horrifying. It was the first and last fight I had in school. I heard one of the kids call Bernard a brat one day on the school yard and that became my nickname for him, Bernard the brat. As my English vocabulary improved, I had some other choice names for him.

In later years, I was told that the principal had never threatened to send me back to Lithuania; my uncle just wanted to make a lasting impression.

I decided after the school yard incident that the best way to stay out of trouble was to stay busy. During recess period I studied. I kept my books with me all day and I studied every available moment. I went to the A&P grocery store and worked after school. And went to night school to learn auto mechanics. At the gas station during slow periods I studied. I stopped listening to *The Lone Ranger* with Uncle Max and instead I studied. I had a purpose now and I wanted to succeed. It paid off and I made not great, but average marks at the end of the year.

Thirty-nine

"B enny, can you teach me how to drive?" I yelled into the garage after I arrived at work. I had been looking at the newspaper and I saw an ad for a used '51 Cadillac. This car became a motivation for me.

"Kid, I can teach you everything about a car that you need to know, but I can't teach you how to drive one because I don't have one myself," he said and went into a coughing fit. His cough was raspy, like a grating sound.

"You might want to ask your uncle about teaching you," he smiled, as he thought about it. "But I'm not too sure he wants anyone but him driving that Buick. He came in here one afternoon with a sad look on his face," Benny continued. "He got a scratch from another car in the parking lot at the grocery store. That's his baby. I thought he was going to cry."

I started to save my money. I had two goals for the summer: I wanted to learn how to drive and buy a car. I worked three jobs that summer, one at the A&P, another at the gas station, and a paper route. I still gave a portion of my earnings to my parents, but I saved as much as I could for my car.

After what seemed like an eternity, I finally had enough to pay for a cheap used car. There was only one problem remaining: I had not yet persuaded my uncle to teach me to drive. Each day I begged, but he was less than enthusiastic. But through my persistence, he finally gave in. He taught me to drive in his small tow truck that was used to pick up disabled vehicles and bring them to the station. I never got to drive his new car. After many trials and tribulations, I learned how to drive and acquired my driver's license.

The day I got my license I bought a used black '37 Dodge from one of my uncle's customers. It wasn't the '51 Cadillac that I had dreamed about, but it was the first car that the Shachnow family had ever owned. When I drove it home and pulled up in front of my uncle's house, my mother, father, and Stanley came out to take a look. We all piled into the car and I made my first legal drive downtown to the ice cream shop. I showed them how I could parallel park. They were all impressed. When we got home, even though the car was clean, I washed and polished it again. Each morning, I would polish and shine my prized possession before I left for work.

During the summer, my parents found a small apartment for the four of us. We lived on the ground level of this home and the owner and his wife lived on the second level. Behind the house was a barn with a horse and wagon.

Barney Gold, our landlord, was a very friendly man. He told me about his year-round independent business. He delivered heating oil year-round and ice in the summer. Soon after we moved in, Barney replaced the horse and wagon with an oil truck. He also arranged the yard so I could park my car next to his oil wagon.

My new school was a couple of blocks from where we lived. Pickering School. It was a more relaxed atmosphere and the students were much friendlier. I continued in the eighth grade. My grasp of the language was still limited, but I could usually understand more than I could speak or write.

One morning during the fall semester, I decided that I would drive my car to school, even though it was only a three-minute walk. I parked the car and went into class with the other students. When the school day was almost over, a lady from the office came into my classroom to talk to the teacher. The class was working on diagramming a sentence and everyone was quiet.

"We've been searching all day for the person that owns a black Dodge. Do you have any idea whose car this might be?" the lady asked my teacher. "If we don't find the owner before the bell rings, I guess we'll just have to have it towed away. It's awfully expensive for the school to have to pay for a tow away."

Since I was sitting on the first row of class, I overheard their conversation. I stepped up to my teacher's desk, feeling like I was probably in trouble again and on my way back to Lithuania. "Ma'am, are you talking about a '37 Dodge?" I asked sheepishly.

"Yes," she turned to me. "Do you know anything about that car?"

"It's mine," I said.

My teacher's mouth dropped open. "You have a car? You brought it to school?"

"Yes, ma'am. Did I do something wrong?"

"Well," the lady put her hands on her hips. "You parked it in a loading zone, young man. We've been trying to find the driver all day. Didn't you read the sign?"

I looked down at the floor, embarrassed. I didn't even see a sign. "I'm sorry. I'll move it right away." I rushed outside and parked my car in a legal space. I cursed at myself as I walked to the car. I was frustrated. I couldn't keep up with the verbs, pronouns, nouns, adjectives, and prepositions of this difficult language and I couldn't even park in the right space. I was convinced that Bernard the brat was right! I was stupid! I was the butt of many jokes after this incident.

Later in the year, I began to make friends with a few guys on the football team. I sat on the bleachers and watched them work out and practice after school. I had never played organized sports, but it looked like an exciting, rough, and rugged game. I had also noticed that the boys who played football were always very popular in school.

"Hey, Shachnow, you wanna try out for the team?" Al Andrews asked.

He was one of my new friends.

"I don't know how to play," I answered.

"It's easy," he said. "All you have to do is catch the ball and run for the goal line. We can teach you the rules."

"Okay," I answered. I felt a sense of euphoria at being invited to join the team.

"Come to the locker room tomorrow after school. You'll suit up and the coach will check you out."

The next day, after school, I showed up at the gym. The coach was standing in the middle of the locker room. He didn't say anything at first. He looked me over from head to toe. "You could put on a little muscle, son. You're tall enough, but skinny."

"Yes, sir," I answered. "I sack groceries and carry the bags four nights a week." I thought I had muscles, at least on my arms.

"In the legs," he said.

"I'm fast," I answered quickly.

He went over to his office and brought out pants, shoulder pads, and a shirt in the school colors of crimson and cream. The number twenty-three was on the back with WILDCATS in print over the number.

On the field I was taller than most of the boys. It was easy for me to spot and catch the passes they threw. I had an advantage in the end zone. I practiced with the team for several days and the coach told me I could play in a warm-up game and if I played well I would make the Pickering School football team.

On the day of the warm-up game I was pumped up. The other team players and I spent the day talking about the game. The adrenaline was flowing. I knew three plays and those three plays would be called during the game.

I asked my father to come to the game. He was at home most of the time during the day since he hadn't been able to find a job.

When the game started all the kids in school had gathered on the outdoor bleachers. I saw Papa standing to the side of the stands. I waved at him, but he didn't see me.

I sat on the bench when the game started. Finally, in the second half the coach motioned for me to go in. In the huddle, the quarterback called for one of my designated plays.

At the line of scrimmage, he called out the numbers and handed the ball off to me. When he shoved the pigskin in my hands, I began to run. I made ten yards, enough for a first down. I looked up in the bleachers beside the field and I heard people yelling and rooting us on. I looked over at Papa and he was smiling.

On the last play of the game, we were trailing 6-0 and were on the forty-yard line of our opponent. The quarterback again called the number of one of my plays. We went to the line of scrimmage and he called the snap. I started running down the field. He dropped back and passed the ball. I watched as the ball sailed through the air and landed in my arms. I was twenty yards from the goal line. I ran as fast and furious as I could and I passed the goal line. As I crossed the white line, I heard the local crowd screaming and yelling. I made the only touchdown of the game.

I held the ball in the end zone, and the entire team ran onto the field and charged up to me. They slapped me on the back, jumped up and down, and screamed and hollered. I was suddenly a hero and everyone was drunk with delight. With the extra point, we had won the game 7-6.

Pa got caught up in the excitement along with the others. He came over and slapped me on the back and hugged me!

The next day at school everyone was saying hello, the guys were congratulating me and shaking my hand. The girls even took notice of me for the first time. I started to feel accepted in my new school. I daydreamed of winning sports letters and trophies. I was sure that someday my picture would be on the front page of the sports section.

Just as my dreams were beginning to solidify, I was met with defeat. The coach pulled me aside, after a routine locker room pep talk one day. He had a very serious look on his face.

"Shachnow," he started off. "I think you have a lot of potential as a football player. You have a very good way of working with the team and I think that you will make a fine citizen some day in the United States."

Because of his serious expression I knew there was something more.

"I'm proud to have coached you, but there's been a complaint by another school. It turns out that you are too old to play in this league," he said, looking at me sadly. "I'm sorry, kid, but those are the rules."

I returned my gear to him and walked out of the locker room, stunned. I had my brief moment of acceptance and it felt good. But now, I felt like I had been punched in the stomach. I had been on such an emotional high for the last several weeks and this was a big letdown.

I went home that night in a defeated mood. My parents felt defeated also. They had not been able to find jobs after looking for months. Our land of opportunity seemed limited. We were on the outside looking in and were uncertain of how to continue. We all sat and ate our dinner in silence.

————

I went to the school yard in the afternoons late, after my paper route. There were older kids from the neighborhood who played softball on the baseball diamond. Each day they would choose up sides. I watched as they played for several days, but no one picked me for their team.

"Hi, I'm Sam Zoll," a guy said to me after a couple of weeks of watching. I hadn't seen him approach the bleachers. He swung onto the bleacher and sat down next to me.

"Sid Shachnow," I said, extending my hand.

"You know how to play?" he asked, nodding toward the field.

"Yeah, sort of," I answered. "I've been watching for a while."

"Want to play second base?" he asked.

"Sure," I said.

Sam briefly explained what my position required. My English was still broken, but I understood most of what he said. The first person to come to bat was Frank Theriault. Frank was one of the best hitters on the opposing team. He always hit the ball and tried to stretch it out. He'd steal bases and take chances to make a single into a double or a triple.

Frank hit a high ball that arced up in the air and came straight down toward me. I tried to position myself to catch it, but it went over my head and out to the left fielder. The outfielder caught it and threw it to me. At the same moment I felt the ball hit my hand and glove, I felt Frank sliding into second base and hit me at my knees. My knees buckled and my face slapped hard into the ground.

When I got up I was still holding the ball and the referee called Frank out. I looked down and saw blood all over my shirt. My nose was broken.

"Frank, what the hell, you think you're in the big leagues?" one of the boys said as he ran up to me at second base. "You okay?" he asked, and looked at my bleeding nose.

I shrugged. "Sure."

"Here, here are some Kleenexes. Hold your head back and put pressure on your nose," Sam Zoll said, running up with the tissues.

"Hey, I'm sorry you fell," Frank said after a while.

"It's okay," I said and smiled, holding my head back.

They all walked with me back to my house. I thanked them for the game and went inside and put cold water on a cloth and pressed it to my nose.

"What did you do to your nose?" Stanley asked as he watched me in the bathroom.

"Broke it," I said.

"Does it hurt?" he asked, staring up at me.

"Nah, it's nothin'," I answered. I told him the story about catching the ball and making an out.

After supper that evening there was a knock at the door. When I opened the door all the kids from the baseball game were standing on our porch.

"We wanted to see if you were okay," Sam said.

"How's the nose? I'm really sorry," Frank added.

"It's okay. Don't worry," I answered. "You want to come in?"

"Nah, we just wanted to know if you could go down to the corner to Eaton's," Albie, the catcher, asked.

"What's Eaton's?" I asked.

"Our hangout at Moody Square," Sam answered. "It's the drugstore."

From that time on I was a part of the Moody Square Gang. Being accepted socially was a help to me. I felt better about school and studying.

Me as a toddler, not a clue as to what would be my fate.

Shachnowski family photo *(from left to right)*: My father, Leon; my mother, Rose, my uncle Abraham, my grandmother Rochel, my uncle Willie, my aunt Frida, my aunt Leni (Uncle Willie's wife), and the dapper individual in the striped jacket is me.

(Above) My mother and me before the war, walking on the main street in Kaunas. We all lived in harmony, not at all expecting what was in store.

(Right) Me, shortly before the start of the war.

(*Above*) Me, my mother, and my brother, Mula, shortly after liberation from the Nazis.

(*Right*) My uncle Abraham and his wife, Tilli, before the war. Both were murdered shortly after the Nazis invaded.

(*Above, left*) Me, shortly after the war.

(*Above, right*) Arlene and me on a bench in Germany shortly after we were married.

RECEPTION STATION

COMPANY A 12·4 FORT DIX N. J. JANUARY 13 1955

A photo taken of my company during my first week in the U.S. Army at Fort Dix, New Jersey. I am sitting in the first row, third from the left. This was the beginning of what would be a forty-year military career.

A photo of me taken shortly after the fight in Junction City. You can still see the black eye.

Me and Arlene in Fort Dix. Is she not beautiful?

Me holding LeeAnne with Arlene. Both women are dolls.

(Clockwise) Parched, dry ground leading to my first tour in Vietnam at Special Forces Camp An Long.

Sergeant Stevens, Intelligence, who collected and analyzed information from the villagers.

Nurses who gave us information on the VC for money.

Sergeant McRae, the most senior NCO, standing over our cook, Don, giving the "best" instructions on how to carve meat.

Sergeant Wiggington, our medic, taking care of the villagers and children.

Sergeant Donald, Weapons, was the hardest worker in the detachment and also the oldest member.

Sergeant Keating, Demolitions, with his ever-present cigar—even in combat!

(Center) French-born Sergeant Uzikow, Heavy Weapons sergeant.

(Clockwise from top left) Me with my firstborn daughter, Shereen.

Relinquishing command of Det A in Berlin, one of the rare times when we were actually in uniform. We normally wore civilian clothes.

Just after landing in the Soviet Kaserne Karl Horst in Berlin. This was the first time a U.S. helicopter landed in this Soviet compound. The cold war was over!

Retired General Bill Yarborough, the most visionary commander in Special Forces, and my wife, Arlene. He took an interest in me as a young officer and remains a dear friend.

(Clockwise from top left) The main artery intersection in the Berlin subterranean system that handled the sewage and rainwater. Going there got me a letter of reprimand.

Walter Momper, Mayor of West Berlin, me, and General John Shalikashvili, in Berlin.

A small, solemn ceremony deactivating Det A in Berlin. Special Forces came quietly to Berlin and left quietly thirty-nine years later.

Presenting an award to General Jörg Schönbohm, who was responsible for merging the East German Army and the West German Army, and deactivating East German forces after reunification.

(Clockwise from top left) The Commander-in-Chief, President Bill Clinton, and me at the closing ceremony of the U.S. Command in Berlin after the fall of the Berlin Wall.

Me with the Chairman of the Joint Chiefs of Staff, General Henry H. Shelton (2001).

Me and Arlene with Deputy Secretary of Defense Paul Wolfowitz.

(From left to right): My daughter LeeAnne, my daughter Shereen, Mirjam Zaborskieni (a fellow survivor from the Kovno concentration camp), my wife, Arlene, and me.

FORTY

Mrs. Mary Barry was my favorite teacher at Salem High School. She was a heavy-set lady in her fifties; a strict disciplinarian, but she also had a great sense of humor. She was standing at the front of the classroom when the bell sounded at 8:00 A.M. I rushed in the door seconds later and sat down at my desk in front of her. She looked at me with arched eyebrows. "Mr. Shachnow, I'd like for you to come see me after school," she said sternly.

It was not a request, but a demand. All through the day, I wondered what I could have done wrong. No one was asked to stay after class unless they were in trouble. Sam, Albie, Frank, and I spent the lunch hour trying to figure out what I had done to deserve this meeting.

"Thank you for coming, Sid," Mrs. Barry said when I appeared at the door. She was sitting at her desk making notes.

"Sid, how are you and your family adjusting to America?" she asked.

"Pretty good, Mrs. Barry. My father has been looking for a job. He's an engineer, but he doesn't speak English well. It makes it difficult for him to find a job. But we're all grateful to be here in America."

"Do you want to be successful here in America?" Mrs. Barry baited me with this question.

"Yes, ma'am," I answered.

"Do you think you will be successful if you don't apply yourself to a goal?" She looked down at me as I sat at the desk.

"Well, no ma'am. But I work very hard if that's what you mean by applying myself."

She shook her head after I said this. "I know you work hard, and I know that you have a busy social life with your friends. I also know you haven't had many breaks in life, but this is all the more reason for what I am going to tell you."

I listened intently. I did have respect for this teacher.

"You are going to flunk my class," she said flatly.

I felt like I had been kicked in the head. I had no idea I was doing so badly. And I desperately needed to finish the tenth grade if I was ever going to graduate.

"You know I wouldn't flunk you if I didn't know that you were far more capable," she said staring at me.

"I'm not very smart, Mrs. Barry," I answered humbly.

"That is a lie! Nonsense! You are very smart and very industrious. But you don't apply yourself. You think you can't learn and therefore you give up before you've even given yourself a chance," she lectured. "You are much smarter than you think you are. Now, young man, correct your thinking and you will solve the problem and graduate."

"How?"

"Getting motivated. Now, would you be willing to work with me after school? And perhaps some other teachers also?"

"Yes," I said emphatically.

"Okay, I'll have a schedule prepared for you in the morning. I'll give you what you need, but you have to stick with it . . . understand?"

"Yes, ma'am," I said and left.

I had to drive fast to get to my current job on time. I had been promoted to stock boy at the A&P. I thought about what my teacher had said as I drove. I felt depressed that I was doing so poorly, but I also felt inspired that my teachers were willing to help me. I wasn't quite buying what she said about being smart. But, who knows, maybe she was right!

After work, I didn't feel like going home. I caught up with my friends at Eaton's drugstore. They were busy clowning around in the street when I arrived. Rocky Sullivan was joking with Albie. Rocky was one of the wildest kids in our school. He was always getting into trouble, but was a very likable guy. He was slim with sharp features and his hair was a little long at the collar and slicked back.

"Hey, Shachnow, wanna go to the orchard and lift some apples?" he said with a mischievous grin. "Remember, an apple a day keeps the doc away."

I smiled back at him, as he did a slide with his shoes and screeched to a stop in front of me. We all piled into Frank's Chevrolet Bel-Air and drove to the orchard.

The orchard was part of an estate protected by a tall, imposing stone wall. The grounds were impeccably manicured with a beautiful stone mansion that sat in the distance surrounded by large bouquets of shrubbery. We had snatched apples before from this orchard, usually at night. Today, it was dusk, not completely dark.

I volunteered to go over the wall. They piled into a human pyramid and I stepped on their backs and hoisted myself over the wall. I jumped to the ground on the other side. As my feet hit the ground, I looked up and saw a speeding form, pounding its way toward me. A barking, growling, bared-toothed German Shepherd dog. I catapulted myself back over the wall before the dog could reach me. I couldn't tell you to this day how I was able to ascend myself. But at the time, I was sure this was what Mrs. Barry meant about motivation.

"Jeez," Frank said standing on the ground as I sailed over the wall. "What's Shachnow doing coming over the wall?"

They all stood in awe as I jumped down. "How'd you do that?" Rocky asked, stunned.

I was gasping for breath. I could hear the German Shepherd growling, snarling, and hurling himself against the wall. I pointed in the direction of the noise. "German Shepherd."

On the way back to Eaton's my friends decided that I had performed a superhuman feat. I tried to explain the concept of motivation that got me over the wall.

FORTY-ONE

I passed the tenth grade with average marks and would attend the eleventh grade when school started in September. During the summer I traded my '37 Dodge for another car that was a little more expensive. I used my earnings from my three jobs to buy a black-and-red Oldsmobile 98. It was my pride and joy. I took a night course at Franklin Technological Institute in auto mechanics to learn everything I could about my car.

"We can't ask him to sell his car, Rose," I heard my father say as I walked in the door after class one night.

"What?" I asked.

My father looked at me with embarrassment.

"We have run out of money, Schaja," she said. She still used my original name. "We can't pay our rent. Uncle Max has given us so much, we can't ask for any more."

"What about the jewelry?" I asked.

"It's already been sold. That's what we've been living on for these months," my father answered.

"My job as a seamstress with Axelrod's clothing isn't enough," she said. "And your father can't find work."

I saw my father grimace when she said this.

"I can work more hours, or maybe find a job that pays better wages," I said, feeling the tension between them.

She nodded.

I walked over to my dad and patted him on the back. "Don't worry, you'll find something," I said.

He took my hand and held it.

This was the plight of many immigrants who arrived in the United States. It was a dreamland for most, with great hopes and aspirations, creating a new and better life when we reached the shores of opportunity. But when reality set in, learning the language and customs was not easy. It was a difficult adjustment; harder than anyone anticipated. I had learned more about Americans since I was in a school environment. But there wasn't the same opportunity for my parents. I talked about what I had learned from Mrs. Barry. She had a long-reaching affect on my psyche.

I wasn't sure if my parents understood what I was explaining. I wondered if they had already faced too much in their lives and secretly wondered if the adjustment to America would be too difficult for them.

Several weeks later, my father came in late one evening. He was smiling from ear to ear. "I have some good news to tell you!"

We all gathered around him.

"I have accepted a position at Pioneer Plastics, Inc. The big manufacturer here," he said.

We all hugged and congratulated him. His tough endurance had paid off. I felt a throb of admiration as I watched him smiling and looking confident again. He was clever, persistent, and educated. I was sure he would do very well at his new job. I was embarrassed that I had ever doubted his abilities. The gloom that had engulfed the house quickly changed to the upbeat and cheerful home of before. I was relieved that I could keep my car.

I took a new job during the summer with a fruit and vegetable vendor, Siple's Mobile Fruit and Vegetables. Mr. Siple was a solidly built, "Mac truck" type of man with a permanent scowl etched on his face. My interview with him lasted three minutes. He asked me if I was fast and strong. He needed somebody to run up and down stairs quickly with boxes and bags of fruit and vegetable deliveries. Second, he wanted someone that was polite, humble, and friendly.

I answered those two questions with a simple, "Yes, sir."

He assumed, from my appearance, that I could fill the bill.

Mr. Siple had a truck. In the enclosed back of the truck, he displayed his produce on shelves, like a grocery store. He insisted that the fruits and vegetables be lined up immaculately and took great pride in the presentation of his goods. He had a system that consisted of him going to an apartment complex, displaying his goods, and then going door to door to take orders. He usually insisted that the buyer come out and view his produce, but he also had customers that had standing orders and he would just put the produce in a box or bag and have me deliver it to them. I usually earned tips.

The job was simple and I liked meeting and greeting the customers. I also was allowed to eat the fruit for free. As a skinny, growing teenager, I had a voracious appetite and my favorite snack was bananas. I couldn't get enough of them. Mr. Siple noticed that I had eaten four or five bananas before the noon break one day.

"How many dos' banana you gonna eat?" he asked.

I looked at him guiltily.

"Lay off da bananas!"

I exercised control and 'lay'd off da bananas!' But one morning I was running late. I had studied until after midnight at an advanced course at Franklin Institute. When I came home and tried to get into my bed, my brother was already asleep and had hogged the entire bed. I had to sleep on the chair and I only managed a couple of hours of rest. When I got to work we had a heavy load of orders to deliver. I raced up and down stairs all morning. We had more than double our usual amount of customers. When Mr. Siple left to go into the apartment complex, I grabbed a banana, then another, and another and another. Then it dawned on me I had to get rid of the evidence. I threw the peels under the truck so that when we pulled away from the apartment complex, Mr. Siple would never see them.

I calmly took the orders that Mr. Siple gave to me during the morning and made my deliveries. When we were ready to leave, he turned the key to the ignition, but instead of going forward he put the gear into reverse for some strange reason. I panicked as the truck backed up and revealed the four banana peels.

I watched Mr. Siple's face turn a scarlet red. Sputtering sounds came from his throat, and gobs of spit began to fly from his mouth as he shouted at me. He looked like a rabid dog ravaging a chain link fence by the time he finished.

I couldn't understand a single word he had said. All I could do was gawk at him with my eyes as wide as saucers. The one thing that I understood clearly was that I no longer had a job. I didn't need to understand words to know that I was fired.

When we finally arrived at Mr. Siple's house he had calmed down. "I like you very much, Se-e-dney, but now I have lost confidence in you. This is why you must leave." He looked at me very sadly and walked off.

I felt lower than a snake. Why hadn't he stayed mad? At least I wouldn't have felt ashamed. I didn't like the feelings of inadequacy and stupidity. I had to do better, I thought to myself.

The rain was pounding on the roof. When I looked outside it was coming down in torrents and the clouds above were heavy and black. My mother came in the room and stood next to me.

"Schaja, why don't you go pick up your father? It will be a long walk home for him in the rain. I'm not sure if he took his raincoat and galoshes with him this morning," she said.

I went out and drove the few miles to my father's place of employment. I liked the sound of the windshield wipers, rhythmically slapping the rain off the windshield. I turned on the radio and listened to music. I saw the turn into the parking lot of the Pioneer Plastics office building. I took a right. I sat watching as a steady stream of black umbrellas filed out of the door. I didn't see my father, as my vision was obscured by the heavy rain. I pulled into a parking space and ran inside the building, leaving a trail of water on the floor.

I stopped a man near the entrance and asked where I might find Leon Shachnow. He looked at me and pointed toward the restroom. I thought my father must be using the facilities. As I approached the door and opened it I saw a man from the back in a gray cotton jumpsuit. A bucket of water sat next to him as he pushed a mop.

"Is Mr. Shachnow in here?" I asked. The man turned around and I saw it was my father. I swallowed hard and tried to make sense of this. "Pa?" I said. My father was an engineer, not a janitor. The thought raced through my head. My expression must have been worse than my thoughts. My father's proud posture drooped when he turned around. He looked at me with defeat and embarrassment.

His hurt look said it all. For the first time in my life I had never seen my father appear so fragile and vulnerable. I felt a stab in my heart, a place so tender and hidden that I cringed with emotion. I fought to find the words, but they wouldn't come.

In bungling embarrassment, Father clumsily put his things away and stood with his back to me.

"Pa, it's raining. I came to drive you home," I said softly.

He said nothing in return. He stood silently, his head bowed down.

I backed out the door of the restroom and stood for a moment. I wanted to run back inside and tell him how much I loved him. I didn't care what he did for a living. But the pain I had seen on his face was evidence enough; he couldn't speak of his humiliation.

We walked to the car in the rain without our eyes ever meeting. I didn't understand anything at this moment. All of the family had thought he was hired as an engineer. He talked about his work as though he were an engineer. I was sure, with his degree and experience, he had been placed in a senior position. How horrible it must have been for him after going through the humiliation from the Nazis to face even more humiliation and rejection in his work. My father had once been proud. He had once been respected. His father had bequeathed him with affluence. Today he was a janitor who had lived a lie to his family to avoid more humiliation. His pride had been shattered by my presence. A terrible thought then rushed through my mind: am I a stronger man than my own father? Or maybe I was a smart-ass kid who thought he knew everything.

My parents were never able to let go of their past completely. And yet that was required in our circumstance. Yesterday was forever gone and we had to learn to move forward without shame or humiliation.

I was abruptly brought back to reality when I heard the door slam and he got into the car. I started the ignition and pulled away in awkward silence. After a few minutes, I discreetly looked in his direction.

He was sitting with his back stiffened, eyes forward, and jaws clenched shut. He was trying to hide his humiliation, but I could see the teardrops streaming down his cheeks.

"I was ashamed," he whispered, and began to sob.

My gut wrenched, and my eyes welled up with tears at the sound of his agony. I put my hand on the seat toward him. He placed his hand on top of mine. We drove home in bonded silence.

FORTY-TWO

It was the first day of school, and I walked into my history class and sat down in the front row. While I waited for class to start, I turned around and looked to see if I knew anyone in the room. I stopped when I saw a girl in the back of the class. I couldn't take my eyes off of her; she had a great smile and long dark blonde hair. Her spirit and personality lit up the room for me. As I watched her during class, she had a confidence that bordered on cockiness. I liked her style. I had never seen her in school before, but I wanted to ask her for a date.

I didn't have a lot of time to date, but every now and then I took a girl to see a movie or to get a soda and ride around the local hangouts in Salem. But none of them were serious relationships.

When class was over, I waited until this girl came down the aisle by my desk. I got up quickly and she ran into me. "Oh, sorry," I said and smiled at her.

She gave me a bright smile back. "That's okay."

"I heard Mr. Green is a very good teacher," I said.

"Um-hmmm, I hope so. History can be so boring," she said.

"My name's Sid Shachnow," I said and stuck out my hand.

"Hi, Sid, I'm Arlene Armstrong," she said and shook my hand.

"You live around here?" I asked.

"Uh-huh. How about you?"

"Not far," I said. "If you ever need a ride home, I have a car," I said clumsily.

"Yeah," she smiled and put a piece of gum in her mouth.

One of her girlfriends came up to her and started talking excitedly about something and I drifted off to my next class.

From then on, I made a point to cross paths with Arlene whenever it could be arranged. She was always pleasant and positive in our short conversations. I was still very shy about asking a girl on a date. It took me awhile to work up the courage to make the phone call to ask a girl out, as I always feared rejection. I always sweated this part of the dating process.

I continued my brief encounters with Arlene, and with every conversation I strongly believed that Arlene and I would get along just great.

I finally worked up the nerve to make that dreaded phone call. I sat next to the phone in our kitchen, while everyone was gone one evening, and rehearsed. When I finally dialed the phone, a lady answered. "Arlene Armstrong, please," I said politely, figuring that this was her mother.

"Just a minute," she said.

"Hello," Arlene spoke into the phone a couple of seconds later.

"Hi, Arlene, this is Sid Shachnow," I said as upbeat as I could sound.

"Sid, how are you?" she asked.

"I'm good, Arlene," I paused for a second. "How did you do on that test in history the other day?"

"I made an A, how'd you do?" she asked.

I had made a C but I wasn't going to admit that to her. "I made an A, too," I answered.

"Guess we're pretty smart," she teased.

"Listen, Arlene, I called because I'd like to go out with you sometime . . . Maybe to a movie, or dancing or dinner. There's a party Saturday night that Frank's giving."

"Oh, Sid, I'm sorry but I have other plans," she said.

I was shot down. "Well, I'll call you some other time."

"Good talking to you, Sid," Arlene said and hung up.

I looked at the phone for a long time after I hung up and decided that I would not give up on Arlene.

The next day she was just as friendly and gregarious as before. We had several conversations in the hallway and at our lockers across the hall from each other. I complimented her on her hair and her clothes.

After several weeks of laying more groundwork, I made the call again. I decided I would invite her to the school Christmas party that was two months away. I was positive she wouldn't have plans this early. Well, I was wrong. I asked, and she turned me down flat.

She was not interested at all in me. I didn't understand it. I was a decent-looking guy, and everyone in school seemed to like me. And most important I had a car. I decided I would talk to her friend Elaine who sat behind me in history class.

"Elaine, I've been trying to get a date with Arlene, but she just isn't interested in me. Can you tell me why she doesn't care for me?" I said to Elaine before class one day. "Is she dating anyone?"

"No, Sid, she's not dating anyone, in particular. She goes out with several guys," Elaine answered.

This didn't help. She went out with a lot of guys, just not me. "You know, Elaine, I have a lot of good qualities that I know she would like. I'm ambitious, I'm dependable, I have a nice car . . ." I went on about my good qualities for a while.

"I'll talk to her Sid. Maybe she just doesn't know you well," Elaine said, as Mr. Green began class.

At the end of the hour, I saw Arlene and Elaine whispering in the hallway. I turned away and went to my next class.

The next day, I got to class before Elaine. I could hardly wait to hear the result of her conversation.

"Well, I told her all of the great things about you and then she just looked at me and threw her head back and laughed. You know what she said?" Elaine asked.

I was hoping that she said something like, "I really made a big mistake . . . I must have been crazy to turn down Sid Shachnow. He's the catch of the century!"

"She said, 'If he's that great, you ought to go out with him,'" Elaine repeated.

A few days later, I heard that Arlene was practically going steady with a guy named Louis Swinuich. He was a handsome, blond-haired athletic type. I thought he was too pretty. I couldn't understand her bad taste in men.

Several weeks later, I heard she was going to the Christmas party with Tony Mento. Again, I was shocked. He was short and not nearly as handsome as me. But he was a four-letter man! I asked Nancy Smith to the dance. She was very smart and very popular.

We passed Tony and Arlene once while we were dancing to the orchestra's version of "Stranger in Paradise." I just shook my head in amazement at her dating that guy Tony! I decided, as I was dancing with Nancy, that I would call Arlene after the Christmas vacation.

"Arlene, this is Sid Shachnow," I said brightly, speaking into the phone several weeks later.

"Hey, Sid," she answered.

"Would you like to go see a movie Friday night?" I decided to skip the chitchat and get to the point.

"Well," she said. "Can you hold on a minute, Sid?"

She left and came back a few seconds later. "Yeah, Sid, I'll go to the movies with you on Friday," she said unenthusiastically.

We went to the movie and we had a great time. I liked to talk to her and she liked my sense of humor. I was right, I knew we would get along and our relationship progressed. She evidently had changed her mind and we started going out frequently.

"Arlene, you really mean a lot to me," I said to her one night, several weeks later. We were sitting in the car. "I like you more and more each time we're together."

"Yeah, Sid, we get along pretty well, don't we," Arlene said.

"But I have to tell you something about this relationship, it can't be a serious one, Arlene," I said.

Arlene looked at me strangely.

"You know I'm Jewish and you're Catholic. It would never work." I looked over at her, very solemnly.

She looked at me for a few more moments and burst into laughter. "You are so funny, Sid."

"What are you laughing at?" I asked.

"I don't want to get serious, Sid," Arlene said, still laughing.

"Would you go steady with me, Arlene?" I blurted out. "It can't be serious, but we can go steady . . . if you will."

She smiled and kissed me. I handed her a steady necklace.

I was on top of the world. Arlene and I were going steady. But I was sure that it would never progress beyond that. I was glad that I had been honest with her.

"Where have you been?" my mother asked demandingly.

It was after midnight, and I was surprised that she was still up. "I've been out with Arlene."

"The shiksa?" she asked nastily.

"She's a nice girl, Mama," I answered.

"Don't get her into trouble . . ."

I walked off and didn't even want to answer her.

"Did you hear me, Schaja??"

FORTY-THREE

I passed the eleventh grade, and had only one more year of school. Uncle Max had asked me to work as many hours as possible at the Texaco station. His business had increased so much that Benny and I both worked as mechanics. I also filled the gas tanks and changed the oil for customers that drove into the station.

One afternoon, when it was hot and humid, I opened the icebox and took out a Coca-Cola. I had acquired a taste for the fizzy soda. I took my handkerchief and wiped the sweat off my forehead. As I took the last sip out of the bottle, I saw a long, black Cadillac drive into the driveway. I realized after a few seconds that it was Max's good friends, Paul and his father, Simon Shapiro. They own the machine shop across the street, and I assumed they were here to see Uncle Max.

"Hi," I said as they pulled to the pump. "It's good to see you."

"Sid," Paul said. "It's nice to see you, too." Paul was suspected of being gay. I felt the only reason he was labeled gay was because he was in his forties and had never married or dated girls. Personally, I could have cared less about this rumor. I liked both him and his father and they were both generous. Paul always slipped me spending money whenever I saw him. Their family had been extremely generous to everyone in the community.

"Would you like a soda pop?" I asked them.

"Yes, why don't you get us one, Sid." He handed me some money and I went to the icebox and got two sodas. One Coca-Cola and one Orange Squeeze that I knew Paul liked.

They were sitting at the table in Max's office when I came back to the office.

"Sit down, Sid," Simon said.

"I'm sorry, Uncle Max isn't here," I said. "He had to go pick up some parts for one of the cars we're working on."

"Oh, that's all right, we didn't come to see him. We came to see you."

"Oh?" I smiled.

Benny sat at the table with us. He looked from one to the other as we spoke.

"Sid, this will be your last year in school before you graduate, right?" Simon asked.

"Yes, sir," I answered.

"You've done very well considering your difficult circumstances. We're very proud of you," Simon continued.

"Thank you, sir. I hope I can graduate with no problems," I said.

"Well, I'm sure that you will. In fact, I think you'll probably come out with pretty good grades. I'd like to make you a proposition."

I opened my eyes wide. I wanted to hear what he had to say.

"I will send you to college, if you graduate with at least a C average. Have you thought about college, Sid?" he asked.

"Yes, sir," I said. "That would be great, I just never thought that I would have the money."

He got up and patted me on the shoulder. "Now you do, son. I want you to work hard, okay?"

Paul jumped up when his father did and smiled at me. He reached out his hand and shook my hand. "Sid, maybe after you graduate you can come work for us at the machinery plant." He slipped me a $5 bill.

In my wildest dreams, I had never considered that I would have the opportunity to go to college. I also never considered the strings that would be attached to this offer.

When I left the station that night I was on cloud nine. I decided to go down to Eaton's and tell my friends before I went to Arlene's house. As I pulled up to the curb in my Oldsmobile, one of the guys started yelling. "Hey Sid, your front hubcap is missing."

I had known the hubcap was not sitting right, but I hadn't heard any noise when it came off. "Damn!" I thought to myself. I got out and looked at the tire with the missing hubcap.

Hopi, a big six-foot kid who was my friend sauntered over to my car. "Yeah, I saw a hubcap just like that at the junkyard this morning."

"What were you doin' at the junkyard?" I asked looking up at his hulking body.

"I go there every so often. . . . I find really neat stuff."

"I bet it's yours, Shachnow," Frank speculated. "Somebody probably picked it up after it fell off and sold it to the yard."

"Someone stole it, Shachnow," Albie claimed. "The whole town is goin' downhill my dad says. Somebody needed money and took it."

"How much do you get for a hubcap?" Rocky asked.

"Probably eight or ten bucks," Albie answered.

I let out a low whistle. "I've got to get it back. I don't have eight or ten bucks to spend."

Before I knew it we were on our way to the yard to reclaim my property. No one considered what the consequences might be if we got caught.

Luckily, the junkyard was only ten minutes from Eaton's. I looked at my gas gauge as I drove, and the needle was resting on empty. It was running on fumes. I parked the car about a block away from the gate to the junkyard and took the flashlight out of the glove box. We piled out of the car and headed for our target.

The junkyard was dark. I shined the flashlight on the gate as we approached, and followed down the fence. It was a chain-link fence with several barbed wire strands spanned across the top. If someone tried to go over the fence, they would be snagged by the barbs. But the gate was lower than the fence, with no barbed wire. The problem was, the gate was lit. We looked around to see if there was a night watchman, and saw no one. We decided to go in at the gate.

Albie went to the street to look out for any problems. Hopi, since he was the tallest and knew where the hubcap was located, hoisted himself over the fence after several failed attempts. Just as he started to move away from the gate and over to the hubcap, we heard a shriek from Albie.

"Cops," he yelled.

We all started running like madmen. Hopi careened over the fence and caught up with us. After several blocks we slowed down.

"Oh man, I've got a cramp in my side," Hopi complained. "I never moved so fast in my life."

"Hey guys, this is nothing. They'll never find us. They're probably still looking in the yard for us," I said, confidently.

Out of nowhere, a police cruiser pulled up next to us. The officer on the passenger side blinded me with his heavy-duty flashlight. "What are you boys doin' out here tonight?"

"We just ran out of gas, Officer, and we're walking home," I answered still gasping for breath from running.

"Where do you live, son?" he asked.

I gave him an answer, but it wasn't my real address.

"Where is your car?"

I gave him another false answer.

"Well," he smiled back at me.

I was relieved as I smiled back at him. We were off the hook.

"If that's where your car is and if that's where you live, you're headed in the wrong direction,"

My alibi was blown.

The officer got out of the car and opened the door to the backseat. There were six of us piled one on top of the other in the backseat of the cruiser. It was a long ride to the police station as we all thought about the consequences. I figured they would call our parents and I dreaded to think what my mother would do to me. If I had a police record I would be finished.

"The longer you boys hold out on your crimes the harder they'll be on you," the officer driving said over his shoulder to us.

"Um, what's the punishment for breaking into the junkyard?" Frankie asked.

I almost slapped my hand over his mouth to keep him from talking.

The officer on the passenger side rubbed his chin. "The punishment for breaking and entering is a year in juvenile detention."

I felt myself almost gasp. I saw my college diploma disappearing.

"The judge will have to decide what will happen to you boys," he said.

I started thinking about what really happened. We never took anything. There was nothing stolen and we hadn't committed a crime. I was sure that everything would be all right from my vast legal experience.

I looked over at Hopi, who was sitting beside me, and gave him a look that meant be quiet. I saw a bizarre and strange expression on his face. His lips were scrunched up, and his face was red. I wondered if he was going to flip out. He squeezed his eyes shut and I saw water coming out of them. He looked like he was in pain.

We finally arrived, and the officers took us into a room and ordered us to sit down at the table. "We'll be back in just a few minutes."

When they came back, they had fingerprint cards, and motioned for us, one by one, to come to the table and put our thumbprints on the card. "You know once this is done, we can't do any more for you. You'll be in the system. Your fingerprints will be recorded forever. No leniency. The judge will take it from here, if we have no confession."

Suddenly, all of us blurted out our confessions.

After the policemen left the room, the tension between the six of us exploded. "If it hadn't been for you, Shachnow, we wouldn't be in this mess," Frankie blurted out. "If you had just read my signals and kept quiet we wouldn't be here."

"What the hell are you talking about?" I asked.

"Didn't you feel me pinching you?" Frankie hissed at me.

"Hell," Hopi shot back. "That wasn't Sid you were pinching, it was me! I couldn't figure out what the hell you were trying to do. I thought you were trying to kill me."

The officers reappeared after what seemed endless hours and let us go. As we went out the door, I heard them laughing.

The next day, I went to the junkyard and bought the hubcap for $6.

Forty-four

My parents were still up and standing in front of me when I walked in the door. It was my senior year, and I had been over at Arlene's house. I looked at the clock and it was after 11:00 P.M.

"Hi," I said. I almost plowed into them when they didn't move.

"Where do you go every night?" my mother snapped.

"I'm out with Arlene," I answered. "We're usually over at her parents' house.

"The shiksa? What do her parents think about the relationship?"

"They like me," I answered.

"You never spend any time here. We're you're family, Schaja," my father said.

I looked up at them defiantly. "I go to school, Papa. I work after school and earn money that I bring home to my family. I have a girl and I spend time with her, and we study together," I said, pulling out my paycheck from the A&P and throwing it on the table. "What more do you want from me?"

"I want you to respect your parents and your religion!" my mother said, raising her voice.

"Just because I'm not here doesn't mean I don't respect you," I said.

"You should be dating a lot of girls, or at least a Jewish girl. We want you to be free while you're young, Schaja. You live in America where you can be free and do many things. It's a time to enjoy yourself," my father said.

"My happiest times are with Arlene. She's my best friend and I love her," I said. My mother looked as if I had thrown cold water in her face.

"You don't know anything about love. You haven't considered the fact that it's just impossible to marry outside of the Jewish faith. It's tradition, Schaja, and I will not allow you to betray that tradition," my mother said.

"I know it won't be easy, Mama. I thought about it. I told Arlene that we could never marry. But we're happy together, and I think that being happy is the most important thing," I said. "What has being a Jew done but cause misery and pain in our lives?"

"Don't talk like that, Schaja," my father demanded.

My mother's face fell to the floor.

"I will not allow you to marry that shiksa," Mother said angrily.

"You don't even know her. She's one of the nicest people in the world. She means a lot to me, and that should mean a lot to you. Don't you care that she makes me happy?" I asked.

"You're too young to know what will bring you real happiness," Papa said.

"I'll be twenty-one years old in a couple of months. I'm no baby," I said.

"Maturity doesn't come with years," Mother said.

I was barely able to keep my eyes open I was so tired. "I'm tired, I have to be up at six in the morning. Can we talk about this later?"

My parents shook their heads and I walked into my bedroom.

Stanley was awake when I got into the bedroom. "They've been talking about you and your girlfriend all night," he said.

I didn't answer.

"Why don't you want to marry a Jew?" he asked.

"It's not that. It's just that they won't even give Arlene a chance . . . they won't allow me to bring her to the house to meet them. They don't want anything but to keep me a prisoner. Any girl I brought home they wouldn't like . . . Jewish or not!" I said angrily.

"Ma's really upset," Stanley said.

"I don't care. I'm tired, and I want to go to sleep."

As it turned out, the next day would make my parents very happy. Arlene and I broke up. She was teasing me about something, and I snapped at her. She got angry and said I was too serious all the time and I wasn't any fun. I told her to go find someone that was fun and grumpily walked off.

Arlene, Elaine, Susie, and Juliet went into the auditorium of the school to talk about the senior prom at the end of the year. They were on the committee that was in charge of the decorations and music. It was November and the first meeting of the committee. It was also a good way to get out of study hall.

"I heard Miss Jackson's will have prom dresses in her store by January," Susie said. "I want to get a baby blue chiffon long gown."

"Let's do the decorations in baby blue, too," Elaine said. "It's my favorite color."

"Who are we going to have to play music this year?" Arlene said.

"Not that same old Manuel's Black and White?" Juliet said.

"Let's get a good band. Let's get The Platters," Arlene said. "They're my favorite."

"Let's go rob a bank to pay for it," Elaine quipped. They all broke into laughter.

"All the guys are already complaining about the tuxedos they have to rent!" Susie said. "Is Sid going to wear a tuxedo?"

"I don't know. We broke up," Arlene said.

"No!" Elaine said.

"Yeah," Arlene answered. "We had a fight."

"You'll get back together, you always do," Susie said.

Arlene shrugged. "I don't know. You know Sid is always so serious and he always wants to talk about the future. I just want to have fun right now. I don't want to think about the future. There's plenty of time for that."

"Yeah, but it's not too far off . . . graduation. What are you going to do after you graduate?" Juliet asked.

"Get a job, I guess," Arlene answered.

"I want to get married," Elaine said.

"To Joey Winston?" Susie kidded.

"He's such a bum!"

"Arlene, out of all the boys here at school, who would you marry?" Elaine asked.

"Sid Shachnow," Arlene answered.

They all broke into laughter. "But you just broke up with him."

"Yes, but he's the most responsible of all the guys here. He is very serious, he's older than these other guys, and he'll make the best husband," Arlene said. "He's a great guy, I already miss him." Arlene burst out laughing and the others did, too.

Arlene waited for Sid at their locker, several days later. "I'm sorry I got mad," she said when he walked up to the locker.

Sid's face softened. "Yeah, me, too."

"Let's not fight anymore," she said seriously.

Sid nodded. "I got tickets to go see Spike Jones in Boston in a few weeks. You wanna go?"

Arlene smiled. "Sounds like fun."

FORTY-FIVE

It was freezing outside, but I spent Friday afternoon after school, polishing and cleaning my '49 Oldsmobile, and several hours perfecting the shine. Arlene and I were driving to Boston the next day to see Spike Jones. She didn't know it yet but I was going to ask her to marry me. I knew that Arlene was the one for me. And I was the one for her. I started singing to myself. "She's the one, and I'm the one for her." For the first time in a long time, I thought of my grandmother and how she used to try to teach me to sing. I knew if she were here today, she would help persuade my parents to accept Arlene.

"What are you doing out here? It's too cold, you'll catch pneumonia!" I heard my father's voice behind me.

"Arlene and I are going to Boston tomorrow to see Spike Jones," I said.

"We've told you that you are forbidden to see that girl any longer," my father violently spat out.

I turned and looked at him. "Why are you so angry about her?"

"Because she just wants to take advantage of you. You don't know women, Schaja. You have no experience. You're naïve when it comes to women," he said in a secretive tone.

"You don't even know her. Let me bring her to meet you, please," I pleaded.

He walked back into the house without an answer to my plea.

That next night, Arlene and I were on our way to Boston. "Arlene," I said after we had stopped at Rosie's Roadside Diner. I had just finished a piece of apple pie à la mode. "I have a question to ask you . . ." I hesitated.

She looked up at me.

"I don't know if you remember that I told you we could never get married . . ." This was harder than I thought it would be. What if she said no?

"But I know that we really get along great, and you're my best friend, and I will always take care of you and I know I love you . . ." I said, rambling.

She looked at me in a strange way. "Sid . . . what are you talking about?" she said hesitantly.

"I don't have an engagement ring or anything to give you. But . . . will you marry me?" I blurted out the question. I had practiced what I was going to say, and this wasn't it, but it would have to do. Standing in front of a mirror was a lot easier than sitting face to face and asking a question like this.

She looked at me and her face became flushed. She flashed a smile and then she had a serious look. "Sid, we haven't graduated yet," she finally said.

"We'll get married this summer," I said.

"What about your parents?" she asked.

"My parents will change their mind, once we are married," I said.

"I've always dreamed of a big wedding. Do you think they would come?" she asked me.

"I don't care if they come or not, Arlene. I love you and I want to marry you," I answered.

"What about college, Sid?"

"I'll work and go to college at the same time. Just like I do now," I said.

"I could get a job, too," she answered, still thinking.

"Well, you haven't answered me? Will you marry me?"

Before I knew it, she came over to the other side of the booth and sat next to me. She put her arms around me and kissed me. I was sure that meant yes. Everybody in the diner was staring at us, and my face was beet red. My hands were shaking when I got up to pay the bill at the cash register. The girl behind the cash register gave me a sly look. "We're getting married!" I explained. "We're getting married!"

She beamed a smile at both of us. "Congratulations!"

We got back to Salem around 2 A.M. Luckily, my parents were in bed because I was exhausted and didn't want to listen to the nightly lecture. The next morning at the breakfast table I made the announcement about Arlene and me. My mother went into hysterics and my father ranted and raved about my foolish decision.

"It is against our faith. Schaja, you just cannot disregard the principles of faith. It is a sin! Why must you make this decision right now? You have college and many years to make a commitment like this. What do her parents think?"

"I don't know," I answered. "I just asked her last night."

"There must be some other reason for you to do this," Mother yelled between sobs. "You are being forced into this."

"I love her, Ma. Nobody is being forced into anything," I answered.

"Is she pregnant?" Papa asked.

"How can you ask a question like that? You are such hypocrites," I said angrily. I turned to my mother. "You and your Russian boyfriends," I said and glared at her. Then I turned to my father. "And you, with your young girlfriends." I stomped out of the kitchen, out the door and to my car. I drove around for a while. I had to cool down. I was furious.

After a couple of hours, I stopped by Arlene's. She answered the door with tears in her eyes. "What's wrong?" I asked immediately.

"Your mother . . . your mother . . ." She began to sob.

Mrs. Armstrong came up behind Arlene and put her arms around her. We all walked over and sat down on the sofa in the living room.

"Your mother called and accused Arlene of being pregnant," Mrs. Armstrong said.

"How could she think that, Sid?" Arlene looked at me.

I shook my head and put my arm around her. I didn't understand why my parents would do this. "I don't understand," I said.

"Your mother offered money for her to have an abortion," Mrs. Armstrong said.

This hit me like a ton of bricks. I wondered why my mother was so mean. Was it because she had gone through so much? I really didn't know, and at this particular moment, I didn't care. All I wanted was to get away from my family.

I went home after that, but I didn't approach my parents about the phone call. I knew they would start their ranting and raving all over again. I went to my room and slept.

The next Friday afternoon, Benny and I worked while my uncle took the day off. I saw a black Cadillac pull in the driveway and recognized Simon and Paul. I waved and smiled. They were not smiling. They parked their car in the parking area, not at the pump, and came into the office.

"Hi, how are you?" I asked, brightly.

"Sid, we would like to speak to you for a moment," Simon said.

We walked over to the table and sat down. Benny was already sitting at the table drinking a cup of coffee. Simon did not ask him to leave.

"We're very disturbed, Sidney, about the rumors we've heard about you wanting to marry outside your religion. Is this true?" he asked.

"Yes," I said. "That is, in fact, my plan."

Paul, looked at me very sternly. "You know we have seen this before, Sid. It never works when you marry outside your faith. There are many problems in bringing up children. Especially since we hear that she is Catholic."

I could feel my blood begin to boil now, but I bit my tongue and continued to listen. I looked over at Benny, who was watching as the conversation went on.

"Will she take the faith?" Paul asked.

"I haven't asked her to, no," I answered.

"What about your heritage, Sidney? It is what you are. You are a Jew and that will not change," Simon said.

"We love each other," I answered.

"This does not solve problems," Simon said shaking his head.

"I'm going to marry her," I said firmly.

"And you will throw away your life . . . your heritage. Look at what you have been through, and all of this for nothing but a shiksa," Paul spat out bitterly.

"You have a bigger responsibility than just yourself," Simon said. "When you marry outside the race, you dilute the entire culture. Foolish decisions like this will dilute our culture, and it will mean the extinction of all Jews."

I stared at him. I couldn't believe that he would say this.

"Sidney, if you turn against your family, I can no longer support you in the future. The offer for a college education will be revoked," Simon said flatly. He and Paul got up and went to the door. Paul walked over to me after his father went to the car and put a $20 bill in my palm.

"No thanks," I said and handed it back to him.

I sat down dumbfounded by what had just happened. I was angry and hurt and I didn't understand this kind of resistance from my family. He had said I was turning against my family. This was beyond anything that I could understand. They misunderstood.

Benny's deep, Appalachian accented voice brought me back to reality. "Don't worry about that college education or any of that silly advice they jis' give you, Sid," he said and then paused for a moment. "I've been suspicious all along that Paul has designs on you. You know he's a little queer, don't ya? That's the rumor, anyhow."

He got up and stretched for a long moment. He puffed out his chest and put his thumbs in his suspenders that fit over his greasy shirt. "As for that college crap, I never went and I did okay," he smiled and went into the garage to tinker with an engine. "If you want to marry the girl, marry her!"

Actually, Benny had never finished high school, but I appreciated his support.

When I arrived home at eight o'clock that night, there was a four-hour lecture waiting for me. It was just past midnight when my father in his finale said they were sure that Arlene was pregnant. I had not said a word for hours. After his untrue comment about Arlene I got up, walked into my bedroom, and picked up some blankets and a pillow. Even though it was cold outside, I slept in the car that night.

Forty-six

"There's six inches of snow on the ground, Sid," my brother said when he opened the bedroom door and yelled at me. "Better get up if you want to put snow tires on your car."

I was tired. As I lay there with my eyes closed, I could hear my parents talking in the kitchen. "Max and Sara are on their way to have Thanksgiving dinner with Pauline. I hope they don't get stuck in the snow," Mother said.

My father chuckled. "Max will have the best snow tires made, he won't let anything happen to that Buick. I bet there's not a scratch on that car."

My mother's voice turned stern as she spoke. "Sid hasn't given me the money for rent. Ask him for it, Leon."

"He'll give it to you, Rose. He always does," my father answered.

I jumped out of bed, and when my feet hit the floor I was angry. All they wanted was my rent payment. They couldn't care less about what I wanted for my own life. I pulled some cash out of the pants hanging over the chair and counted it. Still in my pajamas, I walked out into the kitchen and slapped the money on the counter. My parents just looked at me. I went back into my room and got dressed.

When I went outside, big white snowflakes were falling. The snow was covering the sleet that had fallen the night before. Stanley and I made our way down to the Texaco station to change the tires on my car.

"Hey Benny, I'll be back for my shift at two. I'll bring you a piece of turkey from Thanksgiving dinner. I already okayed it with Arlene's mom," I yelled as we backed out of the station.

I drove Stanley back to the house, and ran inside to change my shirt and put on a tie. I walked into the kitchen and saw four bowls of hot, steaming chicken noodle soup on the table. Stanley sat down and hungrily started scooping the soup out of his bowl.

I looked at my mother. "Thanks, Mama, but you can pour the soup back in the pot. I'm not having lunch here. I'm going to Arlene's for an American Thanksgiving dinner."

My mother turned to me with a rage that I had never before seen. In a flash, and without a word, she picked up the bowl from the table and poured the hot, steaming soup over my head, scalding the skin on my face and burning my arms and chest. I was stunned and backed quickly out the door as she ran toward me waving her fists and screaming. I headed for my car and dove into the front seat and locked the doors.

"Over my dead body! Over my dead body will you marry that conniving woman," she screamed and beat on the windows of my car.

When I regained my composure, I started the ignition and drove off. I left her standing, shaking her fists and screaming. I looked in the rearview mirror, and I saw noodles hanging from my head and resting on my shoulders. I couldn't go to Arlene's looking like this. I drove over to the Texaco station and watched Benny gawk at me when I got out of the car.

"What the hell happened to you? You look terrible," he said.

I was in no mood for conversation. I went into the bathroom and washed myself off. I tried to get the stains out of my white shirt, but it was useless. I threw down the wet paper towels and walked outside again. I was angry with myself. I could have handled the situation in a better way. I could have eaten the soup and then eaten less at Arlene's. But, I didn't.

When I arrived at Arlene's, she knew without asking that something was wrong. My clothes were a mess, my hair was sticking out in different directions, and my face was still burning.

She was shocked when she looked at me. "Hey, Sid, you like to wear your food? Is this the new style?" She hugged me and pulled off a noodle I had missed. She whispered in my ear. "Don't worry."

Her family greeted me as if nothing had happened. We had a joyful Thanksgiving dinner of turkey, dressing, yams, green beans, and pumpkin pie. Mrs. Armstrong fixed a paper plate filled with food for Benny, and I left a little before two to go to work.

I had explained what happened in privacy to Arlene. She felt bad for me and for my mother. We agreed that I could have handled the situation better. But I was in a prison. I had no future. I had to make decisions fast about how to support my soon-to-be wife.

I was sitting at the service station about six o'clock that evening. There was no business, and it was peaceful after the stressful day. I was miserably recounting the events of the day and pondering what I could do. I saw a pair of car lights turn into the driveway and stood up to go serve the driver. But I stopped when the car pulled into a parking space next to the building. When I opened the door of the office, I saw a smiling, heavyset, six-foot-tall man. I knew that I recognized him, but I had to search my memory. It dawned on me. He was the rabbi from our local synagogue.

Rabbi Cohen greeted me like a long-lost friend, even though I barely knew him. He embraced me in a bear hug and talked about the significance of Thanksgiving Day. "Gratitude heals all wounds for us. God loves those who have gratitude. I know you have had a life of obstacles, but you have much to be grateful for today. Loving parents who are concerned for your future . . ."
He paused.

He told me he wanted to put some perspective on my problems. He said my parents had told him of my dilemma.

"I don't think it's my dilemma, as much as it is their dilemma," I said. But I sat quietly and braced myself for another lecture. The only difference between his and the other twenty lectures that I had been force fed was his demeanor. He was calm and polite, and far less emotional or threatening.

"Sid, you have not been in this country long. You are essentially new to this world of freedom. I want to explain to you about America. It's separated into three distinct groups: Catholic, Protestant, and Jewish." He stopped to take a breath.

"You see there are problems in the world today because of marital strife. Divorce is on the rise, and nine out of ten times it happens because of unions that are outside of one's faith. The parents begin to fight over how the children are raised after the honeymoon is long past. This religion that we were raised with has deep roots, and in the end it always comes forth in our lives, no matter how much we think we are in love at the moment, it just won't work. When it comes to marriage, it pays to be practical," he said.

I sat and listened politely.

"In short, Sid, don't marry Arlene, it's a big mistake," he said and looked at me waiting for a response.

"I'm sorry, Rabbi, I don't want to appear rude, but I disagree with you. I think that because of the difference in religions, if we assimilate our beliefs through marriage we will all understand each other better. Instead of three distinct groups, why not just one?"

"You are unrealistic. You are wishing for utopia, and it's not to be," he said. He continued on his line of thought and finally saw that he had said all that he could. "You should consider the impact of what you are doing to your family. You need to think of everyone concerned, not just yourself."

"You know, Rabbi, my parents won't even meet Arlene. For that matter you haven't met her, either," I said.

"It's not the girl, Sid, it's the beliefs. My door is always open to you," he said and left.

As I watched the red taillights of his car disappear I felt the weight of the world on my shoulders. No education or career, no money, no family support. Where in the world could I go and how was I going to get there? The question kept pounding in my head. The hundreds of lecturing voices filled my mind, and then I heard my own voice and I knew that I would find a way. I had to listen to my own heart.

PART III

The American Dream

1955–1994

FORTY-SEVEN

Uncle Max asked me to go to the post office to deliver some packages. It wasn't far from the gas station, so I decided to walk instead of drive. I had not been home since Thanksgiving and that was weeks ago. I had been staying in the Texaco station. Benny knew I was there, but no one else. I was still trying to find a solution to my problems. Of course, I found out later that my parents knew all along where I was staying.

I walked along the sidewalk toward the post office, and I saw that there was a line of customers. It was the Christmas season, and everyone was mailing packages. I stood and leaned against the wall of the post office remembering when we first arrived in Salem at this time of year. It was hard to believe it had been almost five years. As I looked back, something came into focus in my range of vision. It was Uncle Rocky . . . red, white, and blue. I shook my head and realized that Uncle Rocky was pointing at me. The Uncle Rocky character on the army poster always made me smile. But then I read the sign tacked beneath the figure:

UNCLE ROCKY WANTS YOU FOR THE U.S. ARMY. JOIN THE 10TH MOUNTAIN DIVISION AND SEE THE WORLD!

Suddenly I could feel myself grinning from ear to ear. I had found my solution! I walked past the post office and followed the directions to the army recruitment office. I bounded up the steps and into the door that would open to a world that I had never imagined.

When I stepped inside I saw an army sergeant sitting behind a desk. I looked around the room at all the posters showing different branches of the army: infantry, with a soldier carrying his rifle; armor-featuring tanks; artillery firing Howitzers. I looked at the many countries that had U.S. Army bases marked on a map by tacks.

"I'd like to know how I can enlist," I said to the sergeant, who had just hung up the phone at his desk. "I want to join the Tenth Mountain Division."

He smiled and put out his hand. "Sergeant Hubbard," he said.

"Sidney Shachnow, sir," I answered, smiling. "I lived in Germany before I came to the United States. That's where I first saw U.S. Army GIs."

The sergeant took his time. "Well the Tenth Mountain Division isn't going immediately to Germany. There's six months of basic and advanced training. When the unit is combat ready, then you're off to Germany with your division."

"That's perfect for me," I said. This would give Arlene and me a chance to get married before I left for Germany. I had a great feeling that everything was finally going to work out.

The sergeant started asking me questions about my education and age. He asked me why I wanted to join the army. I didn't tell him that I wanted to get away from my parents. I said I had always admired soldiers, which was true.

"I think you would probably make a fine soldier, Sid. But I'm going to encourage you to finish your last year at school and get your diploma."

"Okay," I said. "I can probably take another few months."

"Why don't you drop by every now and then, when you have any questions, I'll always be here from eight to six o'clock, six days a week."

"Okay, sir. Thank you very much."

"Look forward to seeing you, Sid."

I drove immediately to Arlene's house after I left the recruitment office. When she answered the door she was crying and very upset. "What's wrong, Arlene?" I said, my heart leaping into my throat. "What's happened?"

She burst into tears before any words came out. I tried to console her. I put my arms around her.

"Your mother called. She offered to pay me off if I would never see you again. How could she do that, Sid? How could she think that I am that kind of person?" Arlene continued to cry.

I was so angry I wanted to hit the wall. I had to make every effort to calm myself down. Why didn't my mother just pick on me and leave Arlene alone? This was all complete insanity.

I decided at that moment to go back and talk to the sergeant tomorrow morning. I needed to join the army now. It was the only way that Arlene and I could survive.

After Arlene calmed down, I told her my plans to join the army and after she graduated, we would get married. We both agreed that this would be the best thing to do.

I left Arlene's after having dinner with her and her parents. I drove to my house. When I opened the door there was a cold silence, except for my brother, who was always friendly, despite my parents trying to turn him against me.

I walked toward the kitchen and threw my keys to the car on the kitchen counter. My mother stared at me icily. I smiled at her. "Hey, Ma, I'm quitting high school and joining the army. I'll be leaving pretty soon for basic training," I said, expecting a different response than the one I got.

Both she and my father were ecstatic. My brother was ecstatic, too. He wanted to know what I was going to do with my car.

I couldn't believe that no one had said this was some harebrained, pre-posterous act that I was getting ready to embark on. No one cried that I shouldn't throw away all my effort to graduate and become educated. There was nothing but joy about my enlisting.

"One more thing, Mother," I said. "Don't you ever call Arlene again. I guess you found out that she couldn't be bought."

She smiled sweetly at me. "Well, we don't have to worry about her any longer since you're joining the army!"

I laughed. She really thought I was going to leave Arlene behind. As angry as I was at my parents, I understood their attitude, even though I didn't agree with them. It was their way of holding onto the past, a world that wasn't here anymore.

The next morning before 8 A.M., I was standing at the door of the recruit-ment office when Sergeant Hubbard arrived and unlocked the door.

He chuckled when he saw me. "Didn't expect you to drop by so soon!"

"Well, sir, I have some circumstances that I need to talk to you about," I said.

He made some coffee and poured two cups. He brought the cups over to the desk and I began to unravel the story of my life to him. He pulled a pipe out of the drawer, filled it with tobacco, and lit up. I spent the next hour convincing him that the army was the only solution for my life, and I listed all of the reasons why I would make a good soldier. Every now and then he stopped me and asked me a question or two.

The minutes ticked by after I had completed my story. He said nothing and just looked at me. He took a puff on his pipe. He looked up at the ceil-ing. He whistled a tune softly that I didn't recognize. I shuffled my feet, hoping that would draw him out of his trance. Then he got up and left the room. He was gone for about five minutes. When he walked back into the room he had a stack of papers in his hand. He laid them in front of me. "Fill these out," he said and left the room.

It took me another hour to fill out all the forms. After I had completed and signed the forms, the sergeant made several phone calls about my ap-plication. "Shachnow, get over to 320 Cromwell Street. If you pass your preliminary physical, you'll report to Boston Reception Station in two days for more tests and another physical."

I could finally smile for the first time in a month. I passed the preliminary physical and went to Arlene's to tell her the news and promise her that I would show her the world!

Two days later, I wasn't prepared for the emotion of leaving. I felt my own uncertainty of what I had done. I wanted to escape from the problems, but I had suddenly propelled myself into a pathway of drastic change.

My friends at Moody Square were envious. They wished me well on my last night in Salem. My parents were still ecstatic with the thought of Arlene being out of the picture. My brother was thrilled to be inheriting my car and our double bed! And for me, anything was better than the turmoil I had been in with my parents. The best part of leaving was that I knew Arlene and I would soon be together.

Forty-eight

The icy wind whipped my overcoat around my legs as I walked from the train station to the Boston Reception Station. I had to tug on the door the wind was so fierce. When I walked inside the large open hall with cubicles set up as testing and physical examinations areas, I saw an arrow pointing to the short line for induction. I was handed some more papers that I needed to fill out at the end of that line. It took almost four hours to visit each cubicle, take tests, answer questions, fill out additional forms, and finally come to the other side of the hall where I was told to take a seat on a bench.

The long bench was cramped with other hopeful inductees, waiting anxiously for approval. I watched as a couple of the guys lit up a cigarette, stubbed them out, and then lit another one. I wondered what their story was and why they wanted to join the army. I reached in my pocket and took out a piece of gum. I hadn't eaten anything since I arrived in Boston almost ten hours ago. Juicy Fruit tasted delicious.

As the hours passed by each man sitting on the bench with me was called by an officer to a cubicle, not far from where I was sitting. They were given a packet and a slip of paper as they left the cubicle, and then went out the side door of the building. I was getting anxious. Why was I the last one? I didn't have to wonder any longer. I saw two sergeants with grim faces walking toward me.

"Come with us," the sergeant said and motioned to me to follow him.

I jumped off the bench, took the gum out of my mouth, and stuffed it into the trash can at the end of the bench. The two soldiers chatted to each other in whispered tones as they led me to an office on the other side of the building. My hands were sweating and my heart was pounding. I must have flunked one of the tests and they were not going to let me join, I thought to myself. By the time I stepped into the office, I was already trying to figure out what I was going to do next with my life. Or maybe I could persuade them to let me take the test over, and this time I would have to pass. I had limited options.

The sergeant took his place behind the desk. The other sergeant stood with his foot propped behind the desk, and his arms over his knee.

"What's your name?" the sergeant barked.

"Sidney Shachnow," I answered.

He opened a file, rifled through some papers, and looked up at me. "There is nothing in this file that indicates to me that your name is Sidney Shachnow. Now, give me your real name," he said tapping his fingers edgily on the desk.

It hit me like a bolt. "Sir, please let me explain. I'm very sorry, but I didn't even think about this before . . ." I felt his glaring focus on me. "My name in Lithuania where I was born was Schaja Shachnowski. When we arrived here from Germany my relatives gave me the name Sidney Shachnow."

"Did you ever have a legal document drawn up to indicate the name change?" he asked.

"No sir, it was all done over the dinner table at my uncle's house. We had only been in the United States for a few days," I explained further.

He wasn't happy. "Did you ever take a civics class in our American schools?"

"Uhhh . . . I think so . . ." I wondered what his point was going to be.

"Ignorance is no excuse. That's the first lesson in civics class! If you learn nothing else today, try to remember that. You'll avoid a lot of problems," he said and rose from his desk. He took a packet of papers out of his lower desk drawer and handed them to me. "Start over again with your real name."

I missed the induction and the trip to Fort Dix, New Jersey, that day and I spent the night sleeping on the floor of the Boston Reception Station.

The next morning the clerk informed me that since I was not a U.S. citizen and I didn't have naturalization papers I would need a declaration of intention. The papers stated that I intended and desired to become a U.S. citizen.

"Can I have a piece of paper and I will write—" I said, but was interrupted by her.

"It's a legal document that you must get from the Immigration and Naturalization Department. It's about a mile from here," she said and gave me directions.

I hustled over to the government building. After standing in line I received the document and quickly filled it out. They handed me a declaration of intention. I rushed out the door of the building and ran into a soldier that I had seen at the Boston Reception Station.

"Hey, where you rushing to?" he asked after I had apologized for colliding with him.

"Back to the station," I answered.

He put out his hand. "Corporal Bryant."

"Schaja Shachnowski . . . I mean, Sidney Shachnow . . ." I stuttered and stammered.

He looked at me and laughed. "You sure?"

I laughed. "It's a long story."

"If you give me a minute to run this paper upstairs, I'll give you a lift back to the station," he offered.

On our way back I told him a brief story of the obstacles I had met with in trying to join up. "Don't worry, kid. You'll get in."

"I hope so," I said.

"But I'll give you some advice. Don't get into the infantry. You don't want to be there," he said. "Even if we're not at war, infantry is shit."

I had heard this from almost everyone who had ever thought about being in the army. But I wasn't quite sure how I could avoid it if I was assigned to infantry. It's not like they gave you a choice. I just nodded in agreement.

At the end of the day I was told that I had met all of the qualifications required. I breathed a sigh of relief.

"Now," the soldier said. "Go over to the ID counter and they will take your fingerprints for security purposes."

I gulped, as I remembered my police experience in Salem. I wondered if my record would show up when I was fingerprinted. I wanted to kick myself at how stupid it was to try to get a $6 hubcap back.

I then followed the officer over to another office where I was given my preassignment interview.

"Shachnowski, your test scores are excellent! We've looked at your overall aptitude and physical condition, and you are perfect for the infantry!"

I gulped and tried to smile at what he thought was great news.

"You'll be sent to infantry training, which will be of great benefit to you. You're assigned as of today to the Tenth Mountain Division at Fort Riley in Kansas," he said. He then pushed induction papers across the desk. "If you'll sign on the dotted line at the bottom of these papers," he said, and sat back proudly in his chair. "You are on your way to being a private in the U.S. Army! Son, you've got a great life ahead of you."

I quickly signed on the dotted line.

"Congratulations, soldier!" he said and shook my hand.

There were twenty-five of us inducted that day. We stood in a room with an officer standing in front of us on a small stage. He was holding a clipboard. A small light shone dramatically on the U.S. flag. There were military crests framed and hanging on the wall.

"Attention," the officer said.

We all snapped to attention, standing stiff as boards, waiting for the next command. I could feel the excitement building inside of me. I was going to be a GI Joe!

"Raise your right hand"—he paused and looked over the group—"and repeat after me," he said and began to speak.

I do solemnly swear that I will support and defend the Constitution of the United States against all enemies, foreign and domestic. That I will bear truth and allegiance to the same and that I will obey the orders of the president of the United States and the orders of the officer appointed over me according to regulations and the Uniform Code of Military justice, so help me God.

This oath meant a great deal to me. In looking at my past, I realized the grave responsibility of maintaining freedom. To protect the most vital document in the history of the world, the Constitution of the United States, and to follow the orders of my country's president, regardless of his party affiliation.

I thought about Sergeant Mitchell and the beginning of my dream to come to the United States and be a soldier in the U.S. Army. It was an eerie feeling when my dream came true!

I was officially Private Schaja Shachnowski, RA 11294295, U.S. Army Infantry. I was told to memorize my serial number. As we made our way to the bus, I went over the number I had been assigned and all of the events of the day. I looked toward a bright future. The past difficulties quickly became a memory. I was on my own and on my way to a life that I could have never imagined.

My experience at Fort Dix was an initiation into a world that would last more than forty years and take me all over the world.

Forty-nine

O n your feet, ladies!" Sergeant Bowery, the leader of our platoon, shouted as he walked into the barracks at 5:30 A.M. "This morning is the first day of your basic training. You will leave here this bright and shining morning as the pansy that you are . . ." He paused. "And six months from now, you will be a MAN!" He strutted around the room with supreme confidence.

All of us had bolted out of our bed, and jumped to our feet, standing at attention. One of the soldiers still had his eyes closed, and the sergeant caught a glimpse of him. He went over and stood in front of the comatose soldier. He got right up next to his ear and finished his sentence. "OR YOU WILL GO HOME TO MAMA!" he shouted.

The soldier almost jumped out of his skin. He had a long hangdog face that was white as snow. It made him look like a man-in-the-moon caricature. A few of us had to work hard to stifle our laughter. "Yes, sir!" he gulped, and hoarsely got out the words. His eyes were still slits.

The sergeant wasn't going to let go of this bone. "Where you from, honey-boy?" The recruit stiffened at this name. But the sergeant's nose was right up against his nose. I could see the sergeant's saliva hit the private's face.

"Boston, Mass, sir!" the soldier looked straight ahead.

"One of those whiskey-drinkin', hollerin', gut-werenchin', cry-in-your-beer, whimperin', chicken shit, Irishmen?"

The soldier's eyes were as wide as saucers now. "Yes, sir . . . I mean no, sir."

I heard a couple of the others snicker when he bumbled his answer.

"What is it, soldier? Yes or no? What's your name? Maybe that will clear it up for us." He put his thumbs into his pant waist and leaned forward pushing the soldier back.

"MacDougal, sir!"

"Bingo!" the sergeant shouted.

I knew that Mac was in for a hell of a day. I knew we all were.

"Ten push-ups . . . for all of you! Just because MacDougal is an Irish-man!" he shouted and turned to leave. We all hit the ground and did our ten push-ups as his assistant, Platoon Sergeant Rogers, stood and watched.

The rest of the day consisted of a three-mile hike to our field exercise location. These field exercises brought the meaning of hustle to a new level.
Finally, at 10:00 P.M. we all fell into bed. As the days progressed, we were occasionally hit with GI Parties. These were held every Friday night to clean
the barracks to a state of spotless cleanliness. It didn't always turn out that
way, and if Sergeant Bowery found a spot, we would spend Sundays cleaning the latrine with toothbrushes until they shined.

I was sleep deprived and exhausted most of the time. But the regimenta-
tion was not as difficult for me since my childhood experiences had been a
preparation for this training. Some of the guys hated it and had a hard time
relenting to all the orders and demands made on them.

At least once a week I managed to get a letter written and mailed to Arlene. She sent several letters back, keeping me up on all the events in Salem
since I had left. She had seen my brother riding around town in my
Oldsmobile. She was getting ready for graduation in a couple of weeks.

I was sorry that I wouldn't be able to graduate with her, but I knew that
I had made the right decision. I liked the army. This life provided me with
things that in some cases I had never had before. Three square meals a day,
spending money, new clothes, warm shelter, and health care.

I also liked the camaraderie that developed in a unit between soldiers.
Every unit had a comedian, and it turned out that MacDougal was ours. No
matter what he did from the day he arrived until the day he left, he always
pissed off the sergeant. But he had a great sense of humor and had the im-
personation of the sergeant down pat. He could even make his voice sound
like Sergeant Hubbard.

As we neared the end of our training we had more free time. I spent
nights standing in line to use the phone. Arlene had started a job at the
telephone company as an operator after she had graduated. She could take
my calls and it wouldn't cost anything, and we could talk as long as she was
on break.

"Arlene, how are you?" I said, after standing in line for an hour. I listened
to her tell me about her new job and all that was going on in Salem. Usually
our conversations lasted for about ten to fifteen minutes. I was intently listening to her when I heard a click. I turned around and saw a man's hand
on the receiver lever. He was a short, stocky guy with a cigarette hanging
out of his mouth.

"What the hell are you doing?" I snapped at him.

"Your time is up!" he said.

"I was talking to my girl," I said.

"And that's why I need the phone," he taunted. "To talk to my girl."

I put the receiver down and started to redial the number, and he pushed
me aside. When I didn't budge, I saw his right hand form a fist and start to
take a swing. He was standing at an angle as his fist came up toward my
face. I ducked, but not fast enough. His hard fist hit me on the cheekbone.

I didn't try to hit him with my fist; I locked my foot around his leg and pulled his foot out from under him. He was caught by surprise and fell to the ground on his back, and he hit his head on the side of the building. The fall and blow to his head stunned him.

I felt someone grab my arm. "Get the hell out of here, Shach!" It was MacDougal. "The MPs are on their way . . ."

"That guy cut me off on the phone. He started it!" I said.

"You're almost out of here, don't mess it up," he said and pushed me down the path.

Later, that night MacDougal came over to my bunk and told me what had happened after I left. The MPs questioned the guy about what had happened. He told them that he had slipped.

It was many months later before I found out MacDougal, who was bigger than this guy, had persuaded him to tell that story to the MPs.

At morning formation, Sergeant Bowers came up to me and told me that I was to report to Sergeant Jones at the Company Orderly room. I could feel the sweat form on my face. I figured I was in trouble for the telephone incident the night before.

I walked over to the Orderly Room and went into an office occupied by Sergeant Jones. I stood at attention in front of his desk.

"At ease, soldier," Jones said. "Have a seat." He was a handsome, athletic-looking man. His uniform looked like it had been ironed on him. His white-blond hair and blue eyes made him look like a poster boy. Sitting next to him was Sergeant Fitch. Fitch was short and stocky and had piercing brown eyes and a ruddy complexion. He was not a poster boy.

They shot questions at me about my past. How long had I been in Lithuania? How long had I been in Germany? What languages could I speak and write? None of their questions even neared the event of last night. I was relieved and happily answered all of their questions. Then they asked me about my experiences with the Russians when they lived in my house. This shocked me. I was surprised that they knew so much about me. I quickly decided that my origins from Eastern Europe had cast a suspicion on me. Maybe they thought I was a spy.

After I had answered all of the questions, Sergeant Jones leaned back in his chair. "How would you feel about being assigned to the Regimental Intelligence and Reconaissance Platoon?"

I didn't have a clue what this was, but I smiled. "I would be honored," I said. I wasn't going to be in the infantry and I was relieved.

They both smiled at me. "The I&R Platoon serves as the eyes and ears of the regiment. Those who are in this platoon are volunteers and are specially selected, based on the talents they bring to the mission. Shachnowski, your asset is that you've been there, you know the territory, the customs, and can speak the language. You'll be a great asset to us." Jones got up and put out his hand to me. "Thank you for volunteering."

"Yes, sir," I said and turned to leave. Within two days, I was transferred to the Regimental Headquarters Company. The platoon consisted of forty men, mounted in twelve jeeps. The most diverse, rough, and ready group of misfits I had ever encountered. Some of them were so aggressive it was frightening, but I managed to get along with all of them.

FIFTY

S hachnowski," Lieutenant Manus, our platoon leader at Fort Riley, shouted. "I want you to drive me over to the Regimental Headquarters."

I was surprised, but happy. I walked out to his jeep with him. I had not driven since I left Salem and it felt good to be behind the wheel again.

"Private," Lieutenant Manus said after we had driven for several miles. "I think you've got a pretty good head on your shoulders. I'd like you to be my driver," he stopped to see my immediate reaction.

I didn't reveal anything.

"Think you can do the job?" he asked.

"Yes, sir. I'd very much like to be your driver," I answered smiling.

Lieutenant Manus and I had a common bond. We both loved cars. As we drove, we discussed cars that we had both owned in the past. I told him about my experience as a mechanic. When we got out of the jeep he handed me an operator's manual for the vehicle. "In case we ever break down," he said and smiled. He walked off whistling.

When the others in the platoon found out that Lieutenant Manus had chosen me to be his driver, my stock in the motley group was raised considerably.

Joe Zimmerman became my best friend in the platoon. Both Joe and I spoke German, and we were both asked to help the others learn the language. I liked Zimmerman; he was a loner and never said much. We both liked ice cream. A flavor called butter brickle. We would share the responsibility of getting a carton of ice cream each night, and meet on the barracks fire escape with our spoon to share the ice cream right out of the container. We conversed in German to keep our language skills honed.

Joe had many stories about both the eastern and western front happenings in World War II. "I was a teenager in Germany when the war broke out. My father was in the German army."

I listened to the stories about the hardships on the German soldiers. I never spoke to Joe about my past.

———

"We'll be shipping out to Aschaffenburg, Germany, sometime in September. As soon as I have the exact date I'll let you know," Lieutenant Manus told us during morning formation. "You'll have a two-week block leave before we go, so count on being home during August."

I couldn't wait to tell Arlene when I called her on Sunday. We would get married in August.

That Saturday evening Joe and I went into Junction City, a small town outside of Fort Riley. Neither of us drank, but we enjoyed the lively atmosphere at the bars where all the soldiers hung out. As we walked down the street "The Yellow Rose of Texas" blared from the open doors of the bars. It was a popular song on the radio.

Joe and I turned into the bar and opened the glass doors. We were hit with the smell of cigarette smoke and whiskey. The normal Saturday night atmosphere. The street was lined with similar bars. This one was called Pig Pen.

A large, heavy-set black-haired man was sitting at the entrance of the bar and collected the cover charge. Some of the soldiers standing in line tried to talk him out of the $2 fee with no luck. Joe and I handed him the $2.

The place was jam-packed with people, and we squeezed through the maze looking for a table. Tonight it was so packed it wasn't even comfortable to stand and look for a table. Joe and I turned to leave, and I noticed someone waving at us from the far corner of the room.

I recognized Sergeant Fitch, waving his hand frantically and motioning for us to come over to the table. Sergeant Jones was sitting with him. I elbowed Zimmerman. "Hey, Joe, the sergeants want us to come over to their table."

We pushed our way over to them and sat down. We started chatting and I realized that Sergeant Jones was busy making goo-goo eyes at a girl sitting across the table next to us with three other people. She was very attractive, with a knockout body. Jones couldn't keep his eyes off her.

"Can I get you boys anything?" the waitress asked as she fought her way to our table.

"A round, honey," Jones said, never taking his eyes off the girl. She was lapping up his attention and tossed her blonde hair seductively.

The waitress looked at Joe and me, and we both ordered a beer and a sandwich.

The place was so loud that we couldn't hear each other when we tried to talk. But the communication between Sergeant Jones and his girl heated up. I discreetly watched while I ate my sandwich.

Her boyfriend was sitting with his back to our table. He was a big gorilla of a man, and evidently didn't realize what was going on; at least it appeared that way. Jones started blowing kisses her way and she returned the sentiment.

I could hardly keep a straight face. I had heard that Jones was a ladies' man with his sculpted good looks and wild nature. I had never before seen him in action.

She gave him a big, flashy, come-on grin. I think that her boyfriend may have noticed. Just as suddenly, she lost interest in the game they were playing and turned toward the gorilla.

Fitch and Jones paid their tab and got up to leave. Joe and I weren't ready to go and stayed in our seats and sipped at our drinks while we watched the crowd. We said good night to Jones and Fitch. I watched as Jones passed the table of four where the girl was sitting. As Jones passed by the big gorilla boyfriend jumped up and grabbed him by the throat. He began to pummel Jones's head. People started running in every direction.

I leaped up from the table and jumped on the gorilla's back. I reached around his head with my hand and clawed at his face. I hung on to him and he tried to throw himself back against the wall to get rid of me. I poked my fingers in his eyes. Then without warning, he arched his back and propelled backward and slammed into the cinder-block wall. The force flattened me like a pancake with a resounding thud! I sunk to the floor.

I shook my head and regained my vision. I saw Joe charging the gorilla boyfriend as Jones punched at his head. Jones's head and face were gushing blood and the entire front of his shirt was covered with red stain. I ran and jumped on the gorilla's back again and he was waving his hands to get to Jones's face again. When I looked over at Jones, it was hard to believe that a human fist could turn a face into mush.

Suddenly, two state troopers appeared behind Jones with their billy clubs drawn. They meant business and threw all of us up against the wall and ordered us to stand with our face against the wall and our arms spread out. They used their clubs to push us around and kick our feet apart. I heard sirens come to a screeching halt and reinforcements arrived.

The gorilla was taken into custody. The state trooper standing near us took us out to his car and piled us into the backseat. Jones's face looked like hamburger. Joe's teeth were broken and he had a huge gash on his lip. He was spitting blood onto the floor of the car. I handed him my cap to spit into, not wanting to aggravate the policeman. I had no apparent injuries other than being sore. We rode to the station in silence and were placed in a holding cell.

I stared at the wall for what seemed like an eternity. I had no idea what consequence I would face. I wondered if I would be kicked out of the army. I knew they were lenient about brawls in bars, but I wasn't an officer, I was a private . . . low man on the army totem pole.

"MPs won't be here for a while, boys," the police officer yelled into our cell. "Maybe they think you need to cool your heels," he said and chuckled his way back to his desk. A few hours later he returned. "Soldier," he said, looking at Jones. "I just thought I'd let you know the reason your face looks like mincemeat." He pulled out an oversized key covered in blood out of a bag. "Your opponent had a weapon."

It was 11 A.M. the next morning when Lieutenant Manus stood looking at us at the door of the holding cell. We were released into his custody. I was tired, hungry, and had a throbbing pain in my head. But I felt better when I walked out of the jailhouse door and saw sunlight.

Jones got into the front of the car with Manus. I was not asked to drive. Joe and I got into the backseat.

"Lieutenant Manus," Jones said. "We'll need to borrow some extra machine guns for our field exercise on Monday. Ours have been sent out for routine maintenance."

I was stunned. Jones was sitting there with a face that looked similar to hamburger, blood red and scratched, acting as though nothing had happened.

"I think your right, Sergeant," Manus answered. "You take care of that before Monday morning formation. I'll sign the paperwork."

That was all that was said and we rode back to the base in silence.

I spent the day in bed. It was Sunday and we had the day off. I took about five hot, steaming showers and tried to work the soreness out of my body. I called Arlene at her long-distance operator job and told her what had happened. She was as concerned as I was about my future.

"Arlene, if I don't get kicked out of the army, I will have a two-week leave before I ship out to Germany in August," I said into the phone. "What about getting married then?"

I could hear the smile in her voice. "That sounds great! My parents want me to have a big wedding. That doesn't give me a lot of time. But, Sid, you know if you get thrown out of the army . . . Sid, we can elope day after tomorrow," she said, cracking up at her own joke. "Maybe you can get a job at the Texaco station and wear that black hat with flaps."

"Very funny, ha-ha, Arlene. I promised you'd see the world when you married me, paid for by the army," I kidded her. "How did you know about that hat?"

"I saw you when you first came to America. I sat in the backseat of our car and laughed at the way you had the ears flipped out so you could hear," she laughed, remembering that sight.

I had never forgotten that little girl. I couldn't believe it was Arlene. "I remember," I said, kidding her back. "I thought you were flirting with me!"

"Men and their egos!" she said. "Gotta go, Sid. I'll start planning the wedding or maybe the elopement."

I could hear her laughing as she disconnected the line.

FIFTY-ONE

At morning formation Jones, Zimmerman, Fitch, and I were ordered to go to Captain Martin's office. Not a word was spoken until we arrived in his office. We all three saluted and stood at attention. Captain Martin was sitting behind a large mahogany desk. He had a paper in his hand.

"What I am looking at, men," he said. "The Military Police Blotter from last Saturday night. I want to read it to you." He went through the entire description of our brawl. "Now, would one of you like to tell me what happened?" he said. He laid down the paper and stared at the three of us.

"Well, sir, first of all I just want to apologize for this incident," Jones humbly began. "I just feel like the lowest snake in the world for embarrassing this unit and the United States Army for my bad behavior."

I thought he was doing pretty good so far.

"I should have been able to control myself and I guess, Captain Martin, that I need more discipline, but sometimes I just can't," Jones continued looking exasperated about his behavior.

Surely he's not going to tell Martin about the girl, I thought to myself.

"And maybe you can advise me, sir, about what to do when I hear some civie bad-mouthing the U.S. Army in general." Jones looked at Martin with innocent eyes. "If he had just said it once, I could have let it go. But, repeatedly, sir, this man cast a terrible light on the U.S. Army. I just couldn't help myself! I am deeply sorry, sir."

Now, my jaw dropped. I put my head down to conceal my surprise. I couldn't believe that he was trying to pull this off. But I did admire his acting ability.

Sergeant Fitch confirmed the story and explained that he did not see the brawl because he was in the restroom at the time.

But if I remembered correctly the minute the fight started Fitch hightailed it out of the bar.

I started to brace myself for the severe punishment that we were about to receive, since the captain probably knew the true story and realized that this was a load of baloney that Jones had fed him. I was caught completely off guard by the next event.

"Well, gentlemen," the captain said softly. "I would like to commend you on your efforts to always protect the good name of the army. I would think that your behavior was commensurate with the erroneous lies that this man was telling. You are standard-bearers for the truth!" He stopped and took a breath. "You did the right thing. Dismissed."

We saluted and filed out of the office.

Sergeant Jones returned to report the conclusion of the matter to Lieutenant Manus. When Manus walked out of earshot after we returned, Jones turned to Joe and me. "I'll never forget what you did for me. I can't thank you enough!" he said and gratefully shook our hands.

At the end of July we started preparing to deploy from Fort Riley. We packed all of the equipment and personal belongings we would need to take to Germany. Two soldiers in my unit from Pennsylvania and I had decided to buy a cheap car and drive to our homes. If we took turns driving to our destination, we could save money and time. We estimated that driving time would take about thirty hours.

We found a '46 Ford for $200. It was in pretty good shape and still had treads on the tires. We divided the cost of the Ford. At the end of the trip we would sell the car and split the profits.

We could not leave Fort Riley until August 6. At one minute past midnight on August 6 the three of us piled into the car with a healthy amount of No-Doz in our pockets and began our journey. We drove through the Great Plains and over the mountains on an endless ribbon of highway. Our only stops were for coffee, the restroom, and gas. We had not eaten for twenty-four hours when we finally arrived at Jack and Salty's hometown in Warren, Pennsylvania. We stopped at an all-night diner on the highway and ordered bacon and eggs with greasy hash brown potatoes.

I drank extra coffee to keep me awake for the last leg of my trip. I had a few more hours' drive to get to Salem. I was in great spirits as I headed to Salem. I was making plans for the future and listening to the radio. I sang along with the radio while I was driving to keep me alert.

I wondered how Arlene was going to like the way I looked. When I left I was scrawny. After six months of physical exercise and training, my muscles had filled out and there was a hard edge to my body. The army had a phrase for it: fighting shape. I liked it.

BOOOM! As soon as I heard the noise I hit the brakes. It didn't feel like a blown-out tire. I looked toward the hood and saw smoke pouring out from the motor. I pulled off the road and got out. I wrapped a rag around my hand and opened the hood and was hit with the fog and heat of the steam still pouring from the engine. I sat down next to the car and waited for the motor to cool down.

A tow truck traveling down the highway stopped when he saw that I was stalled. We both looked at the engine. It was ruined! I was ten miles outside of Albany, New York, and stuck with no car and only a few dollars.

I offered to sell the car to the tow driver for scrap metal price.

"Where you goin', kid?" he asked.

"I'm trying to get to Salem," I said.

"Hop in the cab of the truck . . . the only way you're getting to Salem is by Greyhound. I'll take you to the bus station." I spent the next two days on the bus to Salem.

When I finally walked into my house after the long trip I was greeted as though I was a war hero! I couldn't believe how glad my parents were to see me. Every one was so nice. My mother started cooking the minute I walked in the door and within an hour I had a feast placed in front of me. My brother offered to let me drive "his" car. Things were going so well that I decided to tell them about my marriage plans. I realized very quickly that nothing had changed in their acceptance of Arlene. Both of my parents started with the lectures and tears of disappointment.

"If you marry that Catholic girl," my mother said in her final rant, "we will declare you dead and have a funeral at the same moment of your marriage. You will no longer be a living member of this family!" This was a Jewish tradition for a child that had disgraced the family. I saw that her feelings were so firmly etched in her mind that she would probably do something as ridiculous as this.

"Ma, Pa," I said. "Why don't you stop complaining and give her a chance. She is a wonderful girl and I love her!"

"She is Catholic," my father said flatly.

"Join the new world," I said angrily. "America, the melting pot. Have you even taken a step into this world? You both live in the past! Have you bothered to learn English? Have you even learned how to drive a car? You are not in Lithuania. You are here . . . you are free in the United States . . . a chance for happiness. What counts is not if we believe in the same God, or any God for that matter. It's important that we love and care for each other and we want to make each other happy. No matter what you say I am not going to let you take my happiness from me." I left without finishing my meal and borrowed my brother's car.

When Arlene opened the door she looked even prettier than I had remembered. She was almost eighteen. It had been more than six months since I had seen her. Both of us had changed and both of us had grown.

After I greeted her parents we got into my car and drove around town and talked. "Arlene, we have to get our blood tests tomorrow. I think we should get married as soon as possible. We've got to get a marriage license, too. I think it takes three days or something like that," I said, my mind racing.

"Maybe, we should postpone the wedding, Sid . . . until you come home from overseas," she said.

I sat in silence. I didn't understand. She said she wanted to get married.

What had happened? "What? What did you say, Arlene?" I gasped. "I thought we decided . . . you said you wanted to get married . . ."

"I do want to get married . . . but maybe . . . we should wait," Arlene said. This was the end for me. I was so confused.

"Sid, I'm not saying no. I just think it might be better if we waited. And your parents might feel better if we waited."

"Why?" I asked.

"You just can't demand a marriage because of your stress. I want it to be a happy time. Not when people are angry. It's just not right, Sid," Arlene tried to explain.

I drove the car back to her house.

"Sid, don't be angry. It's just something to think about," Arlene said.

"Yeah, I need to think a little bit," I said. "I'll talk to you tomorrow." I needed someone to talk to, a sounding board. I was more confused than ever now.

FIFTY-TWO

"Hey buddy, how you doin'?" Frank said when he opened the door. He gave me a big bear hug. "When did you get home?"

"A couple of days ago," I said. He could tell by the look on my face that I had problems. "I need to talk to you, Frank."

"Let's take a ride," he said and got his keys. "Let's take my car."

We took a ride out to Salem Willows, a reserve close to the ocean. There was an amusement park there and Frank listened to my story of what had happened since I got home as we walked through the arcades. We stopped and got a hot dog.

After Frank heard my story he was very positive and felt as strongly as I did that Arlene and I should get married right away. He had an infectious spirit that made me feel confident and sure that everything would work out. He reminded me that I had always pushed to make things happen and sometimes you just had to let things take their course. He made sense and I decided I was going to just let things happen. I was sure that Arlene loved me and we would spend our lives together.

"Sid, I've been going to the dog races on Saturdays," Frank said excitedly. We had just gotten in the car to drive back to his house. "I came so close, Sid, so close to winning a C-note last week."

"What do you mean, Frank . . . a C-note."

"A hundred bucks . . . one hundred simoleans!" he said.

"How? That's a lot of money, Frank," I said incredulously.

"I had a bet on this dog . . . not a favorite, but a good dog. I got a good tip and I bet small money, but the odds were great," he said. "Listen to this, she took off running like the wind, Sid. I'm telling you it was a thing of beauty! Anyway, I'm rooting and cheering for Samantha, that was her name. Good name, huh?" he said looking over at me.

"Yeah, it's a good name," I said smiling at his story.

"She was running on the inside track ahead of the pack," he motioned with his hand that she was moving fast. "Then for some unknown reason she moved to the outside and somehow got confused and lagged behind for the rest of the race. Can you believe that, Sid? If she had won I would have made a hundred bucks in just minutes!"

"What do you think happened to her . . . why'd she move to the outside?" I asked.

"You get the picture?" Frank said. He then went into a demonstration of what happened to the dog. He lifted his hands off the wheel to show me.

I watched his hands move and then I felt a horrendous impact and a thunderous crack. In a split second I propelled through the windshield of Frank's car and lost consciousness.

When Frank looked toward me as he told his story the car collided with some construction barriers, rolled over, and dove nose first into a deep trench. Luckily, none of the construction workers were hurt. When I opened my eyes several workers were standing over me. I tasted blood in my mouth and felt blood running down my face from the injuries on my head.

"Where do you hurt?" one of the workers asked.

I couldn't make sense of anything. I just shook my head. "I'm bleeding," I said. In the next few minutes I felt myself coming into consciousness a little more clearly. "Is Frank okay?"

"He just had some bruises. One of the guys took him to the hospital in his car," a worker answered.

"How long have I been out?" I asked. I saw another man come into view. He was standing over me.

"Jeez, I can't put him in my car. My wife would kill me if I came home with blood all over the car," I heard him say.

"We'll use the dump truck," I heard another man's voice.

Suddenly several arms formed a gurney beneath me and placed me in the back of the dump truck. When they laid me down I felt a warm gooey substance. I realized that the substance was tar! Before the driver took off, I somehow managed to jump out. He didn't realize that I was no longer a passenger. He had just hit the accelerator and drove off like a bat out of hell, honking his horn and blinking his lights.

For some reason it struck me as funny, even though I was in very bad shape. I started laughing thinking how he would have a heart attack when he got to the hospital and went to the back of his truck and I wasn't there.

Finally a man came running with a towel in his hand. He wrapped the towel around my bleeding head. Another man drove up in his station wagon and placed a piece of plastic in the back and transported me to the hospital.

After I arrived at Salem Hospital I was given thirty-two stitches. The wound wrapped around my head and face like a train track. Over one hundred pieces of small glass fragments were embedded in my face, mouth, and gums. When I left the emergency room, I was rolled into a hospital room and moved from the gurney to the bed.

The nurse opened the curtain next to my bed. I was face to face with Frank who was lying in the bed next to me. He took one look at me and burst into nervous laughter. His laughter was infectious. I could only imagine what I looked like to him. I started to laugh even though the pain was excruciating.

Arlene came to the hospital the moment she heard about the accident. She was the only person that I had asked the hospital to notify. She had just arrived when I saw my mother and father come through the door of my room. I'm glad I was lying down because in my wildest dreams I could not have imagined that this would be the way Arlene met my parents.

"Hello, Mr. and Mrs. Shachnow," she said. Arlene walked over and extended her hand to my mother. "I'm Arlene Armstrong." She was poised and gracious as she looked at my mother.

I held my breath and watched my mother.

For some reason she was polite and congenial and so was my father.

"Arlene was nice enough to call us," my mother said meekly. "I'm so glad you're okay."

I told them what happened, and Frank joined in taking blame for the accident.

"Arlene, I want to get married as soon as possible," I said, after everyone was quiet. Surely she wouldn't turn me down with a plea from the hospital bed.

"Maybe it's too fast, Sid," she answered.

"Oh, Sid, I wish you would look at things as clearly as Arlene," my mother said. Now all of a sudden they agreed with Arlene.

"I want you to come with me to Germany. Arlene, it's part of my past. We can see it together. I can show you things and I can see it through your eyes," I pleaded.

"She's a very mature girl, Sid," my mother said. "Listen to her."

I ignored my mother. "You'll miss so much, Arlene, if you're not with me. We'll lose touch."

She looked at me for a long time and then smiled. "I may be mature, Mrs. Shachnow, but I love Sid and I don't want to miss being together in Germany." She looked at my mother. "I hope you understand."

A scene that could have been disastrous had suddenly softened my parents. I knew if they met Arlene they would change their minds. They were not ecstatic, they were not even happy about the marriage, but they consented to attend the wedding.

FIFTY-THREE

On August 28, 1955, Arlene Armstrong and I were married standing in front of a justice of the peace in Seabrook, New Hampshire, not far from Salem. My parents agreed to attend as long as no other member of our family would be invited. This was not a wedding that every girl dreamed of with a beautiful wedding gown, bouquets of flowers, wedding presents, and bridesmaids. Arlene didn't even get a handsome groom. My face was still swollen from the accident and I had to lean on a cane when I spoke my vows. My parents sat silently, sulking during the ceremony. The Armstrongs, however, were very happy and made the best of it. My brother fidgeted during the entire short ceremony, wishing he could be anywhere but where he was. I had asked Frank and his wife, Ginny, to attend. She summed up our wedding perfectly. "It was the saddest wedding I ever saw."

There was no reception, no festivities, no good-luck rice thrown, no tears of joy. But to make up for the sad wedding, I had planned a honeymoon by the ocean. My brother had loaned me the car and I headed for the seaside resort motel where I had booked us a room. As we drove toward the shores on the outskirts of New Hampshire, my adrenaline was pumping. I was driving fast and talking to Arlene. I looked in the rearview mirror as I was coming down the ramp to exit and I saw the flashing red lights.

"Oh, my God," Arlene said. "How fast were you driving?"

"I don't know, I was talking," I said. I slowly got out of the car and secured my cane as I walked to meet the policeman. He was stone-faced as he walked toward me. When he got closer he saw the gashes, stitches, and fully developed bruises on my face. His eyes narrowed with a look of disbelief.

"What the hell happened to your face?" he asked incredulously.

"I was in a very serious car wreck yesterday. I went through the windshield," I answered.

He looked at my car.

"It wasn't my car, officer. I was a passenger," I said.

He nodded and shook his head. "Son, I suggest that you keep your heavy foot off the gas pedal," he said.

He took my license and went back to his patrol car.

After a few minutes he came back and handed me my license. "Well, it's Saturday and the courts won't be open till Monday morning. You'll have to spend the next two nights in jail."

I felt my heart sink. "But Officer, I'm on my honeymoon. I can't spend my honeymoon in jail."

He just shook his head.

Arlene poked her head through the window. "Officer, we've had a hard time with his parents . . . we've had a wedding that didn't even have any music . . . he's leaving for Germany to serve in the army . . . and I don't know what we'll do if we don't have a honeymoon. I may never see him after he's shipped out!" Arlene pleaded dramatically with tears in her eyes.

He looked at me. "I guess you're just lucky she married you lookin' the way you do! I'll let you off this time with a warning, but be careful!"

"Thank you, Officer. Thank you so much," I said after he handed me my license.

I saw the sign of the motel about ten minutes later. When I walked into the office to check in I was greeted by a man who weighed about three hundred pounds with strands of greasy hair on his balding head. I guessed that he hadn't taken a bath since last winter. The smell that hit my nostrils was overpowering. I started having doubts about my honeymoon suite.

When I opened the door to our room I knew I had made a big mistake. It smelled like the three hundred-pound man. The floor was dirty and there was dust on the furniture. The window above the bed was broken. I sat our luggage down and looked around. No wonder it was so reasonably priced.

Arlene closed the door. I put the suitcase on the bed and opened it. I started to take our clothes out and put them in the drawers.

"Sid, don't unpack. Let's just stay here tonight and go back home tomorrow," she said.

I looked up and I thanked God that Arlene had a great sense of humor. We folded over in laughter and discussed the events of our wedding day that were in reality a nightmare!

We stayed awake most of the night and we were back on the road to Salem at 7 A.M. the next morning. The manager returned half of my deposit. We laughed all the way home. Partly because we were happy to be together and partly because so far everything that could go wrong had gone wrong. I knew that whatever our future held for us we would survive with humor.

I slipped the key into the door of my parents' house and opened it. I didn't think anyone was home until I heard my mother's voice.

"Yes, I know," she spoke into the telephone. "I am so sorry that my son married a non-Jew. It is a disgrace to all of our family." Her voice paused for a moment as she listened to the person on the other end of the phone. "Yes, I know he will see the light someday . . . and there will be a divorce . . . but what can we do? He is headstrong." She paused again. "Yes, yes, I know, please give my apologies to your family."

If my mother had put a knife through Arlene's heart it could not have been worse. We both stopped in our tracks as she apologized for our marriage. I didn't know whether to leave or stay and tell my mother what I thought of her conversation.

"Sid, don't say anything," Arlene said quietly. "Give it time."

My mother walked in and her face was flushed. She was civil, but arrogant.

Dear Arlene,

I arrived in Aschaffenburg yesterday. We sailed on an old troop ship, USS Rose. Ironic, huh? My mother's name. This ship was old, Arlene, it reminded me of the one that I arrived in when we came to the U.S., and probably as old. We had pretty smooth seas coming over. It was a big difference from my last trip. I wasn't seasick on this trip.

The guys have already checked out the bars here. The barkeeps love soldiers. What they really love is the money. All the locals look at us with a wary eye. I saw a couple of guys (not guys in our unit) get arrested because they were bothering some women in a bar. Zimmerman is a big hit with the German ladies. He speaks the language and they love the rich American soldier. Maybe he'll end up getting married.

I hope that everything is going well at home and you are already packing. I think about you all the time and I can't wait for you to arrive. I'm living in a barracks that is built of stone. It's an old building but the rooms are large and have very high ceilings. A barracks that looks like a mansion! I would have never believed it! Anyway I'm looking for an apartment when I have a chance. I'll have one by the time you get here. Tell everyone hello.

All my love,
Sid

After we had been in Germany for several months, Sergeant Jones pulled me aside. "Sid, I need to see you in my room at 1400." He looked at me sternly. Usually, even if one of us were in trouble he had a more casual attitude. This was something personal if he wanted me to come to his room.

"Yes, Sergeant," I said to him.

I went to his room at the designated time. When he walked in he asked me to sit down on his bed.

"I need some help in solving a problem," he said.

"Yes, sir," I said.

"I need a doctor," he said flatly.

"There's one at the base hospital that I hear is pretty good," I said.

"I don't want an army doctor," he said and gave me a hard look. "You speak German and I think you can find me someone I can trust," Jones said. "Sid, I've got the clap and I need some treatment."

This was no surprise. Jones, the ladies' man, had a new girl every night. "Yes, Sergeant, I will find a doctor."

I laughed when I walked out of the room. We had received countless lectures about the perils of venereal disease. There are notorious stories circulated about the horrors if you catch this disease. The army conducted inspections to ensure that we were not infected. They're nicknamed short-arm inspections.

Sergeant Jones just last week had roused us up early at 5:00 A.M. "Drop your drawers, gentlemen!" he shouted when he walked in the door. When we saw the medic we knew that it was a short-arm inspection. As each of us stood silently as the medic inspected us, Jones walked up and down the center aisle. "Flies spread disease! So if you catch my drift, keep it buttoned up!"

I assumed he meant barflies, for which he had a healthy appetite. Too bad he didn't follow his own pearls of wisdom. I located a German doctor near the base and made an appointment.

Sergeant Jones didn't want to use an army jeep since he was seeing the doctor on the sly. He thought of all the angles when it came to protecting himself from the wrath of the army. He had experience and was the master of deception. He juggled three or four girls at a time and remembered what he told each one of them. It was like a game to him and he liked it. He said the game kept his adrenaline flowing.

"Damn women," he said, almost to himself.

"You ever going to settle down, Sergeant?" I asked him.

"I'd feel like I was dead if I ever got married," he said and gave me a half grin.

"It's not that bad, is it?" I asked.

"For me it would be. It's not the girls, Shachnow, they'll come and go. They will always be there . . . have been since I was twelve years old. It's the chase and the juggling I like," Jones said as we walked into the doctor's office. "Shachnow, why the hell did you get married?"

"I wanted to spend the rest of my life with her," I answered.

"It's easier being in the army when you're single," he said looking at me. "Why didn't you wait until you were an officer?"

"I just didn't want to be without her," I said.

"How can you trust a broad, Shachnow?" he asked.

"I don't trust many people . . ." I said after a moment. "But I do trust her."

Jones couldn't even conceive what I was talking about. He just shrugged his shoulders.

"You got a place to live?" he asked.

"No, sir," I answered.

He shook his head and the nurse called him to see the doctor.

I had explained to the doctor over the phone what the problem was with Jones. When he came out of the office he was smiling. "Good as new in a few days."

"Shachnowski, come to my room for a minute," Sergeant Jones said after we had returned. When we got to the room, he opened a drawer and took out a small box and handed it to me. "I can't thank you enough for helping me out. I'd like for you to take these. When your wife gets here you can wear them for a night on the town!"

I opened the box as he was talking. It was a beautiful pair of cuff links and tie clip decorated with real turquoise. "You don't owe me anything, Sergeant," I said.

He shook his head. "Shachnowski, I want you to organize the range for field firing tomorrow. You're going to run the range for the platoon,"

"Yes, sir," I said and went out the door.

FIFTY-FOUR

One evening about nine o'clock I was walking the neighborhood streets in Aschaffenburg. I had spent the entire day desperately reading every rental ad, searching for an apartment for Arlene and me. She was arriving next week.

As I walked down one of the blocks to the last rental ad address, it was after dark. I ran up the steps of the house and saw that even though it was late there were several lights on. I took a chance and knocked.

"Who is it?" I heard a man's voice from behind the door.

"I saw your ad for a room for rent, sir," I answered.

The door opened. "It's late!" he said grouchily. He stood in the doorway squinting his eyes at me. "I don't have my glasses on. Come on inside and let me look at you."

I walked in and stood in the entry hall. He walked into his living room and retrieved his glasses. He placed them on his nose and looked me over. I looked him over, too. He had white hair that was combed to the side with an attempt to cover his balding head, a full set of perfect-looking teeth that I found out later were false.

"Who are you?" he asked.

"I'm Private Schaja Shachnowski," I said and offered my hand.

He shook my hand. "I'm Mr. Hartman." His fingers were cold. His grip was slight.

"Follow me," he said and led me to the room for rent.

The light was dim, but the room looked like it was okay. It was small but it would do.

"How much does this cost per month?"

"Fifty dollars a month. You share kitchen and bathroom privileges with the other tenants," he answered. "I rent four other rooms."

"My wife will be here next week. I'll give you $20 now and the rest when we move in," I said.

"I have someone else that wants to see it tomorrow and they said they needed to move right away. If I rent it to you I'll lose $30 if you change your mind," he said, shutting off the light and shuffling toward the front door.

"Okay," I said. "I'll give you the $50 now." This was half of my salary per month from the army.

"I've got no clothes to wear, I need some civilian clothes," I said. I was standing over Zimmerman's bunk, in my underwear. He was half asleep. The only clothes I owned were my pea-green army-issue uniforms. I mailed my old clothes back to Salem to my parents before I left for Germany. I thought my brother could use them.

Several of the guys heard my dilemma. Within an hour I had civilian clothing put together by my platoon. It didn't match. I wore stripes and plaids and three or four different colors, but I didn't care. I just wanted to make the train on time. It was a three hundred-mile train ride to meet Arlene. I didn't want to be late.

I got to the pier long before the ship docked. When it finally arrived, I watched the passengers deboard from the USS *United States* luxury liner. Since the ship was a commercial liner it carried quite a few passengers. I anxiously watched for Arlene. I started getting nervous when the stream of passengers stopped. I ran toward one of the officers on the ship when I saw him leaving.

"Sir, I am expecting my wife on this liner . . . Arlene Shachnow," I said, hoping he might know the name.

He shrugged his shoulders. "I'm sorry, everyone is off the ship," he said and thought for a moment. Then he pointed to another officer on the ship with a clipboard. "Go talk to him. He has the passenger list."

I ran up the ramp to the other officer. "Sir, I'm here to pick up Arlene Shachnowski. Can you tell me if she arrived with the ship?"

He looked at the list, and ran his pencil down the page. He flipped to the second page . . . then the third page. "Ahhh . . . Arlene Shachnowski. Yes, she was a passenger," he said and looked up at me.

"Where is she?" I asked.

"You must have missed her, sir."

"Where would she go around here? She doesn't know anyone and she doesn't speak German," I said. He sensed the edge in my voice. There was no way I could have missed her; I had been standing at the end of the exit ramp since the first person got off the ship.

"The only place she could have gone is the terminal," he said.

For the next two hours, I frantically searched for Arlene. I couldn't find her anywhere. I asked women to go into the ladies' room and search for her. I pulled her picture out of my wallet and showed it to everyone in the terminal.

I sat down on a bench and tried to figure out where she might possibly be. The crowds in the terminal had cleared out. The huge room was almost empty. I decided that I would go back to the ship and ask more questions.

"Schaja Shachnowski," I heard a voice in the distance, calling me. I turned and didn't see anyone. "Schaja Shachnowski . . ." I heard it again. I looked over toward the ship, and I saw a man walking down the strand next to the ship, carrying a sign with my name on it and yelling my name. I ran to where he was standing.

"I'm Shachnowski!" I said, grabbing his arm.

"Sir, you're wife has been trying to find you! She won't get off of the ship, unless she sees that you are here!" he said. "We've been paging you for hours."

"Oh, my God, I thought she was lost!"

"Not on our ship, sir. We take care of our passengers," he smiled, and led me to Arlene.

We arrived in Aschaffenburg the next morning. I was wearing the same clothes from the day before. Arlene kidded me on the train about my extravagant wardrobe. I defended myself saying I had to save my money to fulfill my promise to her about seeing the world. This became a running joke between us throughout our marriage, and my career in the army. Once Arlene arrived, it was as though we had never been apart.

We walked from the train station to the apartment that I had rented. I had a key to the front door. It was the first time I had seen the house in the daylight. I could see that the paint on the house was peeling. I opened the door and we walked to our room; in the daylight everything looked dirty and shabby. I had not noticed how bad this was in the dark. I turned to Arlene and I could see the disappointment on her face. "Not too good?" I said.

She mustered a smile. "Well, it's a roof over our heads."

The room was no more than ten by ten. The bed covered most of the room. We had a small table and two chairs. I had been stupid. I hadn't looked at the room the way Arlene was looking at the room.

"Sid," she said, as she walked across the bed. "How is the room heated?"

I had no idea how the room was heated, I hadn't even thought about it. But I did know that it was cold in November, and would only get colder. I walked toward the living room. "Mr. Hartman," I called to my landlord.

He appeared out of nowhere. He didn't say anything, just raised his eyebrows.

"How do we get heat in our room?" I asked.

He pointed to a coal stove that was open on two ends to the room next door. But the coal had to be loaded from the other room. "The only heat comes from the opening if you use the coal stove," he said.

Arlene's eyes flew open and her mouth dropped in disbelief.

FIFTY-FIVE

Arlene got up early the next morning and went to the kitchen. She was still half asleep. I could hear voices in the distance. Then I heard Arlene when she jumped back into the bed. I turned over and looked at her. I couldn't tell if she was laughing or crying.

"I walked into the kitchen, Sid, and first I see a pair of false teeth sitting on the counter next to the sink in a glass of water. Then I look at the back wall and Mr. Hartman and a young girl are sleeping on a cot together. She turns to me and says, 'Morning' . . . then she gives me a toothy smile, or maybe I should say toothless smile. She had the ugliest teeth you can imagine, with two gaping holes of missing teeth." Arlene covered her face with the pillow.

"Mr. Hartman has a girlfriend. That wrinkled old guy?" I said.

"Yeah, and she looks like she's in her teens," Arlene ended her description. "How could she have lost those two teeth?"

It turned out that Mr. Hartman had quite a few lady friends, and we realized that we would be sharing the bathroom with all of his guests.

Arlene and I moved the next week. She searched every day while I was working to find a new residence, and found a couple that would rent us two rooms at 76 Schweinheimer Strasse. Our new landlords spoke only German, but helped Arlene learn the basics of the language and helped her adapt to her new environment while I was at work.

Within one month Arlene had already developed a network of friends with other army wives. Lieutenant Manus's wife, Jane, became a close friend.

I came in one night, after I left the base, concerned about what I had to tell Arlene. "I got some news today. I have to go on a three-week exercise in the field. I won't be back until the twenty-second of December."

"What kind of exercise is it?" she asked brightly.

I had expected her to be upset that I would be gone. But she took it in stride. "Training exercises in the field. Reconnaissance and intelligence gathering in the field. Like we're in a war, but it's just a game," I said.

"Where is it going to be?" she asked.

"Grafenwohr. It's about three or four hours from here," I said.

"I'll be fine. Jane said when you went on training exercises we would get together. Some of the other wives will be alone, too."

The Eighty-seventh Infantry Regiment, I&R Platoon, consisted of twelve jeeps and forty men. We were scheduled to depart at 0300 for a tactical exercise. The army command in Europe had a rule for everything, and one of them was that we traveled with the windshield of the jeep folded down when operating tactically. It was frigidly cold, and the open front and sides would make it very uncomfortable. I shivered as I felt the icy wind cut through my heavy jacket while I was waiting for Lieutenant Manus. I remembered the last time we were tactical and how my hands started to shake on the steering wheel, it took all the concentration I had to keep driving and get us to our destination.

"Sid, I have a court-martial hearing in an hour, we won't be leaving with the rest of the platoon. I'm going to go inside to speak to Captain Martin. When I get back have those doors and windows on the jeep!" Lieutenant Manus said as he turned and marched toward the administration building.

"Yes, sir!" I answered, and saluted before his back was turned.

Army rules considered this mission to be an administrative move, therefore the windows and doors were allowed and our trip was comfortable. Later in the day, we would go back to tactical and remove the doors.

The hearing went on for several hours. I wasn't allowed to be in the hearing so I hung around in the military courthouse and walked around the grounds. I went back into the courthouse and waited for him.

Lieutenant Manus came bursting through the doors of the hearing room with a canvas sack over his shoulder. I jumped to attention and snapped a salute.

"At ease," he said, and returned my salute. "Put this in the jeep."

He handed me a green duffel bag.

"I won't be long," he said to me and started talking with another officer.

I went to the storage room to wait for him. When I went in the door I saw that the doors to my jeep had been taken while I was gone. "Damn!" I thought to myself. I searched the entire room looking for another pair of doors to replace the ones that had been taken.

"What the hell happened to the doors?" Manus snapped when he saw the jeep.

"I'm not sure, sir," I answered. "They were gone when I got here. There's no more doors, but I thought it would help to put this soft canvas piece over your legs!" I held up the canvas. I thought it was better than nothing.

He gave me a look that spoke a thousand words and made it clear that he definitely did not want to wrap the canvas around his legs. He wanted the doors on the jeep.

I stood at attention. "I'll take care of the problem, sir!"

"Yes, you will! I'll be back in twenty minutes and that jeep better be sitting there with doors or else!"

As soon as he turned and left, I was a maniac moving through the storage room looking for doors. I wish I could've gotten my hands on the jackass that took them! I tried every source I could find to solve my problem, with no luck. The twenty minutes flew by. I had three minutes left. There was no choice. I stood next to the jeep belonging to Captain Martin (Lieutenant Manus's superior) parked ahead of me and removed each door. It took less than a minute to remove and install each door. I then leaned against Lieutenant Manus's jeep, casually waiting for my platoon leader when he returned with a full minute to spare. As I looked calm and collected, I was going through the dire consequences that I would face if it was discovered that I took Captain Martin's doors. But the only indication of my internal panic was a small line of sweat that I felt trickling down the side of my face.

"Hot day, Shachnowski," Manus said looking at me, noticing the sweat on my face, and with a slight smile, he swung into the jeep.

I had promised myself that I would return the doors to Captain Martin's jeep at the first opportunity. It was several weeks after we had finished the exercise and returned to base. I saw his jeep parked in front of headquarters. There was no one around and I thought this was a good time to return the doors. I saw that he had a new set of doors on his jeep, but I thought he could probably use a spare set. I took my doors off and leaned them against his jeep and left before anyone saw me. I pulled away quickly and drove into the motor pool.

In about an hour I saw Sergeant Jones and Lieutenant Manus walking toward me. They were talking in a serious manner and Manus was animated, talking rapidly with great excitement. All of a sudden I saw Jones burst into hysterical laughter. He was still laughing when they approached me.

"Come with me, Schaja. Captain Martin wants to see you," Lieutenant Manus said, shaking his head. "Kid, I tell you what, you have got one pair of balls!"

Sergeant Jones doubled over in laughter.

FIFTY-SIX

When we arrived at Captain Martin's office, Manus and Jones went in first. In several minutes Manus opened the door from Martin's office and told me to come in. The office was crowded with my chain of command. Manus, Jones, 1st Sergeant Wolf, and Captain Martin.

I saluted and stood stiff as a board at attention. Standing behind his desk was Captain Martin. He was angry and his face was bright red. He began to read off in blistering tones the brevity of my crime of "misappropriating government property." He read me my rights and asked how I pled to the charges.

I thought about going through the whole series of events that led up to my taking the doors, but it was just an excuse and I didn't think I would receive much sympathy. "Guilty, sir!" I said.

"Would you like to make a statement of extenuation and mitigation before I read your punishment?" Captain Martin asked.

"No, sir," I answered.

He began to read off the punishment. "Forfeiture of $50 . . ."

That hit me hard.

"Restricted to the barracks for a month . . . extra duty and demotion from private first class to private," he finished.

I barely heard the last sentence of my punishment. There was a freight train of thoughts racing through my mind. I had never heard of so much punishment for such a small crime! I had heard of people who did real crimes that got less punishment than I had received. I tried to figure out how I was going to tell Arlene about the penalties and my own stupidity! I heard the word *dismissed!* I numbly walk out the door with the others.

Manus patted me on the shoulder and turned to go to another office.

"You are lucky, Shachnowski, that he was so easy on you," 1st Sergeant Wolf said.

I was dumbstruck. How could he say easy?

"But if you get into any more trouble, soldier," he continued. "Your ass is grass and I am the lawn mower. Try to remember that!"

Jones and I walked slowly across the grounds together.

"I just don't know how I'm going to tell Arlene," I said and shook my head.

"Why do you need to tell her?" he asked.

"She'll figure it out when we have no money for groceries and fifty dollars is missing, plus working the extra hours, and the demotion," I pondered.

Jones abruptly stopped. "Don't you know what happened back there?"

I looked at him.

"Your punishment was suspended!" he started to laugh. "All that talk he gave you was to scare you. The 1st sergeant and I talked to him before you came in and explained why you had taken the doors."

I started laughing. "You mean I'm off the hook?"

"Just lay low and stay out of trouble and you'll be promoted soon."

A few weeks later I received a promotion to corporal.

"Corporal Shachnowski," Lieutenant Manus said after he had called me into his office. "Colonel Teeters, our regiment commander, is looking for a driver."

"Yes, sir," I nodded, as he paused.

"I have recommended you for the job. I am sorry to see you go but I think it's a good move for you," Lieutenant Manus continued. "You'll interview with Colonel Teeters this afternoon."

He gave me the time and place for the interview.

"Corporal," Colonel Teeters said quietly. "The reason you were recommended was the language issue. I need someone that understands and speaks German. Lieutenant Manus says you are capable."

He looked up over his tortoiseshell glasses as if this were a question. "Yes, sir," I answered. "I lived in Germany after leaving Lithuania for almost six years."

He nodded his head. "We'll be leaving here in about thirty minutes, Steakley, my aide will take you down to the car. Wait there for me," he said. "By the way, you'll be on call seven days a week, but don't worry. I'll make sure you have some time off to spend with your family," he said and closed his file sitting in front of him on the desk. He looked up at me standing in front of him. "Dismissed."

I knew that even though I was on call, it still meant that I would have some days off when Arlene and I could travel around Germany. So far the only part of Germany that Arlene had seen was our neighborhood.

Later the next week I started looking for a car that we could use on the weekends. One of the officers in Colonel Teeter's office said he had seen an old car sitting in his neighbor's backyard. He handed me the address at the end of the day and said the man might be interested in selling the car. I took Specialist Ritter with me. He was the company mechanic.

I could see the car from the street. It was an old Mercedes. I went to the door ready to buy.

"Mr. Lowenstein," I said. "Your neighbor Jack Carter told me that you might have a car in your backyard to sell."

"My car?" he said, a little surprised. He raised his eyebrows after he had thought about it for a moment. "Maybe," he said and shrugged.

He took me through the gate and into his backyard. "It's a '37 Mercedes Benz," he said proudly.

It was sitting on blocks. But considering it was twenty years old, the exterior looked good. Ritter and I walked around the car and looked for dents and dings.

"How long has it been since it's been driven?" I asked.

"A few years," he said. "But it's good car! It belonged to a Nazi senior officer."

"Oh, really," I answered noncommitedly. "Which one?"

He shrugged his shoulders. "I don't remember his name."

Ritter popped the hood and started checking the motor. After a while he gave me the thumbs-up and said it wouldn't take much to get it running.

Mr. Lowenstien and I began our negotiations. "All I've got is $50, Mr. Lowenstein," I said pitifully.

He had a look of shock on his face. "It's worth much more than that," he said. "Mercedes-Benz is the very best: $300!"

"It's twenty years old and hasn't been driven. I'm going to have to spend money to get the repairs done. I have very little cash, Mr. Lowenstein, I'm a soldier."

A light seemed to go off in his head. "You can get American coffee?"

This went on for another twenty minutes and we finally agreed on $100 and six large cans of coffee. I could get the coffee on base.

The next day Ritter and I returned. We took the tires off the car and went back to the motor pool and repaired the holes. When we returned with the tires, several neighbors had gathered to see what was going on with Mr. Lowenstein's Mercedes.

A heavyset German woman that spoke broken English walked up to me. "You buyed dis Mercedezzz?" she asked.

"Yes," I answered and smiled at her.

"How much you pay?" she asked.

It wasn't her business but I told her because I thought it was a great deal. "I paid $100," I answered. I didn't mention the coffee because it was not legal for me to buy the coffee and give it to the old man.

She threw back her head and laughed. "Nice gift for that old man!"

"What do you mean?" I asked.

"The old man took the car over when the owners left it sitting in front of his house. It was some Nazi paper pusher who fled the country for Argentina!"

"He told me it was a senior official," I said.

She waved her hand in disgust. "He didn't even have a title. Lowenstein never even owned the car," she said laughing and walked away.

The Mercedes drank money and broke down frequently. I decided that it was a cursed car because of its Nazi owner. We took it on weekend trips, but I always had a tool box with me for roadside repairs.

Arlene and I traveled every free moment we had. Not only in Germany, but throughout Europe. I kept my promise that we would see the world together. We spent time in Paris, Lisbon, Rome, Vienna, and many other scenic spots. My guide was the Fodor travel book, see Europe on $5 a day. We made the best of our $5.

FIFTY-SEVEN

A rlene," I called out while she was standing in the bathroom on a two-day visit to Paris. "I thought Teeters was the most important man in the army but I met his superior yesterday, General Larson."

"Yeah?" Arlene said.

I could see her applying her mascara, looking in the mirror. "I realized that every rank in the army has a superior. I used to think it was just the enlistees that got their ass chewed out. But Larson chewed out Teeters over one of Larson's friends that is an officer."

"What was it about?" Arlene asked.

"I don't know, it sounded to me just like fights we had when we were kids in school . . . personal stuff . . . personality likes and dislikes."

"Ummmm . . ." Arlene mused.

"They weren't communicating," I said. "Larson and Teeters were like two bulls."

"What would you have done if you were Teeters?"

"I would have found out what the real problem was, not just the way it looked on the surface. That's what Larson wanted. I understood why he got pissed off!"

"Sid, I talked to Jane Manus the other day. She said that you would make a good officer." Arlene stood in the doorway now, the mascara tube still in her hand.

I shrugged.

"Sid, an officer has a much better life in the army. Better housing, more money. You know you're very smart and perceptive about people," Arlene said.

"Yeah, but I only have my high school diploma," I said.

"That's no problem, you can take a two-year equivalency test for college credit. And Sid, you know," she walked into the bedroom and sat down on the side of the bed. "We're going to need more money . . . when we have the baby," she looked at me and smiled.

I sat straight up in bed. "What do you mean?" I asked

"We're going to have a baby!" she smiled excitedly.

When I got to the base the next Monday, I filled out a request to attend officer candidate school (OCS). I arranged to take the equivalency test for college and passed. I hoped that my OCS request would not get bogged down by the usual red tape. In the army an application went through an infinite amount of procedures before it was approved.

"Shachnowski," Colonel Teeters said on our way to his office one day. "We are going to attend a command post exercise next week. We'll be gone for four days," he said. He must have seen my face turn white. This was the first time that I had left Arlene alone since she was pregnant.

"Yes, sir," I said, not as enthusiastically as usual.

"Is there a problem?" he asked.

"No, sir."

"Then why the hell did you turn white and sound like a wounded pup when you answered me?"

"It's just that it's the first time I'll be away from Arlene since she got pregnant," I answered.

"Well, congratulations, son," he said with a genuine smile. "When?"

"In May, sir," I said.

"Well, don't worry about her . . . women know how to take care of those things. My wife practically delivered her own babies. We have four," he said proudly.

"Yes, sir," I said.

He sat for a moment looking out the window as we sped down the highway. "How is your OCS application coming along?"

"Slow. It's going through the process as I understand it, sir," I answered.

The regimental adjutant contacted me the next day. "Shachnowski, I want to let you know that your OCS application is being forwarded back to the States. You'll have your interview here in a few days," he said and hung up the phone.

Colonel Teeters had put the process on the fast track. Within three days I was sitting in front of a five-man panel being interviewed. There was no way to study for this test, but I felt confident as I answered each of their questions. They set up scenarios of events and quizzed me on how I would handle the situation. They covered events that could happen in wartime, peacetime, events between civilians and the military. They basically probed my thought about what an officer should be. After an hour I was excused from the meeting.

A few weeks later I received word that I had been accepted. I was scheduled to report to OCS at Fort Benning in September. I could hardly believe it. A former high school drop out qualifying to become an officer in the U.S. Army! Arlene was the first to know the good news.

A few hours after I had learned that I would go to OCS, Colonel Teeters called me into his office. "Corporal Shachnow, I am putting you and my jeep on loan to General Clark. His driver had an accident in his jeep and will be out for a few weeks," he looked at me seriously. "As you know, General Clark is the commander of the Seventh Army. I want you to consider this assignment a privilege."

I snapped my salute and agreed with him. "Yes, sir."

I ran to the motor pool and cleaned Colonel Teeter's jeep. It didn't take long since I always kept the vehicle spotless. After I checked every detail, I reported to General Clark's aide-de-camp to assume my duties.

Working for General Clark was very different from my job with Colonel Teeters. I was Teeters's enlisted aide. General Clark was insulated by his staff and I went through the tiers of power for my orders. I spent most of my days waiting for orders from his aide-de-camp who was a major, and another aide-de-camp who was a lieutenant colonel. The general was accompanied on all of his trips by one or the other along with me. I listened to their hours of conversation and found it very interesting to be on the fringe area of this powerful man's circle.

General Clark was an early riser. He usually required me to be at his residence at 6 A.M. and we returned late in the evening. My time with Arlene was limited, but she understood and encouraged me daily.

"Our driver is going to OCS in September, General," I heard Lieutenant Colonel Daniels say to the general.

The general sat stone-faced with no comment for the next several miles. He then turned to me. "Have you been to my school?"

I had no idea what he was talking about, but I answered him. I hadn't been to any schools. "No, sir."

"Schedule him for the academy before he leaves," the general said. He turned to his aide and made sure he made note of this order.

The rest of the drive was silent and I wondered what I had gotten myself into.

Fifty-eight

Get that shit-eatin' grin off your face, soldier!" Sergeant Randall roared in my face when I walked into the academy.

"Yes, sir," I said, quickly falling into an attention stance and staring straight ahead.

I could hear the other tactical noncommissioned officers (NCOs) razing the applicants as each one appeared through the doorway.

Another TAC NCO appeared. He was a heavyweight and two inches taller than the other officer. His hands were huge.

"You looking at my mitts?" he roared. He clenched his hands in a fist. "These can pound you into the ground in less than ten seconds," he turned to the Randall. "Is this the corporal?" he said with an edge of sarcasm.

"That's him," Sergeant Randall said, nodding his head.

"Who the hell do you think you are?" he hissed as he bent down and stared eye to eye with me.

"Corp. Schaja Shachnowski, RA112942—" I was interrupted before I spat out my serial number.

"Get a load of this, Corporal. You don't have a chance in hell here . . . we don't let anyone but sergeants in this door and most don't make the graduation, so guess what? We're going to make a living example that a specialist corporal," he almost spat the word out. "Will not survive . . . period!"

I later found out that General Clark was the founder of this school and he personally requested that I be accepted. It was the prestigious Seventh Army Noncommissioned Officers Academy in Munich. This was an important event for an NCO's upward mobility.

The harrassment at the academy was to see how we handled stress; a weeding out process to see if we had what it took to be an officer. It was all about leadership and staying power. They wanted to see if we not only had the emotional stability to be an NCO but also the aptitude.

I had two strong points. One, I am very effective at instructing others. Two, I had the ability to withstand the constant harassment that was dished out on a continual basis.

Our appearance was under scrutiny constantly. Our competence was tested and questioned at every turn. But strangely enough I felt myself becoming a new man. For some reason this ignited my own internal demands from myself.

Of the two hundred students, everyone completed the course, but not everyone graduated. On March 29, 1957, Col. Rex Darnel, the academy commandant, designated me the distinguished graduate of the class and awarded me with an immediate promotion to sergeant. I was twenty-three years old.

The guest speaker at the graduation exercise was Gen. Bruce C. Clark, my former boss and founder of the school. In his remarks he mentioned my name. To my great surprise, everyone applauded wildly. It was an intoxicating feeling for me. I was embarrassed and pleased at the same time. I had never before been recognized by my peers and superiors.

When I returned to my unit there was a marked difference in my appearance and manner. I was very conscious of the appearance and neatness that we were taught. My boots were spit shined and there wasn't a wrinkle in my starched uniform. I started reading military manuals and publications. I was lapping up knowledge like a starved animal. With every task I performed, I took a great deal of pride in doing it right.

"You know, Sid," Arlene said one night, smiling proudly at me. "Before you went to school you were just serving in the army. Since you've been back you're a professional in the army."

But not all people were pleased with my promotion and change of demeanor.

"Here comes Sgt. Shake and Bake," Sergeant Fitch announced loudly one day when I was walking down the hallway toward him and several other NCOs. "Just add water and he's instant sergeant."

"Good morning, Sergeant," I said and walked past the group. They were waiting to see my response, but I kept quiet. I had felt a building resentment from other older sergeants who believed they had to struggle long and hard for their stripes. They didn't like the fact that I hadn't paid my dues the way they had. I made no response. They didn't know it, but I had been paying my dues since I was seven years old.

"If he spoke his mind," Sergeant Fitch said, looking toward the other NCOs, "he'd still be speechless."

Several days later, I came out of Colonel Teeters's office and was walking across the grounds toward my vehicle. Sergeant Fitch seemed to appear out of nowhere and sidle up next to me. "Shachnowski, let me tell you something. I've already forgotten more than your diaper rash, red ass will ever know."

My fists automatically clenched, but I bit my tongue. He was making me angry, but I continued to walk. Any response I made would have just made a bad situation worse. I was learning as an NCO to pull back and look before you leap. I didn't want to make this worse for him or for me.

I woke up and Arlene was shaking me. I looked at the clock. It was almost 10 P.M.

"Do you think it's time?" I asked.

"I woke up just a few minutes ago. It feels like labor pains," Arlene said.

"I'll get the car started," I said and slipped on my trousers and a shirt. "You get your bag ready . . . and get your timer!"

I started to get nervous. I put the key in the ignition of the old beat-up Opel that we had bought to replace the Mercedes. It made a grinding sound. I turned it again. Same sound. "Damn." I hit the steering wheel. "This is no time to be temperamental!" I shouted at the car. I turned the key again and again. It wasn't going to start.

I went back inside. "Arlene, the car won't start . . . I'll see if someone can give us a ride."

"Don't bother, by the time someone wakes up, gets dressed, and comes over here we can walk to the dispensary," she said, quickly moving toward the door.

We walked the two miles to the dispensary. The road was dark and deserted and Arlene set the pace. I prayed that her water wouldn't break and I had to deliver the baby on the side of the road.

When we arrived, the doctor examined her and said we needed to go to Frankfurt to the hospital to have the baby delivered.

"How do we get there?" I asked.

"If the ambulance were here the driver could take you, but he's already on the road with another patient," the doctor answered. "Do you have a car?"

"It won't start. Didn't I see another ambulance sitting in front of the door?"

"Yes, we have two, but no driver, he's off duty," he looked around. "I'll have someone call and see if we can find a driver."

The nurse located a driver. When he walked in the door his shirt was half-buttoned, he was barefoot and weaving. He told us he had been out all night partying and was still a little drunk. The nurse handed him two cups of coffee and he gulped them down.

When I looked at his eyes they were spinning from the alcohol. I hoped that the coffee would clear his head.

"I'm very sorry," he said and looked at me. "I'll do my best to get you there."

It was a harrowing forty-minute trip. I stayed in the front of the ambulance with the driver. He continued to apologize. I felt sorry for him; he looked no older than eighteen years old.

I watched him when his head would drop and grab the steering wheel. I yelled and woke him up. I crawled to the back of the ambulance and I saw a look of horror pass Arlene's face.

"The pain pretty bad?" I asked.

"The pain's not the problem, Sid. Get back up there and keep that drunk driver on the road before he kills all of us!" she said frantically.

Shereen Shachnow was born in the Frankfurt hospital at 8:00 A.M. that morning. She was a beautiful baby girl, weighing in at seven pounds, two ounces.

FIFTY-NINE

Arlene and I returned to Salem from Germany in July with Shereen, who was two months old. We each carried different citizenship. Mine was stateless with military orders, Arlene was a U.S. citizen, and Shereen had a German birth certificate. Arlene was not yet twenty-one and couldn't claim Shereen a U.S. citizen until that time and I had never changed my citizenship. We hit a few final snags before leaving but we boarded the plane and prepared for the homecoming.

It was the first time that either Arlene or I had ever flown. The seats were cramped and the flight was long but we were glad to back in the United States.

We stayed with Arlene's parents. After a few days I went to my parents' house with Arlene and Shereen. My parents were coolly reserved.

"Well, it's not as easy being married as you thought?" my mother said as soon as she got me alone.

"I'm very happy," I said honestly.

"I can see that you are tired," she said, almost accusingly.

"Mama, we flew for hours, the time difference wears you out," I said.

She ignored me. "I hope the baby looks like you. I would hate to have a granddaughter that looks like your wife."

I sighed and walked out of the room and went back to Arlene.

"I'm going to work," Arlene announced when my mother sat down in the living room again.

"I thought your job was to be a mother," my mother snipped at her.

"We need money, Rose," Arlene answered. "The army doesn't pay much . . . but Sid's doing great. And he'll be going to OCS."

"Who will stay with the baby?"

"My mother will take care of her while I'm working. I'll be with Shereen when I come home and on the weekends," Arlene answered.

"How could you get a job so quickly?" Mother asked.

"I had my father send me an application for Stone and Webster Engineering Corporation. They've just opened here in Salem," Arlene said.

My father's ears perked up. "Engineering?" he asked.

"Yes, Leon, you should try to get work there."

"It's not the type of place for Leon," my mother snapped. My father just looked at her sadly.

"Doing a good job alone is not going to get you promoted if you don't demonstrate potential." The TAC officer looked warily out at the group. "Some of you yahoos will never have what it takes to be promoted. But your promotions in the army will be decided by a board of officers. They might not even know you . . . probably won't. They will read your file that contains every recommendation, every demoralizing comment ever written about you, each grade you ever earned in school. Every detail we know about you.

"Longevity counts. Potential counts. Performance and indications of this potential are paramount to progress. And the amount of formal education that you have all play a part in your continuing career in the army," the instructor said as he stood at the front of the classroom.

I winced when I heard *formal education*. I was lacking. I had only a few college credits from courses I had completed during night school and end-of-course tests.

"Shachnowski, are you with us?" the instructor shouted at me.

"Yes, sir," I said and brought myself back from worrying about my school history or lack of it.

"Your first assignment is squad leader!" he said.

I wrinkled my brow and he didn't like it.

"You got a problem with that?" he shouted.

"No sir," I yelled back. "This is one of the most important positions in the U.S. Army and I am proud to perform this duty."

In truth, I would have preferred company commander, 1st sergeant, or platoon leader. Squad leader did not give you the opportunity to shine in officer candidate school. He knew that I had wanted a high-profile assignment.

But then I reconsidered. If you made a big mistake as a platoon leader it would be very noticeable. Squad leader was a good first assignment. I could learn the lay of the land.

OCS was much tougher than the Seventh Army NCO Academy in Munich. I had been greeted with the hazing. It didn't bother me as much as the others. I'm sure that my past had been a preparation. The one thing that did get to me were the rules. In OCS, each officer was graded on his awareness of rules and attention to detail. They were silly rules set up to test each candidate. The purpose was not always clear.

1. Six chin-ups before you entered the mess hall. A TAC officer stood by the bar and evaluated your performance. Unfortunately, this decision was made by personal opinion, depending on personal criteria and mood. But if you didn't pass, you didn't enter the mess hall and you didn't eat.
2. We were instructed to double-time (run) whenever we were outside. It didn't matter if you were loaded down with bundles on your back.
3. If there were two or more candidates moving together, the senior candidate was in charge and had to march the other in formation.
4. Each day they made up other rules that would change from hour to hour.

One evening I had failed to pass my chin-up evaluation. I was tired and hungry and irritated. This officer had it in for me.

The day had gone wrong from the time I got up. At morning formation I had just polished my shoes with the secret trick of using a five-day deodorant pad to give them a shine that made them look wet. When we stepped outside to form up for inspection, a light mist began to fall. The TAC officer took his time during inspection and the rain was falling harder. We were getting drenched. He gave demerits for wet uniforms down the line. When he came to me he stopped abruptly.

"Candidate Shachnowski, where'd you get those college boy saddle oxfords! What the hell army do you think you're in!" he yelled at me.

I looked down at my boots. The shiny black veneer had turned white on the toes and heels. Evidently when the five-day deodorant liquid dries and gets wet again it turns white. All I could do was stand and take the abuse.

"Five demerits for sloppy and dirty boots and five more demerits for failure to set an example, candidate! You are a miserable excuse for a leader. Like the road of good intentions, if they follow your lead they will go down the proverbial road to hell. I want you to apologize to every one of these men!"

We all stood in the rain while I made a personal apology to each of my fellow candidates.

The rest of the day was riddled with problems. I was disgusted after I lost the chance to have dinner. I was starving and out of luck. I was about to dismiss my squad for the day when I heard the TAC officer say, "Get your squad and have them ground their equipment and move them into the broom closet!"

Was he nuts? I thought to myself. Did he really say put my squad in the downstairs utility closet? Doesn't he know they're in the mess hall and

I'm not? I knew better than to voice those questions out loud. Our squad had shrunk to eight men, but putting them in a broom closet was still impossible.

I moved them next door and proceeded to try to pack them in the closet. Two men were still outside the closet, no matter what we did. We reformed and tried again. Still two men left. No matter how I configured the men there was not enough room.

"Candidate, form up your squad!" the TAC officer ordered.

The platoon formed up and he shouted at me. "Candidate," he said. "How do you expect to lead these men into combat when you can't to lead them into a closet properly? No one was even firing a shot." He shook his head in disgust.

I felt like I was in a black comedy. I couldn't believe something so insignificant and impossible as this could cause me so much trouble.

When I got to my room I fell onto the bed, worn out, disgusted, and hungry. I went over the events of the day and I heard footsteps clicking down the hallway. The noise stopped in front of my door and I heard a knock. "The company commander, Captain Reagan, wants to see you Candidate Shachnowski!"

The first thought that crossed my mind was that I had failed as a squad leader and I was going to have to pay for this failure in some way.

Captain Reagan greeted me with a smile and a warm handshake when I arrived in his office. "Take a seat, Candidate."

From his demeanor I knew that this meeting had nothing to do with my closet fiasco. I knew in my heart it was worse.

"I've studied your background thoroughly and I am very pleased with the progress you have made here. You have a great deal of potential," he said. "But we have a problem. Intelligence tells me that you are not a U.S. citizen."

I shook my head and felt my heart sink. I was not a citizen of this country but I never realized that this would interfere with OCS.

He raised his hands, exasperated. "For the last two days I've tried to find a way to expedite your citizenship papers. But we can't. In order to be a commissioned officer, Candidate Shachnowski, you must be a U.S. citizen. That is the law."

I was totally crushed. I just looked at him and shook my head in agreement.

"I know this is very difficult news after going through these last couple of months. But I will have to drop you as a candidate. I hope you will seriously consider getting your citizenship and return. I think you would make a fine officer."

I stood up and saluted. "I apologize for the problem, sir, and I want to thank you. I appreciate all that you've done for me."

We shook hands and I started to leave.

"You'll be sent off tomorrow to a holding detachment."

I realized that I would be sent out with the other OCS candidates that had not qualified.

This was a setback that I had never expected.

SIXTY

"Sid, I know you've worked hard but, nothing is ever lost. You'll have new insight when you go the next time to OCS. It's not anything to feel discouraged about," Arlene spoke calmly over the phone. "While we're at Fort Knox, you'll get your citizenship. You'll benefit in so many ways. Anyway, I can't wait to see you. Shereen has grown so much you won't recognize her."

Arlene always took it in stride. My disheartened mood was greatly lifted by her words. I hung up the phone and went out to the waiting bus to take me to Fort Knox, Kentucky. I filled out my application for citizenship on the bus.

When I arrived I was told I was assigned to the installation honor platoon. I had been requested by name by Master Sergeant Elam.

"Can you tell me where there is a mailbox?" I asked the soldier after he gave me directions to Elam.

"Outside and about fifty yards to your left," he answered and smiled.

I found the box and mailed the paperwork for citizenship. I then went to report to Master Sergeant Elam, commander of the Honor Detachment.

"Goddamn, they act like goons at OCS," Master Sergeant Elam said, shaking his head. These were the first words he said to me. When I got there he was standing in the reception area. He was an impressive, tall, and handsome man. He had been at OCS several months earlier.

"Hell, I've been in the army longer and know more than those mafiosi that run that jailhouse," he ranted.

I smiled. He reminded me of Sergeant Fitch.

"I went in after the first week and turned in my resignation!" That ended his story. "I'm glad you're here, Sergeant Shachnowski. I've heard a lot of good things about you. Tomorrow you'll meet the rest of the unit. This is a job that requires precision and discipline. It's not a physically hard job, but a very busy one. We perform at all ceremonies that require an honor guard or color guard. Military programs, funerals, memorial services, and parades," he said.

The first order of business with Master Sergeant Elam was hours of practice of synchronizing the twenty-one-gun salute. The key to a twenty-one-gun salute was to have only three volleys and each volley sound as one. Elam had ears like a wild animal and could hear if the shot was a millisecond off the mark.

"We have a funeral to prepare for next Friday. A very important funeral for a general and there's going to be some people from the Pentagon here for the services," Master Sergeant Elam told us during our break. "Everything has to be solid . . ." He tapped his fingers on the stone embankment where he was sitting. "Rock solid."

I liked Elam and the men in my platoon, but I didn't like these tedious and constant rehearsals. It was the first time since I joined the army that I was unhappy with my assignment. But I was name requested and I didn't want to appear ungrateful.

The next morning I was in good spirits. Elam was obsessed with perfect synchronization for this funeral and we practiced the movements and salutes up until the very moment we left for the funeral.

When the ceremony began I stood on the grounds of the cemetery and watched as the massive funeral party appeared. First the marching band came into view, then the color guard, then the mourners, the chaplin, and the family. The casket of the general was at the forefront with the widow walking next to it, her hand touching the coffin.

After everything was in place for the funeral to begin the music stopped. There was silence, other than the widow's sobs. The chaplin rose from his chair and began to speak. All the while the deceased's wife continued wailing so loud that you could barely hear the words of the chaplin's prayers and readings.

When he finished and sat down I heard Elam's command. "Ready . . . Fire." Just as the word *fire* was spoken a melee erupted at the gravesite. The grief-stricken wife had thrown herself onto the casket. The weight of her body dislodged the suspension mechanism of the casket and one end was plunged into the open grave. People were jumping out of their seats to help.

In that split second I was distracted. The three-volley sound was anything but synchronized because of my momentary lapse of attention. My timing was off.

As we rode back to Fort Knox there was a cold silence on the bus. I decided that I should transfer out of this unit. Both Master Sergeant Elam and I mutually agreed on this move.

The next day Master Sergeant Elam shoved a note in my face from General Disney, the commanding general of Fort Knox. "It appeared that the synchronization of your twenty-one-gun salute was off yesterday. Please make sure that it does not happen again! Signed, General Disney."

I couldn't figure out how anyone could pay attention to those shots with all the uproar at the gravesite. I was wrong.

I reported five days later to 1st Sergeant Miller in the Initial Training Company, which trained new recruits. Miller was a crusty, weather-beaten soldier who had a lot of experience under his belt. He was intolerant of everyone and thought he knew everything about anything. I did not like his personality. Miller grumbled a few words to me that I didn't understand and led me to my commanding officer, Capt. Pedro Contraras.

Captain Contraras was very impressive: tall, lanky, very physical, with jet black eyes and hair. He welcomed me to his command and assigned me the position of drill sergeant. I was taken to meet my platoon by Field 1st Sgt. Ralph Brakebill.

Within a few weeks my platoon, under my supervision, set many records and received many certificates of accomplishment. Captain Contraras was very pleased and always pointed to me as an example of good leadership. He especially liked my instructional ability. This caused some resentment from other drill sergeants. But I had long ago developed a thick skin and tried not to take any jealousy or anger on a personal basis.

"Sergeant Shachnowski, I've called you here today for several reasons," Captain Contraras said as he arranged the papers on his desk. He was a stickler for detail and he always had things in perfect stacks. "I've been very impressed with your work. You have a very innovative and workable approach with troops. I am going to promote you to first sergeant," he said and looked up.

"Thank you, sir, I appreciate that very much!" I said sincerely.

"I am also going to encourage you to reapply for OCS as soon as you get your citizenship papers," he said. "How is that going anyway?"

"I'm studying for the test and I have given them all the papers they asked for. I should hear when I am taking the test sometime soon," I answered.

"You have the kind of potential that we need in the army and I also know that your four-year enlistment is up next year. You have a good future here and I hope you stay with us," he said.

"Thank you, sir, I'll take everything into consideration. The army has been a great experience for me. I appreciate your interest," I said.

Arlene had arrived several months earlier with Shereen and I picked up the phone to tell her about my promotion. She had even better news for me.

"It happened again . . . we're going to have another baby!"

"Wow! When did you find out?" I asked.

"I just got home from the doctor," Arlene answered.

"This is really great, Arlene," I said. "Two little ones, I'm happy . . ."

"Yeah, me, too, Sid," she said sweetly.

"I love you," we both said it at the same time.

Sixty-one

"Please follow me in the oath of allegiance to the United States of America," said the immigration judge standing at the front of the room.

"I hereby declare, on oath, that I absolutely and entirely renounce and abjure all allegiance and fidelity to any foreign prince, potentate, state or sovereignty, of whom or which I have heretofore been a subject or citizen . . . that I will support and defend the Constitution and laws of the United States of America against all enemies, foreign and domestic; that I will bear true faith and allegiance to the same . . ." I spoke the oath of citizenship with heartfelt conviction.

It was November 21, 1958. I looked around at the sixty other people standing with their hands up repeating this oath of allegiance. It was an inspiring moment. One that each of us standing in this room had worked hard to accomplish. I felt a lump in my throat. I knew that I would protect the freedom of the United States under any circumstance.

"That I will bear arms on behalf of the United States when required by the law; that I will perform work of national importance under civilian direction when required by the law, and that I take this obligation freely without any mental reservation or purpose of evasion, so help me God."

"You are now citizens of the United States of America," the immigration judge announced. "Congratulations!"

There was some whooping and hollering from some of the new citizens, handshakes, hugs, and slaps on the back when we turned to our neighbors. Arlene and Shereen were standing in the waiting area for me. Shereen thought it was quite a party. Her eyes were wide with excitement.

"Here are your papers," a man said and handed me a packet of my official citizenship forms. "Mr. Sidney Shachnow?"

"That's me!" I smiled and hugged Arlene and Shereen.

I went to the central office at the base as soon as I could and handed them my new official name for them to change.

"You know, Sergeant," a large woman said after she looked at the papers. "We're going to have to change every paper in your file!"

"I'm sorry," I said.

"Well," she said feigning disgust. And then she looked up at me and gave a big smile. "Congratulations!"

When I arrived at the hospital twelve days later and filled out papers in the emergency room for the birth of our second daughter at 5 A.M., I was so nervous I signed my former name.

"We're taking your wife up to the delivery room, Mr. Shachnowski," the nurse said.

"Shachnow," I corrected her.

She glanced down at her paper and looked at me strangely. She held the clipboard so I could see what was written on the page. "Your name is Schaja Shachnowski," she said.

"Oh, my God," I said and ran back to the desk.

I explained my mistake to the admissions nurse. They were accustomed to nervous fathers.

Michelle Shachnow was born on December 3, 1958, at Ireland Army Hospital, Fort Knox, Kentucky. A six-pound, thirteen-ounce beautiful baby girl.

I had a lot of things to consider after Michelle was born. My four-year enlistment was up on January 30, 1959.

"What do you want to do, Sid?" Arlene asked me as she was changing Michelle's diaper.

"I don't know," I answered truthfully. "I really don't know what my options are outside the military."

"There's a lot of opportunity. You would be good at just about anything you wanted to do," Arlene answered.

Arlene was my cheerleader for life. She had so much confidence in my abilities.

"I can leave and come back in ninety days and I don't lose my rank," I answered thinking about that possibility. "You sure you want to live in the same town with my parents?"

She shrugged. "You could look around and see if you find any kind of job you would like. It would be great to be back in Salem. Their grandparents would be thrilled. Even Rose will love the babies. I'm sure she and Leon will warm up to us," Arlene said getting excited about returning home.

"Okay," I said.

We bought a house with Arlene's parents under the GI Bill, and I started looking for a job as a civilian. I followed every ad in the paper that looked interesting and applied. I liked some of the positions offered, but they held no challenge for me. There was very little responsibility in these entry-level positions.

We went to my parents' house about a week after we had come home. My parents had not changed their attitude toward Arlene. They barely acknowledged her presence. We talked for a while about the army and the future. My mother pulled me into the kitchen after a while.

"Your children are very beautiful," she said.

"Thank you, Ma," I said. "You'll get to see a lot of them. We're only a few blocks from you."

"Did you put the house in your name?" she asked.

"Ma, what difference does it make?" I asked. "Of course, I did. But it belongs to both of us. Anything that I have is Arlene's and vice versa."

She shrugged. "Always keep something of your own. When the divorce comes—"

I interrupted her. "No divorce, Ma." I walked out of the room.

"I got a job," I announced to Arlene one afternoon.

"What? Where?"

"A manager in a noodle factory," I said and chuckled. "I'll have about ten people under me . . . I convinced the guy if I could run a platoon I could run a work crew."

Arlene looked at me. She had watched me during this time and knew I would not be satisfied with the civilian work sector. "Sid, you're just doing this because of me, aren't you?"

"Well, I want you to be happy. I know Salem is a good place for the girls to grow up," I said.

She shook her head. "Sid, why don't you reenlist?" she said. She came over to me and put her arms around me. "You haven't shown me the *entire* world yet!"

I reenlisted and retained my rank of sergeant 1st class and reapplied for officer candidate school.

SIXTY-TWO

I was assigned to Fort Dix as an instructor of marksmanship. It was an interim assignment until I was sent back to officer candidate school. Arlene and the two girls remained in Salem until I completed school.

Within several months I was given a class date to attend OCS.

I took a deep breath as I walked up the stairs to officer candidate school at Fort Benning. I opened the door and prepared for the worst.

I leaned down to sign my name on the official entry paper and immediately a TAC officer was in my face. "Against the wall," he shouted as he shoved himself into my personal space. This was a technique that they all used to throw you off balance. It was important not to show weakness, and not to show panic or cockiness and indifference. Either way you lost. I maintained my balance and stayed calm.

My TAC officer was Lt. Robert A. Plant, and he would determine my fate from this point on. "Okay, you boobs! Get up to the fourth floor to your room assignments," he yelled. He would continually call us boobs.

OCS assessed and measured a soldier's leadership abilities. I discovered that combat arms soldiers did much better than those who had been in support assignments.

My roommate, Bob Orms, and I had the same goal in mind. Graduate! We worked our schedule down to a synchronization of time management. Since I had already been exposed to this situation before, I knew that time management and attention to detail was key to graduation.

A great amount of attention was paid to neatness and cleanliness. Inspection started at 7 A.M. If the TAC officer noticed anything less than perfect, it could ruin the rest of the day. When Orms and I knew we wouldn't have extra time in the morning, rather than sleeping in our bed the night before, we slept on the tile floor. Huge demerits and reprimands were given if you didn't have every square inch of your bed made perfectly. The TAC officer then checked the latrine every morning thoroughly. If it was not perfect, we were told to reflect on our ability to supervise, lead, and organize and were given demerits.

Orms had a unique secret to keep our floors shining like mirrors.

"Sid, stop at the PX and buy two boxes of Kotex," Bob said on a day when I was leaving to run an errand.

"What?" I asked, giving him a double take.

"Yeah," he said in his slow-talking sound of the West.

"How do they come?" I had no idea if they came in sizes or thickness.

"Just get a couple of boxes," he said.

When I returned with the Kotex, he took out the Johnson floor wax and poured it on the floor. He took out a Kotex pad and used it to spread the wax. When he finished I could see my reflection on the floor. We never got demerits for our room cleanliness.

I tried to keep a low profile. I never raised my hand to volunteer for anything or call attention to myself. I had kept busy with my head in a book to avoid becoming a target.

"Candidate, go down to Captain Kirkpatrick's office, ASAP," Lieutenant Plant shouted at me one day.

No one was ever asked to report to the company commander unless there was a problem. I shook my head. What could the problem be? Was I going to get booted again? Thoughts raced through my mind. Was Arlene or one of the girls hurt? I prepared for the worst. This was not a good sign.

Sergeant Douglas, Kirkpatrick's administrative sergeant, asked me to wait in the outer office. Captain Kirkpatrick was on the telephone. I moved to the side of the room and stood at parade rest. This was a stance between full attention and at ease.

First Lieutenant Brizee, the company executive officer, came out of the door of Kirkpatrick's office. He was a very serious and dry guy. No one had ever seen him smile.

I snapped to attention. He walked straight toward me. I knew I would be inspected for my personal appearance. He stopped about a foot in front of me and looked me up and down. He saw nothing wrong with my appearance.

"Assess yourself three demerits for having a brown ring around your nose, Candidate!" he shouted. "So why are you going to visit the regimental commander?" He turned and walked out of the office. He didn't care about an answer.

I was confused. I had no idea what he was talking about. But I realized that whatever it was about, the problem had gone to the top man. I could feel my pulse beginning to pound.

"Report to the company commander!" the first sergeant shouted.

I walked into the captain's office and stood at attention in salute. "Sir, Candidate Shachnow reports as directed!" I said.

Captain Kirkpatrick returned my salute and sat down. "At ease," he said and handed me a very formal white envelope with my name on the front. I took it but I didn't open it.

"Why the hell would the regimental commander, my superior, invite you to dinner?" he said and leaned back in his chair. "I've never been invited for dinner. What makes you so special?" His voice was thick with sarcasm.

"I have no idea," I answered honestly. I wondered if this was a joke, maybe a test of some kind.

He looked me up and down with a nasty expression on his face.

"Do you know Col. Bernard Teeters?"

Everything fell into place. I grinned and told him that Colonel Teeters was my commanding officer in Germany and I was his driver.

He sat stone-faced while I explained. "Dismissed." He never changed expression.

I didn't know whether to be glad or not about this invitation. I knew I was going to pay.

When I returned to my platoon, there were more repercussions.

"Why did you have to see Captain Kirpatrick?" Lieutenant Plant asked.

I told him the story and was assessed again.

"Assess yourself three more demerits for that brown ring around your nose!"

I arrived at the Teeterses that evening and was greeted like a long-lost friend. There were two other captains at the dinner, one an OCS graduate and the other an ROTC graduate. Colonel Teeters was genuinely interested in what I had been doing since we last saw each other and was very pleased at my progress. Mrs. Teeters made me feel very special and welcome.

I got back to the barracks before 9 P.M.

"Did you have a nice time last night, boob?" Lieutenant Plant asked as I abruptly stopped brushing my teeth and came to atttention.

"Yes, sir," I said and realized that there was toothpaste running down the side of my mouth.

"Did you tell Regimental Commander Teeters that I was the best damn TAC at OCS?" he yelled.

"Yes, sir," I answered loudly.

"Give yourself three demerits for that toothpaste running down the side of your mouth," Plant said. He was having trouble keeping a straight face. "You've gotta work on yourself, Candidate."

I saw a broad grin spread across his face when he turned to leave.

Several days before our graduation from OCS, Lieutenant Plant called me in for my periodic counseling. These were interviews that all candidates went through. The TAC officer listed your good points and bad points. We were expected to correct whatever our bad points seemed to be.

"Candidate Shachnow," he said after I came into the room and sat down.

I took out my notebook and prepared to list my failures. I knew he would give me the good news first, and the bad news last.

"We are very satisfied with your performance in general. You show a lot of potential in leadership. Your peers have rated you very high," he said and looked at me.

This was a good sign for a future in the army.

"Personally, I am most impressed with your performance at the target range. When you took over after the instructor got sick, that was very, very good."

He was referring to an incident with my platoon on the target range when we were supposed to be taught by an instructor on sight picture and sight alignment and steady hold factors concerning marksmanship. When we walked onto the field that day, the instructor was sitting down propped against the wall being attended by a medic. His collar was loosened.

"Your instructor is not able to teach today," the medic said.

I wasn't sure if this was a test or the real thing. But since I was the designated platoon leader that day, it was my responsibility to solve the problem. I had taught this marksmanship course at Fort Dix in my last assignment. I went over the notes lying on the podium and instructed my platoon.

Right time and right place, I thought to myself as I listened to Lieutenant Plant talk about how well I handled the situation.

"At times, Candidate," he said.

Now the bad news.

"You are overcautious, and at times, too opinionated. Stand back and look at things a little before you make a judgment." He finished and closed the book of notes.

"Thank you, sir, for that assessment. I will work hard to improve on my weaknesses," I said.

He looked at me and squinted his eyes. "You're in competition for selection as distinguished graduate of your class . . . you'll hear more about it in a few days. I wish you good luck, Candidate. I think you deserve that recognition. Dismissed." he said.

I saluted and left. I was on cloud nine as I walked to my room. I couldn't believe I might be the distinguished graduate.

Ten days later I graduated from officer candidate school and was named distinguished graduate.

I entered Airborne School the next day as a 2nd lieutenant.

"What can I expect?" I asked one of the seasoned paratroopers that I knew.

"The course last three weeks. The first week is all about physical training, getting your body and mind in shape. That is when we separate the men from the boys," he said.

"What happens in the second week?" I asked.

He paused a minute and stroked his chin. "Well, the second week is spent on various apparatus where you learn how to properly exit the aircraft, descend, and land safely. That is the week where we separate the men from the idiots."

"So what do they do the final week?" I continued.

"On the third and final week," he looked at me intensely, "the idiots jump."

I would find out that airborne paratroopers always had a sense of humor. Why else would we jump out of planes?!

Sixty-three

Rose, I'd like to invite you and Frieda over for tea and cake," Arlene spoke into the phone.

Mother's sister had come to visit from Israel where she had migrated before the war. It had been years since they had seen each other.

"I thought it might be nice for Frieda to meet Sid's daughters," Arlene suggested.

She listened as Rose spoke coldly into the phone.

"Yes, Rose, tomorrow at three would be fine," Arlene listened for a moment. "Yes, Rose, Shereen will be glad to see you, too."

Arlene dreaded it and at the same time she looked forward to it. She had tried diligently to ingratiate herself to her in-laws. She wanted them to be in the lives of our children. They didn't deserve to miss out on having two sets of grandparents. Somehow she wanted to find a way to heal the wounds.

Arlene got up at 5 A.M. the next morning and baked a lemon chiffon cake. She dressed Shereen and Michelle in their cutest outfits and at 3 P.M. everything was ready for the arrival of Rose and Frieda.

At 4 P.M., Arlene looked at her watch. She tried not to get angry. Perhaps they had been delayed for a good reason. She went through good reasons in her mind and continued to entertain the two little girls. At four-thirty both Shereen and Michelle were getting fussy. She waited until five and changed them from their dress clothes to pajamas.

Arlene paced the floor, still waiting for her mother-in-law and relative to arrive. She finally picked up the phone. "Mom," Arlene spoke into the phone calling her own mother. "They never showed up! What can I do? This woman will never like me."

At 6:30 P.M. she started to dial my parents' phone number. She hung up before she finished dialing and sat down. She wanted to be calm before she spoke. She contemplated this and then picked up the phone again.

"Hello," Rose said.

"Rose, this is Arlene."

"Yes, dear, what is it?" Rose said, edging on irritability.

"Rose, what happened this afternoon?"

"I don't know what you're talking about," Rose said.

"You and Frieda were supposed to be here at three this afternoon," Arlene said.

"Oh Arlene, you're confused," Rose said. "We aren't coming until Saturday."

"Rose, we made plans for today. I won't even be here on Saturday!"

"Then why did you agree for us to come to your home?" Rose countered.

"I didn't, Rose. You are mistaken!" Arlene said, knowing that this would make her angry.

"Don't talk to me that way, young lady!" Rose said.

"I'll bring the cake over that I baked for you and Frieda in the morning. I have to take the girls to the doctor!" Arlene said and hung up.

I walked into the post exchange on the base to pick up some things for the kids before I flew home to Salem from Fort Benning.

I rushed out the door and ran into a man I had long ago forgotten. When he saw me he was as surprised as I was. Sergeant 1st Class Fitch from my old I&R platoon. The memory hit me about how he had disliked me and given me such a hard time when I was first promoted in that platoon. Today, after graduating from OCS, I outranked him. Regulations dictated that he salute me. He stood ogling me with a grim expression on his face. We made some uncomfortable strained conversation and he started to turn away. He did not salute. I started to let it go, but then I thought about it and realized that it was more than personal, it was a professional dignity that was at stake.

"Sergeant Fitch, I believe that you've forgotten something," I said smiling.

He knew right away what he had forgotten. His face turned beet red and his expression became contorted. But he snapped me a salute, turned, and left.

I heard him make a comment under his breath as he walked away. Whatever he said I knew it was uncomplimentary. But I was glad that I stood my ground professionally.

"Sid, I think Arlene is having some problems," my mother said. I had returned from Fort Benning after airborne school and had been home for several days with Arlene and the kids. This was the first visit to my parents.

"What kind of problems?" I asked. How would my mother know anything about Arlene?

"Well, I think it's probably because she goes out with her girlfriends at night and doesn't get enough sleep. She completely forgot when Frieda and I were coming to see the children," she said to me.

My father came in to the kitchen overhearing the conversation. "This is the problem, Sidney, when you leave a woman for so long. She's young, she wants to go out," he stated. "I've heard there are many divorces in the army."

"Arlene is busy with two kids, she rarely has time to go out," I answered. Unknown to them I knew that Arlene went out only on rare occasions with her friends. They all had small children and little time for partying.

"I would never leave your mother alone," Leon said and walked out the door.

I nearly dropped my teeth on that one.

"We're selling the house," I said to my mother. "We're being transferred to Erlangen, Germany. I'm being assigned to the Second Armored Rifle Battalion. I'll be a platoon commander." I was glad that we were leaving. They still hadn't changed their attitude about Arlene. I had already heard about the story with Frieda and my mother from Arlene. I realized the only way we could coexist with my parents was to live halfway around the world.

SIXTY-FOUR

Master Sergeant Struble introduced me to the members of my platoon when I arrived in Erlangen. He had been the acting platoon leader before my arrival. He was an excellent platoon sergeant and I was lucky to have him until it was payday. The minute he received his pay, he tried to drink every ounce of alcohol to be had in the bars of Erlangen.

The army with all of the discipline, rules, and protocol tolerated alcohol abuse to a degree. In fact, they encouraged it with happy hours, celebrations, picnics, and parties that centered on competitions and alcohol consumption was always the prize. The army considered a soldier's after-hours life off-limits.

I had been platoon leader for about three weeks, and we were notified of an annual evaluation that would take place in a couple of months. This took a great deal of preparation and the results would affect every man in my platoon. It would also reflect on my leadership ability.

So far everything had fallen into place very nicely since I had arrived. I was in an upbeat mood thinking about Arlene and the kids' arrival next week. Our house had sold quickly and our government housing was available and ready.

I walked toward the platoon as the men were loading the track vehicles for an exercise in the local training area. I saw Sergeant Struble stumbling toward me. I knew he was drunk.

"I'm staying back here," he informed me. He was still slurring from the alcohol he consumed the night before. He smelled like the inside of a bottle of whiskey. "I need to take care of some odds and ends."

I looked at him. "No, Sergeant," I said. "I want you to load up, you're coming with us. I need your help in this exercise." It had pissed me off that he hadn't bothered to ask, but told me what he was going to do. And I hated to be a hard-ass, but I had to have authority over the platoon, including him.

"Listen," he said, spraying saliva into my face. "I'm a senior NCO. Don't treat me like some private that just fell off the turnip truck!"

I put my hand on his back after he finished, and started guiding him toward the vehicle where he normally rode. Instantly, he swung around and violently shoved me backward with a force that landed me on the ground. My head bounced off the tracks of the armored personnel vehicle. The searing pain blinded me for a few moments. The entire platoon had stopped what they were doing, and their eyes were glued on this developing situation. I got up and stood in front of Struble. I knew I could have him court-martialed for hitting an officer, but I knew that this was a very delicate situation. The men liked him and if I didn't handle the situation properly I could lose control of the platoon.

"Let's go to the attic and settle this once and for all," Struble said, as I stared, unblinking. "And you'll know who runs this platoon!"

The attic was a room up at the top of the stairs of the barracks that was equipped with mats and a boxing ring. It was a room where soldiers could exercise and also settle their differences. But a sergeant settling differences with his platoon leader was unprecedented.

"Sergeant," I said. "I will give you one chance to go to your vehicle, join the rest of us in training, and acknowledge your behavior was out of line to the whole platoon and we'll forget this ever happened." I thought this was a generous offer.

"You can take that offer and shove it up your ass, Lieutenant," he shouted. "I had serious doubts about being able to work with you."

With that comment, and against my better judgment, I started walking toward the attic. But I realized that I was in a critical situation of being overmatched. Struble was four inches taller than I was and fifty pounds heavier. I did not want to file a complaint against this man. He was a good soldier when he was sober. He had run the platoon before my arrival and he had called the shots. I understood his resentment of me, but why the hell did he have to challenge my authority in front of the platoon?

He went up the stairs ahead of me. The entrance to the attic was right at the top of the landing. Right before we got to the top stair, I moved quickly around him. He slowed to let me pass. That was his mistake. I turned at the landing and I was standing over him. I was about three inches higher. As he came up the stairs I clenched my fist and swung at him. He ducked from side to side, but I landed one under his left eye. He lost his balance with the impact and tumbled down the flight of stairs.

By this time the entire platoon was standing at the bottom of the stairs. As he tumbled to the floor, I walked down the stairs behind him and out of the building. "In your places, soldiers!" I shouted as I went out the door. From the expressions on their faces, I could see that I had won the battle, but had I won the war?

The next day, Struble, looking awkward and embarrassed, apologized. I accepted the apology and quickly changed the subject. From this time on I never had another problem with Struble, and the platoon followed suit.

After Arlene arrived, she was invited to join a company officers wives' group orientation program. This group met monthly. Ginny Durant, my commanding officer's wife, was an important and powerful person that ran the group.

One evening when I arrived home, Arlene was upset.

"I went to the wives' group meeting today. Mrs. Durant assessed how she thought each of our husbands would progress in the army. You know she makes us all call her Mrs. Durant."

She required as much deference as her husband, I thought.

"She sat there like a fortune teller . . . 'Your husband will go far . . . he will end up a colonel,' she said to one girl, to another she said maybe a general," Arlene took a deep breath. "When she got to me, Sid, she said . . . 'Sid can only hope to end up a captain.' "

"I looked at her, my face was probably disappointed . . . she had told everyone else all these glowing predictions," Arlene continued. "She went on and everyone was listening, Sid. She said, 'Sid has many liabilities, Arlene. He is an outsider because he has come up through the enlisted ranks and OCS. He is not a "West Pointer." ' " Arlene took a breath. "My mouth dropped open, but she continued . . . , 'And Arlene, he does not have any education.' Sid, what could I say! Everyone in the room was embarrassed that they had heard all of this."

It was unfortunate that Mrs. Durant had done this publicly. It would have an effect on the way my peers treated me. And I knew what Mrs. Durant repeated usually came from the captain's own mouth. Even though I was angry, I realized that she had valid points about my lack of education.

It was too late to do anything about West Point. But I could do something about getting educated and earning my college degree. I told Arlene I would look into some classes at universities near Erlangen.

Two days after the incident with Mrs. Durant, Arlene and I received the news that we were expecting our third child. I enrolled in a local university and began taking night classes. I threw myself wholeheartedly into this effort and spent every waking moment either working or going to class. I enrolled in a second college for more night classes. The following months flew by in a haze.

I was transferred to a new assignment after I had served as platoon leader for over a year and became the company commander of a Mechanized Rifle Company (an infantry that moved in armored vehicles), 180 men strong.

During a training exercise in the heat of the summer while I was visiting several of my platoons, the battalion command radio net had experienced transmission difficulties. The rear detachment commander's voice was barely legible through the scratchy static. Finally, after repeating the message several times I learned that Arlene was in labor. She wasn't due for two weeks but while she was at the doctor's office in Nuremberg the doctor sent her immediately to the hospital.

"Report to garrison immediately," was the last thing I heard. I made all the arrangements necessary to leave the exercise. Since the message was broadcast on the battalion net, most of the battalion officers and soldiers listening knew I was about to become a father again.

When I finally arrived at the hospital it was a little before midnight. Arlene and I sat and talked for a couple of hours. Her labor wasn't progressing. I decided I would go home and check on the kids and the babysitter. When I got home everyone was asleep. I crashed on the bed and the next thing I knew it was 6 A.M. and the phone was ringing in my ear. I leaped out of bed and ran to the phone.

"Lieutenant Shachnow, you have a baby girl!" It was the nurse from the hospital.

I rushed out the door and went to the hospital. "I'm looking for Arlene Shachnow," I said, still groggy, when I got to the desk. I looked like hell. I was still in the uniform I had worn for the past two days.

She looks me up and down. "Where were you when we called at 3 A.M.?!"

"I guess I was asl—" she snarled at me before I could finish.

"You men are all alike," she said and led me to the hospital room.

When I walked in, Arlene was sitting up in bed holding a tiny bundle with a full head of black hair. Denise Rachelle Shachnow.

Sixty-five

It was two in the morning and our exercise had just concluded. I rubbed my eyes to ease the heaviness I felt. We were at Grafenwohr, a major military training area not far from Erlangen, Germany. I was preparing to leave the assembly area for the command post to participate in the critique on the exercise by my superior who had given me this assignment, Colonel Waldie.

This field training exercise had been my first major training exercise tactical experience as a company commander and a nightmare for me. I was very disappointed and critical of myself. I didn't think Colonel Waldie could be any harder on me than I was on myself at the moment. Tonight I had lost communications with four of my six platoons. I tried several contingency plans to recover but the problem was unsolvable within the time available. Once the attack was in motion, timing was everything, and my company team had screwed up. Some of my fellow commanders had problems, too, but I was the most junior commander and felt considerable pressure.

"Sir," Lieutenant Perez, my executive officer, said, interrupting my thoughts. "Some of the officers have heard that a classified message came across Colonel Waldie's desk today. It's about combat volunteers. Have you heard anything?"

"No, I haven't," I answered. "How'd they hear about it?"

Perez shrugged. "Word travels, sir," he answered, a little uncomfortable.

"I'll see what I can find out," I shrugged and walked out toward my jeep.

"The old man thinks the exercise went pretty good," Capt. Ed Valence, Colonel Waldie's adjutant, whispered to me out of the corner of his mouth after I sat down.

"Bullshit!" I said.

"I'm not kidding," he said.

I didn't believe him.

Colonel Waldie came into the briefing room a few moments later and sat down at the table near the podium. The room was full but you could hear a pin drop at his presence.

Major Cooper, Colonel Waldie's deputy, walked to the podium. He began his critique. I sat listening, quietly stunned. Valence was right, he praised the exercise. There were a few snags that we discussed briefly, but none of them involved my company team.

After the meeting was over Captain Valence and I walked to his office. I knew he would be the man that had the classified information that Perez was talking about. "Sir," I said. "I heard there was some classified message about volunteering for combat that came in."

He hesitated before he spoke. "You know, that's something Colonel Waldie doesn't really want shown around."

"Why not?" I asked.

"Well, it involved Special Forces and he's really not interested in his men volunteering," he answered.

I had heard about Special Forces and I knew that many regular army officers resisted the elite force. "Well, I would be interested in seeing it." I paused. "Will you show it to me?"

"I can't do that, Sid. The old man would be pissed," he said, and pulled a paper out of a file sitting in front of him. He started looking it over.

I looked at him. I didn't know if he was just going to ignore me so I pursued the subject a little further. "Can you tell me where the combat assignment is?"

He stood up, yawned, shook his head, and gave me a funny look. "I gotta go to the john. I'll be back in a couple of minutes." He tapped his fingers on the message before he left.

I jumped out of my chair as soon as he left the room and went behind his desk. I read the message quickly.

> The army is looking for volunteers to apply for Special Forces. The training is approximately six months to qualify and there will be another six-month training with a twelve-man A-detachment . . . deployment to Vietnam . . . hostile fire area . . . . Fill out form 1041 to volunteer request for immediate transfer.

"Where the hell is Vietnam?" I thought to myself.

I left the room before Valence returned and went back to the assembly area. Perez and several of the platoon leaders were waiting to hear about the "hotwash," a nickname for a critique. I gave them the report a little bit differently than Colonel Waldie had given it to me. I told them we received a lot of criticism. I did this because I was not satisfied with their performance. Mistakes like the ones we made tonight could cost them their lives in real battle. I wanted to make sure my men would stay alive in combat. That was my responsibility as their commander.

I told Perez and some of the others about the classified message I had just seen. They were interested; hostile fire pay was $55 per month extra.

None of them knew where the hell Vietnam was, either. We decided to go to the library the next morning.

When we arrived at the library, we were a convoy of three jeeps. We looked on the world globe in the library and couldn't find Vietnam. We looked in the book catalogue . . . nothing under Vietnam. We finally located the librarian. She pointed out on a new almanac where Vietnam was located. It was barely the size of a pinpoint. She gave us a short history lesson about it being part of the former Indochina area under French control. After political overthrows and new treaties it was named Vietnam. There were continued government overthrows in the tiny country and it split into North and South Vietnam. The northern part of the country was controlled by Communists that were trying to invade the south. We now understood why there was a mission and where Special Forces would be sent: America's enemy was Communism. Our new commander in chief, President John F. Kennedy, had made a pledge to stand firm against this threat to freedom.

Everybody was anxious to apply when we left the library. But as reality set in, some of the men lost interest, some considered the opportunity, but in the end I was the only one to volunteer. I kept this to myself. I didn't want Colonel Waldie to find out that I wanted a transfer. He could block my request. I waited to send in the 1041 form requesting transfer until he took leave.

Maj. Paul Cooper, who was in charge of the command while Waldie was gone, let the request go through. I received notification that I was accepted and assigned to Fort Bragg.

I called Arlene and told her that we were being sent out to Fort Bragg. Denise was only a few months old, but Arlene didn't hesitate, she was ready to move. I had been dishonest with her and hadn't told her that I had volunteered for Special Forces. I let her assume I had been assigned to Fort Bragg and made no mention of Special Forces.

Prior to my departure I made a courtesy call on Colonel Waldie, which is customary in the army. To my surprise, he wished me well.

Gen. William Yarborough, the commanding general of the John F. Kennedy Special Warfare Center and School at Fort Bragg from 1961 to 1964, noticed Sid Shachnow as soon as he arrived as a volunteer for Special Forces. Yarborough knew his background and was impressed by his accomplishments after such difficult beginnings. He watched Shachnow's progress during training and saw he had a personality that Special Forces wanted in a commander: "Precise in what he says and articulate." Yarborough had the feeling from the beginning that Shachnow had a future. "Shachnow was the epitome of what the new Special Forces were looking for in a volunteer." There is a song that says,

"Of the one hundred we will train today, only three will wear the Green Beret." Those who were chosen had a maturity and judgment that was needed for the missions they would be sent to accomplish. Shachnow was made to order. Possibly a great deal of this had to do with his past. But he made choices from the very beginning to overcome even the most tragic event and move forward. This takes character. This is the man that will succeed in life." Gen. Yarborough went on to say, "Shachnow had the skill a combat soldier needed to understand the geometry of the battlefield, somewhat like an engineer, and he also had the charisma. He could combine these qualities to be successful on the battlefield and earn the loyalty of his troops."

Gen. Yarborough was a pioneer in developing Special Forces since 1960 and became an instrumental influence in forming and promoting the elite force. General Yarborough had served in the army in many different capacities from combat veteran to chief negotiator at the peace table in Korea.

Shachnow was unaware that Yarborough had taken notice. But as his career continued to rise, he again encountered Gen. Yarborough and they became friends. A unique and well-earned respect developed between them. When Sid Shachnow was promoted to brigadier general, Gen. William Yarborough pinned his own first star that he earned on Shachnow during the ceremony at Fort Bragg, North Carolina. This was the highest symbol of admiration that one officer could give to another. The admiration and respect was equally felt by Shachnow, who considered Gen. Yarborough the strongest influence in broadening the scope and capabilities in Special Forces. Yarborough refined the art of counterinsurgency and guerrilla warfare into not only a fighting force, but also a diplomatic corps on the ground, a special force that could bring protection, training, and compassion in the liberation of the oppressed.

Sixty-six

Col. Aaron Banks trained the first Special Forces Group in 1952 for guerrilla warfare. It was made up of men who were looking for challenges to conquer. Most already spoke several languages and had achieved the rank of sergeant. They were flagged as the Tenth Special Forces Group and their main mission was to ". . . infiltrate by land, sea, or air, deep into enemy-occupied area and organize the resistance/guerrilla potential in order to conduct unconventional warfare, sabotage, subversion, escape, and evasion operations." These insurgency missions were conducted in uniform or civilian clothing by this small force of well-trained men and began to be recognized as one of the most effective weapons in a potential war with the Soviet Union.

But regular army generals and others resisted the use of the elite force and its symbol of the green beret as time passed. They saw no need for this capability and were of the opinion that conventional forces could do the job. They didn't like the unique philosophy, training, or purpose of these units. They did not fully appreciate the subtleties that Special Forces could bring to bear in war. They thought in conventional terms and refused to accept the possibility of a different kind of war on the horizon that didn't require the traditional approach.

In 1956, Gen. Paul Adams, commander of Fort Bragg planned a major field exercise. The Green Berets were participants in the event at Fort Bragg. During the exercise Special Forces intercepted truck supplies, scrambled communications, convoys were misrouted, and Adams's tactical headquarters penetrated. The Green Berets had done their best work.

But General Adams was not happy with these developments and he was extremely hard on the Green Berets. As far as he was concerned, they undermined the training value of the exercise. Never a supporter of Special Forces, he was now even more convinced that Special Forces was a nuisance and nothing more. He strictly prohibited the headgear from being worn, stating that it was not authorized by the army.

Special Forces soldiers had to hide the symbolic cap after earning qualification. When I trained for Special Forces we had one thing in our favor, the current president, John F. Kennedy, who was a great supporter of Special Forces. He recognized that military expertise in today's world of hot spots needed a smaller elite force that could move fast and handle threats, in the changing environment of warfare. Kennedy had also met a stone wall from regular army to become creative and think outside the box.

Gen. William Yarborough, the commander of the John F. Kennedy Special Warfare Center, was fed up with the resistance by regular army toward the Green Beret headgear and mission of broadening the Special Forces. He felt strongly that the green beret was a symbol of pride to all who earned the beret.

After appealing his case on several occasions to the pentagon with unfavorable results, he decided to take the matter into his own hands. He risked his career in a move to go around Pentagon brass when he made a personal plea to the White House.

General Yarborough had gone to West Point with Gen. Jim Clifton. General Clifton was Kennedy's senior military aide. Yarborough convinced his buddy about the importance of the Special Forces mission. The two men conspired to bring the issues of contention to a head.

General Clifton made the president aware of the continued resistance to Special Forces and the Green Berets and suggested that the president make an official visit to Fort Bragg to see the Special Forces demonstrate their capabilities. Kennedy was anxious to make the visit. He had been frustrated with the army's inability to grasp new and unique ideas.

The day Kennedy arrived would become a historical moment for Special Forces. The troops conducted an incredible show for the president. They displayed their unique training and abilities in counterinsurgency warfare. The president sat through several demonstrations given by the soldiers on unconventional warfare and psychological operations. The ceremony concluded with several hundred Special Forces soldiers standing at attention before the president. The room became eerily silent as the soldiers in unison pulled the berets out of their pockets and placed them on their heads for the president to acknowledge. Conventional senior officers stood by and watched, unable to interfere with the events as the president called it "the symbol of freedom and courage." General Yarborough and General Clifton had accomplished their mission.

When Kennedy boarded Air Force One and was saluted by General Yarborough, he smiled broadly and said, "The soldiers sure looked good in their green berets," and went up the stairs to return to Washington. On April 11, 1962, John F. Kennedy issued a letter to the Pentagon, stating officially that the green beret was the symbol of freedom and badge of courage for all Special Forces (see opposite page). From this time on, green berets were proudly worn with no more resistance from the Pentagon. The army made the green beret authorized headgear for qualified personnel.

THE WHITE HOUSE
WASHINGTON

April 11, 1962

TO THE UNITED STATES ARMY:

Another military dimension -- "guerrilla warfare" -- has
necessarily been added to the American profession of arms. The
literal translation of guerrilla warfare -- "a little war" -- is
hardly applicable to this ancient, but at the same time, modern
threat. I note that the Army has several terms which describe the
various facets of the current struggle: wars of subversion, covert
aggression, and, in broad professional terms, special warfare or
unconventional warfare.

By whatever name, this militant challenge to freedom calls
for an improvement and enlargement of our own development of
techniques and tactics, communications and logistics to meet this
threat. The mission of our Armed Forces -- and especially the
Army today -- is to master these skills and techniques and to be
able to help those who have the will to help themselves.

Pure military skill is not enough. A full spectrum of military,
para-military, and civil action must be blended to produce success.
The enemy uses economic and political warfare, propaganda and
naked military aggression in an endless combination to oppose a
free choice of government, and suppress the rights of the individual
by terror, by subversion and by force of arms. To win in this
struggle, our officers and men must understand and combine the
political, economic and civil actions with skilled military efforts
in the execution of this mission.

"The green beret" is again becoming a symbol of excellence,
a badge of courage, a mark of distinction in the fight for freedom.
I know the United States Army will live up to its reputation for
imagination, resourcefulness, and spirit as we meet this challenge.

Sixty-seven

My hands were raw and stinging as I rappelled down the rope. I was hanging below the helicopter about fifty feet off the ground. There were eleven other Special Forces volunteers waiting to get down the rope as the helicopter hovered. We were being dropped behind enemy lines. It was phase four of Special Forces training called Robin Sage, an unconventional field exercise.

We had been in isolation for days preparing for this mission. We were briefed by intelligence agencies concerning the situation in this conflict. The entire exercise was fictional, but the purpose was to capture what we had learned to date. We went through many rehearsals preparing for this conflict. We studied the ethnic culture and customs of our guerrilla contacts and their associates. It was paramount to understand the nuances that developed in all cultures, in order to communicate effectively.

Robin Sage was fought in the Uwharrie National Forest in the Appalachian Mountain range of North Carolina, a few hours from Fort Bragg. Local residents of this area became the friendly enemy and role-players to make this exercise very realistic.

Each soldier would cross-train the duties of each team member in the detachment. Seasoned Special Forces officers were observing us to evaluate and control. Their assessment would determine our future in Special Forces.

Training of the last six-plus months now became a reality in this enactment of counterinsurgency and unconventional warfare exercise.

My role was detachment commander. I had coordinates for our rendezvous with the guerrilla chief. Our contact point had been vague because of the heavy enemy activity and inclement weather.

I looked down from the helicopter to see if I could identify any of the landscape as I prepared to land. It was pitch black, cold, and raining. The raindrops felt like ice as they pelted my face. It was an unusually cold November day for North Carolina. The helicopter lowered altitude and hovered over a wooded area as we descended. I was the first one to hit the ground and run for cover. I heard firing in the distance. I fell to the hard ground and started to low crawl into the heavily vegetated area. As the helicopter lifted off the ground the door gunners returned fire. The gunfire stopped once we disappeared into the forest.

I thought about Arlene and the kids as I lay on the wet ground. She was not happy with me. After we had arrived at Fort Bragg she had discovered that I volunteered for Special Forces. She was very disappointed I hadn't told her the truth from the beginning.

I made my decision alone. I didn't consider the full effect that it would have on my family. We had three young daughters now under the age of six. Special Forces could possibly take me away from them for years at a time, or worse, forever. In thinking back on this, I'm sure my decision had a lot to do with my childhood. I had watched Jews led to their death without a fight. Few had fought in Kovno, at least not until the very end. When I was younger I questioned this and I still do. It might be a superman fantasy, but I wanted the camp prisoners to fight the Nazis. We could have at least drawn attention to our plight. There would have been casualties but we would have resisted an evil that ultimately killed millions. Fantasy or not, I wanted to make sure that no threat to freedom would go unchallenged again. I believed there were some causes worth the sacrifice.

I started moving in the direction to meet our guerrilla leader at the rendezvous point. Our mission brief said that our contact point would be visible. We stayed alert, very conscious of our surroundings. As we moved cross-country and approached the rendezvous point, I saw a mule standing in the rain. I thought about it for a moment when I saw him . . . could that be our contact? The mule even had a hat on. I shook my head and smiled to myself. As we approached the mule our contact man and his companion stepped out of the shadows. They had mules for all of us to ride back to the guerrilla camp.

It was a long, uncomfortable, and wet trip into the hills where the guerrilla band was waiting. When we arrived the sun was coming up. We sat down to a simple, bland breakfast. In my first conversation with the chief, I determined the needs of his unit: money, weapons, and ammunition. I explained what our goals were and laid out a plan of how we could achieve his needs and our goal. I began to build a foundation of trust and rapport with the chief.

We moved out of the camp later that day into enemy territory. We had to survive hunger, sleep deprivation, ambush, and other elements of warfare while we trained several guerrilla detachments. While we were under enemy fire there were scenarios of injured soldiers to challenge our leadership under extreme emergencies. We were given injuries from flesh wounds to amputation of arms and legs all done while in the field.

We ate whatever we caught or killed. Snakes, birds, fish, squirrel, and any other wildlife in the area and drank from streams using our water purification tablets.

We were ambushed in the middle of the night by enemy government forces and threatened on every patrol. We captured enemy troops and treated them in accordance with the rules of war, while at the same time attempting to extract information and intelligence. During this time we were constantly evaluated on our performance.

Special Forces training was the most intense I had ever experienced in the army. There were many volunteers but few qualified. It required a certain kind of soldier that wanted independence and the opportunity to use his own creativity in a crisis. It took a certain kind of commitment to put yourself on the line every day. The training pushed everyone to the edge, physically, emotionally, and mentally. There were good reasons for this kind of training. We would be called upon to find this strength and courage in the missions that we would be asked to perform. We were trained to be professional soldiers fully prepared to lay our life on the line for one another in defense of our country.

I had encountered many hardships in my life and it seemed that I had been preparing for Special Forces since my childhood.

After I finished Robin Sage, I was promoted to captain and assigned commander of Detachment A-121. The eleven other Special Forces members in my new detachment had been in Special Forces since approximately 1960. My unit was on the road running on a cool day in November when a jeep came racing up the road. One of the men in the back of the jeep yelled out to us that President Kennedy had been shot. We ran like hell back to the base and were stunned to learn that President Kennedy, our commander in chief, had died.

Tempers flared, and some of the soldiers blamed the "Commies" and were ready to go to war that day! But the anger turned to sadness as we watched the president's grieving family. It was a blow to all of us. Kennedy had been a friend to Special Forces and an inspiration to most Americans. It was one of the most emotional events nationally that I had seen since coming to America.

Sixty-eight

O n November 3, prior to Kennedy's assassination, Prime Minister Diem, leader of South Vietnam, and his brother were assassinated during a military coup. The United States supported the new military government and began to see gains in the effort to stem Communism in the region.

With the end of the Diem rule the United States felt that the South Vietnamese Army morale would be restored under the leadership of General Minh and other generals who overthrew Diem. They were being hailed as heroes.

Early in 1964, America began to see progress in the war, but on January 30, 1964, General Minh was ousted from power in a bloodless coup led by General Nguyen Khanh. Khanh became the new leader and was embraced by the United States.

On March 6, 1964, Secretary of State McNamara visited South Vietnam and stated, "Kanhn has our admiration, our respect, and our complete support . . . We'll stay as long as it takes. We shall provide whatever help is required and win the battle against the Communist insurgents." America's prestige and President Johnson's reputation were now on the line.

There would be ten new governments in South Vietnam over the next twenty months.

We arrived in An Long on May 1, 1964. An Long Camp was located in the southern tip of South Vietnam near the Cambodian border along the Mekong River.

This area was controlled by the South Vietnamese but heavily infiltrated by the Viet Cong (VC). The VC infiltrators worked for and were supported by the North Vietnamese Communists and Ho Chi Minh. Our purpose in this area was to stabilize the region on behalf of the Saigon government. We had several simultaneous missions: to train the troops in counterguerrilla warfare; to root the VC out of the area; to help rebuild roads, schoolhouses, and buildings that had been destroyed in the area from the many past civil wars and attacks from the Viet Cong; and to provide a secure environment for economic development.

The flight from Fort Bragg to Vietnam lasted over twenty hours on a C-141 jet aircraft to Saigon and a transfer to a C-130 propellor-driven aircraft to An Long. It had been a long and uncomfortable trip. Lieutenant Blair, Master Sergeant McRae, and I had sat in the small cramped seats discussing the mission ahead of us. We would be replacing a detachment that had already served a tour of duty in An Long.

I stepped to the door of the plane after we landed and felt the sweat running down my rib cage as the hot and humid breeze hit me. Sweat poured off my entire body by the time I reached the runway. I turned around and Lieutenant Blair already had his jacket off and was applying Coppertone to his exposed skin. He was a surfer from Hawaii and felt right at home. I felt like I had walked into an oven. I looked around as I stood on the small, dirt runway and saw endless dried-out rice paddies and parched dry ground.

"Captain, Captain Fontaine says this building to the right is our barracks." McRae looked at me with his crooked half-smile and watery blue eyes. "Gonna feel like an oven, sir."

The building was a twenty-four-by-thirty-six-foot cinder-block and wood building. It had small wooden windows with shutters. It was one long room outfitted with hammocks covered with mosquito nets for us to sleep in. We had no power other than the small generator we used for lights and battery charges.

The bathrooms and showers were community in another building close by. To the left was a building that was our headquarters. The compound was surrounded by a moat, a minefield, and guard towers to watch for any enemy approaching the camp.

To my right were thatch-roofed huts with open sides that housed the Civilian Irregular Defense Group (CIDG). The Hoa Hao soldiers slept on raised flat wooden platforms that served as a bed. The huts housed about twenty to thirty men. There were around thirty huts built on poles to avoid the flooding during the rainy season.

The four South Vietnamese Special Forces officers slept in a small building near our barracks, equipped with hammocks covered by mosquito nets like ours. Beyond the grounds were dense trees and vegetation that led to the muddy and murky Mekong River.

Sergeant Lai, a seasoned soldier in the CIDG, walked with me toward our sleeping quarters. He seemed to read my thoughts when I tapped my foot on the parched ground.

"No worry about drought. In monsoon, water cover land, make soft. All differen' from way it look, Captain. Jus' like war. We know VC here but no find. USA here but VC no' know. Hanoi co suong mu."

"What does that mean?" I asked.

" 'Hanoi fog' in English. No 'ting is way it seem." He smiled and continued speaking in his broken English. "Way of war . . . way of Ve'etnam." His words would come back to me before I finished my tour.

Sergeant Keating, my senior demolition noncommissioned, walked alongside us, and the others followed. He pulled his half-smoked cigar from his pocket and lit up. Keating was never without a cigar; if it wasn't in his hand, it was in his pocket or clenched between his teeth. Even in combat he chomped on an unlit cigar.

"*Defense de fumer!!*" Sergeant Uzakow said, complaining about the heavy smoke. "*Mechant fumee.*" Uzakow was senior heavy weapons specialist. He and Keating were always battling over the best cigars, the best wines, the best cities in the world, and the best weapons. Both were well educated, but Uzakow claimed that he had the edge because of his European heritage. He was born in France, served in the French Legion, and then volunteered for Special Forces.

Sergeant Ayers, junior demolition engineer, walked over to the minefield surrounding the complex.

Sergeant Donald, the hardest worker in the detachment, held two heavy boxes filled with ammunition, weapons, food, clothing, and other supplies. He took them into the barracks ahead of us.

Sergeant Burke, junior radio operator, was antsy and wanted to get into action. He wanted to taste combat. "How the hell did the CIA come up with Civilian Irregular Defense Group name? Why didn't they just use the tribal name?"

"They always have their reasons," I said. "The Hoa Haos take pride in their name and their heritage. They've been fighting wars for centuries. They were royally screwed by Diem and his brother. Their land was taken and that's all they have, Sergeant." He leaned down and patted the top of the crusty ground. "This is it. The tribes always get the short end, don't they?"

I shook my head. Somebody always does.

Sergeants Foreman and Donald moved the radio equipment into our radio room. Foreman started setting up the equipment. Within three hours we were settled.

Since 1960 the Viet Cong had infiltrated tribal villages like An Long in Vietnam. The VC would come into an area and adapt to the tribal customs and eventually persuade or intimidate the people to support their fight against the Saigon government.

But when Ba Cat, a revered and respected tribal leader of the Hoa Haos was allegedly beheaded by the VC, the tribe vowed never to forget. They wanted revenge. The CIA saw their window of opportunity and began to work with the Montagnards (mountain men) and other minority tribes that included the Hoa Hao sect.

The agency persuaded the tribes to fight the VC and align themselves with Saigon. The death of their leader was the only reason they agreed to help the Saigon government. But there was still an underlying resentment from the past. During the early years of Diem's rule the Hoa Haos' land had been taken and their homes seized.

The Hoa Haos, however, did trust the Americans.

The men were paid by the United States to fight. I provided satchels filled with Vietnamese piastas (local currency) to pay the six hundred volunteers each month. We had been told in our predeployment briefings that the Hoa Hao tribe was a religious group, very militant, and with no loyalty to anyone other than Buddha. The Hoa Haos, a sect of the Buddhist religion, originated in the early 1900s in the Mekong Delta. They believed in justice for all people, but they did not believe in the restrictions imposed by a political government.

I walked over to the kitchen, a small thatched hut about twenty yards from our barracks. The sides of the hut were netted to keep the bugs out and still give ventilation. I opened the screen door of the entrance and poked my head inside. There were two South Vietnamese. Both wore the traditional South Vietnamese attire of black cotton pants and white shirts with a white apron tied over their clothes.

"*Toi ten la tam*, Captain Shachnow," I said, introducing myself to them in their native language.

They looked up and smiled.

"*Han hanh gap ong. Toi ten la tam, Don.*" Don responded in Vietnamese.

Ba giggled. "*Daiwee* (Captain) Shachnow, we speak little English," she said in a heavy accent that was barely understandable.

They explained they were helping with preparations for a banquet that was being given the next evening by the Vietnamese military leadership to celebrate our arrival. The counters were stacked with fresh fish, fruits, vegetables, and some items of meat that I didn't recognize. It was apparent that a great deal of expense and effort was going into this occasion.

As I went out the door I watched Ba as she danced on the low tabletop and prepared French bread, kneading the bread dough with her feet. I saw the dough rise between her toes.

The next evening at the welcoming dinner I was seated at the long banquet table next to Major Zahn, a highly respected Hoa Hao tribal leader. The local sect had appointed him commander of the camp. Zahn was about five eleven, his black eyes penetrating. He was a very disciplined man with a great deal of pride in his heritage and his people.

I discovered from our predeployment briefings that he had no prior military training or experience. It didn't matter: his power outweighed his lack of experience and his importance was to lure the other Hoa Haos to join the CIDG. The United States would supply all the tactical experience.

On my other side was my counterpart, Captain Nam, a trained Vietnamese Special Forces officer in the South Vietnamese Army. Captain Nam had been in the military since he was fifteen years old, more than half his life. His family had been killed in one of the many civil wars that had taken place when he was very young. He lived as a beggar on the streets of Saigon until he was old enough to join the army. The army was his life and his career. He was a very dedicated officer.

He explained to me during the evening that his main assignment was to mask Major Zahn's military weaknesses and keep a close eye on him since the Saigon government did not trust any of the Hoa Haos. He said at another time the Hoa Haos would be an enemy. They were militants who did not follow the laws of the South Vietnam government, only the laws of Buddha.

The dissension between the two men was a delicate situation, since the premise of any military action must be trust and loyalty within the ranks. None of the minority tribes in the CIDG program trusted the Vietnamese government. They had suffered under several different regimes, their lands had been confiscated, many had been killed, all leading to the distrust. There was suspicion on both sides, and we were in the middle.

"*Daiwee*, Hoa Haos live by law of Bud'ha," Major Zahn began on my right side when Captain Nam was out of hearing distance. "We live free with our loyalty only to Buddha. We follow law of tribal council. We no trust Saigon gover'ment. Diem and his brother were killers, but we have vengeance for North . . . they kill Ba Cat at Can Tho . . . cut his head off!" He put his finger under his neck to indicate the slice. "We will avenge our leader's death. Hoa Haos trust United States, money from U.S. for CIDG, not South."

I smiled at Major Zahn and changed the subject, not wanting to get into the discussion of financing by the United States. Our orders were to give the Saigon government all of the credit. "Major Zahn, I'd like you to take me into the village. I want to talk to some of the people you depend on for information."

"All the village see and hear. All tribe want VC dead!!"

I sat for a while in silence as the first course of the meal was served. I could see that the Hoa Haos were a proud and passionate tribe. They would probably make very good soldiers. But the passion for revenge and the distrust in place between the two armies could become a double-edged sword.

"We go to village tomorrow," Zahn said, interrupting my thoughts.

"Good, I'll look forward to it," I answered as my dinner plate was filled to capacity with food.

The first dishes served were distinctive and unique fish sauces and rice with sides of vegetables. It wasn't bad. But then came fish and eggs with Nuoc Mam sauce. I smelled it before I saw it. I had been warned about this one. It was made from salt and fish that had been fermenting for about a year. The bowl was placed in front of me and the odor almost knocked me out. I took a small bite and gave my hosts a stiff smile. It was hard to swallow, but gradually I got used to it.

Major Zahn reached for the next specialty dish that was being served and began putting a portion on my plate. It was prepared meat that looked like beef.

"Good. Very good," he kept saying and smiling at me.

"What is this dish, Major?" I asked. As I was putting the meat in my mouth, he called the dish by its Vietnamese name.

"*Ga Chuot,*" he answered.

My Vietnamese was not perfect but I thought I heard mouse somewhere in that name.

Captain Nam turned to me with a big smile. "Rat, *Daiwee* Shachnow," he said, waiting to see my reaction. "Very good."

I smiled back at him. We had been told about many of the dishes served in Vietnam and we were also told that it would be an insult to the host if we didn't eat everything served. "This is excellent," I said. I wasn't about to let them get the best of me. They watched for any crack in the armor. I'm sure they were disappointed at my reaction. They continued their smiles with each new serving. They were smiling even as they took potshots at each other during the evening. They were very polite to each other but below the surface was conflict. Nothing was ever the way it seemed in Vietnam.

I looked at the empty plates around the table and thought that dinner must be coming to an end. I watched my men and I could see they were relieved also. Then I saw more food being served.

Captain Nam placed a bowl of eggs, still in their shells, in front of me.

"I'll show you way of eat," he said, and picked up the egg. He slit a small hole in the top of the egg. He threw back his head and sucked the contents out of the shell. "Swallow, no chew," he said smacking his lips.

I shouldn't have asked, but I did. "What kind of eggs are these?"

"Eggs specially selected . . . how you say, 'gourmet' treat for us. Raw, select just as baby chick form."

Major Zahn with great technique made a small hole in the top of the egg and handed it carefully over to me. I had no choice I placed my mouth over the slit. At first I felt the cool slime enter my mouth and slide down my throat then a more solid liquid that was soft and gooey. The embryo. It went down my throat effortlessly, but the thought of swallowing an embryo was a different story. It stayed with me for a while. I had heard even worse things that had to be eaten to appease the host . . . a buffalo eye . . . drinking from a long straw into the depths of the earth where herbs and roots were grown in tainted water. One soldier instead of receiving longer life as promised, received amoebic dysentery. I felt lucky.

We heard the geese in the moat begin making loud noises. There were probably one hundred geese in the ditch around the camp that were used to alert us to any penetration around the camp. Gunfire suddenly erupted in the distance and we could hear the geese squawking. Then it came closer. My men jumped up from the table at the sound and ran out the

door. Nam, Zahn, and I did the same. We were returning fire within minutes along with the CIDG Rapid Response Team. I looked up at the guard
tower and they were throwing flares into the darkness to reveal the VC. We
fired as the black-pajama-clad VC danced back into the rice paddies. The
firefight ended as abruptly as it began. Perhaps this was a message from the
enemy, a welcome to detachment A-121.

As I lay in my hammock later watching the mosquitoes try to bore their
way through the netting I wondered how the VC could attack unnoticed.
The camp had not been penetrated, nonetheless we had to widen the
perimeter for protection. We had responded quickly, but their action had
to be met with an even stronger response. I wanted twenty-four-hour patrols outside the camp in a more aggressive posture.

I thought about Arlene and the kids. They had returned to Salem and
were living with Arlene's parents. Arlene was going to college and tried to
make contact with my parents. But they had not changed. The only one in
the family my mother wanted to see was Shereen.

SIXTY-NINE

The next day, McRae and I went into the village with Major Zahn. As we drove the jeep we had to make detours and cross the fields where normal roads had once been. The village was filled with the same thatch-roofed huts that were at the camp, only smaller.

Along one dusty sun-baked street a couple of merchants were selling wares that they were carrying on their back, others on the street were begging for food or clothing. They were all wearing very lightweight clothing, mostly white and black.

Major Zahn explained that before the VC had come, the vendors now carrying backpacks once had their own shops, but were chased out after being robbed and some being murdered by VC.

An entire block farther down the road had been attacked and torched by the VC including a string of stores and a schoolhouse set on fire.

We stopped and talked to villagers in the street. We visited the homes of the people used by the former Special Forces detachment. They had been hired to work as our eyes and ears. I spoke to them in Vietnamese and even though I had studied Vietnamese for six months while training with the detachment, my pronunciation was lacking. Most of them giggled discreetly at some of my mistakes.

On our last house visit of the day, a little boy about three years old came running into the room while I was talking to his mother. He stood and stared at me when he realized there were visitors in the room. He ran and touched my uniform with his finger and ran back to his mother. I always carried small candies in my pockets. I reached for one of them and handed it to him the next time he ran over and touched my uniform. His mother spoke to him in Vietnamese.

"Cam on, Daiwee," he said thanking me.

From that day he never forgot who I was and always had his hand out for a candy and addressed me as *Daiwee*.

I got my first letter from Arlene. She and the kids were a little cramped living with her parents, but she was glad to be back. She talked about the news reports concerning Vietnam being on the six o'clock television news every night. Shereen was going to kindergarten and Denise was walking and talking. Michelle was in playschool. She included pictures of her and the girls and her parents. I put them in my wallet and kept them with me.

We trained approximately fifty new CIDG troops for counterguerrilla warfare in eight-week increments. Lieutenant Blair, my executive officer, was in charge of training. McRae and the others rotated each day as assistants. We sustained six companies, 120 men per company.

We started with the basics of discipline. In the army, physical and mental discipline is the key to every other phase of training: push-ups, sit-ups, long marching hikes, left face, right face, climbing up and down ropes, hustling through a mud bed, traveling across a river with gear and rucksack protected, understanding the orders, acting as a team on the order, and following through.

Most of the new recruits had never used a weapon, so Sergeant Donald started with the basics of light weaponry. He was a great teacher. The students immediately trusted him; he was always smiling and very patient. He taught them how to use and maintain their weapons, obtain a good sight picture, sight alignment, how to hold a weapon properly, hand-to-hand combat, how to use a knife effectively, and how to make a silent kill. Then Blair would take them out on a mission. He taught them how to cover each other in battle, how to maneuver as a team, and how to set up security.

The VC periodically attacked during these training exercises. We had some casualties, but gradually as the inductees gained experience, we began to have more and more successes.

We watched recruits that could be trained as leaders. Sergeant Uzakow would train these more advanced recruits in heavy weapons and leadership responsibilities.

Our recruiting was continuous to keep the ranks full, replacing those who were killed, went home, or didn't make the cut. Major Zahn and the elders of the tribe spent many days talking to possible volunteers. All of the volunteers wanted to avenge their leader, but not all were prepared to go through the training.

I wanted four of our six companies on tactical operations twenty-four hours a day to show their presence. We were involved in firefights almost daily, but my plan was proving successful.

Our intelligence informants turned out to be mostly unreliable. When we received information from any of the villagers about Viet Cong activity they were paid money whether the information was good or not. Sometimes, people just made up information because they needed money.

Captain Fontaine, the last detachment commander at An Long, had given me the name of two nurses as informants. The two women worked in the dispensary not far off the base. They were very attractive and good storytellers. After a few initial conversations I realized that they had no formal training as nurses. But I decided that I would watch and see if the information they supplied was valid. They informed us about some VC hiding in an area about eight miles from the village. We went out and discovered there was a fresh camping area, but it had been vacated not long before we arrived. Sergeant Stevens paid the women for the information as we did many other informants.

The second story the two nurses gave was that VC had been seen coming across the Cambodian border. They gave us the exact location and we went in search of the VC. When the troops returned they reported engagement with the VC and captured several prisoners. But the report went on to say that the VC were not surprised by the attack and they were fully prepared when we showed up. We determined that the two women were acting as double agents, taking favors from the VC and money from us. We no longer used their information even though they would try to entice us with their stories.

Other villagers were anxious to give their information and each had their own motives. My intelligence officer, NCO Stevens, had a ratings system for accuracy and reliability of the information. If we gathered two or three bits of the same information we would analyze it and make a decision if it was worth investigating. It was not a 100 percent accurate method, but it was the only one we had. Intelligence received from higher headquarters was seldom useful.

Day-to-day life was a struggle for many in the village. I empathized with them. I knew what kind of life they were forced to lead. I also knew that the North Vietnamese government would brutalize them if they came to power. I became committed to the tribe and their efforts to survive.

I assigned Sergeant Keating and Sergeant Ayers to help with civic projects in the area. We repaired roads, bridges and rebuilt schoolhouses that had been destroyed. We enlisted the villagers, women and children alike, to help. We paid them for their work. There was no heavy equipment available in the area for many projects. We had dirt hauled into the village by ox-drawn wagons and filled the holes in the roads. We cleared roads making travel easier and faster. The rainy season would eventually wash away some of the roads. But when the ground softened in the early rainy season we would lay stone into the dirt roads. My men and I frequently worked side by side with the locals in the area. This built trust between us.

Confidence continued to grow between the villagers and Special Forces. Some of the businesses reopened and children returned to school. We gave all the credit to the Saigon government, but the villagers knew it was the United States and not Saigon helping them.

SEVENTY

On a hot, muggy day in June after I had been in An Long about thirty days, Sergeant McRae and I went with Sergeant Lai's company on a routine operation. It was 8 A.M. and the sun had brought the temperature to at least a hundred degrees. We had been moving since about 4 A.M. So far the intelligence had been incorrect; we had met with no resistance.

Lieutenant Do, who was supposed to be in charge of this command, had become ill the night before. Sergeant Lai took his place and I was glad; I had more confidence in Lai. He was young, energetic, aggressive, and very competent. In addition, he spoke some English.

As we picked our way through the dense tangles we came to a murky canal. "Sergeant Lai," I said. "This canal isn't on the map. Are we in the right place?"

"Sir, I think we've gotten bad intelligence. Let's cross the canal, move in a kilometer then toward the south, and get back to camp," he said as he pointed out the route on the map.

The men started to cross the canal making rafts with sticks and ponchos to carry the radios, machine guns, and ammo boxes. Sergeant McRae entered the deep water first. He swam, uncoiling a long rope as he went across. We all waited crouched down in the thick, wet vegetation waiting for his signal that all was clear. When he and his scouts reached the other side, they disappeared into the thick vegetation with their weapons at the ready to look around.

He came back out and gave us the clear signal and tied the rope to a tree to help move us across.

One by one, holding onto the rope, we entered the warm, muddy water and pulled our rafts to the other side. I motioned to Lai as we were moving that we were extremely vulnerable. We were nothing more than slow-moving targets for the VC.

Sergeant Lai gave arm and hand signals to his men to move faster. As each man got to the other side, he stood and shook the water from his gear and clothes. But they were still targets as they stood silhouetted in the sun. Lai ordered in sign language for them to stay hidden until we were all across the canal.

It seemed to take forever with the thick mud, heavy equipment, and slow dog-paddling through the water. Finally we all crossed the river. I thought there would be more vegetation on the other side. But once we moved past the vegetation that McRae had searched we were in a completely flat area . . . sitting ducks again.

I had a bad feeling. I took a step onto the first rice paddie and the noise exploded in my ear at the same moment. I looked to my right and again heard an explosion of automatic gunfire. Without hesitation I started to run in zigzags toward a dike. The bursts were coming not more than one hundred yards away beneath some dense brush. I hit the ground rolling and started firing toward the brush. The bursts from my M16 were ear-splitting. I heard the explosion of a sixty-millimeter mortar. I rolled up in a ball and covered my head.

I looked around to see where the rest of the company was located. I could barely raise my head an inch off the ground with the bullets ripping over my head. When there was finally a hesitation in the firing from the brush, I realized that my unit wasn't firing yet. I didn't understand why they were waiting.

I finally spotted Sergeant Lai and his radio man about twenty meters away. I crawled toward them. When I saw Lai's face it was pure panic! Now I knew what the problem was in not returning fire. Soldiers have many ways of responding to a firefight. Some are frozen by panic at first, some retreat and run, others unconsciously respond to what their training has taught them. Sergeant Lai had panicked.

I yelled as loud as possible to be heard over the gunfire, even though I was next to his ear. "Direct your men to establish a base of fire and assault into the enemy position."

He looked at me as if I were crazy. His eyes were as big as saucers. Going after the enemy was the last thing on his mind. "We're pinned down," he said. "Pinned down, Captain. There's nothing we can do!" he shouted as bullets flew past our heads. "Get air support, is only way to get hell out."

I shook my head and screamed at the top of my lungs. "There is no air support! We have to get out of this one on our own." I could see from his face I wasn't getting anywhere. I put my arm around his shoulder to reassure him. "I will lead the assault, you and the rest of your company follow me!"

Lai just stared at me blankly. McRae had crawled up next to me. He screamed at Lai. "Don't be a fool. Do what he says!" As McRae finished his sentence, another deafening explosion to our left hit the ground. The impact flipped me over and I felt a searing pain in my thigh. I didn't even look to see if I was injured. For the last time I looked at Lai in the eye and I yelled, "Follow me!"

I zigzagged across the field toward the enemy position, running as fast as my feet would move. The pain in my leg was gone. I screamed at the top of my lungs as I ran, firing my weapon in long bursts toward the enemy. The ground and dirt beside me were ricocheting with enemy fire coming close. The air echoed with gunfire from every direction. I was too afraid to hit the ground with all the gunfire aimed at me until I saw a small, flat shrub with a shallow ditch coming up on my left. I dove into it. I was gasping for breath, my face was so close to the ground I was getting mouthfuls of dust and dirt. Then I felt a heavy thump on my back. I tried to react but the heavy weight had pinned me down.

"Oh, shit," I thought. "After all I had been through in my life I didn't want to die on this battlefield."

Then I heard a familiar voice. It was McRae. "You and I are the only people on this assault!" he shouted, as we smashed against one another to stay protected by the mound of dirt.

I turned and looked behind me. I saw Lai and his men still about fifty meters behind us. I felt the sting of dirt fly up from the VC bullets. Then I saw two VC clad in black pajamas dance through the bushes in front of us. McRae and I both fired. One dove for the ground, the other stumbled and fell forward. We saw their weapons fly in the air.

After Lai and his men saw the two VC go down, I finally heard them yelling and returning fire. I smiled in relief as I watched Sergeant Lai and 120 Hoa Haos firing their carbines wildly, running and yelling at the enemy; fire discipline was nonexistent. If nothing else it had a psychological effect on the VC. McRae and I charged forward with them flanked on each side.

As we got close to the enemy's position, I saw the silhouette of a VC dragging bodies of the men McRae and I shot earlier. With my M16 at my waist, the first burst hit him. He spun around and his AK-47 flew off of his shoulder. The black pajama-clad form fell backward and hit the ground, bounced almost in slow motion, and finally came to rest.

Still moving on adrenaline, I ran into the thicket and saw more dead bodies of VC on the ground. Three bodies lay to my left and another on my right. I tried not to look at them closely.

I heard the sound of our grenades going off and very soon the shooting died down. When I found Sergeant Lai, he was with a group of Hoa Haos, surrounding three prisoners. The medic bandaged their injuries. They were blindfolded and kneeling or squatting on the ground.

The Hoa Haos were shooting their weapons in the air, elated with the victory. Lai's intelligence officer informed me that it was a platoon of thirty VC . . . six were dead and three were captured. I let Sergeant Lai make his own decision of how to deal with the dead. Some wanted to leave them lying on top of the ground to scare others from fighting for the VC. Others wanted a burial. I watched as one soldier cut off the ear of the dead VC. It was his proof of a kill. They finally decided on carrying them back to camp, tied to a bamboo pole.

The next day when I woke up I felt like I had been run over by a semi! My groin was bruised and excruciatingly painful. I realized that the pain in my leg yesterday was because I had hit the ground with an ammo carton in my pocket. The carton had cut and bruised the flesh. The walk back to camp had evidently aggravated the injury, it was funny because I never noticed the pain after the impact until the next morning.

Sergeant Lai came by to see me the following afternoon. He boasted that I owed him one! After all, he had saved my life. McRae was also in the office listening to Lai. I saw a look of amazement cross his face. I smiled as Sergeant Lai left my office and wondered if he had been on the same battlefield.

I was awarded the Silver Star by order of the president of the United States.

SEVENTY-ONE

After one of our eight-week training courses, Sergeant Uzikow and I took the new platoon for their graduation field operation along with Captain Nam and the Second Company. We had about fifty graduates. They wore the new green uniforms with their small rucksacks holding extra ammunition, medical supplies, and rations on their back and an Ml rifle at the ready. Two soldiers carried machetes belted on their hip. We started out a couple of hours before dawn traveling in two columns, separated by a kilometer from Second Company.

We had cleared the area of VC a couple of weeks earlier and expected no contact with the enemy, but our new soldiers were excited and frightened as they ventured into the area. I watched each of the soldiers as they marched through the low brush and rice paddies in two columns. I ordered the two soldiers with the machetes to come to the front as we approached the denser area. They sliced the vines and limbs, clearing the way for the troops. After a few hours we approached a low brush area again. I realized that we were coming close to the Cambodian border that was off-limits to us by policy.

"Charlie One," I whispered into the radio at Nam. "We're coming too close to the Cambodian border, let's move east."

"Charlie Six, I just question a peasant," he was speaking softly but I could hear an anxiety in his voice. "VC are in hamlet several hundred meters up front."

"Do you think it's accurate?" I asked.

"We move to hamlet . . . we check," he said.

Within seconds I heard gunfire.

I took out my binoculars. The fog was too dense and I couldn't see anything.

The radio crackled in my hand. "We make contact . . . Cannot . . . no move forward!"

I didn't understand why. The gunfire was sporadic and he had sixty well-trained men with him.

I turned to Sergeant Uzikow and shrugged. "Why the hell can't he move forward?" Uzikow shook his head and shrugged.

"Charlie One, we'll flank to the left!" I responded.

Uzakow and I turned at the same time and looked at our graduates. We both knew from their faces they were going to be unpredictable in disengagement. Neither of us felt totally confident if there was a serious confrontation.

We started moving as fast as we could to flank the VC and take some pressure off Nam and his men. I heard the gunfire increasing from the M1 rifles and carbines. Captain Nam's troops were firing back. I knew it wasn't the VC; they didn't have that kind of ammunition to waste.

As we moved forward I could see the outline of the hamlet. But it worried me that there was no VC flank security. This could be a trap to draw us into a killing zone.

I brought the men to a halt. "Keep your weapons ready and stay hidden. I need a couple of volunteers to come with me." I looked at the group. No one would even look at me much less jump up and volunteer. "Since everyone volunteered," I snapped, "I'll take you and you." I pointed at two of the soldiers. "Let's move it!"

They jumped out of the brush and fell in behind me. The three of us crept forward crouching low to the ground. Using hand signals I motioned them to stay close but out of sight. I moved into the front of the hamlet and approached the first hut carefully. I strained to hear if anyone was inside. All I could hear was gunfire from Nam's soldiers. I edged carefully against the side of the hut. I held my rifle on automatic, safety off, and ready to fire. My heart was pounding, and I held my breath as I turned into the entrance of the hut. I could feel the sweat running down my face. I let out a quiet sigh of relief after I scanned the empty room.

I could hear gunfire outside erupting more rapidly coming from the left and the right of the hamlet. I stepped out of the hut with my finger on the trigger of my weapon and almost collided with a VC turning into the hut. He jumped back. We were only feet apart. His gun was next to his hip. Our looks froze into each other's eyes, and I could only hear the sound of my breathing and my heartbeat. Instinct took over and I squeezed the trigger. Both weapons exploded. I felt a bullet pass under my right ear. I saw the red stain begin to form on his chest and I realized my bullets were more accurate. He bounced backward and crumpled to the ground.

I stared at him in a trance. There were a thousand thoughts screaming all at once. The white noise in my mind was pierced as Uzikow's voice echoed in my ear.

"Where's Captain Shachnow?" Sergeant Uzikow was shouting at the translator in the distance.

Uzikow saw me and then saw the crumpled body, lying only a few feet away. He cautiously walked over to the VC's body and kicked away his weapon.

"Did he fire?" Uzikow asked.

I pointed under my right ear. "He didn't hit me."

"You're one hell of a lucky man," Uzakow said softly.

"Yeah, luckier than him," I said, feeling that my voice was in a tunnel far away. I paused for a moment and tried to shake myself out of the daze that was still with me.

By now the remaining VC had fled across the Cambodian border. We moved in closer and I shouted to Captain Nam to shift his fire. "Ngrung bao [cease fire] !" I could hear Nam shouting to his troops.

As we moved closer to the main impact area I heard Captain Nam again shouting to his men to cease fire. With the adrenaline still flowing, some of them couldn't stop shooting. I saw four of the new graduates drop as they crossed into the path of friendly fire.

I ran to give them help. I knelt down next to one of the young soldiers. He had been hit in the leg and was bleeding pretty heavily. I could see from his face that he was frightened. "You okay?" I said and patted him on the shoulder. "Okay?"

I saw a smile come across his face through the pain. "Okay, Daiwee." I held onto his hand until the medics took charge. As I left he gave me a salute. I returned the acknowledgment.

By now the sun was beating down on us in full force, sapping our energy. Everything was passing me in slow motion. I could hear nothing but my own thoughts ricocheting through my mind about the man I had killed, and wondering how I was still alive.

I ordered the troops to work their way through the hamlet. Three VC casualties were found.

I walked back over to the body of my kill. He had taken at least a dozen rounds. I had no idea I had fired off that many rounds. I thought about the pain he might have felt but as I looked down at his face, his expression was serene.

The Vietnamese Special Forces intelligence officer began to inspect his belongings. Before he tagged the wallet I carefully picked it up. Inside was a little money, a small calendar, and a snapshot of himself standing next to a slim, attractive woman dressed in a long, white traditional Vietnamese dress. They were both smiling. I fought a sadness as I looked at this man standing next to his loved one. The intelligence officer began silently reading a letter he found.

I wiped the salt and sweat off my face with the dirty bandana around my neck. "What's in the letter?"

"A letter to his wife . . . no finish." He looked up at me. "Sir, you want letter? Some soldiers like souvenir of a kill."

I shook my head and walked away. The warmth and thickness of the hot humid air was making it hard for me to breathe. I couldn't get the man's face out of my head.

My entire childhood had been permeated by killings. I had always thought about myself being the victim. I never thought of myself as the perpetrator. My target was the enemy; now he was human with a wife. I had made a mistake in looking back and making it personal.

As I paced around I noticed that Uzikow was not letting me out of his sight. On our tired journey home he trudged along beside me.

"Sir, I know how you feel. It might help to talk it out," he said gently. "Those shrinks that the army hires say it's better to talk about what you're feeling, but then I doubt if the shrinks ever shot anyone."

I shook my head. For some reason I didn't want to speak. All I could think about was Arlene and the kids. What was I doing in this alien and distant land?

Uzikow seemed to read my thoughts. "I felt terrible after my first kill," he said quietly, looking down at the ground as we walked. "Pisses me off, the guys that hit the target from long distances, it's less personal. Push of a button, pull of a lever, an unseen target. Easier that way . . . they never see the coldness of a dead body."

He was right.

"Stevens's wife wrote him and said a lot of kids in college are protesting us bein' here. I don't know everything, sir, but I don't think any of us like war."

I looked at him and wondered if the kids demonstrating in the streets and flying VC flags understood that we were here trying to find peace and protect the freedom for these people. As we shuffled along in silence, I felt alone and troubled.

Later, by order of the president of the United States, I was awarded the Bronze Star. My deed wasn't a vile act; it was an honorable and courageous one. I had protected my men and subdued the enemy. I sent the medal home to Arlene.

Arlene wrote and asked why I had earned the Bronze Star. I was vague in my explanation. She knew I really didn't talk a lot about why I earned medals. Medals were awarded when you took a risk. I didn't want her to worry about me. I would tell her when I got back home.

She also said that my mother had promised to babysit Michelle one afternoon while she had a dental appointment. Michelle arrived at her house after school and my mother was not home. Michelle sat on the porch until Arlene came by to pick her up. Michelle had been sitting alone for two hours. My mother said that Arlene had not told her that Michelle would be at her house.

She said that my father was not too well, but nothing serious. I knew she was worried about me in Vietnam. She didn't say it, but it was between the lines. The living room war made every army wife worry.

"Ba Cut," the Vietnamese intelligence officer said as he sat down in front of my desk a few weeks later. "That was your kill."

Now I had a name for the man that haunted me. That was something the army couldn't erase. I had trained, prepared, and defended myself and was rewarded for killing this man and yet his face still haunted me. I had defended my own life and the lives of my troops. I really had no other choice. But even now, I wonder what happened to his widow. I wondered if she knew the name of the American soldier who killed her husband. I wondered if she hated the scars of war as much as I did.

Sergeant Lai was right: in this war in Vietnam nothing was the way it seemed.

SEVENTY-TWO

I had spent the morning inspecting the schoolhouses, businesses, and dispensary in the village that we had built up in the last few months. Whenever I was in the village area I liked to walk instead of ride. I would stop at the homes of the locals and talk with them. I was a very visible commander and I felt like my communications had enhanced our efforts in An Long.

I was walking down the main dirt road toward the next hamlet when I saw a small white vehicle with a motorcycle engine aiming itself toward me. My security detail was in a jeep trailing slowly behind me. We came to an abrupt stop and the soldiers drew their weapons.

When the oncoming car saw the weapons drawn, it also came to an abrupt stop. Three small Vietnamese men piled out of the car and lastly a large six-foot Caucasian man. As soon as he spoke I knew he was an American.

"Can I help you with something? Captain Shachnow," I said and extended my hand as he walked toward me.

"You're just the man I want to see," he said smiling. "Bob Rogers, NBC News."

He handed me a letter giving him authorization from headquarters in Can Tho to film at our camp and possibly use us in a news special on NBC.

I groaned to myself. The last thing I needed was a lot of TV cameras following us around, filming our every move and conversation and trying to protect a group of people who didn't have combat experience.

"There are other camps that are probably a lot more exciting. Camps that have a lot more combat than we do," I said trying to discourage his interest.

"Yes, Captain," he said looking at me. "But you are the only commander in Vietnam who has a $50,000 bounty on his head," he said.

Major Zahn and Captain Nam had notified me about this bounty several weeks earlier. That was part of the reason for the drawn guns when these people drove toward me. "I don't know how headquarters feels about publicizing that information," I said.

"Oh, that's where I got the information. They said you must be doing something very right, if you were worth that much to the enemy," he said. "That's why I'd like to film your camp."

I shrugged and hoped that our camp would end up on the cutting room floor.

The next day Ted Yates, the director, showed up with a cameraman. He and Rogers went everywhere with us for five days. Since it was the monsoon season and floodwaters were deep, most of our travel was in sampans or Styrofoam boats. The sampans held two to three people and were very difficult to balance. The Styrofoam boats held six to eight people and would not sink. The cameraman at times managed to capsize the sampan as he moved with his camera to get a shot.

"Captain," Yates said to me after we got off the boats one day. "How long do you think we're gonna be here?" I could see the tape rolling on the recorder. "I mean how long do you think it will take to win this?"

"I don't have a crystal ball," I said and smiled. "Wish I did. We're doing a lot of good here and the people deserve a better life. They've lived in poverty, working to live from day to day. That's not right for anyone. Before we got here, many schools were closed, the businesses shut down, people murdered, harassed, stolen from, tortured by the VC. A gang of bandits. I hope as long as we're doing some good the U.S. will stay here."

"When do you go stateside?"

"I'm on a six-month tour. I'll be home the end of October,"

"Do you miss your family?" he asked. Now he had his camera on me.

"I miss Arlene and the kids every day . . . every time I see one of the little kids here I think of them." I thought about my family halfway around the world from me. "I send them letters as often as I can."

"What do you tell them about war?" he asked.

"Nothing, I tell them about the local animals and the people that live here and the kids that I give candy to every day. Maybe by the time they grow up there will be no more wars."

Not all of our conversation hit the airwaves in 1965. "Vietnam: It's a Mad War," showcased my unit and the bounty story was discussed, as well as our accomplishments. They also showed the dangers we faced daily.

It was a beautiful morning several weeks later and I was scheduled to go up the Mekong with the district chief, Tho. We were going to Hong Ngu, a large town north of our camp, near the Cambodian border.

Before we left, the district chief's bodyguard approached me to explain that we needed to stay close to the shores of the Mekong. I told him that wasn't a good idea, but he insisted that's the way Tho wanted to travel. He finally admitted that the district chief had a fear of the water and didn't know how to swim. I wondered how anyone growing up in this area had escaped learning to swim.

We were halfway to our destination when I head a crack rip through the air. I immediately recognized the sound and knew that we were under attack. Ambushed from the vegetation on the shore. I swung into the water using the boat for cover. I looked over toward the chief and saw that he was hit.

His bodyguard lifted him into the water. Even though the chief did not swim, he dove underwater.

The gunboats traveling with us quickly started to respond. I started returning fire the minute I hit the water along with the rest of the bodyguards. The enemy had already disappeared . . . it was a classic hit-and-run ambush.

When the firing stopped I jumped back into the boat. The chief was on the floor of the boat after his bodyguard took him from the water. His injuries weren't bad and the medic on the trip started bandaging his wounds.

One of the soldiers looked at me with a funny expression on his face. "Captain?" he said and pointed to my leg and shirtsleeve. The crimson red stain of blood had oozed onto my pant leg and blood was running down my arm. I was wounded and didn't realize it. The medic turned immediately and put a tourniquet on my leg to stop the bleeding. "Captain, I think you need to go to the rear and have those wounds taken care of."

I shook my head at him. "No way," I answered. I wasn't going to leave my unit for a minor wound. As far as I could tell it was not serious. I knew that he could remove the bullet in my arm with no problem.

I was awarded a Purple Heart by the president.

SEVENTY-THREE

I looked at my watch as I got ready to leave for a briefing at Can Tho. I was ahead of schedule and had just enough time to go by Sergeant Lai's house, five minutes from the camp gate.

Mrs. Lai had come by my office yesterday while I was out and wanted to speak with me. Mrs. Lai did not speak English, so I invited my interpreter to accompany me.

When we pulled up to the thatched-roof house, Mrs. Lai was squatting in front of her house talking with some girlfriends. This was a traditional social ritual in the neighborhood. She was wearing the traditional baggy, pajamalike clothing. She looked up at me with a very grave expression from beneath her wide dome-shaped sun hat.

I handed her a can of sweetened peaches. She rose and graciously thanked me and invited my interpreter and me into her home. When we walked in I saw the traditional alter covered in red and gold aluminum paper with incense-burning candles, fruit offerings, and pictures of family members were organized on top.

"Mrs. Lai, you came by yesterday to see me. How can I help you?" I said. The interpreter repeated my question.

I saw Mrs. Lai begin to talk excitedly. As her mouth moved I could see the black stain on her teeth from chewing betel nuts.

"She is a very troubled woman. She needs your help," the interpreter said. He continued to listen.

Her eyes were cast down to the floor and she never looked at him as she spoke.

"She believes that her husband is being unfaithful to her," the interpreter said. "She came to you to seek your advice and counsel. She is very distraught."

I thought about the words I needed to say in Vietnamese. I was very surprised about this news. Sergeant Lai was a very positive and likable guy and had always spoken with respect about his family. "Sergeant Lai has spoken frequently of you in our conversations. He has the highest regard for you." I looked at the interpreter, making sure I had made no mistakes as I spoke her language.

"I am a good wife," she said.

The interpreter began translating the last sentence.

She then picked up a machete leaning against the wall as I thought about my response. Before I could grasp what was happening, she swung the machete and severed her little finger from her hand, all the while maintaining a somber face and maintaining her love and devotion for her husband. The act of self-mutilation was the proof.

The interpreter and I frantically grabbed her hand and tried to stop the bleeding. I told him to get the emergency survival kit out of the jeep. We slowed down the bleeding and wrapped a towel around her hand and saved the little finger. We quickly got her to the dispensary. The Special Forces medics then took her into their care.

I heard the chopper blades of the helicopter that would take me to Can Tho. I was still trying to figure out what the hell had just happened. I watched as the pilot eased down to the ground to the landing pad. Then we took off for the thirty-minute trip for an intelligence briefing at Special Forces B team compound in Can Tho, my higher headquarters. I had been notified only twenty-four hours before about this operation.

The compound was occupied by South Vietnamese troops and U.S. Special Forces troops. I walked into the executive meeting room that was filled with intelligence experts, commanders, and other personnel involved in planning an attack that was yet unknown to me.

To my surprise it turned out to be in an area of my responsibility. Direction-finding equipment had located a Viet Cong radio broadcasting station. It was east of the Mekong River along the Vietnam border. I couldn't believe that this facility could be in my area. I had constant patrols on every square inch of land and I had no hint of this broadcasting station. But I didn't want to be negative about their information so I continued to listen.

"We have solid electronic evidence," the intelligence officer continued. "It's a mobile station that can be moved on short notice," he said.

The plan was not simple; everyone wanted to get into the act. A Vietnamese regular army unit would land with Chinooks, large, twin-rotor helicopters. They would touch down about ten kilometers southeast of our target. Then they would do a routine sweep to the north and stop short of the Cambodian border. Upon reaching their destination, one company would separate and, under the cover of darkness, move northwest toward the radio station. The remaining unit would make camp and do so attracting as much attention as possible. That was the plan of deception: while the one company was sneaking west along the Cambodian border hoping to catch the radio station by surprise, others were creating a diversion. My job was to send a CIDG company up the Mekong River that same night to establish a blocking position. The CIDG company would atttempt to prevent the enemy from escaping to the south and southwest.

The Army of the Republic of Vietnam (ARVN) would actually assault the station. In theory, using this element of surprise, the plan visualized the enemy being boxed in. The only escape route would be to move north, into Cambodia, and there was nothing we could do about that. Although not officially sanctioned, it was understood that in "hot pursuit" crossing the border for a short distance was acceptable. The border was very difficult to identify because the Mekong is a tidal river. My unit had not worked with regular Vietnamese army and we spent some time coordinating to ensure that we would not fire on each other. This was an operation that we wanted to keep under wraps since security was a never-ending problem. For all I knew the Vietnamese briefer in the meeting could have been a Viet Cong.

The operation was scheduled to take place in several days.

When I returned that afternoon, Sergeant Wiggington, my senior medic, informed me that Mrs. Lai's finger had been reattached. It would not work as before, but the finger was saved. I was relieved and still stunned by her self-mutilation.

On the night of the attack, the CIDG company departed from camp, heading north. After several hours of marching they changed formation, placing two platoons on line and headed toward the blocking position. If the intelligence was correct, contact would be made in a couple of hours.

The ARVN were dropped ten kilometers south of our convergence point by Chinooks. The soldiers were moving toward us, but they had been traveling all day and were exhausted. They were also encountering many water obstacles, slowing them down and making their journey more difficult than expected. All my darkest fears about this mission were materializing. If they were as fatigued as I thought they were, they would not be as alert as they needed to be for this raid. I knew what it was like to be that tired: you use all of your energy to walk and become oblivious to the hazards lurking around you. Your combat formation gets worse and the soldiers start to bunch up, making themselves easy targets. Most important, the leaders get careless when they are tired. Things were not going well at all.

Our CIDG company unit arrived at the blocking position and, as we suspected, there was no ARVN unit. Our unit was about eight hundred meters from the Cambodian border when they made contact with VC troops. I was still back at the camp when the news arrived over the net. I was convinced they had found the radio station. By now, dawn was beginning to break and the ARVN unit was finally closing in fast. It looked like things might work out after all, and we would have the radio station trapped.

Unexpectedly, another report came through the net from Sergeant Uzakow. "Two Cambodian gunboats have taken us under fire . . . we are in serious trouble . . ."

I radioed my superior, Major Lattimore, requesting air support. Although he endorsed the request, it was disapproved because it was too close to the Cambodian border. Coincidentally, there happened to be a congressional fact-finding group following the efforts of this operation in Major Lattimore's office when my request came in. They had the decision reversed and we were granted air support. In the meantime, I took off with our motorboats on the river with one platoon and one on land following. I was not certain what I could do to help, but I knew I could maintain better communication with a more powerful radio system on the motorboat. In addition, the boats had machine guns mounted, but they were no match for a gunboat.

The static on the motorboat radio was interrupted by the voice of the forward area controller, an air force officer flying a small single-engine spotter plane. His job was to do an air reconnaissance for the approaching jets. He would identify the target and direct the fighter jets' air strikes onto the exact location.

He told me over the radio that he had four F-4 Phantoms and needed clarification of the target. He had the target in sight, but from the air he could not tell if the gunboats were located in Vietnam or Cambodia. I assured him it was Vietnam and told him to confirm it by looking at the map. He said it just did not look right from the air, but agreed with me that according to the map, it was Vietnam and went on to inform the F-4 jets to engage the target.

I was disappointed to hear on the radio that the first jet had missed his target; however, the next F-4 scored a direct hit. The controller reported that the boat began to sink and several people were jumping overboard into the river. Personnel on the second boat were attempting to pick up the ones in the river when it was struck by the lead aircraft on a second pass. The controller flew by and observed the target for a few minutes and declared a "mission accomplished" over the radio. I requested that they make one more pass to ensure that the boats sunk.

In all of the excitement of the gunboat battle, the VC unit on land was forgotten. They, in turn, took advantage of the situation and slipped into the sanctuary of Cambodia. By this time, the ARVN had finally reached the river.

I grounded my boat where the ARVN were and spoke to the commander. His troops were exhausted. He was trying to make arrangements with a ferry boat to transport his troops down the river to save time and energy. Unfortunately, he didn't have enough money to pay the fare. Trying to maintain good relations, I offered to pick up the bill. He was extremely grateful.

Uzekow and the Hoa Haos were about a kilometer down the river. I explained that the ARVN were taking the ferry down the river. The Hao Hoa's were not happy about hiking home while the ARVN got to glide down the river, especially since the ARVN had not shown up at the target on time. As I was starting my way back down the river I was startled when I heard the sound of gunfire.

The long-standing sense of rivalry exploded into resentment. It was a battle that I had not started but I knew I would soon be in the middle.

A few minutes after I left, the boat filled with ARVN floated by the Hoa Haos. Insults were hurled from both sides; gunfire erupted. Several soldiers on the ferry were wounded and a few Hoa Haos were shot.

When Uzakow returned he reported the incident to me. I did not write any of it up as the fault of the Hoa Haos. They had been the underdog for too long.

A report came into the headquarters the next day from the intelligence people who had worked on the radio station fiasco. It stated that we had basically blown it and the radio station was probably repositioned into Cambodia.

Several days later I heard a helicopter hovering over the camp. I walked outside, apparently he was waiting for an "all clear" signal that it was safe to land. One of the NCO's popped a green smoke grenade signaling an okay. I casually walked to the landing pad as the helicopter descended. I was not expecting anyone to visit us.

A tall, slim, tanned man in a white suite jumped out of the helicopter. He introduced himself as being a representative from the U.S. Embassy in Saigon. He further explained that he was looking into the circumstances surrounding the sinking of the Cambodian gunboats. It appeared that Cambodia had lodged a formal complaint, and Ambassador Taylor wanted the facts concerning the incident.

We gathered in my office and I briefed him in great detail on what had transpired. He was polite and listened patiently. When I was finished, he casually said "Are you aware that the Mekong is a tidal river?" I had forgotten that, but as soon as he asked the question, I knew what must have happened.

At high tide the island at the border was entirely in Vietnam. That is how it is also depicted on the map. However, at high tide, a much larger part of the island is exposed, and that part was in Cambodia. The boats in question were actually in Cambodia when we sank them. We screwed up.

I was not ready to admit that. After all, my military chain of command would have to be informed first. So with all the confidence I could muster I said, "Yes, I am aware this is a tidal river."

He asked several more questions, nodded politely, and boarded his chopper. I immediately reported this visit and what transpired to my boss, Major Latimore. He did not seem to be too concerned with the visit or the fact that we made a mistake. Although he was irritated that this individual did not obtain his permission to come out and question me.

Newspapers in America carried the story about the official complaint from Cambodia. They also mentioned that the enemy boats had wandered into Vietnamese waters. After reading several versions of this story, I even started to believe it. I never heard another word about this from my chain of command.

SEVENTY-FOUR

I stood on the scorching red dirt runway before I boarded a C-130 to take us from this strange and exotic land to Saigon and then on to Fort Bragg, North Carolina. I looked around at the hundreds of villagers that had waited for hours in the hot sun to bid us farewell. These people were like my family. I had shared their problems, found solutions, and helped them achieve a better way of life. There were times we mourned together when we lost a tribal member, but we also laughed together in happier times. I had been deeply touched by the beauty of this country and the people.

When I reached the end of the ramp to board the plane, I turned and threw out a final salute to them, stuck out my fist, and gave a thumbs-up. I heard their cheers and watched as the plane lifted and the crowd grew small.

Fourteen hours later we landed at Fort Bragg, North Carolina. When the door to the plane opened, the Fifth Special Forces commander and his staff stood on the tarmac to greet us. As we debarked the Braniff aircraft, Colonel Roy, a tall, dark-haired, six-two commander stood and shook the hand of each detachment member.

"I've heard great things about you, Sid," he said. "I want you to take it easy for a few weeks, enjoy the family, and then I've got something special in mind for you. You'll return to Vietnam in about two months."

I couldn't believe what I was hearing. I had just stepped off the plane. I wasn't prepared for this. How would I tell Arlene? She had a good sense of humor, but not that good! All I wanted right now was to be with my family. I smiled at him. "Yes, sir."

The first night I arrived home Shereen, Michelle, and Denise were standoffish. At bedtime, I went into their room and read them a story. I related the animals in the book to the ones I had written to them about in Vietnam. Their eyes were wide with excitement as I told them about the monkeys and the birds and I imitated the noises that they made. This made them all laugh. But I felt a distance that the absence had created. They weren't sure if I was going to be a permanent fixture like their mom. It took time to regain their trust and confidence and to find my role in the family.

This is not an unusual challenge for soldiers that have been away for a long period of time.

During my return physical the next week, I was diagnosed with a TB virus, typhoid virus, and several other illnesses. I had gotten these diseases from the water that I drank out of the rivers in An Long and probably some of the food I had eaten. These diseases were in the very early stages and I was given countless pills each day to cure the problem and was declared nondeployable. I was off the hook for the return to Vietnam in two months. For several days it was considered that I be put in quarantine, but after more tests it was decided that I was not contagious.

For the next couple of months I was given light duty and placed under medical supervision. While recuperating and watching television in the living room of my home, I was stunned at the portrait painted by the newscasters of the military. The war I was watching of Vietnam was very different from the one I had experienced. I didn't understand why the resistance was building in the press and on the streets. It was contradictory, since Johnson won by a landslide in 1964, but the political battle to save Vietnam was being lost. There was a growing disillusionment among society with our politicians and the military as more body bags came home.

As I watched the resentment and anger being portrayed on the television, I wished every American could have seen the gratitude on the faces of the villagers when we left An Long after my tour was completed. Was the sacrifice too great to help people who couldn't defend themselves? Principles that I formed from my own experience influenced my belief that no sacrifice was too great to protect the defenseless. I had been on the other side of that coin for too many years in my childhood.

Freedom meant different things to different people. To me freedom was the most important thing in a person's life and a cause worth fighting for. To others, who had not experienced any lack of freedom, it was taken for granted. I could see both viewpoints, but I knew that complacency was the biggest threat to any nation and, in reality, Communism was a real threat and it had to be stopped.

The battle was being lost politically, not on the battlefield.

"They wanted to send me back," I said to Arlene as we sat drinking coffee after dinner. "Good thing I got sick."

"When did they want you to leave?" she asked.

"Last month," I answered.

"Oh, Sid, that's too much to ask," she said. "Are they going to want you to go when you get better?"

"I may apply to bootstrap. What do you think?"

Bootstrap was a program offered by the army to service members that were seeking a college degree. It was a leave of absence, without losing your rank or pay.

"I offered to pay for the college courses myself," I continued.

"If they granted it you would get your college degree? Where?"

"What about Nebraska? They have a very active program there," I said. I could be deferred from returning to Vietnam until I graduated. I was thirty-one years old and I needed to get a degree if I wanted to continue my career. I had acquired some college credit hours along the way and it would only take me a year to graduate.

"Sounds good, Sid," Arlene said. She paused a minute. "I heard from your father this afternoon while you were sleeping," Arlene said.

"What did he want?" I asked.

"For you to come visit them," she said.

"Is everyone invited?" I asked.

"No, he asked for you only. He was complaining that you've been home for a while and they've only spoken to you on the phone," she said.

"Well, they'll get the message sooner or later," I answered. I would not go to see them until my family was invited.

"Sid, I have something else to tell you," Arlene said, she smiled and looked up at me. "It's number four."

"What are you talking about?" I looked at her confused.

"Eight months from now we will have another baby!" Arlene smiled and put her arms around me.

SEVENTY-FIVE

S hachnow, you're losing your competitive edge," my assignment man-ager said as he rifled through my file. "You just don't have the education to go much higher in rank." He looked at me. "You screwed around with Special Forces too much. We advise that you stay out of SF and build a solid foundation in the infantry and get your college degree."

An assignment manager in the army is like a counselor in school, they advise on how to further your career, although that is not their primary duty. First and foremost their responsibility is to fill army personnel requirements.

I knew when I volunteered for Special Forces that regular army frowned on the assignment, but I couldn't comprehend why they would consider it a waste of time. I had learned more about combat, survival, interpersonal skills, and teamwork through Special Forces than I had learned to date in my other assignments.

"You better get your degree to compete," he said finally.

"I've applied for bootstrap. I realize that I will have to return to Vietnam after I graduate."

"Good move," he said. "The paperwork could take awhile."

I walked out the door and wondered how I could really take the time to go to school. I had three daughters and one on the way.

I had been assigned to Fort Benning after being selected for the infantry officer advance course.

"Sid, I went to the doctor today in town. I had no idea how bad segrega-tion still is in Georgia," Arlene said with a shocked expression. "At the doc-tor's office there's a separate entrance and separate water fountains for blacks and whites. I noticed that the water fountain for the blacks were dirty and the rooms they used for examinations weren't as nice as for the white side of the office."

"I thought President Johnson had changed all of that." I was as sur-prised as Arlene; after all, the army was integrated and had been for some time.

I told her about my assignment officer's advice.

"Well, Sid, you're competing with the 'ring knockers.' I think you should go for your degree. We'll work out the finances some way. We've always been able to eat!"

We both laughed remembering some of the meager meals we had in Germany when I was a private.

Later that night Arlene woke me up. Lee Ann was born on August 6, 1965.

A few months later, I requested that after my graduation I be assigned to Bad Tolz, Germany, with the Tenth Special Forces. I decided to ignore the advice of my assignment officer. To my surprise my request was approved, and I was given thirty days to report for duty in Germany. Arlene and I packed what we would carry with us and were waiting for the movers to arrive when the phone rang.

"Captain Shachnow, this is Capt. Charles Goodwin, your assignment officer. I'm sorry this is such late notice, but I must inform you that your transfer to Bad Tolz Tenth Special Forces has been canceled. You are being diverted to Fort Dix, New Jersey. This will be your temporary station until further assignment instructions. Your written confirmation of what I have just told you should arrive by mail tomorrow."

I heard him hang up the phone on the other end before I could respond.

"Arlene, we're not going to Bad Tolz . . . we're going to Fort Dix, New Jersey," I said as I turned to face her.

Army wives roll with the punches. She took it in stride and rearranged the packing for the new destination and I notified transportation of the change of plans.

I was assigned as director of infantry training. We were responsible for training combat arms soldiers, most in preparation for Vietnam. I also had the additional duty to support the public affairs speaker programs. We received requests from many different civic organizations to speak on the topic of Vietnam and give it a positive spin. The program was very popular since most of the audiences were supportors of the military. I had two other officers that I sent if I was unable to attend. They were highly decorated Vietnam combat veterans and very good public speakers.

My assistant walked in one morning with a letter of complaint from a Veterans group. They were disgruntled about a speech that was given the prior week at a monthly luncheon. The complaint was lodged against Lt. Don Morgan.

"For being disloyal and an embarrassment to the army . . ." I read the complaint and was surprised. I knew this man and I couldn't believe he was guilty of the accusations. He was a Vietnam veteran, a decorated warrior, and a loyal American.

I called him into my office.

"Yes, sir, I did say some things that might be considered disloyal," he said when I asked him about the charges.

"Can you tell me what you said?" I asked.

"Well, I probably talked about my tour in Vietnam last year," he answered. "I talked to them about what we did there and the capacity in which I served. Then someone asked me, 'Do you think we'll win the war in Vietnam?'"

There was a long pause. "And . . . ?" I asked, urging him to continue.

"'Do we really need to?' I looked at the man who had asked me. 'There's a price for every soldier to pay in a war. They are affected mentally, sometimes physically. The thing to be considered is not whether we win or lose, but whether the price we pay as Americans is worth it.'"

I nodded and let him continue.

"Captain, I was injured in Vietnam and today I can only wish that I had been killed," he said and I saw his eyes fill with tears. "My testicles were blown off when I stepped on a mine! I've lost my wife. I have no hope left. They didn't just blow my balls off . . . they took my life and my future. I'm just a breathing corpse of a man and have had serious complications from this injury. I look at myself in the mirror and I no longer see a man . . ." he said and stopped for a moment. "I can't see that the sacrifice was worth it," he finished softly.

"I'm sorry, Don. I didn't know," I said, sadly.

"What are we fighting for, sir?" he asked. "We're fighting for people who want us to stop destroying their country."

I paused a long moment. "Hopefully we're fighting for a society that has been oppressed and want a better life," I said. "You have suffered immensely, but it doesn't make you less of a man. You must continue your courage that helped you get up out of that hospital bed and gives you the strength to face your problems every day. I'm sure it is no easy task . . ." I looked at him and took a breath. "You have compassion. You're trying to set things straight. These are our only weapons of survival. Our compassion and our courage and our hope. These are the parts of us that cannot be taken away or touched by bullets or mortars. The courage, hope, and compassion that you show can never be extinguished and it will not be silenced."

He looked at me. "I hope you're right, sir. What I've endured is too much when I know were fighting for a society that hates us, a society with a land that we have destroyed with our bombs and our armor," he almost smirked. "I watched a buddy of mine hand a kid a candy bar. The kid handed him a grenade that blew him to bits."

"What you've been through, none of us can really know, and I don't have any black-and-white answers for you. I'm not going to try to minimize what your loss has been. I know the public looks at it like a game . . . winning or losing! We haven't advanced far from the Christians and the lions have we?"

"No, sir. I realized after I came back to the States that this is a political game. I lay in the hospital bed and watched the politicians and the war on the six o'clock news. McNamara has no concern for the soldier, and neither does the president as far as I'm concerned. I wish those senators and representatives and cabinet members would come over and walk through a day with the soldiers," he said bitterly. "Win? Sir, I won a one-way ticket to hell!"

"Well, Don," I said. "I am truly sorry about what happened to you and wish there was some way for me to help you. However, in the meantime I do not want you participating in the speaker program."

He nodded and stood up, saluted, and departed.

I sat in my office after he left. Vietnam had changed since I was there. With the draft in effect, the buildup had escalated with thousands of regular army soldiers doing the fighting. The military leadership was very disappointed that the reserves were not being activated for Vietnam. The structure of the army would be changed in the future. In a major conflict, reserves would be called up to serve their country.

The bombing was stepped up, but it hadn't stopped the North Vietnamese Army and Viet Cong. Vietnam had been at war for centuries and most of the people had only a meager future and little hope. Most of them were Buddhists and believed they would return as another being . . . perhaps a chance to become a being with a better life.

The phone rang and abruptly brought me out of my thoughts.

"Sid, your bootstrap has been approved," my assignment manager said. "You're going to the University of Nebraska in Omaha."

SEVENTY-SIX

I sat in the classroom with the other sixty students almost all about ten years younger than me. I was granted this one-year leave of absence, with the understanding that I would take my second tour in Vietnam after I graduated.

I lost some credits with my transfer, but with advancement tests I could graduate in a year with a bachelor's degree in business administration.

I felt strange being out of uniform in a classroom wearing civilian clothes. It had been almost thirteen years since I had been a civilian. And one of the first times that Arlene and the kids and I could spend extended time together as a family without having to put the military first. We planned activities almost every day after my classes were over. At night, I spent my time at the library studying. I was taking a heavy load in order to obtain my degree in the allotted time.

I phoned my parents after we had settled in. I had seen them in Salem, but only after they had invited all of us: Michelle, Shereen, Denise, LeeAnne, and Arlene. I thought that spring break would give us an opportunity to go to Salem and visit the two sets of grandparents.

"Hello, Mother," I said when she answered.

"Who is this?" she asked.

She always did this. She knew who it was, but this was her game. "It's Sid," I said.

"Schaja," she said. She and my father still spoke their native language and always used my original name. "How are you?" she asked. "How is Shereen?"

"Everyone is fine," I said, disregarding that she didn't ask about the others. "How is Pa?"

"Why don't you drop us postcards?" she interrupted me.

"It's easier this way," I said.

"It's a waste of money. You must be a rich man now," she said. "Anyway, your father is not well, he has some problems with his heart," she said.

"What does the doctor say?" I asked.

"He just tells him to take it easy and gives him pills," she answered.

"What kind of pills?" I asked.

"Pills for his blood pressure," she said dismissively. "Sid, where are you?"

"I'm going to the University of Nebraska. I am going to earn my college degree, Ma," I said.

"None of the universities here in the United States can compare with the Freidberg Poly-Technical Institute in Germany, or any of the schools in Germany," she said.

I ignored her comment. "I thought we might come to Salem in a couple of months . . . maybe the first week in April," I said.

"Whatever you would like, Schaja," she said in a martyrish tone. "We would like to see you and your children."

"I'm sure you'd like to see Arlene also," I said.

There was silence on the end of the line. "Have you seen that movie *Dr. Zhivago*?" she asked. "It's the finest film ever made. Russia was so beautiful . . ."

She loved anything that had to do with Russian literature or the beauty of Russia. She probably saw the movie ten times.

"I want to come see you and Pa before I go to Vietnam again. I'll be leaving as soon as I graduate."

"And Arlene?"

"She'll stay in Salem," I answered.

"You're going to leave her again? After her behavior the last time?" Mother said. "Will you be gone long?"

"Yes, I wouldn't leave my family if I didn't have to, Ma. I also trust Arlene completely. The only bad behavior going on the last time was yours!" I said into the phone. My comment was met with silence. "Ma, do you need anything?" Again silence. "Let me know about Pa." She hung up the phone without another word.

It had been two months since I had spoken to my parents. I recognized my mother's voice even though she was crying.

"Your father has had a heart attack," she sobbed. "He is in very serious condition!"

"When did it happen, Ma?" I asked anxiously.

"He woke up this morning about five. He had pains and then he passed out," she said. "Max called an ambulance."

"What do the doctors say?"

"What do I know, I barely understand English and they do not talk to me, but I think he will be okay," she said. "Max is here now trying to find out about him."

"I'll be there as soon as I can, Ma," I said and hung up. I boarded the first available flight to Salem.

When I walked into the hospital room there was an oxygen tent over my father's upper body. He was pale and weak. He reached out his hand to me and gave me a light squeeze.

"He needs a lot of rest. It will take him some time to recover. He has a heart disease called angina pectoris. He is very lucky to be alive," the doctor said to me as we stood in the corridor outside my father's room.

"Will he make a full recovery?" I asked.

"Well, there has been some damage to his heart," the doctor said. "He will probably live for some years if he takes care of himself and loses a few pounds. He has to stay away from fatty foods, no alcohol, and no caffeine. And he can't exert himself."

I thought about the two steep flights of stairs that went up to my parents' apartment in Salem. Not to mention my father devouring jars of mayonnaise and smoking two to three packs of Camels a day. Things would have to change.

"Will he need help at home?" I asked him

"Maybe he'll need a nurse for his first few days at home, but I don't see any reason for him not to live his years out with just a reasonable amount of adjustment."

When I went back to the apartment that night I sat down with my mother. "Ma, you need to get out of this cold weather. It's hard on you both to go through these winters here in Salem."

She shook her head. "But where can we go? This is our home."

"What about Florida?" I asked. "Frida, your sister, is there and Max is planning to move there. You would have family there"

Her face brightened for a moment. "But we have no money to buy a house; we would need to sell this house. Pa is sick and it would be too much for me" she said. "No, no, we just can't uproot. It's too difficult."

"Ma, those two flights of stairs are impossible now," I said. "And you're going to have to help break some of his eating habits . . . the doctor already said he needs to go on a diet."

She shook her head sadly. "There are so few things for him to enjoy now."

"Arlene and I will see what we can do to help," I said. I didn't have a clue what we would do, but I knew they needed to get out of Massachusetts and into an easier environment.

After I returned home Arlene insisted that we take the $10,000 we had in savings, and put a down payment on a condo near Mother's sister in Florida. Somehow we were able to make the monthly mortgage payments when they were not able. My father recuperated in Florida and lived until March 28, 1978. They were both touched by Arlene's generosity. My mother continued to live alone as a widow for an additional twenty-two years, and passed away shortly after her ninety-first birthday. She was a remarkable woman.

I received my bachelor's degree from the University of Nebraska in December. I also received a promotion to major.

I couldn't attend the graduation ceremonies. I received my deployment orders for my second tour in Vietnam and was assigned to the 101st Airborne Division, the Screaming Eagles.

"It'll be different this time. I'll be in a Battalion with eight hundred men," I said to Arlene at dinner the night before I left.

"Daddy, where will you go?" Michelle asked.

"I'm going to Vietnam, honey," I said.

"Do they still have monkeys that hang in the trees?" she asked.

I was surprised she remembered the letters I had written her about the monkeys in An Long. "I'm sure they do," I said.

"Where will you be assigned in the battalion?" Shereen asked. She was picking up army terms already.

"It's a battalion in the famous 101st Airborne Division, so I'll be on jump status," I said.

They had seen me jump on numerous occasions in the past. Shereen was always fascinated by it and wanted to do it. Eventually, when she grew up into a young woman she did become a paratrooper.

Shereen paused for a moment. "Daddy, do you ever get scared when you jump out of airplanes?"

Arlene looked over at me wondering how I was going to answer.

"Sure, I do, honey. Everyone gets scared, but you learn not to listen to those fears and just do the best you can. I pretend I'm a bird with big wings. People that say they are not scared are liars or stupid," I said, smiling and picking her up. "Remember, you cannot be a hero without being scared first."

She started to laugh watching me wing around the room. Then she became serious. "Daddy, when I get scared I get under the covers and I hold onto Joseph," she took a deep breath. "Do you want me to send Joseph with you?"

Joseph was a stuffed green lizard that she loved very much and seldom left her side.

SEVENTY-SEVEN

I was not able to sleep on the flight to Saigon. It was a long and uncomfortable flight. I thought about the war. From all of the reports that I had received in the United States, it seemed like we were doing pretty good. But there were demonstrations going on throughout the United States Violence was exploding in our own communities in protest of the war. Peaceniks who used the very methods they condemned. Violence. I thought about Lieutenant Morgan and his immense sacrifice with a future that held nothing but agony. I wondered where it would all end and what fate had in store for me.

But regardless of the political debate about the war, I had a job to do and I would not shirk the responsibility that I had to my country. This time I would be stationed in the northern tip of Vietnam, close to Hue. I reported to the 101st Airborne Division and was assigned to the 502nd Airborne Battalion (First Strike) as the operations officer.

Lt. Col. Jack Bishop was my first battalion commander. He was a crusty veteran who had served in Korea. He seldom smiled and barked his orders, but he merited respect since he was an officer with considerable combat experience. He was very good to the soldiers in the field and they loved him. He was adamant that the soldier came first. On the other hand, he gave the officers under his command hell. Since I worked under his direct supervision and in close proximity, I was a convenient target.

It had been two weeks since I arrived and the annual Tet holiday ceasefire was approaching. We heard rumors that there was a strong NVA and VC buildup, but intelligence could not gather any significant data. I would consult our S2, the intelligence officer on a daily basis, but there was no specific information about any upcoming attack.

I was sitting on a pile of rocks just outside the command bunker. It was at around 5 A.M., and I was sipping a fresh coffee I had made myself, it was still dark. The sounds of the birds chirping echoed through the air and then the deafening blast of mortar rounds suddenly ripped the atmosphere. I jumped up and grabbed my M16 and heard rockets heading toward the camp. I ran back into the command bunker and Bishop was already shouting orders. I looked out and saw soldiers running in every direction. Some barely had time to zip up their pants when the sound of attack jolted them out of their sleep and into their fighting positions.

We could not get a clear picture of the damage and activity on the perimeter from the radio reports. Colonel Bishop directed me to go down and make an assessment and report back.

I left the bunker with my radio operator to the area of the camp that was receiving the heaviest gunfire. As I ran down the hill I could see we had some casualties. I shouted to the medics to help the wounded. When I got to the perimeter bunker at the edge of the camp, I saw it had been damaged. One side had collapsed. I thought it must have received a direct hit. But farther down I found an injured soldier who had apparently run into the post framing the entrance of the adjacent bunker. In his haste and panic he cut the corner and slammed into the post, seriously injuring his face and head. It was almost comical as he lay on the ground in his underwear, bare feet, ammunition belt slung over his chest, clinging to his rifle in an unconscious state as the medic tried to revive him. After the dust cleared, it was determined that most of the injuries had been self-inflicted, but the VC and NVA certainly got our attention.

We could see rifle flashes in the distance. I returned fire with my M16, but the VC quickly eluded our fire.

A paratrooper, who informed me that I was wanted on the field phone in the bunker, interrupted me. It was my operations sergeant. "Sir, the old man wants a situation report," he yelled into the phone. I shouted over the small arms fire, "The perimeter seems to be secure. There has not been a penetration. There is no incoming fire. What you hear is us firing. No enemy in sight. Casualties are minor, mostly inflicted by accidents not enemy fire."

"How the hell could they surprise us like this? Was security on the outside asleep?" Colonel Bishop yelled in the background.

The fire base was at full alert and we dispatched several patrols, but they made no contact and did not have anything to report. For the remainder of the day, Colonel Bishop was in a lousy mood and very unpleasant to be around. We later discovered that there were 70,000 VC and NVA committed to the surprise operation. The South Vietnamese took the brunt of the attack, although Americans lost over 1,550 soldiers, either killed or missing, and 7,760 wounded. This attack had hit thirty-four of the forty-four SVA/U.S. camps in Vietnam, and in Saigon the U.S. Embassy was attacked. This event began an escalation of the war that lasted until the end of February and marked a distinct change during my twelve-month tour. Our kills of VC were staggering and they never ran out of recruits, but the VC were destroyed as an effective force. The price was high for all concerned, 750,000 were made homeless, the enemy losses ranged between 35,000 and 50,000. But we as Americans lost politically. Although it was a military success in the end, the enemy's capacity to mount a coordinated attack nationwide at a time when we were claiming that the end was near came as a traumatic experience to the American public. I was oblivious to the total picture and lived in my own small world.

It was a warm day in July when my helicopter touched down in Quang Dien district. I was visiting the district chief, a routine meeting where we exchanged information and frequently he would ask me for assistance. Today was no exception; he asked me to transport some building materials from one village to another and I accommodated this request by providing a truck. As I was preparing to leave the chief asked if I could drop a small group of district soldiers off near a patrol base where they were setting up an ambush for the night. I agreed to take the eight soldiers. These soldiers had never been in a helicopter and most were excited; some were, a little scared as we lifted off. Soon we reached an open area and I instructed the pilot to land.

As the troops disembarked the chopper I could hear heavy gunfire. The pilot powered up so fast I almost fell out of the craft. We circled at a safe altitude and I could see that the troops were engaged in one hell of a firefight. We returned to the base and I brought back six soldiers I rounded up and returned to the firefight. As the chopper blades cut through the air, I kept my eyes peeled on the ground. I saw that the enemy was breaking contact and moving toward a wood line. I had the pilot land the aircraft on the other side of the wood line and move with the small group to intercept the fleeing enemy. I was able to anticipate the route of escape they would take and set up my own ambush. But as the enemy approached our ambush, one of the soldiers fired before the enemy was in the kill zone. Then all hell broke lose . . . a violent firefight ensued and lasted for about ten minutes. As quickly as the firefight had started it suddenly ended, leaving a deafening silence. I carefully crept toward the enemy position and found four men dead with their weapons still in their hands or near their bodies.

I motioned for the others to come forward. When they saw they had defeated the enemy, they were elated. This was the first time they had tasted victory in a very long time. We loaded the dead men on the chopper and returned to the district. The chief was beaming with pride as his soldiers came off the helicopter. He shook each of their hands and congratulated them. He thanked me for my help.

In January of the next year, in a small ceremony, I was awarded by the direction of the president of the United States a Bronze Star for heroism.

About two months later, I was on another routine reconnaissance flight in our area of operation. I had my radio operator and two paratroopers for protection, my pilot, and two door gunners. My radio operator nudged me and pointed toward the ground. There was a light haze hovering above the treetops. There was no mistake . . . someone had a campfire lit below. I saw a flicker of a small fire in between the treetops when I zeroed in on the area with my binoculars.

"Go back over that area one more time," I said to my pilot

"Yes, sir," he said.

He circled the area.

I knew the area was controlled by the enemy but I wanted to make sure that it wasn't one of ours.

"Yeah, that's not us," I yelled. "Open fire."

The door gunners started firing. As we hovered above the treetops I spotted a sampan. The pilot began to get nervous because the large aircraft was exposed. Just as I was about to tell the pilot to gain altitude I spotted several men in black pajamas running through the woods. I fired my weapon in their direction marking the area I wanted the door gunners to take under fire.

"Put us down," I said to the pilot. "We'll go after them on foot."

He looked at me like I was crazy, but he followed my orders. Four of us jumped out of the aircraft and started running after the enemy. At a point when they could see the four of us they began firing. There was one hell of a firefight and I began to question my judgement in pursuing the VC on foot. I had the radioman inform the aircraft that we were going to assault the position and shift the fire from the door gunners so they would not hit us.

When we started to assault the enemy we were all screaming and cursing and firing at the same time and this was too much for the VC. As they started to run a VC turned and fired. I saw my bullet hit him. Most of them were shot but some made it to the sampan and escaped.

I walked toward the body of the man I had shot. He was lying on the ground, motionless; his weapon had fallen away from him, but was within reach if he was alive. I approached him cautiously, but elation was pulsing through my body. It was a strange juxtaposition of emotions. I had cheated death . . . dodged the bullet . . . I was not a statistic in a body bag. Being alive, pulling through in a combat situation was an incredible high. It was a different feeling from my last experience.

The helicopter returned with troops and destroyed the VC base camp.

"Hey Major Shachnow, how about a picture with your kill?"

I looked around, the adrenaline still pumping. I was standing in the middle of the dead soldiers as they were being lined up on the ground.

"Yeah," I said and looked at him, thinking he was going to snap a shot of me as I was standing in front of him. I waited for him to snap the shot.

"No, Major, how about squatting down next to your kill?"

I squatted down.

"Lift him up a little bit," he said.

I could hear people in the background shouting congratulations to me, showering me with compliments.

"Major, you are one brave son of a gun," one of the soldiers said and put out his hand to me. "You single-handedly brought down this VC camp!" He walked off shaking his head.

"Major, how the hell did you spot them?" another soldier said.

"It's all up here," another soldier said pointing to his head looking at the other soldier. "He's a hell of an officer!"

I felt like an observer caught up in a moment that seemed surreal. The picture was snapped and we left the area. When we arrived back at headquarters word had already spread and everyone was talking about the event.

That evening I was leaning against a wall made of sandbags listening to Sergeant Tsabota whistle. He was good at it. He suddenly stopped and looked up at me.

"Sir, do you have a death wish?" he said softly.

I didn't answer, but realized that I did behave irrationally and irresponsibly toward my family. As I thought about it, I was surprised that there were no inhibitions on my part to go into battle since I had serious questions about killing on the battlefield in my first tour. Could it be that one gets used to it and grows callous?

The army awarded me a Silver Star for gallantry in action and I was given a parade for this accomplishment. For several weeks everyone looked at me in awe. It was strange in retrospect, because I never intended to become a hero when I went on the mission.

SEVENTY-EIGHT

S hachnow, who the hell gave you the authority to make that goddamn decision?" Colonel Bishop shouted as he came storming into the bunker.

I thought he was talking about going into a skirmish with only three men, but that had been days ago.

"No one, sir," I said.

"No one, Shachnow? You are pretty presumptuous!" he continued to rant with an angry scowl on his face. "You ordered A Company to move without consulting me."

"Yes, sir," I said. "You were not here, so I made that decision assuming that is what you would have done had you been here."

"You assumed? Well, let me tell you about assumption. Assumption is the mother of all fuck-ups. I make all operational decisions! I am in command here! Do you understand?"

I did not respond.

"I'm going to have you relieved from my command, Shachnow!" he said and left the bunker.

He had threatened to have me relieved on about fifteen occasions, along with many other officers, too. But he never acted on his threats. And I never changed in doing what I thought was right.

Colonel Bishop left Vietnam after four months. I was the only continuity in the battalion in the twelve-month period of my tour. We had three different battalion commanders, one approximately every four months. This was very hard on the soldiers. Each colonel had his own ways and methods and it became a constant process of adjustment. I tried to make each transition as smooth as possible. I went out on operations frequently with the units. Most of the soldiers were adaptable and learned to take change in stride. The frequent change in command was an army philosophy to produce as many combat-experienced commanders as possible. This was done at a considerable price and later the army admitted that it was not a wise policy.

Since the army is a microcosm of the American society, it was not surprising that much of the debate and dissension was going on within the

ranks. Discipline was at an all-time low. There were rumors of officers being shot or fragged (grenade throwing at an officer). When I was in the rear
a guard would be assigned to protect me while I slept in my tent. Morale
was the worst I had ever seen in my career. And I had my own doubts about
the war by this time, not in purpose but in execution.

Back home the public was berating and insulting the military. We became a pawn in the political struggle. It was not easy to be a soldier in these
times, although there were many who were very supportive and generous.
Arlene wrote and told me that our family orthodontist would not send us a
bill for Shereen's braces because I was serving in Vietnam.

I went with my men on a brigade operation one morning. We now had
about five thousand helicopters in Vietnam and were able to transport
large troop formations at a moment's notice anywhere in the country. This
operation involved hundreds of helicopters and thousands of troops. Our
battalion was one of the units in the operation.

The men were absorbed in their thoughts as we deployed to our destination. The hypnotic rhythm of the rotor blades was the only noise we
could hear. It sliced into any conversation. The atmosphere was thick with
emotion. For some it was fear, others were lost in thought about their loved
ones, some would close their eyes to mask their feelings. Some would talk
nonstop, sometimes to themselves or others, with neither the listener nor
the talker able to understand the conversation. It was just an outlet.

"Ten minutes out," the copilot turned and shouted.

In ten minutes, we will be in the midst of the battle. We all knew what we
had to do. It was rehearsed over and over and over again. I knew it in my
sleep.

Our chopper started its descent and we landed in a prepped landing
zone. There were helicopters all around us. We were carrying about ten U.S.
soldiers. We could hear that some of the other units had already made contact. The sound of gunfire could be heard over the rotors of the aircraft.
Most of the soldiers were off the chopper immediately, as they were trained
to do, but I saw one soldier at the back of the aircraft holding onto a strap
with no intention of getting off. I guess he had no intention of taking part
in the operation.

"Soldier, get out . . ." I shouted and stared at him.

He didn't respond.

"Get your goddamn ass out!!!"

He held onto the strap and shook his head at me. I could see and smell
his fear. It was in his eyes and pouring from his body.

I grabbed him by the harness and looked at him hard as I drug him toward the door. "Get out there."

I knew he was scared . . . everyone was. But I also knew that when one soldier doesn't do his job, it jeopardizes every other life on the field of battle.

"No, sir, I don't want to go," he said. I could hear his voice trembling.

I pulled him forward. He hung onto anything he could grab. I moved behind him, braced myself with my back against the wall, and kicked him off the aircraft and onto the ground.

As soon as he was on the ground he took off running toward the others. I followed him and looked up to see the chopper lift off the ground and the pilot give me the thumbs-up.

I could have had this soldier court-martialed. For a moment he was a coward and a traitor. As a soldier you assess a responsibility toward your fellow soldiers. It's an important bond, and he violated that bond. If I saw him today I would have greater compassion and understanding. I was not as tolerant when I was young. Today I have a different understanding of courage.

When I got back to our firebase, I found the picture that had been taken some time ago with my kill. I was sick when I saw it. I was holding the VC up like he was an animal or a trophy. I was smiling and looking happy. What had I turned into? I didn't hate this man. I never hated any of my enemies. I was doing my duty as a soldier, as I was trained and sanctioned by our society.

That night when I was lying on my cot, I looked at the picture again. I had killed others in battle, but I didn't have a photograph to remind me. I had learned from my first tour not to personalize kills. I was thirty feet away from the man in the picture and I had my M16 on full automatic. Most of the magazine went into him. What was I thinking? I didn't want to ever see this picture again. It was painful enough that this event would be etched in my mind forever, and I certainly couldn't send it home to Arlene. What in the world would my family think of me? I started to tear it up and throw it away, but I stopped because I realized that now this was something that was part of me. It showed something about me that I wasn't proud of, but it was an experience. Remembering this might help me become a better man. A piercing reminder of humility.

Many years later, long after Vietnam, I came across a photograph of a woman holding a small baby. She was standing crouched shielding the child in her arms. Standing behind her was a German soldier, rifle aimed, getting ready to kill her. A chilling photograph, but what was written on the back of the picture was even more chilling. "My contribution toward eliminating the Jews." The German officer mailed this home to his family during World War II with pride. I thought about the picture I kept from Vietnam and realized there was a vast difference between the pictures, but there were also similarities.

My tour was coming to an end in early October when I went on a night patrol. We had been out since dark and the sun was now beginning to rise. I was moving cautiously in the thick, dense shrubs and I saw a VC coming toward me, moving along a narrow path. He was in the crosshairs of my rifle. Suddenly I saw him look right at me; there was no question that he spotted me. He was walking with his weapon along his side. He knew there was not enough time to get his weapon up to a firing position. I started to squeeze the trigger and saw an expression cross his face . . . a look of resignation as he dropped his weapon to his left side. His pace slowed, but he continued to walk erect and I could tell he was prepared to die. I stood with him in my sights for a moment as many thoughts crossed my mind. Sweat dripped from my hand and the trigger became wet. A short distance before he reached me he turned to the left and walked across a footbridge arching his back as though he expected a round to penetrate him any minute. I could not force myself to pull the trigger. I lowered my rifle and walked away.

This was a troubling experience for me. I questioned my effectiveness as a soldier and an officer. Had I run out of courage? Was my bucket empty? Could I still be effective on the battlefield? I desperately wanted to talk to someone, but I could not go to my superiors or my subordinates, or for that matter my peers. I had to put all of these things into the same hidden place with the Holocaust. Something I couldn't talk about for now.

I left Vietnam in 1969. I was troubled, but not ashamed of what we did there. As a soldier one has options in combat. You can fight, flee, posture, or surrender. I thought that in the final analysis I stayed and fought. Throughout history, military training has been devoted to breaking down the resistance to taking another human being's life. However, when men kill in combat, it is normal to suffer profound revulsion afterward. Killing is so deeply repugnant that society has traditionally offered absolution by honoring veterans with parades, decorations, veterans associations, and memorial rituals that offer psychological compensation for the enormous emotional cost incurred by wartime killings. I was no exception: I came home with a chest full of decorations.

The American people saw the full horror of that conflict on their television screens in great detail. As the draft increased and more young Americans were drawn into the conflict, opposition to the war grew stronger, until the whole nation seemed to have split in dispute over the war. It became the most dominant issue in U.S. politics. When Richard Nixon became president in 1968, he initiated a policy reducing our involvement. It meant Vietnamization of the ground war with massive U.S. airpower support. As the American troops were gradually withdrawn from Vietnam, the nature of the war changed. To the surprise of many, the South Vietnamese held their own, even when the North Vietnamese Army invaded the south.

The Watergate scandal rocked the American political system and our commitment became dubious. By 1975 we could make the claim of never having lost a battle, but losing the war. This experience would have a profound impact on the military and on me as an individual. I no longer trusted the political leadership and questioned the will of our nation. It did not seem like we had the staying power to fulfill our commitments and promises in Vietnam. Some prominent senior officers have stated that using Special Forces early on, along with a political initiative to work with Ho Chi Minh, could have produced a different outcome. Ho Chi Minh was not a die-hard Communist, but there came a time when we boxed each other in with no way out. Of course, the army leadership was distrustful of Special Forces and considered them of marginal value, a side show. We did not have a mentor or sponsor to make our case. John F. Kennedy was dead and no one picked up the mantle.

SEVENTY-NINE

Gentlemen, I am Maj. Sid Shachnow, your instructor for the next four hours. During this block of instruction, you will gain a better appreciation of the enormous arsenal designed for large-scale conventional war that must be adapted to win a small-scale struggle against shadowy guerrilla fighters. This is the problem that faces us in Vietnam and it presents a challenge and difficulty that we really have not yet solved."

After I returned to the United States I had been assigned as the tactics instructor at the Infantry School at Fort Benning, Georgia. I was a principal instructor teaching infantry officers, primarily captains and lieutenants. This was considered a very desirable and career-enhancing assignment for a combat arms officer. I was delighted.

"A whole range of electronic devices have been developed to support you in the field. Helicopters are in new formations. Artillery has been grouped into mutually supporting firebases. But the essential problem remains: how do we as infantrymen fight the Viet Cong on the ground, in the forest, in the swamps, and in the villages? This knowledge will help you to be more effective as a soldier and will increase your chances of survival."

After the class I walked into my office. The secretary handed me a message from Col. Bud Sydnor. He was head of the combat arms branch and handled the careers of all infantry, armor, and artillery officers in the army from the Hoffman Building in Washington, D.C. He was also in charge of all assignments for officers who were making a career of the army. Colonel Sydnor was a highly decorated and well-respected war hero. He was the ground commander of the daring San Tay Raid, an effort to rescue U.S. prisoners of war in North Vietnam. U.S. intelligence had identified this camp west of Hanoi as an active prisoner camp. Unfortunately, the intelligence was faulty and all that would be rescued was an abandoned prison. Nonetheless, the operation was a classic precision execution and later used as a model. Colonel Sydnor was a legend.

"Sid," he said when I got him on the phone. "You were selected to attend the Command and General Staff College in Leavenworth." He paused. "I heard you told them you wanted to decline or go later. Is that correct?"

"Yes, sir. I've been here at Fort Benning for only a few months. I like what I'm doing and I thought since I had been away from my family so long—"

"That's a stupid move, Sid," he said interrupting me. "You'll lose your competitive edge, and you'll probably stay a major. You've overcome tremendous obstacles during your career after starting as an immigrant. Sometimes I don't understand how an opportunity can be served up on a silver platter and you turn it down."

"I'm sorry, I didn't look at it that way, sir," I answered.

"It's one of the most prestigious institutions for a career officer to attend," he said frankly.

"I understand, sir," I said.

"You are about to screw up, big time! I want you to reconsider your decision."

When I hung up the phone I thought about what he had said. I had a great deal of respect for this man and I had to admit that he was right.

I went home that night and told Arlene. As usual she was optimistic and encouraging. Arlene saw it as a real plus that the army was looking at me with the idea that I had potential to go further in the military.

On my last day of teaching at Fort Benning, Captain Washington, one of the better students in the class, walked up to my desk.

"Major Shachnow, sir, could I have a few minutes of your time?" he asked.

"Yes, Captain. Have a seat," I said and motioned to the desk in the first row of the class. I walked around to the front of my desk and hoisted myself onto the top.

"What've you got on your mind?" I asked him.

"I'm not sure if I should say anything, Major, but I am concerned about the men's morale. Not only their morale, but mine. The demonstrations . . . every time we turn on the television . . ." He paused. "All I see are people against the war. It makes me wonder, sir, about what's right . . ." He trailed off. "It's hard to know, sir."

"We all have taken an oath. Your duty and responsibilities are clear. At the same time, it's natural for a soldier to wonder what he is doing. I've felt the same conflict that you have. In my opinion, it doesn't lessen our loyalty to our country or to our service in the army if we question things. In fact, I think it's healthy. But in the final analysis, you must follow the legal orders that you have received. That is what discipline is all about. Failure to do so can have serious consequences for not only you, but others as well, and it is totally unprofessional," I said. "Throughout our history there has been resistance to war by some segments of society. That is normal in a democracy."

He sat and looked at me, considering what I had said.

"I don't know if you've ever thought about what it would be like if we didn't have the freedoms that we take for granted," I said, remembering

Lithuania. "Remember, freedom is not free. Each generation pays a price. At one time you decided to place your most precious possession, your life, on the line, in order to defend the Constitution and this country. That is a most selfless act and you can be proud of yourself. If you can no longer do what you set out to do when you volunteered to be a soldier, you must resign."

He shook his head. "I've always lived here. I've always been free."

I gave him some of my background and what it was like not to be free.

He stood up after I finished. I stuck out my hand. "I'm glad we talked, Captain."

This officer had a lot of courage when he asked to talk to me considering he did not know how I would react. I had a great deal of empathy for him, for there was a time when I had a need to talk to someone in confidence and I did not have the trust or courage to do so. I only hoped that our talk gave him some peace of mind.

After I graduated the Command and General Staff College, the army was facing the biggest morale problems since the beginning of its existence. The changes we faced were because of Vietnam and the continuing resistance to this war. Military budgets were being slashed. Society didn't want to see or hear about a soldier or the military. We were treated as villains. Vietnam was winding down and the press portrayed us as losing the war. However, in truth, we never lost a battle, but we lost the war. This created the beginning of a transformation of the army.

EIGHTY

W here's your boss?" General Miller said, peeking his head in the door of my office. My boss was Col. Tom Fallon and I was assigned as his deputy G3, in the Berlin Brigade.

"He's tied up, sir. Can I have him contact you—" I was interrupted as he moved past me and opened the door to Fallon's office. General Miller was a tough, wiry guy who didn't put up with a lot. I could tell he was annoyed with my answer.

When he walked inside the colonel's office, I could hear him shouting. "What are you doing standing in your goddamn underwear!?" He said a few more harsh words to the colonel and walked out again, slamming the door.

Even though it was 10 A.M., Colonel Fallon had just gotten to the office bearing the aroma and dress of the night before. Colonel Fallon, a bachelor, was a party animal and a ladies' man. He did not allow duty to interfere with his social life. This was a problem that had been brewing for a long time and this incident was about all General Miller was willing to accept.

"Sid, are you up to taking Colonel Fallon's job?" General Miller asked as I stood in front of his desk the following morning.

I was shocked. I was flattered and apprehensive at the same time. I was only a major and it was a position for a senior lieutenant colonel, a War College graduate. But that didn't stop me. After all, this was an opportunity that may not come again. "Yes, sir, I would be honored," I heard myself saying.

When I left the office later that afternoon the word had already spread about Fallon's dismissal and my replacing him. There was quite a bit of resentment about me taking over his position, being a junior officer. There were a number of senior colonels who felt they should have the job. Some complained to General Miller, but he stood his ground and I stayed.

Colonel Fallon was reassigned to Heidelberg, working on the staff. He died several months later of a heart attack. Of course, rumors were that his lifestyle and appetite for women ultimately got the best of him.

I was working for around six months when General Miller called me into his office and informed me that he had received orders for me to assume command of Detachment A. I took the command several months later.

Det-A was a "black" Special Forces unit, a covert unit. Our true identity as a Special Forces unit was to be concealed or permit plausible denial. The detachment was imbedded in the Berlin Brigade, and only those with very high security clearance even knew of its true purpose or existence. The detachment was put into place in 1956 and was active until the end of the Cold War.

The importance of Det-A was part of the history of Berlin and the U.S. Army. Berlin today is a modern metropolis that has been center stage throughout the twentieth century. Unified Berlin is the capital of a united Germany and populated by eighty-two million people. A large, spiraling city, located in the heart of Europe, it is culturally rich and the center of European politics, science, and business. About 3.5 million people live in a thirty-eight-by-forty-kilometer area.

But this has not always been the case in the history of this 765-year-old city. Its past has been both turbulent and deadly. World War I stopped all cultural, economic, and social development when Germany suffered a humiliating defeat. After this, there was a short flirtation with democracy, until Adolf Hitler was elected state chancellor in 1933. He consolidated his power as a dictator, and on September 1, 1939, unleashed World War II. His success was short-lived and he was faced with defeat when Allied forces converged on Berlin in April 1945.

Field Marshal Zhukov commanded the first Belerussian Army and launched the attack on Berlin. His command included 2.5 million soldiers, 42,000 artillery and mortars, 6,200 tanks, and over 8,000 aircraft. The Germans put up a stubborn resistance inflicting over 102,000 casualties (not including the wounded) of Russian soldiers. As the battle was waging, Hitler married Eva Braun on April 29, 1945. Both committed suicide the following day.

On the night of May 8, German field marshal Keitel signed the unconditional surrender at Karlshorst in a nondescript building that was an engineering school. Later that building was designated a museum by the Russians. After the dust settled it was claimed that the Soviet soldiers were responsible for over ninety thousand rapes.

As a result, in three separate conferences the Allies divided Germany and Berlin into four zones. One zone for each victorious ally: Russia, United States, England, and France. In addition, within the zone the respective power would have supreme authority.

With Berlin still in ruins, confrontation began to take shape. For U.S. Army troops to reach our sector in Berlin, located 110 miles inside the Soviet zone, we needed Soviet approval. When the Second Armored Division of the U.S. Army attempted to reach their sector, the Russians refused to allow the transit. After diplomatic negotiations and intervention by President Truman, the troops were allowed to pass. They took control of their sector on July 4, 1945.

Several years later, the Germans were unhappy under Soviet rule and by 1953 there were riots in the streets protesting Soviet oppression.

At this point, the intelligence community determined that there was considerable resistance potential against the Soviets that could be exploited. Based on this analysis, in November 1953 the Tenth Special Forces were stationed in Bad Tolz, Germany, to exploit the weakness of Soviet rule. In 1956, six modified operational detachments, totaling approximately eighty-five Green Beret commandos, were positioned in Berlin, in a covert status. This was the beginning of Det-A.

Their purpose and mission were classified. The execution would be directed on specific orders and could precede actual hostilities. The detachment plan was organized and equipped to attack specific strategic targets and then would continue to engage in targets of opportunity. They dressed in civilian clothing made in East Germany and carried Eastern European documentation and identification. The unit was allowed relaxed grooming standards, and the training included behavior that would allow the personnel to blend in with their operational environment. The intelligence community provided pertinent and continuous information to the six teams.

The targets in East Berlin and East Germany that were to be destroyed on order were selected by the staff of the European Supreme Allied Commander and were of significant strategic value in order for the special forces to take the extraordinary risk. Each target would be heavily guarded and difficult to penetrate; consequently, the intelligence requirements asked for great detail. Because the information could only be obtained by HUMIT means, and the intelligence capability was limited in the human field, we had to make assumptions. After the Cold War ended and there was an opportunity to verify the correctness of our assumptions, it was determined that we were right on the mark. We had more luck than brains on that issue.

Periodically we would conduct reconnaissance to visually determine any changes in our targets. We photographed and updated various changes we observed.

We were on high alert twenty-four hours a day, every day. We knew we would only be called upon on or before the commencement of hostilities. Each day we got up knowing that we needed to be prepared when the call came. We would be asked to put our lives on the line, but we believed what we were called upon to do was important. We weren't sure that if we reached a target we would have any chance of getting out alive, but that was the cost of freedom and we had all made the commitment. We were all volunteers, there was not a ball and chain holding us down. We all knew that we had the option to quit. Each one of us knew the risks; there was never a quitter. Most of the members of Det-A were foreign born, making it easier to blend into the area.

We were divided into a number of teams. Each team had its assigned target and trained in preparation for the mission. The team missions were compartmentalized and not discussed between the men; Unit 1 did not know what Unit 2's responsibility would be and vice versa. They were each staffed with soldiers who had specific skills, talent, and ability needed for the particular target. I was the only one who knew all the missions of Det-A. If any of my men were caught behind enemy lines in civilian clothes, they were at risk of being declared a spy.

Each man in the unit had extensive training and was chosen because of his skill in demolition, weapons, tactics, electronics, or communications. The most important asset needed was a grasp of the language and the ability to blend into the landscape. This is why we studied the enemy environment in considerable detail. I insisted that they learn to eat like the East German, walk like them, and talk like them. If they were stopped during a cursory check, it was critical that they know their cover and handle themselves in a manner to not attract attention or suspicion. This was all vital for the individual survival and accomplishment of the mission.

We created scenarios, devised contingency plans, and war gamed each possible situation. If A soldier was wounded or killed, B soldier would take this position. If soldier A were carrying five pounds of demolitions and soldier B was carrying five pounds of demolitions, and both were killed, how would we continue to accomplish the mission? Would we have all soldiers carry demolitions? And how many pounds? Should we provide three times the supplies we needed to cover any loss? C soldier would be designated to take A and B's responsibilities. We created the problem and worked to find the solution to cover any situation. Det-A soldiers had to think creatively on their feet.

We had at our disposal for operational purposes, $25 million worth of gold coins, stored not far from our headquarters.

When I took over the Detachment from Colonel O'Malley, I was very conscious of not making unnecessary changes and maintaining continuity. It is disruptive to the soldiers and the organization to have dramatic changes whenever a new commander takes charge. But the world around us was changing and we had to be flexible and prepared for the new challenge: terrorism. We carefully examined new techniques and tactics in order to confront this new threat. We placed greater emphasis on marksmanship and sniper training. The standard army's sniper rifle was not as accurate as we needed; we bought commercial rifles and had them modified to achieve greater accuracy.

We were provided with schematics for most commercial airlines. We learned where all exits and doors were located. We perfected our plans of rescue to avoid loss of life of the passengers. We perfected blowing doors off an airplane with minimum damage to the interior. The research on this type of rescue at the time was scarce. We wanted to bring it into an exact science. Reflecting on the capability that we possess now in special operations, our state of preparedness at that time was amateurish. But it was all we had. We did not begin developing and emphasizing our capability in this field until the failed mission to rescue the fifty-three American hostages held by the fanatical followers of the Ayatollah Khomeni on April 24, 1980.

On one particular exercise we were training on clandestine communications. The purpose was to assure secrecy or concealment of the operation and communications that were taking place. One element was scheduled for their blind contact. This meant that they had to quickly send a status report at a predesignated time and date on a specified frequency by radio.

The men were staying in a rented room in a German gasthaus serving as a simulated safe house. The four men had checked in earlier, tired after a grueling day of phsical activity. They had hit a target and had moved by foot for fifteen miles. They were in the safe house and scheduled to make contact in order to report what they had accomplished. They were basically living the simulated cover for this exercise.

Inside the room, they encoded the message and set up the radios, waiting for the designated time to send the message. They had several options when they powered the radio. One was to use a hand-cranked generator, which required some physical exertion and hard work; or go to the easier alternative and use the electrical power outlet in the room. The collective decision the men made was to use the electric power; after all they were tired and had a hard day. Why not use the easy route and conserve energy? The room was pitch black, preventing anyone from seeing from the outside what was going on. They checked the antennas that were strung across the room and correctly oriented. These were directional antennas used to reduce the probability in intercept and detection. The cable was connected to the electrical outlet and the radio had power. Now it was only a matter of waiting for the arranged time to send the message. At the designated time, the radio operator started keying the radio and sending the message using Morse code. Since the room was dark, the team did not realize that every time the key was depressed all of the lights in the gasthaus blinked on and off. Soon after, the fuse blew and everyone was in darkness. Suddenly, all of the guests were outside and complaining to the management. The management was frantically trying to find out why the blackout occurred.

This was a good lesson for all of us in the detachment. During hostilities people are at a much higher state of alert. We could have been easily compromised and missions affected. Fortunately, this was a training exercise and we were in West Germany. No officials were called and we were able to leave the gasthaus undetected. But it did demonstrate the importance of physical fitness, thinking clearly when fatigued, and the lazy, easy way is not necessarily the most effective.

A concern for Det-A by all who commanded this unit was how to infiltrate our teams with their equipment to reach their targets undetected. Our war plans estimated that Berlin would fall in a matter of days unless our main forces went on the offensive early and made some remarkable progress. We planned to go to numerous, predesignated hide sites and safe houses. Where we would stay and allow the enemy to roll over us, at an appropriate opportunity we would surface and move to our targets. We hoped to be able to take advantage of the confusion and the fog of war to infiltrate our objectives within the first twenty-four to forty-eight hours of the conflict. This was not an ideal scenario, but at the time it was the best plan available. There was a need to always look for new alternatives.

Arlene and I had been invited to a Sunday afternoon social event at one of the Berlin District Mayors' homes. In Berlin there was always a celebration event on most weekends. It was a buffet and I was standing at the table covered in platters of food. As I was going through the line there was a man standing behind me who I began to talk with.

"You're an American?" he said, smiling. "Are you in the military?"

"No," I answered. "But I do work with the military."

"Ah, in what capacity?" he said and stuck out his hand to introduce himself before I had a chance to answer. "Dr. Bertran Wiecarek."

"I am in public safety with the Provost Marshall's office," I said as I loaded my plate with food. "I'm Sid Shachnow."

I set down my plate and we shook hands. "What kind of work are you in, Herr doctor?" I asked. This was a very common exchange; after all, it is the profession that defines who you are at these events.

"I'm with Berlin Wasser Betriebe, the Berlin Water Works," he answered.

I must have looked puzzled. He began to explain.

"Whenever it rains, water goes under Berlin through miles of canals. There are approximately five hundred miles of canals under the city, actually," he went on to explain. "There are two separate systems, one takes care of the sewage and the other the rainwater."

"How do you get down to that system?" I asked.

"Well, there are openings on the street for drainage," he said.

"What if something has to be repaired?"

"Well, there are some entrances aboveground. You've probably seen them. They are little cement buildings," he said. "The irony is that although people can not travel to the East without permission, the sewage and rain-water flows freely between East and West."

We were interrupted in our conversation as we reached the end of our buffet line and someone else began talking with Dr. Wiecarek. But I made a mental note to follow up on this subterranean system and the possibility of using it as a route of approach to our targets. I vaguely remembered that one of my officers, Capt. Rolf Kreucher, had raised the issue that we needed to explore the possibility of using the sewage system as a route. However, at the time of his suggestion, I didn't realize the system was five hundred miles long, traversing the entire city, East and West. Meeting this man was a godsend; it could provide us with all kinds of alternatives.

I went to the office the next morning and we started researching the possibility of moving troops underground as the armor of the enemy was moving above us on the streets of Berlin. It could be a brilliant opportunity and I was excited about this new possibility. We had limited information on the subterranean system, not enough to make a decision. I decided not to seek permission to make a reconnaissance of the system. From some of the documents I had seen in our files, it appeared that the place was off limits. If I had asked the request would have to go through a series of channels and I probably would not have liked the answer. I decided that in this case ignorance was bliss.

We found an entrance location, and four of us smuggled ourselves underground into the subterranean system. We were equipped with flashlights and compasses, maps, markers, and knives. We took no weapons because I did not know what to expect and if something went wrong, I did not want to aggravate what would certainly become an international incident.

The underground was more than I had expected. You could walk four abreast through the huge pipes. In the main arteries, a truck filled with ammunition could be driven through the tunnels. We did not see any signs of human activity. But I was not surprised, since we had chosen Sunday for that very reason.

It was difficult to know our exact location since we had no reference points. On several occasions we got lost and the trip was taking much longer than I expected. Through trial and error we finally reached the points separating the West from the East. There were signs warning us not to trespass and a thick iron grill closed off the opening. We measured the thickness of the grill to compute the amount of demolitions needed to blow our way through.

I told my men the story of going under the Nuremberg Castle when I was a kid. They each had their own stories of sneaking into banned locations. As we walked back to our point of entrance, we were all very enthused about our find. There was no doubt that the tunnels were a perfect option for our plans.

The next day I made plans to have a team go back and further develop the routes, map the different arteries of the system, and then possibly cache some equipment down there. It was almost midmorning when I received a phone call from Colonel Bradley, the deputy commander.

"Sid," he said into the phone. "Have any of your troops been down into the subterranean system . . . the canals below Berlin?"

I knew the colonel very well and had a great deal of respect for him and I wasn't about to lie. "Yes, sir, I was down there yesterday. I'd be more than happy to come over and explain in more detail," I said, not wanting to discuss classified matters on an open line. You never knew who might be listening.

"Not necessary, Sid, but you need to go and explain it to the old man. He is not happy," he said.

The old man that he was referring to was the commanding general, Cobb. I was surprised and I could not figure out why he would be upset. It looked like a great opportunity to me. "When should I go see him?"

"I'll call you back with the time, but don't bug out, I know it will be to-day," Colonel Bradley said and hung up the phone.

Thirty minutes later the general's secretary called and scheduled the meeting for one o'clock.

As soon as I entered the office, I knew that this visit spelled trouble. The general, who normally was an outgoing, friendly man, had a stern look on his face. There was no doubt that he was upset. Off to his side, sitting on the leather couch, was George. I knew that he had a last name, but it was a mystery to me what it was at the moment. He was the CIA station chief in Berlin. He had the same pissed-off look as the general.

I saluted the general and he returned my salute. However, he did not offer me a seat. I remained at attention.

"Major Shachnow, what the hell were you doing down there?" he asked.

As I tried to explain the purpose of being down there, I was quickly cut off.

"You stupid son of a bitch!" George interrupted aggressively. "You fucked up one of my operations!"

I was taken back at his emotional outburst and insulted. I was ready to leap on that tub of lard. George was overweight!

The general saw the conversation was quickly spinning out of control. He also knew that I did not work for him. I was a tenant unit and had to comply with his policies, but my boss was outside of Berlin. He then interrupted George.

"Major, the agency has a very sensitive operation going on down there. When you approached the divide and the heavy grill you mentioned, you set off some East German sensors. They deployed a quick reaction force and there is a good possibility that this highly classified operation is compromised," he said and paused.

At this point, George had calmed down and I had regained my composure.

"Did you not see my policy about going down there?" the general asked.

I was splitting hairs, but I had not *seen* the orders, only heard about them. "No, sir, I did not see your policy."

"I do not want you or anyone from your unit down there without my personal and written permission. Is that clear?" he continued.

"Yes, sir, it is perfectly clear," I said, without hesitation.

There was a long and awkward silence that seemed to last an eternity. The general was staring at me and not a word was spoken.

"You are dismissed," he finally said.

I saluted and left his office.

On my way out, I stopped at Colonel Bradley's and briefed him on what had transpired. As I was leaving his office, walking down the hallway and out of the headquarters, George came alongside of me.

"Shachnow," he said politely. "I want to apologize for that emotional outburst. It was not called for and I am sorry."

I was pleasantly surprised. "No sweat, forget it." I almost started to like the man; it took a lot of character to apologize. As for screwing up his project, I didn't feel too bad. It's just the cost of doing business when you keep things compartmentalized. We had not done a good job of sharing information.

Several days later, Colonel Bradley asked me to come by his office. He handed me a general officer's letter of reprimand, signed by General Cobb. He faulted my judgment and failure to comply with his policy. I was stunned!

"Sid, I'm sorry," Colonel Bradley said. "Just keep your nose to the grindstone and you'll be able to overcome this."

That was easy for him to say. But I knew that this letter would bring my career to a screeching halt. Getting a general officer's letter of reprimand was serious business and the promotion boards in Washington, D.C., looked at it as a showstopper!

Several months later, while attending a parade, I saw Colonel Bradley. He had just returned from the Pentagon.

"Sid, how are you . . ." he greeted me warmly. "Congratulations are in order. You've been selected for early promotion to lieutenant colonel!"

Needless to say, I was flabbergasted. "How can that be? The last time I saw you I was given a letter of reprimand!"

He smiled at me. "That letter never left Berlin. You're too good of an officer to be destroyed by an incident like that. The old man just wanted to close the case out and give you a scare," he said and chuckled. "He thought you were getting a little too cocky! And about the promotion, keep that under your hat. I was on the board in Washington that promoted you," he said and patted me on the shoulder and turned and walked away.

I was on cloud nine.

I commanded Detachment A until 1974. The Special Forces Det-A story ended in 1990. The Green Berets departed, quietly, with no fanfare or parade. I presided over the deactivation of the unit as the commanding general of U.S. Army in Berlin. The ceremony took place in an empty room with only a handful of people present. This was a small, covert unit, staffed with incredibly talented people willing to make the ultimate sacrifice for America. They served on the front lines of the Cold War and never fired a shot in anger. No force of its size in history has contributed more to peace, stability, and freedom. Interestingly enough, the commanders that followed me after 1974 were never able to obtain permission to pursue the subterranean option.

I was promoted to lieutenant colonel when I left Det-A and sent to Washington, D.C., and assigned as chief of Army Personnel Action Division. I spent two years in Washington, D.C., working with predominantly civilian personnel. It was my first experience being responsible for and working with civil service employees. Before I arrived, I heard many uncomplimentary stories about these people. However, my experience proved that they were dedicated, hardworking men and women. I learned a great deal during this time since I had never worked in an administrative personnel management position. The job broadened me as an officer and it also introduced me to Washington, D.C.

I was then moved to Fort Hood, Texas, and assigned as commander of the 1-12th Cavalry, First Cavalry Division. As we were packing for our move to Fort Hood, I came across the letter of reprimand. I destroyed it.

EIGHTY-ONE

Lieutenant Harris looked at me with concern as he stood in front of my desk. "Sir, we have a problem."

I had been commander of the 1-12th Cavalry, First Cavalry Division, at Fort Hood for several months. It was one of the most enjoyable commands I had encountered in the army. I had twelve hundred troops that I was responsible for maintaining in a combat-ready state.

"What's the problem?" I asked.

"We're missing a forty-five-caliber pistol, sir."

I got up from my desk and we walked over to the weapons room in another building. The armorer that was responsible for the weapons checkout showed me the missing weapon slot. Normally a soldier turns in his weapons card when he checks out a weapon. The card would be in the slot and exchanged when the weapon was returned.

The NCO pointed out the slot, and it was empty . . . no card and no weapon. The soldier had no idea how both had disappeared.

The unit had come in about an hour earlier from range firing. All the men had turned in their weapons. "Lieutenant Harris," I said. "Have the commanders assemble the men." Not all soldiers lived in the barracks. The ones who were married usually lived off base with their families. "Have them assemble in the auditorium."

When I walked into the auditorium, I heard a low mumbling among the soldiers. The word had already spread about why I was talking to them. "We have a weapon missing. If anyone has accidentally taken the weapon, now is the time to turn it in and there will be no repercussions. It was a mistake, nothing more." I stood at the podium. I waited for a few minutes before I spoke again. "I'm not sure if you realize the seriousness of this matter and the consequences if we have to call in the criminal investigators. It is army regulation that all weapons be accounted for at all times. If this weapon is not found, all soldiers will be confined to the barracks until it is found. This means that you men that have families will not be going home. It's December 10 and I know this is a very special time for you and your families. This also means that I will not be going home, and that makes your commander very unhappy!"

I paused for a moment.

"Look, whoever has the weapon, give it back. This is not funny, I have a wife that is supposed to deliver our baby before Christmas. Give me a break on this," one of the NCOs said. He looked around the crowd. No one volunteered any information. He shook his head and sat down.

I felt bad for him, and for that matter all of them. "Okay, you've made your choice, you are now restricted to your company areas! No one leaves!" I walked out of the theater. I heard the rumbling complaints and felt their glaring eyes as I left. I hoped that by morning the problem would be resolved.

It was havoc that night in the barracks. There were not enough beds for the extra soldiers. They were sleeping on the hallway floors. The mess hall was in chaos trying to accommodate the extra men.

Since there was no confession, the Criminal Investigator agents came the same day and started the investigation, narrowing down the list of suspects to seventy, but, still, everyone was subject to investigation. The purpose of a lockdown was that inactivity would get on the soldiers nerves and peer pressure would force the person to come forward or someone would give us information. However, the soldiers demonstrated extraordinary initiative and imagination in making the most of the situation.

After several days, I realized that they were having a great time. I thought the lockdown would demoralize the soldiers, but instead, it was like a vacation. The wives were a different story. I received calls every day from the wives begging me to let their husbands come home. Some had good reasons for their husbands to be at home and I felt bad. But if I gave in the whole concept would fall apart and I would be on the hook if the gun was ever used for illicit purposes. After a while some of the wives had some choice names for me and conversations could become downright nasty.

Lieutenant Harris asked me to come to the window one morning several days later. I looked outside in the parking lot and there were ten Dallas Cowboy cheerleaders, thirty wives, and several reporters. One of the wives saw me standing in the window. She shot me the finger. I smiled and waved to her.

I discovered the cheerleaders had been hired by a car dealer for a promotion at his dealership in Killeen, Texas. The wives had gone to the cheerleaders and told them the situation concerning their husbands being in lockdown on the base. The cheerleaders came to the headquarters in support of the wives, and demonstrated in opposition to the punishment. This assured plenty of press.

"We want Shachnow!" "We want Shachnow!" "We want Shachnow!" The cheerleaders yelled and pranced up and down the sidewalk with the wives and some of the kids in tow. Television cameras were rolling, and reporters were snapping shots of the protesting cheerleaders. They also interviewed the wives.

I sent the adjutant out to explain why I couldn't let the soldiers go home. He was a tall, handsome New Yorker, and the cheerleaders in their blue-and-white uniforms posed for pictures with him. The next morning the shots were in the newspaper.

After the news hit the newspapers and television news hours, I was referred to as Mr. Grinch. There was a personal interest story about the pregnant wife of a soldier. She tearfully complained that he would be deprived of seeing his first child born. There would be no one to take her to the hospital when her labor pains began and everyone blamed me.

On December 21, I went to my commander, General Todd, and explained the situation to him. I told him I did not want to keep the men in lockdown because it was serving no purpose.

"You know the investigation isn't complete," he said.

"It can be finished in January," I answered. "There will be a couple of soldiers transferring out to Hawaii before January, but that was scheduled six months ago. The CI agents can interview them when they get there."

"Do what you think is best. I'll back your decision," he said, and I was dismissed.

His answer still left me on the hook if a soldier went out with that weapon and held up a bank. But I felt it was worth the risk.

I assembled my battalion on the parade field. I stood in front of the twelve hundred men. "I would like to wish all of you a very happy holiday. I'm sorry that one of you has created a great inconvenience for the other 1,199 soldiers. I can assure you that the army will get to the bottom of this mystery. But that will have to wait until later. You are all free to go home when you are released by your chain of command," I said and smiled at them. I saw the expressions change from glum to joy, and just as suddenly, I had changed from Mr. Grinch to Santa Claus.

When the Criminal Investigators in Hawaii interrogated one of the suspects that had been transferred, he confessed during a polygraph test that he took the weapon. He had sneaked it into his jacket when the armorer had turned away from him to put another weapon into the rack. The soldier was court-martialed and dismissed from the army.

After the holidays that year, much to my surprise, my oldest two daughters, Michelle and Shereen, began dating two officers in the battalion. Lt. Bill Chadwick and Lt. John Batiste were good friends and roommates that had graduated from West Point. Fort Hood was their first assignment since they were commissioned in the infantry. They shared a trailer off base.

In my wildest dreams, I never thought these relationships would become serious, since both girls had made it very clear to Arlene and me, as they were growing up, that they never wanted to marry a soldier. Their hair was too short and they looked dumb with those haircuts. They didn't dress in the style of the times. They used to poke fun at some of the officers if their heads were shaped funny after they had buzz cuts. However, the real reason was that I never looked at them as young women . . . they were our kids.

I was running late one evening when I got home, hurrying to get ready to attend a military function. When I arrived at my house I had only a few minutes to put on a suit and go to the promotion dinner for one of my senior officers.

"Sir," Lieutenant Chadwick said as I walked quickly through the living room. He was escorting Shereen to the same function and was already dressed and ready to go. He looked a little nervous as he spoke. "Could I have a few minutes of your time, I need to talk to you about . . ." He hesitated.

"How about later?" I said.

"Dad, Bill and I would like to get married and we would like to get your and Mother's blessing," Shereen said.

I looked over at the two of them. Bill looked like he would have preferred being in a combat zone getting shot rather than going through this moment. He almost looked scared.

All sorts of flares went off in my head. I knew they were seeing each other frequently; but, marriage? This was not something that I had time to think about at the moment. "I'm running late . . . let's talk about it a little later."

"Yes, sir," Bill said.

I could almost hear a sigh of relief . . . from both of us.

"Arlene?" I said when I got to the bedroom. "Do you know Shereen and Bill want to get married?"

She raised her eyebrows. "Well, I knew they were pretty serious."

"This serious?" I asked, shaking my head. "They're too young, Shereen is barely twenty."

"Yeah, but remember we were younger than that."

"Times were different," I said. I didn't want to sound like my mother, but times were different, weren't they?

After we had been at the party for a while, Arlene and I decided to break away and go to the officer's club and discuss how we were going to handle this meeting about marriage. Bill and Shereen had been watching our every move throughout the party. They were inseparable, as if there was greater strength in sticking together. Shereen intercepted us as we were leaving.

"See you at the house," she smiled brightly.

"We'll be there in a few minutes," I said.

Fortunately, the club was not crowded and we found a private area. I felt that I could throw cold water on this idea when it came to Bill, but Shereen I was not so sure. She was a strong-willed child, but the more I thought about it the more I decided that I could delay a marriage. Arlene, on the other hand, was not so sure about our degree of influence. She knew they were young and in love. She would rather gain a son-in-law than loose a daughter by standing in the way of their wishes.

We were deep in conversation when I spotted Michelle and John heading toward us. Lt. John Batiste was my antitank platoon leader. An extremely capable officer. It was not a surprise that he later became a major general and commanded the famous 1st Infantry Division in combat. In my judgment, he is a brilliant warrior and combat-tested veteran. But at this moment, I was not interested in seeing either one of them. Thoughts were racing through my mind as to how I would tell them to take a hike and that Arlene and I needed some time alone. But I was abruptly interrupted.

"We've been looking all over for you," Michelle said. "We need to talk to you."

"We're talking about something pretty important right now," I said. "Maybe this could wait till later."

"Sir, I want to marry your daughter," I heard the sound of a male voice to my left.

Two in one night! Arlene and I were flabbergasted. I listened as John told me how much he loved my daughter Michelle and that he would do everything he could to make her happy if I would give him permission to marry her.

As the old saying goes, "You gotta know when to hold and when to fold." Arlene was right, there was no way of stopping them. We gave them our blessings. Before the evening was over, they laid out the plans . . . a double wedding.

On June 11, 1977, I walked down the aisle giving away my two girls in a double-ring, military wedding at the First Cavalry Division Chapel at 1200 hours . . . noon in civilian time. The chapel was packed and the press was out in full force. It was later described as a "fairy-tale classic with a military twist . . . two sisters walked down the aisle with two lieutenants serving in their father's battalion . . ."

For months I was kidded that the marriages were arranged by using "command influence."

Eighty-two

A rlene, get ready to pack your bags. We're moving to Carlisle, Pennsyl-vania," I said into the phone. I had just hung up from talking to my commanding officer. He had informed me that I had been selected to attend the Army War College in Carlisle. This was a very prestigious institution in the army. All lieutenant colonels in the army were considered for selection by a senior officer panel for this college, but only 10 percent were chosen.

It was an unstated requirement for all general officers, and a great honor to be chosen. I did not anticipate becoming a general, but I thought it might help me achieve the rank of colonel. There was little advancement for Special Forces officers, plus I was forty-six years old. By the time I would be considered for general officer I would be too old. At least that's what my career manager told me. I had been in the army for twenty-five years, and I anticipated I would be forced to retire in about five years.

As we prepared to move to Carlisle, Arlene encouraged me to continue my college studies and get my master's degree. Carlisle was close to Harris-burg and Gettysburg, Pennsylvania. Shippensburg University was not far away and the school offered a master's degree program.

During the day I attended the War College, and in my spare time went to Shippensburg to earn my master's degree. By the end of the year, I had graduated from the War College and received my master's degree in public administration from Shippensburg University.

We also received sad news at the end of that year. Shereen and her hus-band had separated and their divorce was final. Arlene and I were very concerned. We knew that the split would be hard on both of them. We were sorry that it did not work out. Shereen had moved in with her sister, Michelle, while she decided what she needed to do with her life. She ulti-mately earned her master's degree at Southern Georgia University in early childhood education and joined the army. In a way, the divorce made her stronger and more determined. She joined the army as an enlisted soldier and then obtained a commission in the Adjutant General Corps. She com-pleted Airborne school and became an outstanding and highly respected officer, retiring from the U.S. Army Reserve as lieutenant colonel.

I was promoted to colonel in 1980 and was assigned to the 197th Infantry Brigade as the deputy commander. Approximately a year later, I was given my own command, the Infantry Training Group. I was responsible for all initial entry infantry training at Fort Benning, Georgia. This was a challenging and enjoyable command with a few surprises.

One morning the secretary informed me that two Alcohol, Tobacco, and Firearms (ATF) agents were outside my office requesting to see me.

"Sir, do you have an officer in your command named Don Grace?" the ATF agent asked me.

"Yes, I know him. He is one of my better officers. What about him?"

At this time another agent joined us. I recognized him; he was a military criminal investigator (CID). I had worked with him before.

"We think there is a problem, Colonel," the CID officer said.

"Grace is alleged to be one of the leaders of the Alabama Ku Klux Klan," the ATF agent said. "We think he's misappropriating government equipment and ammunition and providing it to the Klan. There is no smoking gun . . . and we have no proof . . . that's why we're here."

"You've got to be kidding?" I said, stunned.

"No sir," the CID agent said. "We would like to put an undercover ATF agent in his unit and see if we can substantiate the allegations. We need your permission and support."

"He's never shown any kind of prejudice toward the black officers or myself. He's an excellent soldier," I said. It was hard for me to accept these accusations. I had attended countless social functions where he and his wife were present. His wife was a beautiful, kind, and charming woman, and an officer in the air force. I was skeptical; the allegations just did not fit the individual. However, I did fully cooperate.

A month later, he was arrested. The ATF caught him with hand grenades in the trunk of his private car. When the evidence was presented to me, I had no choice but to take disciplinary action. He was brought to my office where I served him with court-martial charges. After I read him his rights and the charges and before I dismissed him, he looked at me.

"Colonel Shachnow, I have no ill feelings about this," he said. "You've always been fair and just with me as an officer. I have always respected you, even though you were a Jew."

It stunned me that he could be such a chameleon. He had shown me a totally different side of himself than the Ku Klux Klan had seen. And I knew that people are not born with prejudice, they are taught, and none of us are, in truth, free of prejudice. Several months later Brig. Gen. Joe Lutz phoned me and told me he was in command of First Special Operations Command at Fort Bragg. He informed me that he had requested me to be assigned as his chief of staff.

I looked forward to this assignment. However, before I reported to Fort Bragg, I was given a mission in Nigeria working with Gen. Muhammad Inuwa Wshishi, commander of the Nigerian Army. Our mission was to improve their commando forces. Nigeria was an oil-rich country and our cooperation was in our national interest.

I was also sent to Liberia to improve their armed forces, working with the "madman," His Excellency Commander-in-Chief Samuel Kanyon Doe, head of state and chairman of the People's Redemption Council. This was a memorable experience and an eye-opening one to the corruption that can rule third-world countries.

Sgt. Samuel Kanyon Doe had been trained by Special Forces in Liberia. We trained him so well that he soon decided that he could run the country. He staged a coup and established himself as head of state. Doe had ultimate respect for Special Forces.

The United States needed votes in the United Nations during the Cold War and this influenced many international relationships. We would get in bed with some strange people in order to keep them on our side.

Eighty-three

The complexity of terrorism was just beginning to surface into the headlines in 1983. Terrorists had been hijacking airlines, and on occasion killing passengers since the 1970s. But with the bombing in Beirut, terrorism had reached a new level of sophistication in technique and execution.

At the same time, Special Forces was in the process of expansion and restructure of organization, recruitment, purpose, and philosophy. Our first step was to become a separate branch of the military. There were three officers who worked diligently to make Special Forces unique and independent during this time period. Their contribution was critical in developing the force to its fullest potential.

I often compared this expansion to a horse race: Gen. Joe Lutz was in the saddle when the horse left the gate; General Suddath took us through the long haul of adjustments, focusing on discipline, cultivating relationships within the ranks, and fine tuning the organization; Gen. Jim Guest, a focused, no-nonsense, and determined commander, took us down the final stretch and unified the branch. I assisted each general during this time, and watched Special Forces take on a new and powerful importance in the army.

General Lutz had already been in command of Special Forces about a year before I was asked to come on board as chief of staff.

As his chief of staff I supervised, coordinated, and directed the six hundred men and women making up the command staff. I took care of routine details in order to free up time for the general to devote his efforts to complex tasks. This was a demanding and time-consuming position. Of course, we had some very competent people on the staff who were specialists in a various number of fields covering a spectrum from personnel, intelligence, operations, logistics, engineering, medical, legal, electronics, public affairs, and aviation. In addition, I was often called upon to brief army brass, politicians, state department, and CIA officials about issues and projects. Some projects were classified and sensitive.

We monitored all of our deployments, which frequently accounted for several thousand Special Forces soldiers in thirty to forty countries around the world. At the same time, the army looked at Special Forces with suspicion and at times outright hostility. We were not considered a core army requirement and subsequently had problems getting funded in the army budget. Our voices were often unheard by the Department of the Army at the Pentagon

Several months after I arrived, we had gone to the Pentagon to negotiate funding requirements. During the meeting in the Pentagon one of the senior officers raised the possibility that it might be better for Special Forces to report directly to the Department of the Army. This was an arrangement that we would like. It would eliminate many of our problems. After a lengthy discussion the subject was dropped, but not closed. General Lutz was delighted with this development. The seed had been planted.

The next day we were scheduled to brief General Lutz's boss, General Cavazos.

"Sid," General Lutz said. "Include what transpired at the Pentagon yesterday. Slip the issue of command relationship in there, but don't make a big deal of it. I hope that the boss doesn't notice it. I know he won't support it."

"Why mention it at all?" I asked him. "We didn't raise the subject, the Army Department did. Let them tell General Cavazos."

"No," he said. "I want to be up front with it. Put it in the briefing slides." He smiled. "But bury it."

Several of us flew in a small aircraft to Atlanta, Georgia, where our higher headquarters were located. A van drove us to the briefing and I set up the projector and prepared for the briefing.

The staff and general officers straggled in and took their seats. At the prescribed time, a voice shouted, "Ladies and gentlemen, the commanding general!"

Everyone in the room rose and stood at attention. General Cavazos, a four-star general, entered the room. He then asked us to take a seat. He walked over to General Lutz and gave him a warm and friendly greeting. He shook hands with me, exchanged some small talk, and then took his seat. I could see that he was in a good mood. I was hopeful that the briefing would be smooth sailing.

"Go ahead, Sid, let's hear what you have to say," General Cavazos said with General Lutz at his right side.

About the third or fourth slide was the command relationship issue, buried in the middle. I casually mentioned that during our visit to the Pentagon a general mentioned the command relationship change. I quickly picked up the next topic and thought I was home free. I was dead wrong. General Cavazos was not asleep at the wheel.

"HOLD IT!" the general bellowed. "This will never happen!" he said and turned and pointed his finger into General Lutz's chest. "Do you understand, Joe?"

General Lutz nodded his head in the affirmative.

General Cavazos turned to his staff. "This briefing is over! General Lutz, I want to see you in my office, now!"

General Lutz followed General Cavazos out of the briefing.

I packed up the slides and projector and went downstairs to wait in the van. General Lutz appeared about ten minutes later and we drove off. There was dead silence as we drove to the airport. General Lutz was pale and in no mood for conversation.

We boarded the plane and had been airborne for about twenty minutes when I turned to General Lutz. "How did it go in his office?"

He was silent for a while. He then spoke. "I don't know, but I think I have been relieved."

The remainder of the flight was in silence.

If our Special Operations Command were elevated we would be on equal status with General Cavazos's command. It was clear that he wasn't going to take to this idea without a fight.

When we arrived at the office the next morning, both of us were anxiously waiting for the next shoe to drop. When someone is relieved of command it is done in a formal process, through channels. General Lutz would get reassignment orders and a new commander would be appointed. Normally, the chief of staff is chosen by the new commander and if Lutz were reassigned, I would probably also be replaced.

We were on edge for several days. Finally, we received instructions from General Cavazos's office. "If this topic was ever raised again we were not authorized to comment on it and would refer it to General Cavazos's headquarters."

We breathed a sigh of relief. General Lutz had recovered. He called me in and gave me his guidance. We would follow the directions of General Cavazos's letter, but our objective to become a major command would not change. We would pursue this objective with all our energy.

"Work smart and don't get me in trouble," he said, smiling. He had regained his sense of humor and was himself again.

Joe Lutz never stopped pushing the envelope. He had a vision of First Special Operations Command becoming a major command reporting to the Department of the Army. Consolidating all Special Operations under this command. That included Green Berets, Special Operation Aviation, Rangers, Civil Affair, and Psychological Operations forces. It also included classified units not listed by the army. He also wanted to make Special Forces a branch allowing the focus to be primary and single in becoming a Green Beret. At this time, the men had to maintain proficiency in a principal branch such as infantry, armor, or artillery. Special Forces was an additional skill that had to be mastered.

During this time we were also embroiled in an investigation concerning Katie Wilder, a female army officer who had volunteered for Special Forces. She was admitted in accord with the existing regulation. But we had never envisioned that a woman would apply. We attempted to rewrite the regulation after the fact and were faulted for it. Katie Wilder was treated very badly and every effort was made to have her fail. It became an emotional issue with some of the trainers and they were determined to make her quit. But she was a tough young woman and she had the last laugh.

There was a formal investigation by the Department of the Army and General Lutz was faulted. As the commander he was responsible for everything that occurred or did not occur under his command. This investigation and his aggressive push to achieve his vision derailed his promotions and he retired as a major general. He paid a price.

I felt then and do now that women should be in Special Forces. Not necessarily in an operational A Detachment, but within the Special Forces structure. I have heard all the arguments against it, but most do not hold up. Our thinking has softened somewhat, and I predict that we will see women wearing the green beret. It will be a very special woman that will accomplish this. Katie Wilder was ahead of her time.

General Joe Lutz was reassigned to Greece. He was replaced by Gen. Leroy Suddath.

When the command was told that General Suddath would replace General Lutz, he was not well known in the Special Forces community. Replacing a very popular and highly respected commander like Joe Lutz was not an easy task.

General Suddath was very well known in the airborne community. Some of the officers had heard about him. Suddath had a nickname: "Sudden Death" . . . his reputation preceded him. If you didn't meet his standards he was hard on subordinates. His limited Special Forces experience was also discussed.

"He'll be the worst thing that ever happened to Special Forces," an officer said. "He is too conventional!"

Rumors also surfaced that he was coming to "put us in our place!" Joe Lutz's vision was dead.

I had never met the man and had no reason to believe that he knew about me. I decided that my tour as chief of staff was about to come to an abrupt end. I called my career manager and told him that I would probably be reassigned after Suddath came on board. I was sure that he would bring his own chief of staff.

My manager told me it really wasn't any consequence to my career if he wanted to use someone else as chief of staff. I had reached my potential and was too old to become a general. I was fifty years old and had been in the army for twenty-nine years, more than half of my life. He complained once again that I had spent too much time in Special Forces.

I had heard all of it before, but I loved serving in Special Forces, since the day I volunteered to become a member of this elite fighting team. I felt it was the most important part of the army.

On the first day that General Suddath arrived, he called me into his office. "Sid, I want to keep you on as chief of staff. You know what needs to happen and when it needs to happen in this command. I would appreciate it if you would stay," he continued. "You helped to keep me informed, before I took the position, and it has made the transition smooth. Are you agreeable to staying?"

"Yes, sir, I appreciate your confidence!" I said. General Suddath and I developed an excellent working relationship, and I began to see that he was without a doubt the best thing that ever happened to Special Forces. He gave us confidence, pride, and brought a sense of discipline to the command.

I walked into General Suddath's office one day after he had just hung up the phone and I could see that he was angry. "Why can't those guys just take care of business and be professional!" He looked at me, his jaws clenched as he spoke. "That was a call from the U.S. Embassy in Thailand . . . a Thai official registered a complaint about one of ours! They had a celebration at the end of the mission in the officer's club. Seems like some of our men challenged their counterparts." He continued, looking disgusted. "There was plenty of alcohol and one of our guys decided to have a contest to see who had the best equipment!! Personal equipment, you know what I mean. Well, he and a few of the others pulled 'it' out and whoever was the 'smallest' bought the next round! Someone who witnessed it filed a complaint."

He shook his head. "Why can't these guys just be quiet professionals?"

At the staff meeting later, I mentioned the Thai incident. I told them the old man was upset, he wants us to be quiet professionals. I used the analogy of the Lone Ranger, who accomplished his good deed and rode off into the sunset with his horse, Silver. And you heard the question, "Who was that masked man?" A true quiet professional. For some reason that term *quiet professional* resonated and is used to this very day to describe Special Operations Forces.

Gen. Leroy Suddath never wavered from the direction and vision that Joe Lutz had set. His tenacity and perseverance allowed him to make incredible progress toward our goals. In that effort, he did not endear himself to some in powerful positions. Without a doubt, he should have been promoted to three stars. But like Lutz he paid a price. General Suddath had taken the reins of progress from Joe Lutz and continued to build and amplify the force in preparation of the twenty-first century.

General Suddath was largely responsible for my promotion to brigadier general when others felt I was too old. He was a tremendous asset to Special Forces and it was a sad day when he retired. I was commander of troops for his retirement ceremony.

Gen. Jim Guest, a contemporary of mine, assumed the duties of Leroy Suddath. I was his deputy commanding general. Early on, Jim Guest told me that we would push for the vision of Joe Lutz. Jim was an unpredictable commander with a short fuse. He prized loyalty above all else. Officers who did not support his established agenda were dealt with severely. He was the right man at the right time for the Special Forces. He ruthlessly maintained momentum established by Suddath and Lutz. One may argue about his leadership, style, and techniques, but no one can argue his success and effectiveness. It was under his tenure that Special Operations became a MACOM (Major Command) and Special Forces became a branch. It was also under his tenure that we made the final touches of consolidating all Special Operations Forces under the Army Special Operations Command. He also retired as a two-star general. In my opinion, he also irritated enough people and paid the price. Without doubt, today's "achievements" in Special Operations are traceable to wise decisions made years ago.

I was proud to serve under, support, and contribute to the agenda brought forward by these three men in setting the standard for Special Operations that we know today.

This was also an exciting time for the family. Our daughter, Denise and Capt. Joseph Smith, decided to get married. They had been dating for about a year, having met at Fort Benning, Georgia. While Joe was serving as a tactical officer at the Officers Candidate School, he volunteered for Special Forces. I could not be prouder of him, he would later command the 1st Special Forces Group, and be a combat tested, decorated professional. They were married December 3, 1983.

About this time Shereen has been dating a young West Point officer, Capt. Ron Gillette. Ron was a Black Hawk pilot and accomplished infantryman. We were delighted when they decided to get married on July 7, 1984. Ron later left the army to pursue a carrier in corporate America, and did so most successfully.

EIGHTY-FOUR

I had reluctantly assumed duties as the director of U.S. Special Operations Command, Washington Office. Like many other military personnel, an assignment to Washington and the Pentagon was not on my "wish list." My preference was to stay with troops. However, orders are orders and I complied. My staff was composed of army, navy, and air force personnel. My responsibilities were to serve as the principal representative of the Special Operations Commander in Chief in the national capital. My duties were to coordinate with the Office of the Secretary of Defense, the Joint Staff, the services, Congress, intelligence community, and other governmental and nongovernmental agencies on all aspects of special operations. I also represented the boss to the National Security Council. Here again I surprised myself, but not Arlene. Much later even my boss, Gen. Jim Lindsay, told me that I exceeded his expectations. He never explained what his expectations were. We must have been pretty effective if you used the number of people who resented us and wanted the general officers position eliminated, as a gauge. Eventually they succeeded; I was the last general assigned to that office.

Arlene and I had bought a house in Alexandria, Virginia, and we hoped that I would stay in this job for several years in order to recoup our investment. But no such luck. I received a call from General Lindsay one day. "Sid, I put your name in to be the commander in Berlin, Germany. I hate to lose you but I thought this was too good of an opportunity for you to let pass. If you are accepted you will have to move on a short fuse. I am giving you a heads-up." Although I got to like my assignment in Washington, this was something I had never contemplated and loved the idea of returning to Berlin, as the commander. Later I found out that in a meeting of four-star generals, General Saint, the commander of army forces in Europe, asked if anyone knew of a general who could do a good job in Berlin. General Lindsay responded that he had a man who would do an exceptional job, but he did not want to release me. Apparently he changed his mind.

I now attended countless briefings and conferences at the State Department, CIA, and in the Pentagon bringing me up to date on Berlin. None of the briefings and estimates were able to predict and anticipate what really did happen. We just did not appreciate the deplorable financial and economic state of the Soviet Union and the power of the people.

I could not have picked to arrive in Berlin at a more exciting and historic moment. No one seemed to fully understand the developments as they unfolded. Only several years earlier, in 1987, President Reagan challenged the Soviet leader Mikhail Gorbachev "to tear down this wall." I don't think even he knew, that was going to happen.

There had been demonstrations in East Germany beginning in August 1989. They were growing larger and louder. The demands were actually modest: they wanted freedom of travel. As sophisticated as our intelligence community was, it did not recognize the vulnerability of the Communist system at that moment and the forces of the dissatisfaction. Suddenly on November 9, 1989, Politburo member Gunter Schabowski casually mentioned at an evening press conference the opening of the borders. The press showered him with questions. Schabowski was not prepared for some of the questions. When he was asked when the borders would be opened, he shuffled with his papers, and stated that it would be immediately. Unfortunately he was reading from a draft document. The bureaucracy and the border security units were not aware of that policy and consequently procedures were not in place. The hours that followed are unforgettable to anyone who experienced them. Thousand of Berliners descended on the checkpoints, the guards were not prepared and were unable to get instruction on what to do. So they stood aside and let the Berliners have free passage. Of course, the rest his history.

My tour in Berlin was filled with irony. My headquarters was Hermann Göring's, the number-two man in Nazi Germany, Air Force Headquarters, not a shabby place by any standard. Our residence was a magnificent large estate. It was the confiscated home of Nazi general Fritz Reinhardt. An economist by trade, he was appointed as the Nazi finance minister. After the war he was declared a "main offender" under the denazification laws. The United States retained the right to use the home. It was the designated home of the U.S. commander. It was strange to roam through the same rooms that at one time entertained Adolf Hitler and his cronies. The home was staffed with nine employees, all at the expense of the West German government.

Times have changed and indeed the beginning of a "new world order" was taking shape. I was entertaining my Russian counterpart, Gen. and Mrs. Alexander Nicholiovich Evtew. He brought his "friend" with him, General and Mrs. Dulenko. I knew of General Dulenko: he was a KGB officer. I first heard of him operating in Lebanon where he was stationed some ten plus years ago. There was no effort to introduce him as an intelligence officer, but I knew and he knew that I knew. Arlene had taken the ladies off on a tour of the house. We were being served drinks by the butler, when General Etew said, "You know, Sid, we were talking earlier and commenting what a satirical situation this is." I must have looked puzzled for he continued. "Here you are a Jew, a survivor, who was imprisoned by the Nazis. Brutalized by them. Liberated by the great Soviet army. You join the Americans, come here to Germany, and defend the very people that did you so much harm. You do that by being prepared to fight and kill the very people that have freed and saved you." I must admit I had never thought about it that way. I was going to say, "Only in America," but decided against it. My vocabulary in Russian was limited and I did not want to get too deep into that subject. The subject then turned to the inevitable German unification and the city's half century of quadripartite occupation. Contrary to the U.S. position, the Soviets did not like it and feared it. Dulenko said, "Mark my words, it is only a matter of time before they will start 'goose-stepping.' We will fight them again. Maybe not in our lifetime, but we will fight them." Arlene and the ladies rescued me by announcing that dinner was ready.

I must admit that even in those early days one could see the 'anti-American' feelings just lingering below the surface.

During the Gulf War there were thousands of demonstrators converging in front of my headquarters expressing their support for Saddam Hussein and his dysfunctional police state, while at the same time vilifying the United States. For some reason they did not have the same need to express themselves with my French and British counterparts.

If I had to identify a memorable but sad event, it would be my visit to the Wannsee Villa. At one of our first dinners honoring the West Berlin officials, I was seated next to the governing mayor of West Berlin, Mayor Momper. After coffee was served, he pulled me aside and spoke to me privately. He had been briefed before my arrival concerning my past history with Germany.

"General Shachnow, I would like to offer you a private tour of something I think you might be extremely interested in."

"What would that be, Herr Momper?" I asked.

"Our city owns the Wannsee Villa, and although it isn't occupied at the moment or available to the public, I'd like to arrange for you to see it."

"Of course, Mayor Mompar, it certainly would be something that would interest me very much," I answered, almost unable to comprehend that I would be in the villa where the plans were finalized to conduct the extermination of the entire Jewish race.

"Please have your staff phone me at my office and we will make the arrangements," the mayor answered.

"Thank you, Herr Momper, I appreciate your offer."

The next week I arrived at Wannsee Villa. I rode in my car, along with my aide-de-camp, Lt. Brian Fenton and driver, Corp. Andy Andrews. We arrived around noon. I was followed by my personal security detail that accompanied me whenever there was a threat against my life. I very rarely knew the specifics of the particular threats, but they were taken seriously.

The villa was hidden by high stone walls and heavy iron gates. When we turned into the driveway the tall, black gate was opened by a German police officer. He greeted us by name and checked our credentials. The security detail followed us through the gates. The officer escorted my aide and I to the entrance of the villa.

The mayor had arranged for a historian to conduct the tour. He was a tall, younger man, wearing glasses and speaking English with a thick German accent. He said he was a student of the Nazi era and was with the university.

He began to talk about why the villa was significant. He went through the plans that had been made here by the Nazis. I was well aware of this, and listened for a few moments, but my mind was elsewhere. I began to visualize the fifteen or more cars entering the driveway almost fifty years ago, and each man entering the villa. I was familiar with the face of each Nazi present at that meeting. I had studied these men so thoroughly that I felt as though I knew them, even though I could never understand them.

I stood in the fireplace room and looked around. This was where the ministers had eaten their lunch and drunk schnapps in shot glasses, toasting to the führer, exchanging ideas, telling a few jokes, all the while determining the efficient means of the extermination of the Jews. I turned away and looked out the window.

The historian handed me a translated version of the Wannsee Conference Protocol packet that had been placed in front of the secretaries on that day, before their lunch by the staff of Reinhard Heydrich, chief of police and security. The protocol packet was a summary of what transpired and was agreed upon during the conference. I stopped and read a few of the pages:

Under appropriate standards of accomplishment, the Jews should come in the course of the final solution to engage in work service in the east, in a suitable manner. Separated by sex, Jews capable of work will be led into the areas in large labor columns to build roads, whereby a large segment will doubtless fall away through natural diminution. The remnant that finally survives all this, because here it is undoubtedly a question of the segment with the greatest resistance, will have to be treated accordingly, since this segment, representing a natural selection, would have to be considered as the germinal seed of a new Jewish build-up, were it to attain freedom. As part of the practical execution of the final solution, Europe will be systematically combed from west to east. The entire territory of the Reich, including the Protectorate of Bohemia and Moravia, will have to come under consideration first if only for reasons concerning the questions of living space and other sociopolitical necessities.

Step by step, the evacuated Jews will be brought, first, to so-called transient camps; from there they will be transported farther east.

An important precondition for carrying out the evacuation success-fully will be a precise determination of just which groups of persons are considered.

It is intended not to evacuate Jews over the age of sixty-five, but rather to place them in a camp for the aged. Theresienstadt has been chosen for this purpose.

In addition to these groups, of the 280,000 Jews present in Germany and Austria as of October 31, 1941, approximately 30 percent are older than sixty-five. The Jewish camps for the aged will also receive Jews se-verely handicapped in WWI and Jews who have received military deco-rations. By means of this effective measure, the many instances of outside interference will be neutralized with one blow.

After I had read these pages the historian explained further. "These organ-izational parallel lines would be executed only to gather all the Jews 'east to west,' the ultimate goal of extermination was being hidden in language and action, but each man knew clearly what it meant," the historian said. "Nei-ther Hitler, Himmler, nor Gzring, or Goebbels attended this meeting. Not a single principal. Bureaucratically, the meeting was held under the title of 'Conference of State Secretaries.' But the orders were clearly given by Hitler."

There was only one copy ever found. All the participants were told to memorize the plan and destroy the papers. The only one who did not do this was Martin Luther, representing the Ministry of Foreign Affairs. But the irony of his life occurred when he was sent to Sachsenhausen Concentra-tion Camp in 1944 for conspiring against Ribbentrop, his boss. His own people turned on him.

I was fascinated with the language that couched the horror of their clan-destine actions in cold and dispassionate bureaucratic words. "Diminution" for death, "remnant" meaning survivors, "germinal seed" for the procre-ation of Jews. It was hard to imagine these men as human beings. At the time, they conducted this entire meeting in a cloak of secrecy. No one read-ing this document, outside the meeting, could have seen their full intent.

I looked around at the empty rooms, the paneled walls and high ceilings. I wished the walls could talk and answer the questions that all mankind asked today. How could these men carry out the plans of a tyrannical mad-man without reservation? How could a fellow human being devise such heinous crimes with no just cause except hatred? But why is always the question. I had no answers. Neither did the historian.

He continued with the history of Wannsee Villa after the war, and the plan to make proper use of the villa as part of an educational institution.

———

I was again confronted by my past with a visit to the Nazi Document Center, a property owned by the West German government now under U.S. control. I was now responsible for the center's security. The head of administration was Dr. Joseph Marvel, a representative of the U.S. Justice Department. The center employed fifty to sixty people, researching and preserving all of the captured Nazi papers of the Third Reich. The facility was protected by a contingent of the military police (MP) under my command. Dr. Marvel was named to research all information discovered after the fall of Hitler. The United States also knew that we would need to turn over all documents to German authorities eventually whenever unification occurred. There was in the past a great deal of apprehension and fear from the older generation of Germans who had bloodlines that were traced to the Nazi party and their deeds. They did not want these documents released. If they fell into the wrong hands it could be used against them. Some had things to hide and did not know how much was documented.

The center was an unassuming structure, with a flat roof and plain windows. My aide and I walked into the unmarked doorway. There was a small sign on the building, in small letters: DOCUMENTATION CENTER.

There were two MPs sitting behind the desk in the entryway. They stood and saluted and then led us down a hallway to a narrow, dimly lit stairway. After several flights of stairs, Dr. Marvel greeted us at the doorway. He then took us through several rooms containing documents filled with rows and rows of filing cabinets. There were genealogy documents, medical documents, death certificates, and historical documents on almost every Nazi that ever belonged to the party with hundreds of thousands of documents tracing the lineage of all Nazis and their wives, to determine if they were of pure blood.

Dr. Marvel handed me a file marked Dr. Menegele.

Dr. Menegele was classified as an anthropologist, not a medical doctor. He was a very enthusiastic supporter of Hitler. The documents outlined, detailed experiments of barbaric proportion that he performed on the "guinea pigs" they called Jews. Experiments that required bone fragments to be taken from twins with no anesthetic. He measured the effect of pain on one twin compared to the other twin; he would watch as one would die a death of agony. He opened their brains before they were dead, with no anesthetic, to compare the two.

I read the report and found it to be incredible. How could they make the document look so respectable and his deeds defined as medical science? We drove back to my office in silence. I still couldn't understand how it could have happened. We were all humans, with a heart, bones, blood, and muscle. Where does this kind of hate come from?

The most regrettable event of my tour in Berlin started with a phone call.

One morning, Gen. John Shalikashvili was on the phone telling me that General Haddock, my predecessor, had called him issuing a complaint against me. He told me that Haddock accused me of misappropriating government property by taking items for my personal use and inappropriately reversing his decision to return the house he previously occupied to the West German government. He suggested that a search be done of my house and they would probably find these missing effects in my home.

General Haddock had a strong personal sense of importance about his position and contributions. He made an extravagant display when he left his post as commander. During a special ceremony he had arranged to take place in front of his home, he lowered the American flag and replaced it with the flag of Germany. The band played the respective national anthems. He gifted the symbolic key of the house and all of its contents to a representative of the finance minister of Germany. He left freezers of food, furniture, artwork, and a wine cellar with over two hundred bottles of wine inside the house, plus a staff of nine.

Several weeks after his departure a representative from the German government contacted my chief of staff, Col. Al Baker. He explained to him that they were embarrassed, but it was impossible to accept the contents of General Haddock's home, as well as the staff. They could only take the house back when it was emptied. She asked if he could help her with this problem.

After I heard the story, I understood the problem and ordered Baker to store the furniture that was in the house, have the two hundred-bottle wine cellar delivered to my house for official entertaining, and find jobs in other areas for the nine servants.

Haddock had heard about the items not going to the German government and he was angry. He had the perception that I had deliberately reversed his decision and somehow benefited from doing it. I gave General Shali and his boss, General Saint, a detailed account of what actually transpired. I also made the report in writing. Both were satisfied and told Haddock that his allegations could not be substantiated. I then had an inquiry from Ambassador Walters, the U.S. ambassador to Germany, who also received the allegations. Since he was also in my chain of command I gave him the same explanation.

Haddock was unrelenting, calling the ambassador and General Shalikashvili and General Saint and amplifying his allegations. The calls irritated them. I tried to figure out why he was so bent on causing a problem, and I wondered if it was personal. Did he have a vendetta against me? None of those questions seemed right. I wished I could have spoken to him directly, but he had set the wheels in a different direction. He allegedly began telling people that he was returning to Berlin once I was asked to leave as a result of my misconduct.

When he determined that he would not receive satisfaction from my superiors, he filed a formal complaint with the Department of the Army Inspector General. That put the accusations on full automatic. With the formal complaint, an investigation was required. At the same time all favorable actions concerning me were stopped, to include my pending promotion. Two colonels from the Pentagon came to Berlin to conduct the investigation. All parties concerned were interrogated under oath with tape recorders running. That included Arlene as well as the Germans. In all the years in the army this was the first time I experienced being the subject of an investigation. After two weeks of questioning the investigators departed, without telling me of their findings.

In the meantime Ambassador Walters related his findings to Haddock. It didn't help; he still complained. He continued to call and finally Ambassador Walters bluntly told him that there was no truth in his accusation. He ended his last phone call with Haddock in a very stern reprimand. "Everything is in order, now just let go, Haddock!"

Pending the outcome of the investigation my upcoming promotion to major general was frozen. The investigation continued for about six months. It was very embarrassing, for my promotion was common knowledge, and when it did not happen rumors were flying. Ultimately, I was purged of all charges and promoted to major general with an adjusted date of rank. Having a general make an unfounded allegation against another fellow general is most unusual in the army. I suspect that Ray Haddock did not endear himself with many senior generals acting so irrationally and irresponsibly.

I don't imagine that Politburo member Schawbowski realized that with his press conference he uncorked the collapse of Communism, the unification of Germany, and dramatically changed the events of our world. I recall attending a symposium by the prestigious Aspin Institute. The conclusion was that this new world order minimized the need for a military. We could now take all that money and focus on many pressing needs that have gone neglected in the past. It all sounded interesting but I had to deal with reality confronting us today.

The next challenge was to facilitate German unification and a new relationship with Russia and Eastern Bloc countries. During the unification process, I became friends with the same men that were bitter enemies only months earlier.

I got to know them as human beings as well as their families. We had spent most of our adult lives preparing to do battle with each other, even to kill one another if necessary, but both sides discovered there were no differences in our human aspirations.

West Germany tasked Gen. Jorg Schonbohm with the mission of dismantling and deactivating the East German army and all their equipment.

This was a formidable task. However, they picked the right man to do it. Not only did he have to deactivate the 103,000-man-strong East German army, which had faithfully served the Soviet doctrine and stood against every democratic principle we believe in. He also had to close down many military facilities, renovate others, and rehabilitate and integrate a small portion of the army into the West German army and most importantly secure and control countless tons of weapons, ammunition, and equipment.

My instructions were to cooperate with him and be as helpful as possible. I did just that and he always appreciated it. So it was no surprise when I received a phone call from him. "Herr General Shachnow, I think I have something you may find very interesting. We have in our possession the war plans and the manner the East German army was to attack Berlin. You can come to my headquarters in Potsdam and read them. Regretfully, I cannot give them to you." I took him up on his kind offer. I was surprised to find that a primary approach was using the city's sewage system. Elements of the First Motorized Infantry Division led by a sapper unit (a specially trained engineer unit in overcoming obstacles and demolition techniques) were actually right underneath our brigade's defensive positions. We would have never known it until they surfaced behind us. It would have been catastrophic.

Although all our kids visited us in Berlin and we enjoyed them immensely, there was one visit that had our full attention. Our youngest daughter, LeeAnne, came with her boyfriend. We knew they were serious but there had not been any discussion of marriage. We had not met him to date. Needless to say Arlene and I checked him out in great detail. Yes, he was on the examining table. At the same time it did not seem like he was eager to impress us or really cared whether he passed the test. He had never been in the military and that hurt his score. He was working for a small Internet company called AOL, I never heard of it. When he discussed his work, it seemed like he was talking in a foreign language. I was not certain he would be able to provide for my daughter and future grandchildren. Well, they did get married at Fort Bragg on July 4, 1992. And I was wrong, he did extremely well with this company and turned out to be a wonderful and generous son-in-law.

At the end of my service in Berlin, a traditional ceremony was held to commemorate the change of command. The troops marched, and dignitaries from our allies, France, Germany, England, and Russia, were present, along with General Shalikashvilli, General Saint, and General Yates, who was assuming the Berlin command.

The president of the United States, authorized by an act of Congress, July 9, 1918, has awarded the Distinguished Service Medal to Maj. Gen. Sidney Shachnow, United States Army, for exceptional meritorious service in a position of great responsibility. Major General Shachnow distinguishes himself by exceptionally meritorious service from December 1989 to August 1991 in multiple roles as commander of the United States Army, Berlin; commanding general, Berlin Brigade; and community commander of the United States Military Community Activity, Berlin. General Shachnow quickly assessed the environment of Europe and Berlin and formulated a solid plan on which the command could set its course in a period of rapid global change and transition. His unique capabilities as a soldier led to unequaled levels of readiness and an increased quality of life for soldiers and family members in Berlin. He established an atmosphere of trust and respect with the British, French, German, and Soviet military leaders in Berlin, forming a dynamic partnership. His influence in the civilian community was graphically illustrated during operations Desert Shield and Desert Storm, when donations from all walks of life were received. General Shachnow's genuine concern, commitment, and mission accomplishments have resulted in one positive result after another, in a diverse and challenging assignment. Maj. Gen. Shachnow's accomplishments and performance of duty are in keeping with the highest traditions of military service and reflect great credit upon himself and the United States Army.

I stood proudly as General Shalakashvilli awarded me the Distinguished Service Medal and pinned the decoration on my chest. But I was even more grateful for the next award.

The Department of the Army has awarded the Outstanding Civilian Service Medal to Arlene Shachnow, in recognition of outstanding volunteer contributions to the Berlin Community from December 1989 to August 1991. Mrs. Shachnow devoted countless hours of care of soldiers, airmen, civilians, and their families. She has been an essential member of the Berlin-American Women's Club and Allied Wives. Mrs. Shachnow developed and implemented a network of command advisors to ensure the community and the brigade programs were provided excellent service to the command. She made Berlin American High School one of the top schools by establishing a national and recognized program of excellence which motivates students through a system of rewards and recognition. Mrs. Shachnow's volunteer contributions reflect great credit upon herself and the entire Berlin community and the United States Army.

Arlene's award was well deserved. She had endured many sacrifices. I was proud to see her honorably recognized by the army. There is no greater asset to a professional soldier than a wife that stands with him and beside him. It is a partnership that enriches a marriage, a career, and a life.

EIGHTY-FIVE

I returned to Fort Bragg as commander of Special Forces in 1991. I had been in Special Forces for almost thirty years. This position gave me an opportunity to contribute to the soldiers and their capabilities and share my philosophy from a position of authority.

The command was comprised of approximately 14,000 troops, stationed throughout the United States and deployed in thirty to forty different countries on any given day. Since the fall of the Berlin Wall we were facing a very different threat. It was global and despite the geographical distances, cultural, religious, and political systems, there was one common denominator: they were all directed against democracy, freedom, and the United States and its interests. We were at war, a war of attrition for which we have had little patience or understanding—and even less taste. It was different in that there were no definitive front lines. No direct involvement of major forces, governments, or use for nuclear deterrent.

Yet despite the consequences, it was almost a silent, forgotten war that was waged without public awareness, little political support, and with no recognized populace understanding. As a result, a battle or terrorist act won or lost might catch the public eye for an hour or a day and then get buried under piles of other information of public interest. The confrontation we were engaged in was fought without political consensus, without the backing of the media or congress and without the proper means by which to defend ourselves.

To ensure that the Special Forces command was properly trained and focused to face this ambiguous environment, I traveled to the widely dispersed units and shared with them my strongly held philosophy as to why Special forces was different and why we were a full-spectrum force.

On one occasion I was scheduled to visit the First Special Forces Group at Fort Lewis, Washington. I was still formulating how I would state my philosophy to the assembled troops. While cleaning the garage, I found an abandoned golf ball. Out of sheer curiosity, I cut open a Titleist golf ball to see how it was constructed. It was primarily made up by three principal components: a small hard rubber ball was the core; the rubber ball was bound by a rubber string that made up the second component; and finally the third component was the thin dimpled white outside cover. Several days later I decided to use the composition of the ball as an analogy to explain what Special Forces was all about and that it was critical that we maintained those skills in order to be ready and relevant for the future. The golf ball story, although a dozen years old, is still remembered by a number of old-timers.

The center hard rubber ball and the first component symbolizes the Special Forces volunteer, already a seasoned, responsible soldier qualified in a particular skill. He is healthy in good condition and has already demonstrated a capacity to learn. After all, we are talking about an NCO or a captain. The officer as a rule has graduated from college, completed the basic and advance courses, and has established himself in his branch. Many volunteers are already airborne qualified and have attended Ranger School. During Special Forces assessment and selection, the John F. Kennedy Special Warfare Center and School cadre assisted by technical personnel will make the final check to see if the volunteer is properly motivated and has the right character and temperament to serve on a operational A detachment. Surprisingly many do not make it—more than 60 percent. That does not mean that they are poor soldiers; it is a subjective evaluation by the Special Forces experienced personnel. This close evaluation has determined that they are not the right people to serve with this kind of unit performing Special Forces missions. At this stage the volunteer is a candidate but he is not Special Forces.

The Special Forces capability starts and is symbolized with the second component of the golf ball, the rubber string winding. This stage essentially equates to the Special Forces Qualification Course. The emphasis is on the five accessions occupational skills, weapons/tactics, medical, communications, engineering/demolitions, and command skills for officers. The course further develops the warrior traits, an aggressive effective fighter, and prepares the individual for assignment to an operational A team.

Finally, after what seems like an endless period of time the individual attends the ceremonial regimental supper, where he dons his coveted beret in a memorable but simple ceremony, listens to a speaker who frequently is a cure for insomnia and consumes a reasonable meal. The next day is graduation. The individual walks across the stage and is given a diploma, and listens to a speaker again, who delivers a message for the graduates, but several hours later no one can remember what he said.

However, even though a year may have elapsed and the individual has the green beret, he is not yet Special Forces qualified! The simple reason is that the critical skills that distinguishes a Special Forces qualified individual from some other fine, outstanding soldiers have not been mastered. Yes, this highly trained individual is tactically and technically proficient but is not Special Forces. He is lacking some critical ingredients.

The third and final component is the 336-dimpled outside cover and backspin that makes a "golf ball" and permits it to stay airborne twice as far as a smooth ball hit with the same force. It distinguishes the golf ball from all other balls. So it is with the third component, armed with it the individual becomes Special Forces. The three areas making up this component are critical to his qualification, his ability to be a force multiplier and be able to effectively work with, and through indigenous forces. Developing a working knowledge of these disciplines allows him to paint the landscape of his operational area and understand its dynamics.

1. Regional Orientation

Since each unit is focused a specific region of the world, it only makes sense that the members who are about to join the unit know something about the region. That includes geography, not merely memorizing place names, but developing a working knowledge of climate, topography, drainage, natural vegetation, soils, and minerals. However, the focus is not limited to the physical foundations. A Special Forces soldier must also have an appreciation for culture and society. Religion in some areas of the world is so pervasive that it practically is the culture. Government, law, food restrictions, family life, art, and economic activity all fall under the prescription of religious teaching. As we have seen in recent times, frequently cultures are in the process of expanding are stronger than those with whom they make contact. The result usually leads to the weaker culture being substantially changed through this contact. Perhaps the most global example of this process is the Westernizing of certain parts of the world and the resistance of Islam. There is also a need to understand the political dynamics within which the people in the region live.

2. Language

There has been an appreciation for the importance of language in the Special Forces from its inception. Language training consumes considerable time and money. It is a perishable skill that needs constant maintenance. Simply put, a Special Forces fully qualified soldier is bilingual. There can be no compromise with this requirement. It is ironic that the army has always recognized incentive pay for a host of skills that are not mission critical, but have neglected language incentives until recently and are doing it inadequately. Maintaining language proficiency is a shared responsibility by the institution, the unit, and the individual.

3. Interpersonal Skills

Mastery is critical to achieve effective operations. Unfortunately it is not always clear what we mean by interpersonal skills. I am simply talking about "people skills," such as empathy, graciousness, and the ability to read a social situation. Understanding one's own feelings and empathy for the feelings of others and controlling ones emotions in a way that enhances relationships. It also includes negotiations; it is back-and-forth communications designed to reach an agreement when you and the other side have some interests that are shared and others that are opposed. Principled negotiation is an all-purpose strategy, that must be learned. Understanding negotiation techniques and developing these skills will be a critical component of one's career success and personal success.

Ability to persuade and teach are frequently used tools of Special Forces, we use these skills more frequently than we use our weapons. It only makes common sense that we should be good at it. Finally, it has been estimated that as much as 70 percent of all communications is nonverbal. In addition where there is a conflict between what is said and what the body language reveals, nonverbal communications are more accurate. It has also been established that it is crucial to take into consideration cultural and environmental differences. The average person unschooled in cultural nuances of nonverbal communications often misinterprets what he sees.

That was my message from the first day I took command and is something I firmly believe to this day. For the contemporary conflict at whatever level is essentially a "social conflict." Since the fall of the Berlin Wall the emphasis has shifted toward social, political, and psychological factors, rather than pure military. This does not mean violence is being discarded, but that it will be complementary rather than controlling. Striking a proper balance of mastering all three components will allow Special Forces to understand and effectively operate in this complex environment and ultimately it is what makes them unique. That was the core of my command philosophy but it is not embraced by all senior Special Forces leaders. There are some who feel that the emphasis must remain on the war fighting skills, the other less warrior activities they would address as time and money allows. This dispute which is at the very core of what Special Forces are all about is alive to this very day.

In 1993, I was assigned as commander of the John F. Kennedy Special Warfare School and Center at Fort Bragg. It was here that I had the opportunity to influence the Special Forces doctrine, equipment, research development, organization, purpose, and training. The position acted as an extension to my prior command. I was able to institutionalize some of my ideas and philosophy.

Over ten thousand students trained there each year. We had over one hundred students from foreign countries undergoing training. The institution was looking at some leading-edge technology to enhance the capabilities of the soldier. It was an institution with a superb reputation. I would frequently seek the council of retired senior leaders like Col. Aaron Banks, the founder of Special Forces, and Gen. Bill Yarborough, who had a profound impact on the force. It was a most fascinating and satisfying assignment. What a way to close out a military career.

I received an invitation to return to Germany not long before I retired.

EIGHTY-SIX

President Clinton smiled at the crowd as he rose to take his place in front of the microphone. This was the final farewell for the Berlin Brigade. Shortly after this ceremony all allied troops would depart Berlin and the symbolic unification of Germany would be complete.

Arlene and I had been requested by the White House to attend the ceremony. I was told that President Clinton wanted me in the audience when he spoke my name. He began his speech by welcoming the political, military, and allied dignitaries

He talked about the unification of Germany and the great strides that had been made in the world since the Cold War began in 1945.

I listened while he listed contributors along the way. "They were people like Col. Gail Halverson, who dropped tiny parachutes carrying candy to the children of Berlin during the 1948 airlift; and Sid Shachnow, a Holocaust survivor, who became an American citizen after the Second World War . . . Here, in Berlin . . ." He looked toward me and smiled. "He became better know as General Shachnow, the brigade commander . . ."

After the ceremony I was positioned on the aisle by one of the presidential aides. He told me I would have two minutes with the president. Arlene and I both stood and waited.

I arrived two days early for the ceremony. The individual in charge of the advance team offered to show me and Arlene the effort and complexity of preparing for a presidential visit. It was a fascinating experience; I had never seen such a finely choreographed event. Everything was designed and timed down to the second. Where he would walk, who he would talk to, when to take a left turn, when to take a right turn. I was impressed. The security requirements were difficult to appreciate unless you see what goes into protecting the U.S. president. There were over six hundred people involved.

When the president approached me, I told him what an honor it was to meet him. In his personable way, he stopped me and said it was his privilege. We chatted for several minutes, much longer than I expected. When he spoke to Arlene, she asked to meet Mrs. Clinton. He turned and called his wife over and she graciously congratulated Arlene on her accomplishments in service to the army.

I had worked for many, but never met a president in my career. But no matter who the president is, we in the military take an oath to serve the Constitution and the president and it has always been my belief as a soldier that you owe your loyalty and support to the commander in chief, regardless of his political beliefs or his policies. I was honored to meet Pres. William J. Clinton at this important and significant ceremony.

I retired on October 31, 1994, at Fort Bragg, North Carolina. There were parades and speeches. Arlene, my daughters, and grandchildren sat in the front row. I handed over the command of the John F. Kennedy Special Warfare Center and School to Maj. Gen. Bill Garrison, a distinguished Special Forces warrior and a veteran of many battles, including Mogadishu and Somalia. I was presented with the American flag that waved proudly at Fort Bragg on the last day of my command.

My career had passed quickly. Coming up through the ranks had given me invaluable experience and an understanding of what it meant to be a soldier. I had enjoyed every assignment and had spent my lifetime in service to the freedoms I had found when I came to America.

I had served double the twenty-year norm of service required for retirement. In the army, I found opportunities beyond my greatest expectations. I married the woman that I loved beyond description and raised a family. I always wondered when they called me with a new assignment if they had forgotten how long I had already served; I never reminded them. When I approached my fortieth year, someone finally noticed.

Gen. Wayne Downing, the commander in chief of the U.S. Special Forces Command, walked to the podium to make the farewell remarks. This four-star general was the ultimate Ranger and epitome of a soldier. I considered him not only my boss but also my friend.

Sid Shachnow has a very, very distinguished career . . . many of you know that career as well as or better than I do. You've read his bio and seen his accomplishments. The only thing you can say about Sid Shachnow is that he has truly done it all! From private to major general, almost forty years of service all over the world, in every corner of the world, and not only in corners where we have American troops . . . in peace and in war . . . in every capacity, in every kind of unit you can think of; straight leg infantry, airborne infantry, mech infantry, Special Forces, duty and civilian assignments, sensitive posts, twice in Germany as commander of a detachment and later as commander of Berlin forces. Duties in the arduous and harrowing corridors of the Pentagon;

the State Department in Washington D.C., commander of Special Forces and commander of the John F. Kennedy Special Warfare Center and School.

By any measure that we apply to a successful officer, Sid Shachnow has been an inspiring success for aspiring young officers to emulate.

Of course, there's more to the story. To fully understand Sid Shachnow and what he has achieved from the path he has walked, you've got to understand where he came from and how he got to this country. Sid Shachnow was born in Kaunas, Lithuania. He grew up in World War II. . . . notice . . . I did not say during World War II. Sid Shachnow lived in the midst of World War II. As a young boy, he saw his country overrun by Germans. He saw himself and his family, because of their religion, because of their creed, put into a German concentration camp. After the liberation by the Soviets, he was once again imprisoned and escaped through the German and Soviet lines to Allied occupied forces on the eastern front in a six-month trip with his mother and brother.

Sid is a Holocaust victim. A survivor of the most unspeakable, tolitarian brutality. A situation that most of us cannot begin to comprehend. I had the experience of going to the Holocaust Museum with a group of general officers, escorted by Sid. We walked with him through the historical exhibits. He gave us his personal recollections and answered our questions. He showed me where he was born on a map of Lithuania and pointed out where Kovno Camp was located. It was an afternoon I will never forget. A man who had endured and experienced the absolute worst in mankind, but was able to rely on and trust his fellow human beings. And is able to talk and share and inform me and others the kind of things he thought we should know.

He was able to love: love his family, love his fellow human beings, and love his country. A man who truly understands freedom because he knows what freedom means more than many, many other of our citizens. Sid knows freedom is not free. He knows freedom has got to be paid for and it's got to be diligently protected.

Sid's saga represents the best of the human race and the best of America's boundless opportunities. A destitute immigrant to this country, he has through sheer determination, hard work, and native talent risen to the highest level of his profession in one of the most competitive fields in the United States.

A survivor of Nazi and Soviet occupation, internment, and persecution, he knows the value of our freedom and has generously given of his considerable talent to ensure that Americans never have to go through what he was subjected to as a youth in war-torn Europe . . .

The United States was blessed the day Sid Shachnow entered this country and blessed again the day he joined this army . . . Everyone who *has ever known him or been around him has been affected by Sid. His wry sense of humor, which he cannot keep under control in the most serious of situations, breaks the tension. He brings an insight that you're never going to get without that sense of humor.*

I listened while General Downing traced the events of my life in his speech. I had seen the world change, dramatically, and suffer many triumphs and many failures. Oppression was still an enemy. But I realized how important it was to keep hope, courage, and perseverance, and we would someday erase this scourge from society.

I remembered how American GIs had inspired me as a young immigrant boy and ignited my dreams for freedom and a better life. This sparked my imagination and brought my dreams into reality. Freedom is a reality that everyone deserves.

It was hard to believe where I had come from and how lucky I have been. I will always be grateful to this country for giving my the opportunities and choices.

I know of no one in our military or public service in the United States that has contributed more of himself to our nation than Sid has . . . I know of no one who knows the blessings of our freedom more than Sid Shachnow and maybe that is one reason his service has been so distinguished, and why so many of us admire him and are inspired by him . . . Your example has affected two generations of soldiers . . . I predict that you will join the rank of Aaron Banks, Bill Yarborough, Leroy Suddeth, and Berrato, to name a few, as one of the pioneers that brought Special Forces into a prominent role in the twenty-first century. You have created a force that can do it all. It can fight and function in the complex operations we find ourselves faced with today throughout the world. A force that is culturally attuned, language skilled, with the ability to go anywhere in the world with precision effectiveness.

The ceremony included recognition for Arlene and her help to military families throughout her career. The torch was passed and it was a new day for Special Forces and a new beginning for me. I decided to return to Lithuania, it had been more than fifty years since I was smuggled out of the country.

EPILOGUE

It was warm and sunny as I walked through the streets of Kaunas. I saw that many things had changed for the better, but my memory of the past lingered. The scars were tender as I visited my original home on the square and my grandmother's house where we lived until we were taken to Kovno Camp. I traveled across town to Uncle Jacob's where he and his family had been massacred. I went to the location where Abraham and Tili had been burned alive. Other than my original home in my grandfather's building, the others had transformed into new buildings and parking lots, or piles of rubble.

Kovno Camp was now a memorial. Fort IX was a beautiful park with impressive monuments, built to mask the ugly events. The deep ditches where my grandmother had been shot to death and then thrown into the pit was now a green meadow. I shuddered with the fear she must have felt. I said a prayer and placed a small handful of dirt into an envelope in remembrance of this horrible experience and chapter in my life. Time had passed but it all seemed like yesterday to me.

I felt tears spill onto my cheeks. As I looked to my side, I saw Mirjam, a fellow inmate of mine who had never left Lithuania after being liberated by the Russians, crying along with me. We hugged and quietly mourned.

Against my better judgment, my mother and other family members prodded me to return and claim my grandfather's property. It required documents to be presented and a long paper trail of proof to unravel the past. Forms had to be filled out and endless statements submitted. I was assured that the matter would be resolved quickly. Although the politicians were saying all the right things, anti-Semitism was very apparent in Lithuania. I had to attend one more meeting in this process and I would gladly board a plane and return to my small horse farm in Southern Pines, North Carolina.

Eight years have passed since I left Lithuania with a promise that my grandfather's property would be restored to me. Rose, my mother, passed away in February 2000. I was sorry she hadn't seen the return of her beloved home before her death.

In one of my phone calls, through my own channels of information, I was told that the person working my property claim allegedly said, "I'll do everything I can to keep that Jew from getting his property . . ."

The war never ended.

Rose Shachnowski continued to live in Florida and was somewhat of a celebrity in her community as a Holocaust survivor. She didn't like phone calls from her sons. She preferred postcards, feeling that talking on the phone was risky and expensive. She carried many scars, suspicions, and fears from the past. Her years of oppression became a battle that was never quite forgotten. She was ninety-three years old when she passed away.

Leon Shachnowski, General Shachnow's father, passed away in 1979 while living in Florida. He died of a heart attack.

Uncle Willie died of a heart attack in 1955 while living in California.

Appendix

Entitlements of Major General Sidney Shachnow,
U.S. Army (Ret.)

1. Individual Decorations and Service Medals

Distinguished Service Medal, two awards
Silver Star, two awards
Defense Superior Award
Legion of Merit
Bronze Star, two awards
Bronze Star with "V" for Valor
Purple Heart, two awards
Meritorious Service Medal, two awards
Air Medal, 12 awards
Army Commendation Medal with "V" for Valor
Army Commendation Medal, two awards
Good Conduct Medal
Army Occupation Medal
Armed Forces Expeditionary Medal
National Defense Service Medal
NCO Professional Development Ribbon
Army Service Ribbon
Overseas Service Ribbon
Vietnam Service Medal
United States Special Operations Command Medal

2. Unit Awards

Army Presidential Unit Citation
Army Valorous Unit Award
Army Meritorious Unit Award
Republic of Vietnam Presidential Unit Citation
Vietnam Gallantry Cross Unit Citation
Vietnam Civil Actions Unit Citation

3. Badges and Tabs

Combat Infantry Badge
Expert Infantry Badge
Master Parachutist Badge
Special Forces Tab
Ranger Tab
Expert Marksmanship Badge (Rifle and Pistol)

4. Foreign Awards

Republic of Vietnam Gallantry Cross
Republic of Vietnam Campaign Medal

German Parachute Badge
Russian Parachute Badge
Thai Parachute Badge
Canadian Parachute Badge
Belgium Parachute Badge
Korean Parachute Badge

5. Other Recognitions

Doctor of Laws (Honorary Degree)
Four Chaplains Legion of Honor
Military Lay Leadership Award
California Senate
  Resolution/Commendation
Distinguished Service Medal
  of Alabama
Inducted into the Infantry Officers
  Candidate Hall of Fame

6. Institutional Education and Training

B.S.—Business Administration
M.S.—Public Administration

Seventh Army Noncommissioned
  Officers Academy
Army War College
Command and General
  Staff College
Capstone Course
Personnel Management Staff
  Officer's Course
Infantry Officers Candidate Course
Infantry Officers Advance Course
Special Forces Qualifications
  Course
Ranger Course
Jumpmaster Course
High Altitude Low Opening Course
  (HALO)
Counter Insurgency/Special Warfare
  Staff Officers Course
Creative Leadership Course
Harvard Executive Management
  Course
Sniper Course
Communications Course—
  Negotiations and Persuation
Language Courses (Vietnamese and
  German)